# School-Based Interventions

## The Tools You Need to Succeed

**Kathleen Lynne Lane**
*Peabody College at Vanderbilt University*


**Margaret Beebe-Frankenberger**
*University of Montana*

PEARSON

Boston • New York • San Francisco
Mexico City • Montreal • Toronto • London • Madrid • Munich • Paris
Hong Kong • Singapore • Tokyo • Cape Town • Sydney

**Executive Editor:** *Virginia Lanigan*
**Editorial Assistant:** *Robert Champagne*
**Executive Marketing Manager:** *Amy Cronin-Jordan*
**Production Editor:** *Paul Mihailidis*
**Manufacturing Buyer:** *Andrew Turso*
**Cover Administrator:** *Kristina Mose-Libon*
**Electronic Composition:** *Stratford Publishing Services, Inc.*
**Editorial-Production Services:** *Stratford Publishing Services, Inc.*

For related support materials, visit our online catalog at
www.ablongman.com.

Library of Congress Cataloging-in-Publication Data

Lane, Kathleen L.
    School-based interventions : the tools you need to succeed / Kathleen Lynne Lane,
  Margaret Beebe-Frankenberger.
        p.   cm.
    Includes bibliographical references and index.
    ISBN 0-205-38605-9
    Problem children—Education—United States.   2. Problem children—Services
for—United States.   3. School psychology—United States.   4. School violence—United
States—Prevention.   I. Beebe-Frankenberger, Margaret.   II. Title.

LC4801.5.L36 2004
371.93—dc21                                                                2003054849

Printed in the United States of America
10  9  8  7  6  5  4  3  2  1      07  06  05  04  03

*This book is dedicated to*

*My grandfather, William Paul Frank, M.D.*
*The best naturally occurring intervention*

K.L.L.

*My grandsons, Howie, Andrew, & Mason*
*The most socially important outcomes in this grammy's life!*

M.E.B.-F.

# Contents

Acknowledgments     xi

About the Authors     xiii

## 1. Designing Effective Interventions: Introduction and Overview     1

Levels of Prevention     2
Primary Prevention     2
Secondary Prevention     3
Tertiary Prevention     5

Key Features of Effective Interventions     5

Summary and Purpose     8

## PART I • Reviewing Linking and Monitoring Strategies     15

## 2. Linking Interventions to Assessment Results     17

What Is Assessment?     19
Administrative versus Functional Assessments     19
Assessment versus Testing     22
Standardized versus Skills-Based Tests     23
What Is and How Do I Identify a Replacement Skill/Behavior?     24

What Does It Mean to Link Intervention to Assessment Results?     25
Linking Assessment to Primary Intervention     25
Linking Assessment to Secondary Intervention     27
Linking Assessment to Tertiary Intervention     29

Why Is It Important to Link Intervention to Assessment Results?     31

How Do We Link Intervention to Assessment Results?     32
Primary Interventions     33
Secondary and Tertiary Interventions     36

Summary     50

## 3. Monitoring Changes during Intervention     53

What Does It Mean to Monitor Changes?     53

Why Is It Important to Monitor Changes?     57

*How Do We Monitor Changes?*    **58**
    Outcome Measures    58
    Measurement System    61

*How Are Skills/Behaviors Measured?*    **62**
    Define Skill/Behavior by What It Looks Like: Topography    62
    Define Skill/Behavior by Dimension    64
    Define Monitoring Method    65
    Topography, Dimension, and Method Combined    66
    What Is "Response to Intervention"?    69

*Who Monitors Interventions and How Do They Do it?*    **69**
    Teacher    69
    Student    71
    Parent    75

*Summary*    **78**


**PART II • *Introducing the Core Components Model*    83**


**4.**  *Social Validity: Goals, Procedures, and Outcomes*    **85**

*What Do We Mean by Social Validity?*    **85**
    Pre-Intervention: Social Validity Components    85
    Post-Intervention: Social Validity Components    88

*Why Is It Important to Assess Social Validity?*    **90**

*With Whom Do We Assess Social Validity and Why?*    **94**
    Teacher    94
    Parent    95
    Student    96

*How Do We Assess Social Validity?*    **97**
    Self-Report Rating Scales    98
    Interviews    98
    Direct Observation and Social Comparison Techniques    101
    Repeated Use    101

*How Do We Interpret Social Validity Surveys?*    **101**

*Summary*    **102**


**5.**  *Treatment Integrity: Is the Intervention Really Happening?*    **128**

*What Do We Mean by Treatment Integrity?*    **128**

*Why Is It Important to Monitor Treatment Integrity?*    **130**

*Why Aren't Interventions Implemented with Integrity?*    **132**

*How Do We Assess Treatment Integrity?*    **133**
    Direct Observation Procedures    133
    Behavior Rating Scales    137

Self-Reporting Strategies    137
Permanent Products    141
Manualized Interventions    141

*Which Methods Should I Use?*    **141**

*Summary*    **144**

**6.**  *Generalization and Maintenance of Treatment Outcomes:*
*Making It Last?*    **147**

*What Is Generalization and Maintenance?*    **147**

*Why Is It Important to Consider Generalization and Maintenance?*    **148**

*How Do We Program for Generalization and Maintenance?*    **151**
Topographical Approaches    151
Functional Approaches    159

*Did the Intervention Outcomes Last?*    **161**
Data-Based Decision Making    161
Programming for Generalization: Comprehensive Guidelines    162

*Summary*    **164**

**PART III • *A Summative Example*    167**

**7.**  *Putting It All Together*    **169**

*Key Tools*    **170**

*A Three-Tiered Model of Prevention: A Hypothetical Sample*    **172**

*Primary Intervention*    **172**
Identifying the Intervention Target Areas: Pre-Intervention Assessment    174
Intervention Planning Activities    174
The Primary Intervention Plan: Design, Preparation, and Implementation    181
Monitoring Student Progress    183
Results    184
Identifying Nonresponsive Students to Participate in Secondary
Prevention Efforts    185

*Secondary Intervention: Academic Target*    **185**
Identifying the Intervention Target Areas: Pre-Intervention Assessment    185
Intervention Planning Activities    194
The Secondary Intervention Plan: Design, Preparation, and Implementation    194
Monitoring Student Progress    195
Results    196

*Secondary Intervention: Social Skills Target*    **203**
Identifying the Intervention Target Areas: Pre-Intervention Assessment    203
Intervention Planning Activities    204
The Secondary Intervention Plan: Design, Preparation, and Implementation    204

Monitoring Student Progress    205
Results    205
Identifying Nonresponsive Students to Participate in Tertiary
  Prevention Efforts    207

***Tertiary Intervention: Functional Assessment-Based Intervention    207***
Identifying the Intervention Target Areas: Pre-Intervention Assessment    207
Intervention Planning Activities    216
The Tertiary Intervention Plan: Design, Preparation, and Implementation    218
Monitoring Student Progress    219
Results    219

***Multilevel Interventions: Summative Findings    220***
Question 1: To what extent did the three-tiered model of intervention help upper and
lower elementary school students improve academically?    220
Question 2: To what extent did the three-tiered model of intervention help upper and
lower elementary school students improve behaviorally and socially?    220
Question 3: Did the three-tiered model of intervention differentially influence
students with low-, moderate-, and high-risk status as measured by the Student Risk
Screening Scale?    221
Question 4: To what extent was risk status affected by the three-tiered model of
intervention during the school year?    221
Summary    221

***Summary and Conclusions    221***


***Appendix: Reproducibles    225***

*Reproducible 2.1    **Preliminary Functional Assessment Interview    226***

*Reproducible 2.2    **Student Functional Assessment Interview    231***

*Reproducible 2.3    **Sample Observational Assessment of Student Inappropriate
Behavioral Events    235***

*Reproducible 2.4    **Observation Measure of the Learning Environment: Schedules
of Reinforcement    236***

*Reproducible 2.5    **Sample Observational Assessment of Classroom Learning
Environment    237***

*Reproducible 3.1    **Problem-Solving Worksheet    238***

*Reproducible 3.2    **Weekly Summary Intervention Monitoring    239***

*Reproducible 3.3    **Generic Frequency Count Form    240***

*Reproducible 3.4    **Self-Monitoring Pleasant Events    241***

*Reproducible 3.5    **Self-Monitoring for Neat and Complete Work Assignments    242***

*Reproducible 3.6    **Self-Monitoring Behavior during a Class Period in
Middle School    243***

*Reproducible 3.7    **Progress Monitoring Grid    244***

*Reproducible 3.8    **School-Home Progress Note    245***

*Reproducible 4.1    **Treatment Acceptability Rating Profile-Revised
(TARF-Revised)    247***

*Reproducible 4.2*    *Intervention Rating Profile-15*    *250*

*Reproducible 4.3*    *Children's Intervention Rating Profile (CIRP)*    *251*

*Reproducible 5.1*    *Sample Treatment Integrity Protocol: PATR*    *252*

*Reproducible 5.2*    *Weekly Treatment Integrity: PATR*    *253*

*Reproducible 5.3*    *Behavior Rating and Self-Evaluation Scale*    *254*

*Reproducible 5.4*    *Treatment Integrity Rating Scale: Percentages*    *255*

*Reproducible 5.5*    *Independent Group Contingency Plan with a Response Cost*    *256*

*Reproducible 5.6*    *Treatment Integrity: Permanent Product Evaluation*    *257*

*Reproducible 5.7*    *School-Home Note*    *258*

*Reproducible 6.1*    *Programming for Generalization: Topographical Approaches*    *259*

*Reproducible 6.2*    *Generalization Guidelines*    *260*

*Reproducible 6.3*    *Schoolwide Intervention: Social Skills*    *261*

*Reproducible 6.4*    *Homework Reminder Form*    *262*

*Reproducible 7.1*    *Primary Intervention Planning Guide and Checklist*    *263*

*Reproducible 7.2*    *Secondary Intervention Planning Guide and Checklist*    *268*

*Reproducible 7.3*    *Tertiary Intervention Planning Guide and Checklist*    *273*

*Index*    *279*

# Acknowledgments

We would like to thank the exceptional people who trained us in school-based intervention research: Frank M. Gresham, Donald MacMillan, Richard Eyman, Keith Widaman, and Sharon Borthwick-Duffy. We would also like to acknowledge Katherine Falk and Lauren Lunsford for their detailed edits on earlier versions of this text. Finally, we would like to thank the students with whom we worked in the past and those whom we hope will benefit from this book in the future.

The authors would like to thank the reviewers for their time and input: Rita Mulholland, California State University, Chico; Tamarah Ashton, California State University, Northridge; and Monica M. D'Angelo, Iona College.

# About the Authors

## Kathleen Lynne Lane, Ph.D.

Dr. Kathleen Lane is an Assistant Professor in the Department of Special Education at Peabody College of Vanderbilt University and an Investigator in the John F. Kennedy Center for Mental Retardation at Vanderbilt University. She earned her master's degree and doctorate in education from the University of California, Riverside. Prior to entering academia, Dr. Lane served as a classroom teacher of general and special education students for five years and provided consultation, intervention, and staff development services to five school districts in southern California for two years in her role as a program specialist. Dr. Lane's research interests focus on investigating the relationship between academic underachievement and externalizing behaviors with students with, or at-risk for, emotional and behavioral disorders (E/BD). She has designed and implemented several school-based interventions. These interventions focus on addressing the academic, social, and behavioral needs of students with, and at-risk for, antisocial behavior. Dr. Lane is also the primary investigator of a directed research project studying positive behavior support at the high-school level and a co-principal investigator on a doctoral leadership grant designed to prepare students to assume leadership roles as researchers and practitioners in the area of behavior disorders. Dr. Lane also serves on the editorial boards for *Journal of Emotional and Behavioral Disorders*, *Journal of Positive Behavior Interventions*, and *Preventing School Failure*.

## Margaret Beebe-Frankenberger, Ph.D.

Dr. Margaret Beebe-Frankenberger is an Assistant Professor in the Department of Psychology at the University of Montana (UM), Missoula, where she serves as the Director of the School-Clinical Psychology Program. She is engaged in the expansion of the current NASP/NCATE accredited MA/EdS. school psychology program into a combined school-clinical doctoral program, enhanced by the existing APA-accredited clinical psychology program at UM. Dr. Beebe-Frankenberger earned her doctorate in education as a school psychologist from the University of California, Riverside. She served as a school psychologist, behavior specialist, and intervention consultant in several school districts in southern California. Her work in school districts focused on high-profile cases necessitating systemic assessment and intervention to effect outcomes for children with and without disabilities. Prior to her current position, Dr. Beebe-Frankenberger served as project director of two longitudinal research projects funded by the U.S. Department of Education and conducted at the University of California, Riverside, by nationally recognized scholars in the fields of learning disabilities, mental retardation, and emotional/behavioral disorders. The first project examined the effects of grade retention on academic and social competence, and the second studied development of mathematical problem-solving in students at risk for math difficulties. Dr. Beebe-Frankenberger's research interests focus on academic and social competence, particularly as related to a family systems approach, emphasizing positive parental support and involvement.

# 1

# *Designing Effective Interventions*
## *Introduction and Overview*

When students begin formal schooling, there is an expectation on the part of teachers, administrators, parents, and the students themselves that they will acquire knowledge across a variety of content areas, develop a range of skills (e.g., be able to read, express themselves in writing, and use problem-solving skills), and expand their abilities to interact successfully with others (O'Shaughnessy, Lane, Gresham, & Beebe-Frankenberger, 2002). Clearly, educators are faced with enormous demands. The scope of the curriculum has expanded not only to include basic academic content areas such as literacy, mathematics, science, and social studies, but also to address such areas as social skills, anger management, conflict resolution, violence prevention, health awareness, and drug prevention. Principals and other educational leaders are expected to promote growth in all academic areas, maintain a positive school climate, and eliminate school violence. Teachers are expected to create learning environments that allow *all* students to achieve the specified district and state standards. With the trend toward inclusive programming for students with special needs (Fuchs & Fuchs, 1994; Lane & Wehby, 2002; MacMillan, Gresham, & Forness, 1996), teachers are asked to meet the educational needs of an increasingly diverse student population. Further, school psychologists are charged with implementing evidenced-based interventions (Stoiber & Kratochwill, 2001) that have previously demonstrated effectiveness in addressing academic and social concerns based on empirical criteria set by the Task Force on Evidenced-Based Intervention in School Psychology (Lonigan, Elbert, & Johnson, 1998; Stoiber & Kratochwill, 2001).

In light of these varied demands facing today's educators, it is essential that intervention efforts be carefully constructed. Due to limited resources (e.g., time, personnel, and materials), interventions must target meaningful goals, be implemented precisely with attention to detail, and evaluated wisely to draw accurate conclusions. Further, with the increased emphasis on providing proactive, rather than reactive, support inclusive of early detection and early intervention, schools are fast becoming an important context for addressing many of students' and society's needs (Lane & Wehby, 2002; Nelson, Rutherford, Center, & Walker, 1991; Walker & Severson, 2002). In fact, there has been a recent shift toward looking at the *school,* rather than at the individual student, as an agent for change (Lewis & Sugai, 1999; Walker et al., 1996).

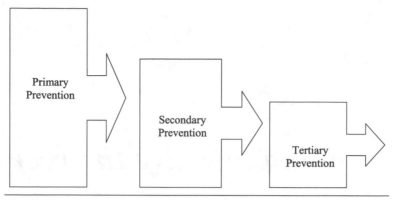

**FIGURE 1.1**   *A Three-Tiered Model of Support*

With careful planning, schools can provide comprehensive, multi-level interventions that can be used to prevent and remediate numerous problems (Kamps, Kravits, Stolze, & Swaggart, 1999; Walker & Severson, 2002) and fulfill the school's mission. Specifically, schools can implement *primary, secondary,* and *tertiary* prevention programs in a data-driven, coordinated fashion (see Figure 1.1) to provide progressively more intensive support to address the academic, behavioral, and social needs of today's students (Caplan, 1964; Forness, Kavale, MacMillan, Asarnow, & Duncan, 1996; Walker et al., 1996). By implementing an integrated system of early detection and progressive levels of support, schools can effectively address the full scope of learning and behavior problems in an organized, efficient, and effective manner. This model of multi-leveled support also has been proposed and recommended by renowned researchers who are studying methods to better identify and serve students with behavior disorders (Walker & Severson, 2002; also see Figure 1.2) and learning disabilities (Gresham, 2002; also see Figure 1.3).

## Levels of Prevention

### Primary Prevention

The first level of support, *primary prevention,* focuses on preventing academic and behavioral problems from occurring by providing all students with a given intervention. Examples of primary intervention programs include schoolwide literacy programs (Lane & Menzies, 2002), positive behavior support (Lohrmann-O'Rourke, Knoster, Sabatine, Smith, Horvath, & Llewellyn, 2000; Scott, 2001; Taylor-Greene & Kartub, 2000; Turnbull et al., 2002), anger management and conflict resolution programs (DeBaryshe & Fryxell, 1998), social skills programs (Jones, Sheridan, & Binns, 1993; Lewis, Sugai, & Colvin, 1998), discipline and management plans (Canter, 1990; Canter & Canter, 1992; MacGregor, Nelson, & Wesch, 1997), and violence prevention plans (e.g., *Second Step Violence Prevention Curriculum,* Committee for Children, 1992). Students are neither screened for eligibility nor do they have to meet some set of criteria to participate in these primary interventions. By virtue of being enrolled in the school, they are involved. Because every student in the school engages in the primary level of support, the learning and behavioral expectations are clear. Essentially, the playing field is leveled in an

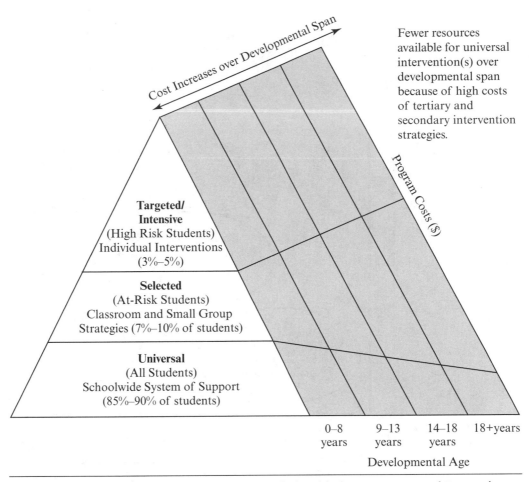

**FIGURE 1.2** *Three-Tiered Model of Support: Relationship between Costs and Prevention Focus Across the Age Span*

*Source:* Reprinted with permission from H. M. Walker & H. Severson (2002), "Developmental Prevention of At-Risk Outcomes for Vulnerable Antisocial Children and Youth." In K. L. Lane, F. M., Gresham, & T. E. O'Shaughnessy (Eds.), *Interventions for Children with or At Risk for Emotional and Behavioral Disorders* (pp. 171–194).

effort to reduce risk (Walker & Severson, 2002). An often cited analogy in the medical field is the use of inoculations. The intent of inoculating children for smallpox is to universally prevent or reduce the risk of small pox. Colvin, Sugai, and Kame'enui (1993) estimate that approximately 80 percent of students should respond to primary interventions.

## Secondary Prevention

The next level of intervention, *secondary prevention,* is focused on reversing harm (Walker & Severson, 2002). Secondary prevention provides more intensive, focused interventions for students who do not respond to primary intervention efforts or who are identified as at-risk learners. Students are typically grouped together by common skill or performance deficits (Elliott & Gresham, 1991). Skill deficits, also referred to as acquisition deficits, are skills that are simply not a part of the child's repertoire. In contrast, performance deficits are skills that are a part of

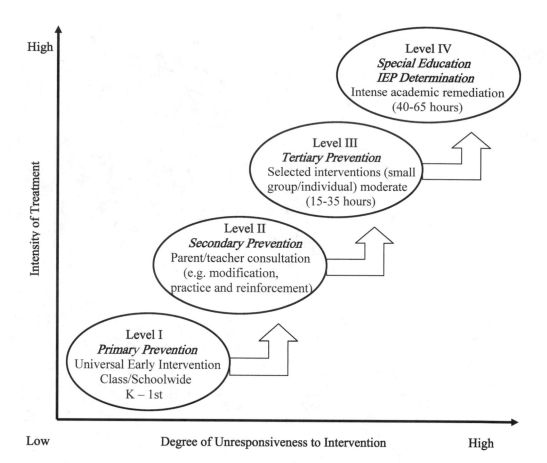

**FIGURE 1.3**   *Degree of Unresponsiveness and Intensity of Treatment*

*Source:* Reprinted with permission from F. M. Gresham (2002). "Responsiveness to Intervention: An Alternative Approach to Learning Disabilities." In R. Bradley, L. Danielson, and D. Hallahan (Eds.), *Identification of Learning Disabilities: Research to Practice* (pp. 456–529). Mahwah, NJ: Lawrence Erlbaum.

the child's repertoire but are not used either frequently enough or in the current context. Consequently, no amount of encouragement (or chocolate!) is going to prompt the desired behavior because the problem is a *can't do* (skills deficit) rather than a *won't do* (performance deficit) problem (Elliott & Gresham, 1991).

Once the children are grouped, suitable interventions are designed and implemented based on common areas of concern. Examples of secondary interventions might include focused interventions such as phonological awareness training for children with poor early literacy skills (Lane, Wehby, Menzies, Gregg, Doukas, & Munton, 2002), social skills training for children with acquisition deficits (Lane, Wehby, Menzies, Doukas, Munton, & Gregg, 2002; Lo, Loe, & Cartledge, 2002), and anger management (Dwivedi, & Gupta, 2000; Feindler, 1995; Kellner, & Tutin, 1995; Presley & Hughes, 2000). Researchers estimate that approximately 10 to 15 percent of students will need secondary prevention support (Gresham, Sugai, Horner, Quinn, & McInerney, 1998).

### Tertiary Prevention

The final level of intervention, *tertiary prevention,* is focused on reducing risk (Walker & Severson, 2002). Tertiary prevention programs are individualized interventions based on specific students' needs. Students who are either nonresponsive to secondary prevention programs or who are exposed to multiple sources of risk such as low cognitive ability (Haskins, 1986; Richardson, 1981), parents with low levels of involvement (Reid & Patterson, 1991; Walker, Zeller, Close, Webber, & Gresham, 1999), and low socioeconomic status (Coutinho, Oswald, Best, & Forness, 2002; Kauffman, 1999) are likely to benefit from this level of support (Lewis & Sugai, 1999; O'Shaughnessy et al., 2002; Walker et al., 1996). Examples of tertiary interventions include functional assessment-based interventions (Dunlap, Foster-Johnson, Clarke, Kern, & Childs, 1995; Dunlap et al., 1993; Kern, Childs, Dunlap, Clarke, & Falk, 1994; Umbreit, 1996), intensive, individualized reading instruction (Torgesen, Alexander, Wagner, Rashotte, Voeller, & Conway, 2001), and home-school interventions such as *First Steps to Success* (Golly, Stiller, & Walker, 1998; Walker, Kavanagh, Stiller, Golly, Severson, & Feil, 2001).

Many schools are currently providing these levels of support for their students. However, some schools are challenged with key issues such as the following: How can we implement these levels of support in a coordinated fashion? How can we determine how well these interventions are working? How do we decide which students need more intensive levels of support? How do we know if these interventions produced lasting outcomes? How do teachers, parents, and students feel about the results of these interventions? These questions can be addressed and the overall quality of the interventions enhanced by incorporating key features into the design, implementation, and evaluation of primary, secondary, and tertiary levels of prevention.

## Key Features of Effective Interventions

There are a variety of specific features that have the potential to enhance intervention outcomes. This book will introduce and provide you with suggestions for implementing each of the following key features: (a) linking interventions to assessment information; (b) evaluating student performance; (c) assessing social validity; (d) monitoring treatment integrity; and (e) attending to issues of generalization and maintenance (Lane, Beebe-Frankenberger, Lambros, & Pierson, 2001; see Figure 1.4). Each of these features will be introduced in brief.

First, it is important to *link interventions to assessment information*. Rather than deciding to implement a schoolwide program on conflict resolution just because

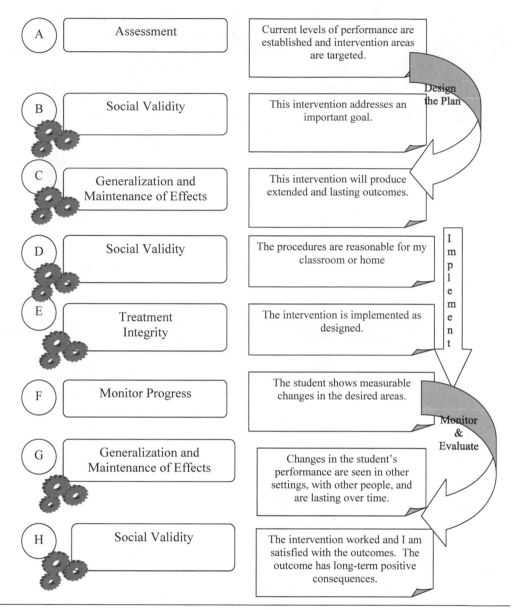

**FIGURE 1.4**    *The Intervention Process*

such a program is available, examine existing information or data to decide if such a program is warranted. For example, in looking at the number of disciplinary contacts that have resulted due to poor problem solving skills or limited anger management skills, one should consider the following questions: Is this a problem that is specific to students in certain grade levels? To students in one or two teachers' classrooms? Or to students in the school as a whole? If it is the latter, then a primary intervention may be justified. If the scope of the problem is limited to a given grade or to specific classrooms, then a secondary intervention may be more appropriate. Similarly, when deciding how to focus a district-wide literacy program, examine a variety of measures ranging from test scores at the state level, curriculum-based measures (Fuchs & Fuchs, 1999; Stecker & Fuchs, 2000), and work samples at the individual student level. This information can then be used to determine areas that warrant additional emphasis.

Second, once the intervention plans are in place, it is important to *monitor student progress* to determine the degree to which the interventions are producing the desired changes. For example, in order to examine the effectiveness of a school-wide positive behavior support intervention, it is important to monitor student progress. As a faculty, the decision might be made to monitor average weekly disciplinary contacts with the vice-principal and average weekly attendance. Further, you might decide to keep track of the percentage of completed assignments to see if there are any changes in academic performance that occur as a collateral or "side effect" of improved school climate (Cushing, 2000). Similarly, if you have designed and implemented a functional assessment-based intervention for a student with an emotional disturbance who is receiving services in a general education first-grade classroom, you will want to determine how well the intervention is working; namely, is the child showing decreases in the problem behavior (e.g., disruptive behavior) and increases in the desired behavior (e.g., participating in class activities)? In this case you would need to use frequent, repeated assessment to monitor student progress on both the problem and the desired replacement behaviors.

Third, prior to implementing intervention and at the conclusion of the intervention, *assess social validity* (Kazdin, 1977; Lane et al., 2001; Wolf, 1978; also see Figure 1.4). Social validity refers to the degree to which the involved parties view the intervention goals as significant, the intervention procedures as acceptable, and the outcomes as important. Social validity is an important, and often overlooked, component of developing effective interventions. Assessing social validity at both time points allows the treatment agents to identify common goals, come to a consensus about the feasibility of various intervention procedures, ensure a commitment from all involved parties to carry out the necessary procedures, and assess the likelihood of (onset) and actual (end) intervention outcomes.

Fourth, when putting the intervention in place, it is important to *monitor treatment integrity* (Gresham, 1989; Lane et al., 2001; Yeaton & Sechrest, 1981; also see Figure 1.4). Treatment integrity refers to the extent to which the intervention plan was implemented as designed. Rather than assuming that the intervention is taking place as originally constructed, it is important to monitor the extent to which each component or step is happening. This information allows more accurate conclusions to be drawn about treatment effectiveness. It may be that a specific intervention (e.g., anger management groups for middle school students) may not produce the desired outcomes. If information about treatment integrity is not collected on a regular basis, then it is difficult to determine if the intervention was ineffective because it was a either a poor intervention or a good intervention that was not implemented correctly. Given that schools have limited resources, we need to invest our monies, personnel, and materials in interventions that help to achieve their intended goals.

Fifth, because the goal of intervention is to produce lasting changes that continue across time and under circumstances that deviate from the training environment, it is also important that attention to *generalization and maintenance* issues be addressed before interventions are implemented (Horner & Billingsley, 1988; also see Figure 1.4). Frequently, current school-based interventions are put in place and the desired goals (e.g., increased oral reading fluency, fewer disciplinary contacts, and improved playground behavior) achieved. Yet, when the intervention concludes, the effects seem to disappear. Why? Because the intervention was not designed to maintain outcomes. Fortunately, it is possible to implement procedures to promote generalization and maintenance of the newly acquired skills and target skills that will increase the likelihood of meaningful, lasting changes.

Finally, it is critical that professionals have a precise, concise method of *presenting intervention outcomes*. With the increased emphasis on performance and achieving district-level and state-level standards, district personnel, principals, and teachers alike need to have a method for documenting data-based student outcomes. These reports need to clearly state (a) the intervention goals and objectives; (b) a justification of these goals and objectives; (c) a detailed description of the intervention, including training and implementation procedures; (d) information on treatment integrity of the intervention procedures; (e) information on social validity of key persons at the onset and conclusion of the intervention; (f) data on student performance before, throughout, and beyond the intervention that includes information about the reliability of the data collected; and (g) recommendations for future interventions.

## Summary and Purpose

There are a wide range of interventions implemented in schools today. As previously mentioned, these interventions range from (a) *primary prevention*—broader scale interventions such as schoolwide positive behaviors and violence prevention programs; (b) *secondary prevention*—small group interventions targeting specific areas of concern such as social skills, anger management, and conflict resolution; to (c) *tertiary prevention*—individualized interventions proposed and implemented by the prereferral intervention team, the special educators, or school psychologists. Unfortunately, oftentimes these interventions do not incorporate the essential components necessary to accurately evaluate intended and unintended intervention outcomes. Specifically, plans to assess social validity, treatment integrity, and generalization/maintenance are often overlooked when designing interventions. Yet these are the tools essential to designing, implementing, and evaluating multilevel school-based interventions (Figure 1.5). Without these components it is diffi-

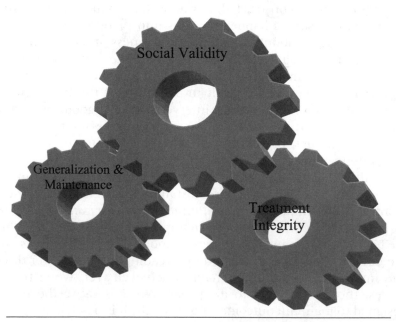

**FIGURE 1.5**  *The Core Components Model: Key Tools for Designing, Implementing, and Evaluating Multilevel School-Based Interventions*

cult to draw accurate conclusions about intervention outcomes. In an era of increased accountability, these components provide professionals the ability to document outcomes that will drive the decision-making process about students' educational programming. This book will define each of these concepts, explain the importance of each, and provide a step-by-step guide to using these tools. Application of these tools will improve the effectiveness of school-based interventions generated by various assistance teams and professionals (i.e., student study teams, functional assessment-based interventionists, and school psychologists). The process will enable professionals to comply with legal mandates set by the federal government (*Individuals with Disabilities Education Act,* IDEA, 1997), such as establishing a student's responsiveness to instruction (Fuchs, Fuchs, & Speece, 2002) and resistance to intervention (Gresham, 1991, 2002), while providing effective tools to document intervention outcomes.

The intent of this book is not to recommend a particular program or intervention, but instead to provide a complete guide to practitioners and researchers in an attempt to refine the intervention process. This text will introduce strategies to incorporate the above-mentioned essential components of intervention design, delivery, and evaluation that will improve the effectiveness of intervention outcomes for primary, secondary, and tertiary levels of prevention.

More specifically, the next two chapters will review recommended practices for linking intervention to assessment results (Chapter 2) and monitoring changes during intervention (Chapter 3). These foundational elements are typically part of intervention. We include a review of these key factors about intervention because we contend that these tasks are often performed without a great deal of understanding *why* they are essential, *what* are current recommended practices for assessing and monitoring performance, and *how* these practices link to outcomes.

Chapters 4, 5, and 6 each explain key tools of our *core components model:* social validity, treatment integrity, and generalization and maintenance, respectively (Figure 1.5). Witt and Elliott (1985) presented a working model of major variables that influence treatment acceptability, stating that use and effectiveness of treatment is bidirectionally influenced by integrity of implementation and acceptability. This model extends the Witt and Elliott model by suggesting that assessing and evaluating the key tools presented in the core component model promote treatment effectiveness and provide a means for providing documentation for treatment accountability. Moreover, when the three key tools of the core component model are incorporated into each level of prevention programs, they reinforce the use of each other. In brief, if pre-intervention measures of social validity are administered, evaluated, and incorporated in intervention, then the interventions are likely to be implemented with integrity. When treatment integrity is measured, then not only is the intervention more likely to be implemented as planned—thereby resulting in the desired changes—but generalization of new skills is more likely to occur and long-term maintenance is likely to be fostered because the new skills will have many more opportunities to be practiced and reinforced naturally. When methods are used to program generalization and maintenance into the intervention, post-intervention assessment of social validity is likely to demonstrate positive treatment outcomes of previously identified, socially significant goals. Finally, the model suggests that when treatment agents find an intervention successful with socially important outcomes, they tend to not only accept future intervention efforts, but also recommend and support intervention for others. Thus, the key features of the core components model individually and collectively reinforce the use of the next component and increase the probability of achieving the desired outcomes while providing concrete evidence of treatment accountability. Figure 1.4 is an extended visual representation of the key tools of the core component model (Figure 1.5) that illustrates when and how each of these tools are used in the intervention process. Figure 1.4 will be reproduced and referred to in Chapters 4, 5, and 6.

In sum, this book addresses the need for educators to provide evidence of intervention effectiveness for universal, secondary, and tertiary interventions. Specifically, *School-Based Interventions: The Tools You Need to Succeed* provides a rationale for and specific steps necessary in designing interventions based on assessment results. We offer a practical, user-friendly method of putting into place best practices for successful implementation of interventions so that educators can document and evaluate intervention results with confidence.

The basic principles and methods reviewed in the book are universal to academic, behavioral, and social areas and are applicable to intervention projects for all students, regardless of ability level, across the preschool to young adult age span. In addition, this book is intended for use by a wide range of interventionists. It can be used by general educators, special educators, chairs of prereferral intervention teams, counselors, school psychologists, behavioral specialists, and researchers.

By following the strategies and guidelines presented in the pages to follow, you and the students you serve will be more likely to benefit from the interventions (primary, secondary, and tertiary) available at your school site. These strategies and guidelines will help you to design more effective interventions to achieve the intended goals specified by those in leadership positions as well as the goals specified by you, your parents, and your students. Further, you will acquire the data necessary to document your efforts and to demonstrate accountability for results.

## *References*

Canter, L. (1990). *Lee Canter's back to school with assertive discipline.* Santa Monica, CA: Canter & Associates.

Canter, L., & Canter, M. (1992). *Lee Canter's assertive discipline.* Santa Monica, CA: Canter & Associates.

Caplan, G. (1964). *Principles of preventive psychology.* New York: Basic Books.

Colvin, G., Sugai, G., & Kame'enui, E. (1993). *Proactive schoolwide discipline: Implementation manual.* Project PREPARE, Behavioral Research and Teaching, College of Education, University of Oregon, Eugene.

Committee for Children. (1992). *Second Step: Violence prevention curriculum for preschool-grade 9.* Seattle: Author.

Coutinho, M. J., Oswald, D. P., Best, A. M., & Forness, S. R. (2002). Gender and sociodemographic factors and the disproportionate identification of culturally and linguistically diverse students with emotional disturbance. *Behavioral Disorders, 27,* 109–125.

Cushing, L. S. (2000). *Descriptive analysis in the school social culture of elementary and middle school students.* Doctoral dissertation, University of Oregon, Eugene.

DeBaryshe, B. D., & Fryxell, D. (1998). A developmental perspective on anger: Family and peer contexts. *Psychology in the Schools, 35,* 205–216.

Dunlap, G., Foster-Johnson, L., Clarke, S., Kern, L., & Childs, K. (1995). Modifying activities to produce functional outcomes: Effects on the problem behaviors of students with disabilities. *Journal of the Association for Persons with Severe Handicaps, 20,* 248–258.

Dunlap, G., Kern, L., dePerczel, M., Clarke, S., Wilson, D., Childs, K., White, R., & Falk, G. (1993). Functional analysis of classroom variables for students with emotional and behavioral disorders. *Behavioral Disorders, 18,* 275–291.

Dwivedi, K. N., & Gupta, A. (2000). "Keeping cool": Anger management through group work. *Support for Learning, 15,* 76–81.

Elliott, S., & Gresham, F. M. (1991). *Social skills intervention guide.* Circle Pines, MN: American Guidance Service.

Feindler, E. L. (1995). Ideal treatment package for children and adolescents with anger disorders. *Issues in Comprehensive Pediatric Nursing, 18,* 233–260.

Forness, S., Kavale, K. A., MacMillan, D. L., Asarnow, J. R., & Duncan, B. B. (1996). Early detection and prevention of emotional or behavioral disorders: Developmental aspects of systems of care. *Behavioral Disorders, 21,* 226–240.

Fuchs, D., & Fuchs, L. S. (1994). Inclusive schools movement and the radicalization of special education reform. *Exceptional Children, 60,* 294–309.

Fuchs, L. S., & Fuchs, D. (1999). Monitoring student progress toward the development of reading competence: A review of three forms of classroom-based assessment. *School Psychology Review, 28,* 659–671.

Fuchs, L. S., Fuchs, D., & Speece, D. L. (2002). Treatment validity as a unifying construct for identifying learning disabilities. *Learning Disability Quarterly, 25,* 33–45.

Golly, A. M., Stiller, B., & Walker, H. M. (1998). First Step to Success: Replication and social validation of an early intervention program. *Journal of Emotional and Behavioral Disorders, 6,* 243–250.

Gresham, F. M. (1989). Assessment of treatment integrity in school consultation and prereferral intervention. *School Psychology Review, 18,* 37–50.

Gresham, F. M. (1991). Conceptualizing behavior disorders in terms of resistance to intervention. *School Psychology Review, 20,* 1, 23–36.

Gresham, F. M. (2002). Responsiveness to intervention: An alternative approach to learning disabilities. In R. Bradley, L. Danielson, & D. Hallahan (Eds.), *Identification of Learning Disabilities: Research to Practice.* Mahwah, NJ: Erlbaum.

Gresham, F. M., Sugai, G., Horner, R., Quinn, M., & McInerney, M. (1998). *Classroom and schoolwide practices that support students' social competence: A synthesis of research.* Washington, DC: Office of Special Education Programs.

Haskins, R. (1986). Social and cultural factors in risk assessment and mild mental retardation. In D. C. Farran & J. D. McKinney (Eds.), *Risk in intellectual and psychosocial development* (pp. 29–69). Orlando, FL: Academic Press.

Horner, R., & Billingsley, F. (1988). The effect of competing behavior on the generalization and maintenance of adaptive behavior in applied settings. In R. Horner, G., Dunlap, & R. Koegel (Eds.), *Generalization and maintenance: Lifestyle changes in applied settings* (pp. 197–220). Baltimore: Paul H. Brookes.

*Individuals with Disabilities Education Act Amendments of 1997.* Pub. L. No. 105–17, Section 20, 111 Stat. 37 (1997). Washington, DC: U.S. Government Printing Office.

Jones, R. N., Sheridan, S. M., Binns, W. R. (1993). Schoolwide social skills training: Providing preventive services to students at-risk. *School Psychology Quarterly, 8,* 57–80.

Kamps, D., Kravits, T., Stolze, S., & Swaggart, B. (1999). Prevention strategies for at-risk students and students with EBD in urban elementary schools. *Journal of Emotional and Behavioral Disorders, 7,* 178–188.

Kauffman, J. (1999). *Characteristics of emotional behavioral disorders in children and youth.* Upper Saddle River, NJ: Merrill-Prentice Hall.

Kazdin, A. E. (1977). Assessing the clinical or applied significance of behavior change through social validation. *Behaviour Modification, 1,* 427–452.

Kellner, M. H., & Tutin, J. (1995). A school-based anger management program for developmentally and emotionally disabled high school students. *Adolescence, 30,* 813–825.

Kern, L., Childs, K. E., Dunlap, G., Clarke, S., & Falk, K. B. (1994). Using assessment-based curricular intervention to improve the classroom behavior of a student with emotional and behavioral challenges. *Journal of Applied Behavior Analysis, 27,* 7–19.

Lane, K. L., Beebe-Frankenberger, M. E., Lambros, K. L., & Pierson, M. E. (2001). Designing effective interventions for children at-risk for antisocial behavior: An integrated model of components necessary for making valid inferences. *Psychology in the Schools, 38,* 365–379.

Lane, K. L., & Menzies, H. M. (2002). Promoting achievement and minimizing risk—phase I: The impact of a school-based primary intervention program. *Preventing School Failure, 47,* 26–32.

Lane, K. L., & Wehby, J. (2002). Addressing antisocial behavior in the schools: A call for action. *Academic Exchange Quarterly, 6,* 4–9.

Lane, K. L., Wehby, J., Menzies, H., Doukas, G., Munton, S., & Gregg, R. (in press) Social skills training for students at-risk for antisocial behavior: The effects of small group instruction. *Behavioral Disorders.*

Lane, K. L., Wehby, J. H., Menzies, H. M., Gregg, R. M., Doukas, G. L., & Munton, S. M. (2002). Early literacy instruction for first-grade students at-risk for antisocial behavior. *Education and Treatment of Children, 25,* 438–458.

Lewis, T. J., & Sugai, G. (1999). Effective behavior support: A systems approach to proactive schoolwide management. *Focus on Exceptional Children, 31,* 1–24.

Lewis, T. J., Sugai, G., & Colvin, G. (1998). Reducing problem behavior through a schoolwide system of effective behavior support: Investigation of a schoolwide social skills training program and contextual variables. *School Psychology Review, 27,* 446–459.

Lo, Y., Loe, S. A., & Cartledge, G. (2002). The effects of social skills instruction on the social behaviors of students at risk for emotional and behavioral disorders. *Behavioral Disorders, 27,* 371–385.

Lohrmann-O'Rourke, S., Knoster, T., Sabatine, K., Smith, D., Horvath, B., & Llewellyn, G. (2000). Schoolwide application of PBS in the Bangor area school district. *Journal of Positive Behavior Interventions, 2,* 238–240.

Lonigan, C., Elbert, J., & Johnson, S. B. (1998). Empirically supported psychosocial interventions for children: An overview. *Journal of Clinical Child Psychology, 27,* 138–145.

MacGregor, R. R., Nelson, J. R., & Wesch, D. (1997). Creating positive learning environments: The schoolwide student management program. *Professional School Counseling, 1,* 33–36.

MacMillan, D., Gresham, F., & Forness, S. (1996). Full inclusion: An empirical perspective. *Behavioral Disorders, 21,* 145–159.

Nelson, C. M., Rutherford, R. B., Center, D. B., & Walker, H. M. (1991). Do public schools have an obligation to serve troubled children and youth? *Exceptional Children, 57,* 406–415.

O'Shaughnessy, T., Lane, K. L., Gresham, F. M., & Beebe-Frankenberger (2002). Students with or at-risk for learning and emotional-behavioral difficulties: An integrated system of prevention and intervention. In K. L. Lane, F. M. Gresham, and T. E. O'Shaughnessy (Eds.), *Interventions for children with or at risk for emotional and behavioral disorders* (pp. 3–17). Boston: Allyn & Bacon.

Presley, J. A., & Hughes, C. (2000). Peers as teachers of anger management to high school students with behavior disorders. *Behavioral Disorders, 25,* 114–130.

Reid, J. B., & Patterson, G. R. (1991). Early prevention and intervention with conduct problems: A social interactional model for the integration of research and practice. In G. Stoner, M. R. Shinn, & H. M. Walker (Eds.), *Interventions for achievement and behavior problems* (pp. 715–739). Silver Spring, MD: National Association of School Psychologists.

Richardson, S. A. (1981). Family characteristics associated with mild mental retardation. In M. J. Begab, H. C. Haywood, & H. L. Garber (Eds.), *Psychosocial influences in retarded performance* (pp. 29–43). Baltimore: University Park Press.

Scott, T. M. (2001). A schoolwide example of positive behavior support. *Journal of Positive Behavior Interventions, 3,* 88–94.

Stecker, P. M., & Fuchs, L. S. (2000). Effecting superior achievement using curriculum-based measurement: The importance of individual progress monitoring. *Learning Disabilities Research and Practice, 15,* 128–134.

Stoiber, K. C., & Kratochwill, T. R. (2001). Evidenced-based intervention programs: Rethinking, refining, and renaming the new standing section of *School Psychology Quarterly. School Psychology Quarterly, 16,* 1–8.

Taylor-Greene, S. J., & Kartub, D. T. (2000). Durable implementation of schoolwide behavior support: The high-five program. *Journal of Positive Behavior Interventions, 2,* 233–235.

Torgesen, J. K., Alexander, A. W., Wagner, R. K., Rashotte, C. A., Voeller, K. S., & Conway, T. (2001). Intensive remedial instruction for children with severe reading disabilities: Immediate and long-term outcomes from two instructional approaches. *Journal of Learning Disabilities, 34,* 33–58.

Turnbull, A., Edmonson, H., Griggs, P., Wickham, D., Sailor, W., Freeman, R., Guess, D., Lassen, S., McCart, A., Park, J., Riffel, L., Turnbull, R., & Warren, J. (2002). A blueprint for schoolwide positive behavior support: Implementation of three components. *Exceptional Children, 68,* 377–402.

Umbreit, J. (1996). Functional analysis of disruptive behavior in an inclusive classroom. *Journal of Early Intervention, 20,* 18–29.

Walker, H. M., Horner, R. H., Sugai, G., Bullis, M., Sprague, J. R., Bricker, D., & Kaufman, M. J. (1996). Integrated approaches to preventing antisocial behavior patterns among school-age children and youth. *Journal of Emotional and Behavioral Disorders, 4,* 193–256.

Walker, H. M., Kavanagh, K., Stiller, B., Golly, A., Severson, H. H., & Feil, E. G. (2001). First step to success: An early intervention approach for preventing school antisocial behavior. In H. M. Walker, and M. H. Epstein (Eds.), *Making schools safer and violence free: Critical issues, solutions, and recommended practices* (pp. 73–87). Austin, TX: Pro-Ed.

Walker, H. M., & Severson, H. (2002). Developmental prevention of at-risk outcomes for vulnerable antisocial children and youth. In K. L. Lane, F. M. Gresham, & T. E. O'Shaughnessy (Eds.), *Interventions for children with or at risk for emotional and behavioral disorders* (pp. 177–194). Boston: Allyn & Bacon.

Walker, H. M., Zeller, R. W., Close, D. W., Webber, J., & Gresham, F. (1999). The present unwrapped: Change and challenge in the field of behavior disorders. *Behavioral Disorders, 24,* 293–304.

Witt, J. C., & Elliott, S. N. (1985). Acceptability of classroom management strategies. In T. R. Kratochwill (Ed.), *Advances in school psychology* (Vol. 4, pp. 251–288). Hillsdale, NJ: Erlbaum.

Wolf, M. M. (1978). Social validity: The case for subjective measurement or how applied behavior analysis is finding its heart. *Journal of Applied Behavior Analysis, 11,* 203–214.

Yeaton, W., & Sechrest, L. (1981). Critical dimensions in the choice and maintenance of successful treatments: Strength, integrity, and effectiveness. *Journal of Consulting and Clinical Psychology, 49,* 156–167.

Part **I**

# Reviewing Linking and Monitoring Strategies

The intent of the following chapters is to provide you with an opportunity to revisit two important components of designing interventions: linking interventions to assessment results and monitoring student performance.

# 2

## *Linking Interventions to Assessment Results*

As educators, we frequently observe our students and notice their various levels of performance in a variety of areas. We see some students making great strides in the area of reading (e.g., the first-grade student who reads *Harry Potter and the Chamber of Secrets* [Rowling, 1999] during sustained silent reading), others who are on par with the rest of the class (e.g., the second-grade student reading an emergent-level text), and others who struggle with tasks that are below grade-level expectations (e.g., the fifth-grade student who cannot decode the word "ship"). We use this information to make decisions about how to group students for reading instruction, when to modify lessons for students who are struggling or provide supplements for students who need to be challenged, and how to evaluate student performance at report card time. Educators have made these types of comparisons and subsequent decisions not only about individual performance, but about system-wide performance as well.

The Leave No Child Behind Act of 2001 signed into law by President Bush on January 8, 2002 (Fournier, AP 2002), places a new demand on educators with the mandate for all states to institute standards-based testing to demonstrate grade-level academic proficiency by the year 2005. Statewide testing is to be implemented to monitor the extent to which standards in reading and math are met, and results will be used to judge student, teacher, and school performance. The pressure is on educators to raise student performance levels across the board (Linn, Baker, & Betenbenner, 2002). Failure to do so may result in a school losing federal funding and, in turn, students could receive funding to seek tutoring support or permission to transfer to more successful public schools (Beebe-Frankenberger, Bocian, MacMillan, & Gresham, 2002; Fournier, AP 2002).

Clearly, educators must demonstrate student growth—and not just on standardized measures such as state assessments (e.g., Academic Excellence Indicator System, AEIS, Texas; Florida Comprehensive Assessment Test, FCAT; Massachusetts Comprehensive Assessment System, MCAS; Oregon Statewide Assessments; Standardized Testing and Reporting, STAR, California; Tennessee Comprehensive Assessment Program, TCAP). Schools must also document student responsiveness to various curricula, programs, and interventions that have been implemented in order to produce optimum opportunity for student success. We cannot wait for yearly results on statewide standardized testing to detect increases in academic performance levels. Student progress must be monitored frequently and accurately to assess growth. No longer are informal assessments (e.g., work samples and informal observations) used in isolation from data-based methods sufficient for informing curricular decisions and monitoring student progress. There is a call for accountability for what is taught, how instruction is delivered, and more precision when monitoring student progress toward learning.

Fortunately, the field of education has made great strides in assessment with the validation of Dynamic Indicators of Basic Early Literacy Skills (DIBELS, Kaminski & Good, 1996), curriculum-based measurement (CBM; Fuchs & Fuchs, 1986; Shinn, Rosenfeld, & Knutson, 1989), performance-based assessment (PBA; Greenwood, Terry, Marquis & Walker 1994), and direct observation technology such as Multiple Option Observation System for Experimental Studies (MOOSES; Tapp, Wehby, & Ellis, 1995). These assessment tools enable frequent, repeated assessment to monitor more subtle changes in student performance, which is essential in light of the call for increased accountability and educational improvement (Linn et al., 2002). Progress monitoring provides systematic, formative feedback that informs instructional practices and planning (Fuchs, Fuchs, & Hamlett, 1993, 1994). By monitoring student progress, the information can be used to (a) evaluate existing programs, (b) inform those in leadership positions as to which programs or interventions are producing the desired changes and which are in need of modification, (c) identify students not making sufficient progress in primary intervention, (d) determine what types of interventions would be beneficial for students who are not responsive to primary intervention efforts, (e) evaluate the effects of secondary interventions such as reading comprehension groups or anger management groups, (f) identify students who might need intensive, tertiary interventions, and (g) evaluate the effects of tertiary interventions. Thus, each level of prevention—primary, secondary, and tertiary—is linked or connected to assessment information. Decisions about how, when, and with whom to intervene should not be arbitrary decisions; they need to be informed decisions linked to assessment results.

As you read this chapter, keep in mind that each level of intervention is targeting a desired area for improvement. In the case of primary prevention efforts, the focus of intervention efforts should be determined after reviewing the available data. Examples of data that are frequently available to schools include the following: state assessment measures of reading, written expression, language, mathematics, social studies, and science skills; attendance rates; disciplinary contacts such as referrals, suspensions, and expulsions; and percentage of students receiving free and reduced lunch. By reviewing this information, it might be evident that students are failing to perform in the area of reading as evidenced by state test scores, and that students appear to demonstrate rather high levels of physical aggression as evidenced by disciplinary information. In this case, the school might decide to design, implement, and evaluate a schoolwide literacy program along with a violence prevention program. In order to evaluate how students are responding to this new primary prevention program, data would be collected frequently (e.g., weekly, bimonthly, or monthly) to determine which students are benefiting from this instruction. If a group of students demonstrates minimal progress in the area of decoding as measured by limited progress on oral reading fluency passages, a secondary intervention such as a small group intervention to address this skill deficit might be proposed. The *focus* of the secondary intervention is determined by evaluating the data collected to monitor student responsiveness to the primary intervention. Again, intervention is linked to assessment results.

As with the case of primary interventions, student responsiveness to secondary interventions is monitored by collecting data on behaviors or skills that are targeted in the secondary intervention (e.g., the number of words read correctly in a one-minute passage, the number of sight words read correctly per minute, or the percentage of comprehension questions answered correctly on a weekly basis). Results of secondary interventions are interpreted to identify students who might need even more intensive, tertiary support.

Tertiary prevention might include functional assessment-based interventions (e.g., see Dunlap, Foster-Johnson, Clarke, Kern, & Childs, 1995; Dunlap & Kern, 1996; Ervin, DuPaul, Kern, & Friman, 1998; Kern, Dunlap, Clarke, & Childs, 1994; Umbreit, Lane, & DeJud, in press) or individualized interventions. As with secondary interventions, data are collected frequently with the use of repeated assessments (e.g., direct observations or curriculum-based measures) to monitor the degree to which students are benefiting from the intervention.

In each level of prevention, decisions about *who* needs intervention, *what* type of intervention, and the *level of intensity* are made by examining data. Thus, each level of prevention is linked to assessment results.

The intent of this chapter is fourfold. First, we will broadly define what is meant by the term "assessment." Second, we will explain specifically what it means to link interventions to assessment results. Third, we will discuss the importance of linking interventions to assessment results. Fourth, we will offer procedures for connecting interventions to assessment results at each level of prevention (primary, secondary, and tertiary).

## What Is Assessment?

Simply stated, assessment is a process of gathering, synthesizing, analyzing, and interpreting information about a student, a class of students, or the whole student body using a variety of reliable and valid instruments and methods for the purpose of making sound decisions (Airasian, 1996). When assessment is completed, the information collected is presented in data format and used to guide the decision-making process, which includes intervention design. Assessment data provide the basis for deciding whether there really is a problem, and if so, the data are used to measure progress during intervention and attainment of the intervention goal.

### Administrative versus Functional Assessments

Educational assessments can be academic and/or behavioral and are used primarily for two purposes: (a) administrative decisions, such as diagnosis, prognosis, and eligibility, and (b) evaluative decisions to understand the effects of teaching and/or intervention (Mash & Terdal, 1988).

Assessment for the purpose of diagnosis, prognosis, and/or eligibility is *administrative assessment* and results in a global judgment about the overall condition of a student, class of student, or a student body. An example of schoolwide administrative assessment may be a summary statement that there is low morale among students. Results of administrative assessment cannot be linked to a specific intervention because no specific cause for the low morale is detected in an administrative assessment.

Assessment for the purpose of evaluating of effects of teaching or intervention is *functional assessment* and results in the identification of a specific academic or behavioral deficit that is the cause of the "problem" and thus can be linked to intervention with data (Bastsche & Knoff, 1995). For the student body with low morale, a functional assessment would determine the specific conditions producing low morale, such as data concerning the number of aggressive incidents on campus during a week or the number of students who failed core classes.

Thus, the administrative assessment confirms an overall problem while the functional assessment provides data about behaviors or skill levels that contribute to the overall problem. Both types of assessments are used to make decisions about intervention. Administrative assessments are useful to determine a system-wide problem and then can be used to apply a primary intervention. More specific information, or functional assessment, is necessary for secondary and tertiary intervention.

An everyday situation that illustrates how an administrative assessment and a functional assessment differ in kind is as follows: A child looks pale and feels hot to the touch. A mother uses a thermometer to confirm that her child has an elevated temperature and is ill. This is an administrative assessment from which a global judgment can be made: her child is sick. The elevated temperature is a symptom of a specific illness and can be treated without the knowledge of specifics. The mother could apply a primary intervention and give her child aspirin to bring the temperature down (a primary intervention we've both used many times!). However, if the cause of the elevated temperature is meningitis rather than the flu, the aspirin will not be effective. If her child's temperature returns to normal within twenty-four hours or so, she may assume that it was just the flu, without any further harm to her child. However, if the temperature does not respond to the aspirin and more time passes, a serious condition could worsen by waiting an additional twenty-four hours before seeking help from the doctor to pinpoint and treat the specific illness. The mother also decides to call the doctor for an appointment for further assessment to find out the specific cause of the fever. Without the doctor's assessment, no specific treatment is inferred. She is asking the doctor to identify the *function* of the high temperature. The fever is a clear symptom that signals *something* is wrong, but not *what* is wrong with her child. The doctor's assessment will be used to evaluate what is wrong and what is an appropriate treatment for the specific illness. Should it be aspirin, fluids, and rest for the flu, or more intensive specific treatment in the hospital for meningitis? The doctor's medical assessment data will *link* the type of treatment selected to restore the child's health. Medical data will be used to monitor whether treatment is working.

In education, an example of the outcome of an administrative assessment is a diagnosis of Attention Deficit Hyperactivity Disorder (ADHD). Nothing specific is known about a child with a diagnosis of ADHD, nor does the label lead to a specific treatment. As a matter of fact, diagnosis categories specified in the Diagnostic and Statistical Manual of Mental Disorders (DSM-IV; APA 1994) are designed to be "shorthand" among diagnosticians. The diagnosis indicates the presence of a sufficient number of the typical cluster of symptoms of a disorder to qualify for educational or medical services. A diagnosis alone does not give information about the specific deficits or performance levels of the individual. Thus, the specific treatment that is valid for any one individual is not necessarily indicated by an administrative assessment. In other words, merely knowing that the child has ADHD does not provide explicit information that can be used to design an effective intervention to help that child attend to instruction in school. By contrast, if results of a functional assessment showed that a student, Bryce, exhibits low rates of academic engaged time when asked to complete twenty minutes of independent seat work in math, the data could be used to help design and monitor an intervention for his unique needs. In this example, one possible intervention to address Bryce's ADHD decreased attention span would be to create shorter tasks for Bryce (e.g., complete the first five problems) that could be checked by the teacher during the twenty-minute interval.

Similarly, in general education, teachers may identify through standardized testing that a student is low functioning in reading. A student scoring 78 on a standardized reading test (where a score of 100 is the average score) would be a signal to the teacher that there is a problem with the student's reading skill. The score of 78 does not give the teacher any information about what specific reading skill the student is deficient in and what skill needs to be targeted by intervention to raise the student's overall reading skill. Is the student reading so slowly that comprehension is difficult, or is the student deficient in phonemic awareness and is not reading the words correctly to comprehend text? One cannot *link* an administrative assessment (in this example a low reading score) with intervention because the generalized score does not identify or measure the specific deficit skill, and therefore does not infer specific treatment for the student. Skill deficits that are unique to the student need to be assessed to make hypotheses about replacement skills/behaviors that can be taught in intervention to promote skill acquisition and proficient skill performance levels.

*Functional assessment* provides specific data about a deficit or area of concern. For secondary and tertiary interventions, we are referring to *functional assessments* that yield data related to specific deficits so that assessment is linked with intervention and can be used to monitor academic progress. Results of functional assessment are used to make a hypothesis about a replacement skill/behavior—the *link,* which is designed to solve the problem or address the area of concern. Not only are we identifying the deficient skill, but also the extent of the deficit so that intensity and duration of intervention can also be hypothesized. Should we expect the student to reach the intervention goal after three weeks of treatment or after ten weeks? Should the treatment be applied twice daily or twice weekly? These types of questions are answered by evaluating the results of functional assessment. The example in Box 2.1 describes a student who used off-task behavior to mask an underlying problem of deficient writing skills. This is a prime example of functional assessment. The assessment identified a specific writing skill deficit that was the *function* of off-task behavior. Data collected relative to the deficient writing skill performance level and rate of off-task behavior link assessment to intervention design, monitoring, and accomplishment of the goal. A realistic skill level for an intervention goal can be set for the student based on the original assessment of writing skill deficiency. The functional assessment provides the baseline writing skill level measurement used to assess and monitor student progress toward the final writing goal (see Chapter 3, Monitoring Changes).

In summary, educational assessment can be *administrative* or *functional.* Administrative assessment is useful when a system-wide (school, district) problem is present. This type of assessment results in a global judgment about a condition for which primary interventions are appropriate and will rectify a problem for the vast majority of students. When more specific intervention is necessary (secondary or tertiary), more specific assessment data need to be collected so that appropriate replacement skills/behaviors are targeted. Functional assessment provides the data to evaluate the specific deficit and extent of an underlying problem and then links intervention with a realistic and appropriate replacement behavior and mechanism for monitoring intervention effectiveness. A school psychologist uses both types of

**BOX 2.1  •  *Practical Application of Linking a Tertiary Intervention with Assessment Results***

A student is referred to the Student Study Team because of excessive off-task behavior (e.g., out of seat, talking to peers) during writing activities. The teacher has exhausted his repertoire of behavior management techniques. The student is evaluated through a variety of assessment procedures including direct observations, interviews with the teacher and the student, and a school record review. It is hypothesized that the off-task behavior is due to deficient writing skills. The student avoids writing by using competing behaviors of talking to peers and walking around the class (if you're talking or walking, you can't be writing). Although the referral "problem" is off-task behavior, the root problem is a writing skill deficit. The assessment collects data about the occurrence of off-task behavior (frequency, intensity, etc.) and also data about writing skills. The assessment is linked to intervention when treatment is designed to improve the student's writing skills to a realistic level that will make the student successful. The link is the *replacement skill* (improved writing skill) that is being taught through intervention, which is the "solution" to off-task behavior. The student's willingness to write is increased, decreasing the need for avoidance accomplished by off-task behavior. During the intervention, data are collected to monitor both off-task behavior and writing skill. The initial assessment data are compared to monitoring data to judge whether progress is being made. If off-task behavior decreases as writing skill increases, the replacement skill is working. The positive intervention outcome will be improved writing performance and reduced time off task; thus, student success is promoted.

Conversely, had the off-task behavior problem been targeted for reduction by using punitive techniques, and the deficient writing skill not detected as the root cause of off-task behavior, the intervention would not have been successful in the long term. In a way, the student is unconsciously using off-task behavior as a survival technique, taking attention away from a true writing skill deficit while showcasing social skills among peers (talking and being a social butterfly around the room). A behaviorist would say we would assess for and design an intervention to target the *function* of the off-task behavior, which is *avoidance* of the writing task that is onerous to the student because of deficient writing skills. The *link* connecting the assessment information to a writing intervention is established. Namely, the focus of the intervention is to teach writing skills to a predetermined proficiency level that is realistic for the individual and that will promote student success. Off-task behavior is a symptom of the real problem—writing skill. The intervention goal will be to increase writing skill that will decrease off-task behavior during writing tasks. Off-task behavior and writing skill are monitored during intervention using data so that all parties to the intervention can make judgments about the ongoing intervention and then make decisions about changes, if necessary. Assessment data inform the entire process, providing both feedback and accountability.

assessment during a thorough formal evaluation of a student for special education services. In this manner, both eligibility and appropriate replacement skills/behaviors can be evaluated so that teachers and parents have both types of information available when formulating future educational plans and specific goals for a child.

### Assessment versus Testing

Further confusion about assessment takes place when the terms "testing" and "assessment" are used interchangeably. To clarify, testing is just one part of assessment. Testing refers to a "formal, systematic, usually paper-and-pencil procedure for gathering information" (Airasian, 1996, p.5). Assessment relies on four sources of information: (a) review of records, (b) interviews with persons familiar with the student and/or responsible for the intervention, (c) observation of the student and others in the learning environment, and (d) tests of student skill performance (Batsche & Knoff, 1995). Assessment utilizes multiple sources of information that together can be used to design an intervention. The best instructional technique for a particular student can also be determined through the assessment.

It is important to recognize that a skill may be affected by the *teaching strategy* rather than by student *ability* to learn. One focus of assessment may be how best to teach a skill to a student. Consider, for example, the case of Bryce, a student with ADHD. Bryce has the ability to learn, but his short attention span and impulsive behaviors require a different teaching strategy: shorter, but frequent, learning sessions. Comparing the student's acquisition and/or performance level of a skill using one teaching strategy versus another may help the assessor determine which strategies may be more suitable for the individual student. In this manner, assessment is linked with intervention by teaching technique; we know what to do to help the student acquire and master a skill.

### Standardized versus Skills-Based Tests

Tests can be standardized or skills-based (Batsche & Knoff, 1995). Standardized tests make comparisons between an individual student and other students exposed to the same educational material, usually the same grade or age. For example, a student scoring at 74 percentile on a math proficiency test is evaluated as demonstrating math skills that exceed 73 out of 100 students taking the same test. Skills-based tests assess an individual student's performance of a specific skill. For example, how many words does the student read correctly per minute? Although the results of skills-based testing can be compared to another student or to all students in a class, the purpose of collecting the information is to evaluate a student's progress toward learning the skill. A second-grade student who is measured as reading twenty correct words per minute may have an intervention goal of sixty words per minute with benchmarks of thirty, forty, and fifty as interim intervention targets. The skills-based test will be used to monitor progress toward benchmarks and the goal.

Parents and teachers are informally assessing and making *normative* comparisons all the time by using their experience of how an average child performs or looks. This is based on their exposure to a number of children over time. The more children a teacher or parent is exposed to, the greater the ability to make informal judgments about one child's performance relative to others. Administrative assessments use normative comparisons and standardized testing to compare one child to all children of the same age and/or grade. This is accomplished by administering an assessment instrument that is normed on a national sample comprised of students in the same regional and ethnic proportions as the national population. One example of this is an intelligence test that results in a full-scale IQ for an individual student. An IQ of 85 is relative to the normative sample of the IQ testing instrument. Thus, one can say that the individual student is performing below the average student (an IQ of 100 is average) in the United States. The standardized score gives a relative standing to others. "Typical tests provide information about whether one student is performing better or worse than other students. This does not help very much when designing instruction except to say that *something* needs to be done about a low-performing student" (Witt & Beck, 1999, p. 7). The use of skills-based testing as part of a functional assessment is needed to make decisions about what replacement skill/behavior will be the focus of an intervention. Skills-based testing provides the performance level data to begin intervention, the data to monitor progress, and the data to determine intervention effectiveness.

Curriculum-based assessment (CBA) is a skills-based assessment used to measure the students' current levels of performance on the curriculum to which they have been exposed (Fuchs, Fuchs, & Stecker, 1989; Shinn, Rosenfeld, & Knutson, 1989). By using the local curriculum as a basis for gathering information about students' performance levels, CBA has been termed an "edumetric" tool (Carver, 1974) and is more relevant to students' immediate educational needs than are nationally standardized tests such as the Woodcock-Johnson III (W-J III; Woodcock, McGrew, & Mather, 2001), a standardized test used to compare student performance in the population. CBA has been used for at least four different purposes: (1) as an alternative to standardized tests for placement purposes (Elliott & Fuchs, 1997), (2) as a means for monitoring progress, (3) to identify where to begin instruction, and (4) to determine the types of errors a student makes. CBA provides specific data from which to design instruction, beginning at the student's current level of functioning. Curriculum-based measurement (CBM) is one type of CBA and uses probes to measure learning of specific skills; thus, it can be categorized as skills-based testing, or measurement. For example, one-minute reading probes from the class reading text can be used to measure reading fluency performance levels. CBM yields invaluable data for monitoring ongoing progress during intervention, facilitating students' knowledge of their own performance, enhancing student motivation for learning (Fuchs, Butterworth, & Fuchs, 1989), and producing data to make adjustments when necessary during intervention (Fuchs, Fuchs, et al., 1989; also see Chapter 3, Monitoring Changes). CBM measures are relative to the individual student, are brief and easy to administer, and can be used repeatedly over the course of intervention (O'Shaugnessy, Lane, Gresham, & Beebe-Frankenberger, 2002). The replacement skill/behavior is selected using functional assessment, of which CBA is a component, while CBM is one type of CBA used to measure and monitor progress toward acquisition of academic skills.

### What Is and How Do I Identify a Replacement Skill/Behavior?

In the case of secondary and tertiary prevention, assessment data link to intervention by providing sufficient information (data) to hypothesize about an academic or social *replacement skill/behavior* that will be the solution to the identified problem or area targeted for growth. The focus of successful proactive interventions is a replacement skill/behavior that is taught and practiced until a prespecified performance level, determined by assessment data, is attained.

It is almost always apparent what is *not* acceptable, or what students should *not* do. The focus for treatment is the correct skill, or sufficient skill level that replaces the wrong skill/behavior. An intervention, whether primary, secondary or tertiary, designed to teach what *not to do* is doomed for eventual failure because it only creates a void; there is no instruction about what *to do* in that same space of time. A prime example is the "Just Say No" campaign during the 1980's used to address teenage drug use. Although implemented with good intentions and reverberated through every public school, "Just Say No" brought the drug abuse issue to the forefront, but it did not decrease teenage drug use. Why? Because the negative consequences of using drugs were not addressed (Fishbein, Hall-Jamieson, Zimmer, Von Haeften, & Nabi, 2002) and because no alternative behavior/skill was taught to teenagers as an effective way to "say no," or as an alternative to drug use.

Using assessment data to decide upon an appropriate and socially acceptable (see Chapter 4, Social Validity) replacement skill/behavior is essential to the success of intervention, linking assessment results to intervention.

## What Does It Mean to Link Intervention to Assessment Results?

When assessment results are linked with intervention, the intervention has *treatment validity* (Gresham & Lambros, 1998; Sulzer-Azaroff & Mayer, 1991; also see Box 2.2). More specifically, treatment validity refers to the extent to which assessment information contributes to useful treatment outcomes (Gresham & Lambros, 1998; Hayes, Nelson, & Jarrett, 1987). The treatment is generated from assessment data to produce a specific outcome, or goal of intervention. The treatment is not arbitrarily designed. Decisions about what skill/behavior to target for change and the corresponding replacement skill/behavior selected to train during intervention to produce the change are linked with assessment by data, not by hunch or whim. Data are numbers that represent real-life situations and provide the measure of need for treatment, progress toward treatment goals, and eventual attainment of goals. Regardless of whether the intervention is primary, secondary, or tertiary, the replacement skills/behaviors trained during intervention to achieve a goal are the link between the problem or desired area of improvement and the solution or method of attaining that goal and are based upon assessment data. The entire intervention process is a dynamic process that moves and shifts as a result of treatment. Assessment data prior to intervention, during intervention, at the end of intervention, and as a follow-up help us monitor success (see Box 2.3).

### Linking Assessment to Primary Intervention

When schools use a proactive approach to provide an optimal learning environment, educators conduct schoolwide assessment in certain areas to get an indication of system-wide academic and social health. A schoolwide assessment may entail evaluating (a) schoolwide mean proficiency levels for reading, math, and writing, (b) number of discipline referrals, (c) number of suspensions, (d) absenteeism rates, and (e) number of accidents on campus (see Jones, Sheridan, & Binns, 1993; Lewis, Sugai, & Colvin, 1998; Lohrmann-O'Rourke, Knoster, Sabatine, Smith, Horvath, & Llewellyn, 2000; Scott, 2001; Taylor-Greene & Kartub, 2000 for

**BOX 2.2** • *Treatment Validity Defined*

***Treatment Validity***
Treatment validity refers to the extent to which
assessment information contributes to useful treatment outcomes.

(Gresham & Lambros, 1998; Hayes, Nelson, & Jarrett, 1987)

**BOX 2.3 • *Linking Assessment to Intervention Results***

The "link" between assessment and intervention is using the information collected about the behavior targeted for improvement and then designing an intervention that is hypothesized to be a probable approach for reaching the desired behavior changes.

*Note.* [a]Target area refers to the focus area (e.g., literacy skills) for the primary prevention and the specific skill or performance deficit identified in the secondary prevention (e.g., social skills) and tertiary prevention (e.g., academic engaged time) support.

examples of schoolwide interventions). Once an assessment is complete, school professionals use the evaluation to make decisions about areas of strength and areas for improvement. It is important to assess whether weaknesses are widespread across classes and students or more unique to specific classes or students. If assessment reveals a widespread area of concern, then a primary intervention is appropriate. Areas of system-wide areas of concern become the target for a *primary intervention*—an intervention that takes place across classrooms and students and that will build skills/behaviors that support a positive environment in which to learn. Assessment data is used as the beginning point. Then data are examined, and a realistic proficiency level by the end of intervention is determined and specified in the form of an objective. Treatment is designed to facilitate learning in the targeted skills/behaviors so that levels of the targeted weakness are increased from the beginning point, or deficient level, to the end point, or proficiency level. Assessment prior to, during, and after intervention yields the data to monitor student progress. In such a manner, assessment is linked with a primary intervention, and the treatment will have legitimacy, or *treatment validity.*

An example of a primary intervention implemented schoolwide by linking assessment to intervention is as follows: Proactive school professionals decide to look at the previous school year's schoolwide records for attendance, discipline, and safety records to identify any areas of weakness that might have affected student academic performance. Using the previous years' data, the school team identified high rates of absenteeism as an area of weakness; the average days absent for the previous school year of 180 days was thirteen days per student. The high rate of absenteeism meant less time exposed to the curriculum and less time to learn, which may explain why school performance levels on statewide testing did not reach anticipated levels. It was determined that high absenteeism was widespread across classes and students. Although the intervention could target specific students, that approach would be costly. Thus, the school team decided to implement a primary intervention so that all students would be targeted to help improve attendance, whether their own attendance or that of their peers. An intervention goal to reduce absenteeism by 70 percent, to an average of four days per student, was set as a realistic goal. The primary intervention used several procedures to increase attendance rates: (1) a schoolwide assembly about the importance of good school attendance, (2) implementation of a rewards system for good attendance (free ice cream at the end of the week for being at school all five days), (3) teachers reinforcing good attendance with class rewards (extra fifteen minute recess on Friday if 95 percent of the students have perfect attendance for the week), and (4) parent education about the link between achievement, school dropout, and attendance.

The beginning point of the intervention period had a baseline measure of thirteen days average absenteeism. Weekly rates of absenteeism were monitored as the intervention proceeded to detect progress toward the final goal of four days. Data provided the feedback as to whether the intervention was working. This primary intervention has *treatment validity* because the decision to target absenteeism was made by evaluating schoolwide attendance records, and the procedures implemented to decrease schoolwide rates of absenteeism were a direct result of the assessment. Decisions about treatment methods, procedures, and final goals were linked with the original and continuing data from assessment. A decision to target attendance was not made on a hunch or because someone thought it was a good idea; it was based on actual school records. Thus, a *primary intervention* is linked with assessment and has *treatment validity* when the methods, steps, procedures, and goals of a system-wide (district, school, or whole classroom) primary intervention target an assessment-identified area of system-wide weakness and data about the weakness are used to assess progress toward a goal (see Box 2.4).

### Linking Assessment to Secondary Intervention

A secondary intervention involves a subset of the system-wide population (e.g., school or classroom) who either did not respond to a primary intervention (recall that about 20 percent will need more assistance to change according to Colvin, Sugai, & Kame'enui, 1993) or who were identified because of poor response to the curriculum or social situations. Change is facilitated through small group instruction so that only the students demonstrating deficient skill/behavior levels receive the intervention. The group of students share a common problem; a deficient skill/behavior that impedes progress thus becomes the target of intervention. The skill/behavior is assessed and measured prior to intervention to obtain data that represent average group performance at the onset of intervention. Again, the intervention is linked to assessment by the data that indicate the extent of a problem and that can be used to design, implement, and monitor the intervention toward the data-based goal.

Taking the example from the primary intervention a step further to the secondary intervention level looks like the following: By the end of ninety days, the school reduced absenteeism rates by 50 percent, or down to 6.5 days on average per student. However, they achieved this rate at the sixty-day mark, and so were stalled in progressing toward the final goal of four days per student. Monitoring attendance data provided formative feedback during the ninety-day period to

**BOX 2.4  •**  *Linking Primary, Secondary, and Tertiary Intervention with Assessment Results*

The diagram displays how primary, secondary, and tertiary interventions (addressing the initial problem of excessive absenteeism used as an example) were linked by assessment data to intervention procedures and goals.

### Schoolwide Problem:
**Excessive Absenteeism, Impeding Schoolwide Student Academic Progress**

**Assessment of Problem:**  Thirteen days absent per student per previous school year.
**Primary Intervention:**  Implement schoolwide, all students: (a) a schoolwide assembly, (b) free ice cream at end of a "no-absents" week, (c) extra 15-minute recess on Friday if 95% of the students in class have perfect attendance for the week, (d) parent education about the link between achievement and attendance.
**Result:**  Absenteeism at 90-day mark reduced 50%; 80% of students improved.

**Assessment of Problem:**  Three classrooms: homework triggers excessive absences.
**Secondary Intervention:**  Implement with all students in 3 classes:(a) teach study skills; (b) limit homework to10 mins./subject, increase max. of 20 mins./subject, maximum of 60 mins. total/day; (c) extra points for homework completed on time; (d) classwide reward for 95%; (e) letter home to parents about study skills in home.
**Result:**  Homework completion increased by 85%; Absenteeism reduced 90% in 3 classes; Schoolwide = 65% reduction.

**Assessment of Problem:**  Nine students display various deficient skills; Billy has read-aloud anxiety due to deficient reading fluency skill.
**Tertiary Intervention:**  Implement individually for Billy: (a) increased tutoring; (b) parent involvement, rich reinforcement; (c) reduced requests to read aloud until skill sufficient to do so; (d) rich reinforcement from teacher.
**Result:**  Reading fluency increased to average level; Billy absent 0 days; Absenteeism reduced 75% for 9 students; Schoolwide = 70% reduction.

**Target Goal: Reduce Absenteeism by 70%; 4.5 Days Average**

detect change toward increasing rates of attendance. Attendance records were examined once again at the end of the primary intervention and revealed that two fourth-grade classes and one fifth-grade class still had much higher rates of absenteeism when compared to all other classes in the school. If these three classes were omitted from the school average, the average days of absenteeism fell to 3.5 days per student! The three classes were assessed for potential reasons for the excessive absenteeism. Assessment results uncovered a trigger for poor attendance in all three classes; students were not meeting teacher expectations for homework assignments and thus were staying home from school. Data collected about the number of homework assignments completed and days absent provided the base rate for change. It was decided that a *secondary intervention* would be implemented to target only the three classes (a subset of the school population). A secondary intervention was designed using the following procedures that would be used with the three classes only: (a) teach students homework study skills, (b) limit amount of homework to ten minutes per subject, slowly increasing amounts to a maximum of twenty minutes per subject area with a maximum of sixty minutes total homework per day, (c) implement extra point rewards for students who complete and turn in all homework assignments on time, (d) allocate class-wide rewards when all students complete and turn in homework on time, (e) send a letter home to parents regarding importance of homework completion and explanation of student study skills to be used at home. All students in the three classes received the intervention. The students in the three classes who already had good attendance and turned in homework would be good role models, coaches, and supply encouragement for their classmates' success. Homework completion and attendance were monitored weekly for sixty days during the intervention period. At thirty days, students in the three classes increased homework completion by 85 percent and had reduced absenteeism by 90 percent. The schoolwide absenteeism rate had been reduced by 65 percent overall by the end of the secondary intervention. Thus, a *secondary intervention* has *treatment validity* when the methods, steps, procedures, and goals address the academic or social deficit that a subset of students has in common at the onset of intervention as identified through pre-intervention assessment activities. Data describe the extent of the deficit, detect progress, and signal attainment of the intervention goal (see Box 2.4).

## Linking Assessment to Tertiary Intervention

In the case of tertiary interventions such as functional assessment-based interventions, data link problem assessment information to the *replacement behavior skill, level, or behavior* hypothesized to raise skill or behavior from a deficient to proficient level. The foremost intervention outcome is successfully teaching a *replacement skill, skill level, or behavior* in place of an assessment-identified deficit that increases the probability that a student will be successful. Assessment data are used to evaluate the nature and extent of a problem, to design and monitor the intervention, and to assess attainment of the intervention goal. Assessment activities might include monitoring student work, conducting curriculum-based assessments, and observing the child in the classroom or recreational settings.

Regardless of whether the problem is related to an academic or social deficit, assessment should also be used to determine if the problem is a skill deficit or a performance deficit; a "can't do" versus a "won't do" problem (Elliott & Gresham, 1991; Noell & Witt, 1999). The two deficits require different types of interventions.

Specifically, a skills deficit requires skills-based training, whereas a performance deficit would use motivational factors to shape skill performance during the intervention. A number of methods have been demonstrated through educational research as quick, yet accurate ways to determine the nature of the deficit (Ayllon & Roberts, 1974; Daly & Martens, 1994; Daly, Martens, Dool, & Hintze, 1998; Daly, Martens, Hamler, Dool, & Eckert, 1999; Lovitt, Eaton, Kirkwood, & Pelander, 1971; Umbreit, Lane, et al, in press; Witt & Beck, 1999). Quite simply, something that is highly reinforcing to the student, such as choice of reading material or choice of order in which to perform various tasks, is offered to perform an academic or social skill. If the student cannot perform a skill even under highly reinforcing conditions, then the deficit is assumed to be skills-based, and specific training of the skill is appropriate as the intervention. Conversely, if the student increases performance of the skill when reinforcement is present, it indicates a performance deficit and an appropriate intervention would address motivational factors. Linking assessment to intervention to ensure treatment validity makes it necessary to determine the nature of the deficit. The intervention is linked to assessment by using the data that indicate the nature and extent of a problem. Thus, data link treatment to the replacement skill/behavior that is selected and monitors the intervention toward the data-based goal.

Returning to the previous example of the school with the goal of increasing attendance, a tertiary intervention would take the following form: At the conclusion of the secondary intervention, the school attendance clerk made a list of students who still exhibited excessive absenteeism, in spite of previous intervention. Eleven students in various classrooms made the list. The students' teachers were asked to generate ideas about why these particular students were absent so often. Two students had chronic illness and were under the care of a physician, as verified by the school nurse. However, nine of the students appeared to be resistant to coming to school. The school psychologist was asked to assess potential reasons for the nine students' excessive absenteeism. Using best practices for multimethod, multi-informant assessment (see the next section), the psychologist and teachers found a variety of reasons for the absenteeism. Tertiary interventions that targeted each student's unique problem were designed and implemented as a result of assessment data. We will take one student as an example here: Through evaluation of assessment data, it was determined that Billy had an aversion to reading aloud in class because of his reading skill level. In spite of the fact that the teacher worked with Billy on raising his rate of reading fluency, he was embarrassed to read in front of his peers. This was problematic given that he was required to read aloud during daily reading groups. He suffered from anxiety over reading aloud to the extent that he was physically ill many mornings, and his parents kept him home from school. The tertiary intervention targeting Billy's sensitivity to reading aloud coupled with emerging reading fluency skills was designed. The treatment included (a) increased time in one-on-one tutoring for reading fluency to raise Billy's skill level more quickly, (b) meeting with Billy's parents to encourage him to read aloud at home each night and to train the parents to reinforce and reward him with a rich schedule of verbal praise and high-incentive rewards, (c) reduced requests and quantity of passages for reading aloud in the beginning of intervention, slowly increasing the number and the amount of time requested to read aloud as the intervention proceeded, and (d) the teacher using high rates of reinforcement to encourage Billy. Within thirty days, Billy had increased his reading fluency rate and his tolerance level for reading aloud in front of peers to the extent that he no longer became ill at the thought of doing so. Billy became eager to read and attended school every day toward the end of intervention, even after high rates of praise and reinforcement were faded. Natural reinforcers maintained Billy's enthusiasm for reading aloud, which generalized to reading aloud everywhere he went (grocery store, church; see Chapter 6 on Generalization and Maintenance). Assessment data indicated the reason for Billy's excessive absenteeism—reasons that were not addressed by the techniques used for the school's primary or secondary interventions. The other eight student's attendance concerns were addressed with tertiary interventions. By addressing each students' reasons for not attending school, the school reached their target of reducing absenteeism by seventy percent overall. As a result, academic statewide testing scores increased over time (see Box 2.4). In each of the above examples, the nature and level of the intervention was linked to assessment results. In the section that follows, we will discuss and illustrate the importance of linking, or connecting, interventions to assessment results.

## Why Is It Important to Link Intervention to Assessment Results?

Societal pressure for educators to be accountable for educational outcomes makes intervention for poor academic and/or behavioral performance the highest of priorities (Linn et al., 2002). "The *outcome-based* education movement within the school reform process has triggered a general call for accountability in all aspects of education" (Batsche & Knoff, 1995, p. 570). When a problem is apparent or an area is targeted for improvement, educators assess the problem and find solutions. The problem can be for an individual student (e.g., failing math), for a classroom of students (e.g., excessive absences), or schoolwide (e.g., low morale). It is important to link intervention with assessment using the data that are collected about the problem and the replacement skill/behavior to be taught during intervention. The data help us decide what form intervention should take, what the replacement skill or behavior should be, at what rate we should expect learning to take place, and what realistic skill/behavior level to set as the goal of intervention to rectify a problem. Regardless of whether the intervention is primary, secondary, or tertiary, all interventions need to be designed using assessment data. For example, high rates of aggression may be measured during pre-intervention assessment in the form of the number of referrals to the principal's office for aggressive behaviors. The number of behavioral referrals for the entire school will inform violence prevention efforts by providing the excessive number of referrals that are to be reduced as a result of intervention (administrative assessment). The data also inform what the intervention should focus on. Specific replacement behaviors will be designed as a result of assessment data that quantify the behaviors that are causing referrals (functional assessment), the antecedent conditions that set the stage for the behavior, and the consequences that serve to maintain the target behavior (Mace, 1994; Lane, Umbreit, & Beebe-Frankenberger, 1999). Data help decide what intervention should be done and then are used to monitor the progress toward the intervention goal. Data are used on an ongoing basis to determine how well the schoolwide violence prevention intervention is working. And, finally, the data provide evidence of effectiveness and success; in one word, accountability.

For special education professionals, the reauthorized IDEA (1997) mandates that assessment be linked to specific intervention skills/behavior by data in the form of Individual Educational Plan (IEP) goals and benchmarks. Low scores on standardized reading, math, or writing tests cannot be *directly* linked to intervention. Norm-referenced standardized tests are not designed to be administered repeatedly so cannot be used to monitor progress, which is essential in determining benchmarks toward a goal. Functional assessment, in the form of curriculum-based assessment (CBA) can be used to link academic assessment to academic treatment benchmarks and goals by providing specific areas for the focus of intervention and data upon which to judge adequate progress. The term *curriculum-based assessment* (CBA) is defined as any measurement using "direct observation and recording of a student's performance in the local curriculum as a basis for gathering information to make instruction decisions" (Deno, 1987, p. 41). Using a CBA measure simply means that a student is tested for his rate of learning of what is being taught in that particular classroom. The replacement skill, or proficiency level, is determined from CBA data, which also provide the baseline for monitoring progress. For example, if it is evaluated through CBA that a student is under-performing in reading because of deficient decoding skills, a decision to explicitly teach decoding strategies would be made and a realistic goal for rate of learning can be set for that particular student. CBA is the overall term for any assessment that is based on local curriculum, and several models have been developed over the years (Shinn et al., 1989).

One form of CBA that is gaining empirical evidence through research as an effective academic assessment method is curriculum-based measurement (CBM; Witt, Elliott, Daly, Gresham, & Kramer, 1998). CBM uses brief probes of local curriculum to measure student progress in learning. CBM probes have been developed for reading, math, and writing. The teacher uses CBM probes to establish the student's initial level of learning and to set realistic learning goals, then uses these probes to check how the student is progressing toward the goal. If little or no progress is made, the goal can be altered; or, the need for more in-depth assessment may be indicated. Conversely, the goal can be increased if progress is being made much faster than expected (see Chapter 3, Monitoring Changes; also see Deno, Fuchs, Marston, & Shinn, 2001; Lane, O'Shaughnessy, Lambros, Gresham, & Beebe-Frankenberger, 2001, for studies that have used CBM procedures).

It is also important to link assessment results to intervention so that inappropriate interventions are not targeted or unrealistic expectations are not established (Batsche & Knoff, 1995; Sulzer-Azaroff & Mayer, 1991). Replacement skills/behaviors should always be within the child's physical, mental, and developmental range. For example, assessment results may provide information about a previously unknown physical problem of a student that may interfere with a treatment that would otherwise be planned. For instance, the records review may reveal that a former school's nurse detected a hearing loss in a child, but that no referral for further evaluation had been made. It may be that the hearing loss is the reason the child does not always respond to teacher requests, and may be at the root of behavior problems. With the assessment data about hearing loss, further evaluation can be made; the resulting intervention may include teaching the child to sit closer to where instruction is taking place and training the teacher to get eye contact with the child when making requests. Without the data concerning hearing loss for this particular child, the intervention may have taken on a completely different form and thus would probably have been unsuccessful.

## How Do We Link Intervention to Assessment Results?

The field of school psychology has long adhered to a problem-solving model based on behavioral consultation. In traditional behavioral consultation (Bergan, 1977; Bergan, 1995; Bergan & Kratochwill, 1990) and in the more recent model of direct behavioral consultation (Watson & Robinson, 1996; Witt, Gresham, & Noell, 1996), the consultation process is comprised of four stages: *problem identification, problem analysis, plan implementation*, and *plan evaluation*. According to the traditional approach, the intent of the *problem identification* stage is to (a) identify and operationally define a socially significant target behavior, (b) determine the frequency, duration, or magnitude of the target before beginning an intervention, (c) identify which data-collection procedures will be necessary, and (d) establish the discrepancy between the current and desired performance levels (Bergan & Kratochwill, 1990; Martens, 1993). The second stage, *problem analysis,* focuses on (a) identifying why the problem behavior is occurring, (b) designing an intervention plan based on the assessment results, and (c) confirming the use of data-collection procedures. The third stage, *plan implementation,* focuses on (a) implementing the intervention as originally designed with treatment integrity (Gresham, 1989) and (b) monitoring the extent to which the target behavior and replacement behaviors are demonstrated. The final stage, *plan evaluation,* consists of (a) evaluating the intended goals, (b) assessing social validity from multiple perspectives, and (c) assessing generalization and maintenance.

Interventions are linked to assessment results by using the data collected to identify the intervention most likely to maximize the likelihood of achieving the desired outcomes. Moreover, "how" to link is related to the *problem identification* and *problem analysis* phases of the consultation model regardless of whether the target area is specific to a student, a class, or the entire school. The preliminary information gained about the characteristics and function of the target skills/behaviors in the problem identification phase and the more in-depth information about the circumstances that prompt (antecedents) and encourage (consequences) the target behavior provide the information necessary to design, implement, and evaluate an intervention that is linked, or connected to, the assessment results.

Batsche and Knoff (1995) offered the acronym RIOT to represent the assessment process as it is linked to intervention efforts. The steps included in RIOT include (a) review records, (b) interview, (c) observe, and (d) test. "Assessment practices that focus on the development of hypotheses that link the problem to the conditions under which the problem occurs, automatically provide a link with the desired intervention and the methods; Review, Interview, Observe, and Test (RIOT)"(p. 571). According to this model, there are six conditions that should be considered when assessing an individual child's problem so that multimethod, multi-informant data are available to make the best decision about secondary and tertiary intervention procedures and goals. These conditions are (a) child characteristics, (b) teacher characteristics, (c) peer characteristics, (d) curriculum issues, (e) school environment issues, and (f) family/community factors (Batsche & Knoff, 1995). Relevant conditions should be assessed to provide data and considered when making hypotheses about appropriate replacement behavior/skills taught during treatment. Box 2.5 lists the specific areas of concern for each of the six conditions. Assessing the suggested areas, when relevant, provides the data to make hypotheses about replacement skills/behaviors and conditions and potential intervention goals.

The problem-solving model delineated by Bergan and Kratochwill (1990) can be applied to all levels of prevention, as can the RIOT process. In the sections below, guidelines for linking assessment information to interventions are offered.

## Primary Interventions

As previously discussed, *primary interventions* are applied to the whole population to prevent potential problems or address a specific area of concern (e.g., school violence or literacy skills) that is system-wide (district or school). Steps toward linking assessment results to primary intervention require that data need to be collected

**BOX 2.5 • *Six Conditions to Assess for Secondary or Tertiary Interventions***

| Conditions/ Characteristics | Areas of Concern | Specific items suggested to question/assess: |
|---|---|---|
| Child | Cognitive | • Academic skill level<br>• Attention span<br>• Self-monitoring skills |
|  | Behavior | • Self-control<br>• Social Skills<br>• Impulsivity<br>• Oppositionality |
|  | Health | • Hearing, motor, vision<br>• Overall health<br>• Medication side effects<br>• Medication schedule |
|  | Other | • Absenteeism<br>• Native Language |
| Peer |  | • Reinforce inappropriate behavior?<br>• Provide appropriate model?<br>• Academic skill relative to student?<br>• Social skill relative to student?<br>• Teased, neglected, ignored by peers? |
| Curriculum |  | • Too easy or too difficult?<br>• Not relevant?<br>• Presented too fast for understanding?<br>• Congruent with student learning style?<br>• Sufficient opportunity to practice taught skills?<br>• Sufficient model/feedback?<br>• Assignments too long for attention span?<br>• Curriculum developmentally appropriate?<br>• Homework is for mastery of skills?<br>• Homework is appropriate in length? |
| Teacher |  | • Expectations too high/low?<br>• Positive reinforcement too low?<br>• Negative reinforcement too high?<br>• Insufficient rehearsal time, direct instruction time, teacher guided practice?<br>• Teacher fatigue, tolerance results in higher negative, less frequent feedback?<br>• Teacher unfamiliar with curricular methods necessary for child?<br>• Level of supervision too low? |

**BOX 2.5** • *Continued*

| Classroom/ School/District | Classroom | • Seating arrangement fosters learning?<br>• Rules/expectations clearly stated and posted?<br>• Rules stated in positive manner? |
|---|---|---|
| | School/District | • Schedule of daily activities inconsistent?<br>• Disorganized physical space?<br>• Temperature too high or low?<br>• Lighting not conducive to learning?<br>• Areas not adequately supervised areas?<br>• Playground supervision adequate?<br>• Bus ride too long?<br>• Problems at bus stop?<br>• School motto and/or mission posted?<br>• School safety rules posted?<br>• Access to school grounds/classrooms monitored? |
| Family/ Community | Parent/Family | • Level of parent discipline (too much, not enough)?<br>• Conflict between student/parent or family?<br>• Lack of or low levels of supervision?<br>• Expectations and/or values differ from school?<br>• Parent academic skills to support student?<br>• Reading/academics promoted & practiced in the home?<br>• Parent difficulties (drug abuse, marital discord, etc.) interfere with supervision, parenting?<br>• Parent expectations reasonable for child?<br>• Parent cooperative with school?<br>• Parent unwilling/unable to meet health/nutrition basic needs of student resulting in absences, tardiness, etc.? |
| | Neighborhood | • Delinquent activity in neighborhood?<br>• Level of adult supervision available in neighborhood? |

*Source:* Adapted from G. M. Batsche and H. M. Knoff (1995), "Best Practices in Linking Assessment to Intervention," in A. Thomas and J. Grimes (Eds.), *Best Practices in School Psychology*. Washington, DC: National Association of School Psychologists.

concerning the target area and hypotheses made about the overall solution. Data are collected primarily from existing information readily available to the school, such as school statewide yearly testing scores, attendance records, number of behavioral referrals, and district multiple measures (e.g., reading comprehension and written comprehension skills). The data that are reviewed to make decisions about appropriate intervention are relevant to the problem. Interventions conducted today frequently focus on providing positive behavior support (see Lohrmann-O'Rourke et al., 2000; Scott, 2001; Taylor-Greene & Kartub, 2000; Turnbull et al., 2002). However, school-based interventions (such as the one described in Box 2.4 that targets excessive absenteeism as a reason for low academic performance scores on state standardized testing) are also designed as a result of careful review and use of assessment data. Although defined more extensively in Chapter 3 (Monitoring Changes), the steps to link assessment data to primary intervention include:

**a.** Identify the specific area targeted for improvement
**b.** Evaluate the degree and intensity of the identified problem or area for improvement
**c.** Develop appropriate replacement skills/behaviors in a corresponding intervention plan
**d.** Identify the best monitoring measure for the treatment
**e.** Set benchmark goals of the monitoring measure
**f.** Develop a reasonable and appropriate performance level of the replacement skill/behavior deemed as the proficient level when intervention is concluded.

### *Secondary and Tertiary Interventions*

Steps (a–f) shown above are used to link assessment data to intervention for secondary and tertiary interventions. However, more detailed information relevant to the unique needs of the small group or individual student is necessary when designing secondary and tertiary interventions. Student needs are assessed through functional assessment procedures that yields data linked to replacement skill/ behaviors, monitoring, and goals. Using the RIOT multimethod, multi-informant approach is one technique that can be used to identify the appropriate target behavior/skill of intervention (Batsche & Knoff, 1995).

***RIOT: Review.*** Although a variety of methods can be used to review students' cumulative records, one empirically validated tool is the School Archival Records Search (SARS; Walker, Block-Pedego, Todis, & Severson, 1991). The SARS is a systematic recording procedure for school records that yields data relevant to school performance including (a) attendance, (b) achievement test scores, (c) number of grade retentions, (d) disciplinary contacts, (e) within-school referrals for academic, behavioral, or speech problems, (f) out-of-school referrals (medical, counseling), (g) negative narrative comments, (h) demographics (gender, grade, ethnicity), (i) certification for special education (IEP on file), (j) placement out of regular classroom, and (k) free/reduced lunch services provided (yes/no). SARS has been demonstrated to be a reliable way to quantify student cumulative record information and can be used to distinguish between students who are and are not at risk for different types of problem behaviors (e.g., internalizing and externalizing behaviors; Walker et al., 1991).

***RIOT: Interview.*** Interviewing the teacher, parent, and student (when possible) makes it possible to collect information about the nature, extent, and intensity of a problem. An essential part of the interview process is to ascertain the social validity (see Chapter 4) of the problem, the solution, and the acceptability of treatment. Form 2.1 is an example of a structured functional assessment interview for a problem behavior referral. Structured interview can be used to interview the teacher, parent (see Form 2.1), or student (see Form 2.2). The interview yields data that can be used to quantify the problem and the replacement behavior/skill.

*Positive Behavioral Support*
...for Children
and Their Families

TIME STARTED: _____

PRELIMINARY FUNCTIONAL ASSESSMENT SURVEY

Instructions to PBS Staff:  The following interview should be conducted with the student's teacher. Prior to the interview, ask the teacher whether or not the Classroom Aide should participate. If yes, indicate both respondents' names. In addition, in instances where divergent information is provided, note the sources attributed to specific information.

Student: _____    Subject #: _____

Age: _____    Sex:  M _____    F _____

Interviewer: _____    Date: _____

Respondent(s): _____

   1.  List and describe behavior(s) of concern.

      a.

      b.

      c.

      d.

      e.

   2.  Prioritize these behaviors (which is the most important?)

      a.

      b.

      c.

      d.

      e.

   3.  What procedures have you followed when the behaviors first occurred?

      a.

      b.

      c.

      d.

      e.

**FORM 2.1**  *Preliminary Functional Assessment Interview*

*Source:* Reprinted with permission from Glen Dunlap. Interview was referred to in G. Dunlap, L. Kern, M. dePerczel, S. Clarke, D. Wilson, K. E. Childs, R. White, & G. D. Falk (1993), "Functional Analysis of Classroom Variables for Students with Emotional and Behavioral Challenges." *Behavioral Disorders, 18,* 275–291.

4. What do you think causes (or motivates) the behavior?

   a.

   b.

   c.

   d.

   e.

5. When do these behaviors occur?

   a.

   b.

   c.

   d.

   e.

6. How often do these behaviors occur?

   a.

   b.

   c.

   d.

   e.

7. How long has this/these behavior(s) been occurring?

   a.

   b.

   c.

   d.

   e.

8. Is there any circumstance under which the behavior does not occur?

   a.

   b.

   c.

   d.

   e.

9. Is there any circumstances under which the behavior always occurs?

   a.

   b.

   c.

**FORM 2.1**    *Continued*

d.

e.

10. Does the behavior occur more often during certain times of the day?

a.

b.

c.

d.

e.

11. Does the behavior occur in response to the number of people in the immediate environment?

a.

b.

c.

d.

e.

12. Does the behavior occur only with certain people?

a.

b.

c.

d.

e.

13. Does the behavior occur only during certain subjects?

a.

b.

c.

d.

e.

14. Could the behavior be related to any skills deficit?

a.

b.

c.

d.

e.

---

**FORM 2.1** *Continued*

15. What are the identified reinforcers for this student?

    a.

    b.

    c.

    d.

    e.

16. Is the student taking any medication that might affect his/her behavior?

    a.

    b.

    c.

    d.

    e.

17. Could the student's behavior be signaling some deprivation condition (e.g. thirst, hunger, lack of rest, etc.)?

    a.

    b.

    c.

    d.

    e.

18. Could the behavior be the result of any form of discomfort (e.g., headaches, stomachaches blurred vision, ear infection, etc.)?

    a.

    b.

    c.

    d.

    e.

19. Could the behavior be caused by allergies (e.g., food, materials in the environment, etc.)?

    a.

    b.

    c.

    d.

    e.

**FORM 2.1**    *Continued*

20. Do any other behaviors occur along with this behavior?

    a.

    b.

    c.

    d.

    e.

21. Are there any observable events that signal the behavior of concern is about to occur?

    a.

    b.

    c.

    d.

    e.

22. What are the consequences when the behavior(s) occur?

    a.

    b.

    c.

    d.

    e.

TIME COMPLETED:_____

TOTAL TIME:_____

COMMENTS

**FORM 2.1** *Continued*

STUDENT ASSESSMENT

Student: _____

Date: _____          Administration Time: _____

Target Behavior: _____

_____

1. When do you think you have the fewest problems with _____(target behavior) in school?




   Why do you not have problems during this/these time(s)?




2. When do you think you have the most problems with _____(target behavior) in school?




   Why do you have problems during this/these time(s)?




3. What causes you to have problems with _____(target behavior)?




4. What changes could be made so you would have fewer problems with _____ (target behavior)?




5. What kind of rewards would you like to earn for good behavior or good schoolwork?




---

**FORM 2.2    *Student Functional Assessment Interview***

*Source:* Reprinted with permission. L. Kern, G. Dunlap, S. Clarke, & K. E. Childs, (1994). "Student-assisted Functional Assessment Interview." *Diagnostic, 19,* 20–39.

Rate how much you like the following subjects:

| | Don't like at all | | Fair | | Like very much |
|---|---|---|---|---|---|
| Reading | 1 | 2 | 3 | 4 | 5 |
| Math | 1 | 2 | 3 | 4 | 5 |
| Spelling | 1 | 2 | 3 | 4 | 5 |
| Handwriting | 1 | 2 | 3 | 4 | 5 |
| Science | 1 | 2 | 3 | 4 | 5 |
| Social Studies | 1 | 2 | 3 | 4 | 5 |
| English | 1 | 2 | 3 | 4 | 5 |
| Music | 1 | 2 | 3 | 4 | 5 |
| P.E. | 1 | 2 | 3 | 4 | 5 |
| Art | 1 | 2 | 3 | 4 | 5 |

What do you like about _____?

What do you like about _____?

What do you like about _____?

What do you like about _____?

What do you like about _____?

What do you like about _____?

What do you like about _____?

**FORM 2.2**   *Continued*

What could be done to improve _____?

What do you like about _____?

What do you like about _____?

What do you like about _____?

What do you like about _____?

Is there any type of _____ you have ever done that you've liked?

What could be done to improve _____?

What do you like about _____?

What do you like about _____?

What do you like about _____?

What do you like about _____?

What don't you like about _____?

Is there any type of _____ you have ever done that you've liked?

What could be done to improve _____?

---

**FORM 2.2**   *Continued*

## STUDENT ASSESSMENT

Student: _____     Date: _____

Interviewer: _____

| | | | |
|---|---|---|---|
| 1. In general, is your work too hard for you? | always | sometimes | never |
| 2. In general, is your work too easy for you? | always | sometimes | never |
| 3. When you ask for help appropriately, do you get it? | always | sometimes | never |
| 4. Do you think work periods for each subject are too long? | always | sometimes | never |
| 5. Do you think work periods for each subject are too short? | always | sometimes | never |
| 6. When you do seatwork, do you do better when someone works with you? | always | sometimes | never |
| 7. Do you think people notice when you do a good job? | always | sometimes | never |
| 8. Do you think you get the points or rewards you deserve when you do good work? | always | sometimes | never |
| 9. Do you think you would do better in school if you received more rewards? | always | sometimes | never |
| 10. In general, do you find your work interesting? | always | sometimes | never |
| 11. Are there things in the classroom that distract you? | always | sometimes | never |
| 12. Is your work challenging enough for you? | always | sometimes | never |

**FORM 2.2** *Continued*

A number of interviews are currently used in the functional assessment process to assess the magnitude of the behavior, generate a hypothesis as to why the problem behavior is occurring, and identify possible replacement behaviors that are functionally equivalent to the target behavior. Some examples of interviews include the Preliminary Functional Assessment Survey (Dunlap et al., 1993; also see Form 2.1), the Functional Analysis Interview Summary Form (O'Neill, Horner, Albin, Sprague, Storey, & Newton, 1997), and the Student Functional Assessment Interview (Kern et al., 1994; also see Form 2.2).

Other types of measures such as behavior rating scales can be used to obtain teacher and parent perspectives about students' behaviors. For example, the Social Skills Rating System (SSRS; Gresham & Elliott, 1990) is a nationally normed instrument that quantifies student performance from teacher, parent, and student perspectives. Each version of the instrument provides valuable information that can be used alone or with other indicators to identify skill or performance deficits in social

**ABC EVENT RECORD**

Student:_____

Date:_____ Start Time:_____

Observer:_____ School:_____

Grade:_____ Intervals:_____

| Time H:min | ANTECEDENT and SETTING What happened *before* the behavior? | OFF-TASK BEHAVIOR (check) | | | | | CONSEQUENCE(S) What happened *after* the behavior? |
|---|---|---|---|---|---|---|---|
| | | Side Talk | Out of Seat | Stare Off | Head on Desk | Other | |
| | | | | | | | |
| | | | | | | | |
| | | | | | | | |
| | | | | | | | |
| | | | | | | | |
| | | | | | | | |
| | | | | | | | |
| | | | | | | | |
| | | | | | | | |
| | | | | | | | |
| | | | | | | | |
| | | | | | | | |
| | | | | | | | |
| | | | | | | | |

**FORM 2.3**   *Sample Observational Assessment of Student Inappropriate Behavioral Events*

skills (e.g., cooperation, assertion, and self-control), the presence of problem behaviors (e.g., internalizing, externalizing, and hyperactivity), and an evaluation of academic competence. Still other rating scales, such as Durand and Crimmins (1988) Motivation Assessment Scale (MAS), can be used to identify the hypothesized function of the problem behavior. At the tertiary level, this information can be used to determine if the behavior is helping students to seek or avoid a task, a social situation, or a sensory experience (Umbreit, Ferro, Liaupsin, & Lane, in preparation).

*RIOT: Observe.* Observation of the student, peers, and the learning environment are essential to the problem identification and problem analysis phases of the behavioral consultation process. Observations can be structured in many ways; however, it is important that the observation system identify antecedents that precede and the consequences that follow the target behavior. Namely, what is happening prior to the behavior that sets the stage for the behavior to occur (antecedents)? And what is happening following the behavior that encourages the behavior to continue (consequences)? In the functional assessment literature, this is referred to as A-B-C data (Bijou, Peterson, & Ault, 1968). Form 2.3 is an example of an observational tool used to identify what events or activities (Frankie alone at recess) immediately precede a student's inappropriate behavior (Frankie grabbing the ball away from Joey), and what immediately follows the inappropriate behavior (Frankie gets Joey's and the yard supervisor's complete attention) that guarantees the behavior will happen again in the same situation.

Observations can also be conducted to obtain information about the classroom environment itself. An example of a structured observation of the learning environment can be seen in Forms 2.4 and 2.5. Form 2.4 yields data about how much positive versus negative reinforcement is present in the student's classroom. This is important to assess not only in relationship to other students in the classroom but in the classroom as a whole. Although the amount of positive reinforcement that is present may be sufficient for many of the students in the class, more may be required to shape the replacement skill/behavior for the referred student. Form 2.5 is a structured observation of the classroom that yields data about the nature of the present learning environment for the referred student. Both types of data are essential to problem identification and in developing the design of the treatment.

***RIOT: Test.*** Results of standardized testing are useful in describing the extent of an academic problem (scoring below the 10th percentile on a standardized reading test indicates the performance level and severity of the problem), but not what the specific skill deficit(s) might be that produce the low reading scores. The use of skills-based tests, such as CBA/CBM mentioned previously, are necessary to pinpoint specific deficits that will be targeted by secondary or tertiary intervention, are relative to the specific student, and can be used to measure student performance often. Other skills-based tests that are increasingly used to evaluate reading include the Woodcock Johnson III Tests of Achievement (Woodcock et al., 2001); the Comprehensive Test of Phonological Processes (CTOPP; Wagner, Torgesen, & Rashotte, 1999), that measures phonological skill areas and yields data to indicate whether there is a strong likelihood of future reading problems and a need for intervention; and the Dynamic Indicators of Basic Early Literacy Skills (DIBELS; Kaminski & Good, 1996), which measures fluency on several key indicators of early literacy acquisition (O'Shaugnessy et al., 2002).

At the secondary prevention level, this information can be used to form small intervention groups to target common skill or performance deficits. For example, students with common social skills deficits might be grouped together for purposes of direct instruction in identified acquisition deficits (see Lane, Wehby, Menzies, Doukas, Munton, & Gregg, in press), or students could be grouped together to receive instruction in early phonetic skills (see Lane, Wehby, Menzies, Gregg, Doukas, & Munton, 2002). At the tertiary level, information gleaned from the problem identification and problem analysis phases can be used to design, implement, and evaluate functional assessment-based interventions that are ideographic or individualized (see Dunlap et al., 1995; Dunlap et al., 1993; Kern et al., 1994; Umbreit, Lane, et al., in press).

REINFORCEMENT ASSESSMENT

Positive Reinforcement: _____ Yes _____ No    Frequency: _____ per _____

Types in Use:

Praise_____ Close Proximity ____ Tokens _____ Points _____

Other: _____

_____

Negative Reinforcement: _____ Yes _____ No    Frequency: _____ per _____

Types in Use:

Ignore_____ Activity Withdrawal ____ Tokens ____ Points ____

Other: _____

_____

Punishers:            _____ Yes _____ No    Frequency: _____ per _____

Types in Use:

Time-Out _____ Detention _____ Office _____ Parent _____

Other: _____

_____

Frequency count positive/negative teacher/aide statements in classroom:

Duration of recording:_____    Time of day:_____

|          | Target Child | All Others |
|----------|--------------|------------|
| Positive |              |            |
| Negative |              |            |

**FORM 2.4    *Observation Measure of the Learning Environment: Schedules of Reinforcement***

## LEARNING ENVIRONMENT ASSESSMENT

**Physical Setting:**

Number of Students _____     Teacher/Aides: _____     Size of Room: _____

Furnished with (desks, tables, bookcases, bean bag chairs, toys, etc.): _____

_____

_____

Student Location (where does student normally sit in the class relative to peers and teacher?):

_____

Lighting (good, fair, poor?): _____ Number of Doors: ___ Number of Windows: __

Class Rules Posted: _____ Y _____ N      Rules are (list): _____

_____

_____

Schedule Posted: _____ Y _____ N      Schedule is (list): _____

_____

_____

Student Work Displayed: _____ Y _____ N

Definitive Areas: _____ Y _____ N Briefly describe or sketch (e.g. play area, reading area):

_____

_____

Time Out Area: _____ Y _____ N
If yes, where . . . describe (location relative to teacher & peers): _____

_____

Point System Displayed?: Group ____ Individual _____ Description of point system:_____

_____

_____

**Social Setting:**

Supervision for peer interaction? _____ Y _____ N

Classroom conducive to social interaction? _____ Y _____ N

Interaction facilitated by teacher/aide? _____ Y _____ N

**FORM 2.5**   *Sample Observational Assessment of Classroom Learning Environment*

## Summary

At each level of prevention, assessment is linked to intervention by obtaining, examining, and analyzing reliable and valid data obtained in the problem identification and problem analysis phases of behavioral consultation. Moreover, data continue to link assessment with intervention as treatment is implemented and monitored throughout the intervention period and then assessed again at the end and follow-up to intervention. Data provide information about the nature and extent of intervention outcomes and measurable quantities to demonstrate progress. Replacement skills/behaviors are taught as an intervention for problematic skills/behavior to provide optimum opportunity for student success. Educators demonstrate accountability for student outcomes by linking assessment with intervention.

## References

Airasian, P. W. (1996). *Assessment in the classroom.* New York: McGraw-Hill.

American Psychiatric Association (1994). *Diagnostic and statistical manual of mental disorders,* Fourth Edition (DSM-IV). Washington DC: American Psychiatric Association.

Ayllon, T., & Roberts, M. (1974). Eliminating discipline problems by strengthening academic performance. *Journal of Applied Behavior Analysis, 7,* 71–76.

Batsche, G. M., & Knoff, H. M. (1995). Best practices in linking assessment to intervention. In A. Thomas & J. Grimes (Eds.), *Best practices in school psychology—III.* Washington DC: National Association of School Psychologists.

Beebe-Frankenberger, M. E., Bocian, K. M., MacMillan, D. L., & Gresham, F. M. (submitted 2003). Sorting second grade students with academic deficiencies: Characteristics differentiating those retained in grade from those promoted to third grade.

Bergan, J. R. (1977). *Behavioral consultation.* Columbus, OH: Merrill.

Bergan, J. R. (1995). Evolution of a problem-solving model of consultation. *Journal of Educational and Psychological Consultation, 6*(2), 111–123.

Bergan, J. R., & Kratochwill, T. R. (1990). *Behavioral consultation and therapy.* New York: Plenum Press.

Bijou, S. W., Peterson, R. F., & Ault, M. H. (1968). A method to integrate descriptive and experimental field studies at the level of data and empirical concepts. *Journal of Applied Behavior Analysis, 1,* 175–191.

Carver, R. P. (1974). Two dimensions of tests: Psychometric and edumetric. *American Psychologist, 29,* 512–518.

Colvin, G., Sugai, G., & Kame'enui, E. (1993). *Proactive schoolwide discipline: Implementation manual.* Eugene: Project PREPARE, Behavioral Research and Teaching, College of Education, University of Oregon.

Daly, E., & Martens, B. K. (1994). A comparison of three interventions for increasing oral reading performance: Application of the instructional hierarchy. *Journal of Applied Behavior Analysis, 27,* 459–469.

Daly, E., Martens, B. K., Dool, E., & Hintze, J. (1998). Using brief functional analysis to select interventions for oral reading. *Journal of Behavioral Education, 8,* 203–218.

Daly, E., Martens, B. K., Hamler, K., Dool, E., & Eckert, T. (1999). A brief experimental analysis for identifying instructional components needed to improve oral reading fluency. *Journal of Applied Behavior Analysis, 32,* 83–94.

Deno, S. L., (1987). Curriculum-based measurement. *Teaching Exceptional Children, 20,* 41.

Deno, S. L., Fuchs, L. S., Marston, D., & Shinn, J. (2001). Using curriculum-based measurement to establish growth standards for students with learning disabilities. *School Psychology Review, 30,* 507–524.

Dunlap, G., Foster-Johnson, L., Clarke, S., Kern, L., & Childs, K. E. (1995). Modifying activities to produce functional outcomes: Effects on the problem behaviors of students with disabilities. *Journal of the Association for Persons with Severe Handicaps, 20,* 248–258.

Dunlap, G., & Kern, L. (1996). Modifying instructional activities to promote desirable behavior: A conceptual and practical framework. *School Psychology Quarterly, 11,* 297–312.

Dunlap, G., Kern, L., dePerczel, M., Clarke, S., Wilson, D., Childs, K. E., White, R., & Falk, G. D. (1993). Functional analysis of classroom variables for students with emotional and behavioral challenges. *Behavioral Disorders, 18,* 275–291.

Durand, M., & Crimmins, D. (1988). *Motivation Assessment Scale.* Topeka, KS: Monaco.

Elliott, S. N., & Fuchs, L. S. (1997). The utility of curriculum-based measurement and performance assessment as alternatives to traditional intelligence and achievement tests. *School Psychology Review, 26,* 224–233.

Elliott, S., & Gresham, F. M. (1991). *Social skills intervention guide.* Circle Pines, MN: American Guidance Service.

Ervin, R. A., DuPaul, G. J., Kern, L., & Friman, P. C. (1998). Classroom-based functional and adjunctive assessments: Proactive approaches to intervention selection for adolescents with attention deficit hyperactivity disorder. *Journal of Applied Behavior Analysis, 31*(1), 65–78.

Fishbein, M., Hall-Jamieson, K., Zimmer, E., Von Haeften, I., & Nabi, R. (2002). Avoiding the boomerang: Testing the relative effectiveness of antidrug public service announcements before a national campaign. *American Journal of Public Health, 92,* 238–245.

Fournier, R. (2002, January 9). Education overhaul signed. *The Associated Press syndicated article in The Riverside Press Enterprise,* pp. A1, A9.

Fuchs, L. S., Butterworth, J., & Fuchs, D. (1989). Effects of curriculum-based progress monitoring on student knowledge of performance. *Education and Treatment of Children, 12,* 21–32.

Fuchs, L. S., & Fuchs, D. (1986). Effects of systematic formative evaluation: A meta-analysis. *Exceptional Children, 53,* 199–208.

Fuchs, L. S., Fuchs, D., & Hamlett, C. L. (1993). Technological advances linking the assessment of students' academic proficiency to instructional planning. *Journal of Special Education Technology, 12,* 49–62.

Fuchs, L. S., Fuchs, D., & Hamlett, C. L. (1994). Strengthening the connection between assessment and instructional planning with expert systems. *Exceptional Children, 61,* 138–146.

Fuchs, L. S., Fuchs, D., & Stecker, P. M. (1989). The effects of curriculum-based measurement on teachers' instructional planning. *Journal of Learning Disabilities, 22,* 51–59.

Greenwood, C. R., Terry, B., Marquis, J., & Walker, D. (1994). Confirming a performance-based instructional model. *School Psychology Review, 23,* 652–668.

Gresham, F. M. (1989). Assessment of treatment integrity in school consultation and prereferral intervention. *School Psychology Review, 18,* 37–50.

Gresham, F. M. (2002). Responsiveness to intervention: An alternative approach to learning disabilities. In R. Bradley, L. Danielson, & D. Hallahan (Eds.), *Identification of learning disabilities: Research to practice.* Mahwah NJ: Erlbaum.

Gresham, F. M., & Elliott, S. N. (1990). *Social skills rating system (SSRS).* Circle Pines, MN: American Guidance Service.

Gresham, F. M., & Lambros, K. M. (1998). Behavioral and functional assessment. In T. S. Watson & F. M. Gresham (Eds.), *Handbook of child behavior therapy.* New York: Plenum Press.

Harcourt Brace Educational Measurement (2000). Technical data report. *Stanford Achievement Test Series,* Ninth Edition. San Antonio, TX.

Hayes, S., Nelson, R., & Jarrett, R. (1987). The treatment utility of assessment: A functional approach to evaluating assessment quality. *American Psychologist, 42,* 963–974.

*Individuals with Disabilities Education Act Amendments of 1997.* Pub. L. No. 105-17, Section 20, 111 Stat. 37 (1997). Washington, DC: U.S. Government Printing Office.

Jones, R. N., Sheridan, S. M., & Binns, W. R. (1993). Schoolwide social skills training: Providing preventive services to students at-risk. *School Psychology Quarterly, 8,* 57–80.

Kaminski, R. A., & Good, R. H. (1996). Toward technology for assessing basic early literacy skills. *School Psychology Review, 25,* 215–227.

Kern, L., Dunlap, G., Clarke, S., & Childs, K. E. (1994). Student-assisted functional assessment interview. *Diagnostic, 19,* 20–39.

Lane, K. L., O'Shaughnessy, T., Lambros, K. M., Gresham, F. M., & Beebe-Frankenberger, M. E. (2001). The efficacy of phonological awareness training with first-grade students who have behavior problems and reading difficulties. *Journal of Emotional and Behavioral Disorders, 9,* 219–231.

Lane, K. L., Umbreit, J., & Beebe-Frankenberger, M. E. (1999). A review of functional assessment research with students with or at-risk for emotional and behavioral disorders. *Journal of Positive Behavioral Interventions, 1,* 101–111.

Lane, K. L., Wehby, J., Menzies, H., Doukas, G., Munton, S., & Gregg, R. (in press). Social skills training for students at-risk for antisocial behavior: The effects of small group instruction. *Behavioral Disorders.*

Lane, K. L., Wehby, J. H., Menzies, H. M., Gregg, R. M., Doukas, G. L., & Munton, S. M. (2002). Early literacy instruction for first-grade students at-risk for antisocial behavior. *Education and Treatment of Children, 25,* 438–458.

Lewis, T. J., Sugai, G., & Colvin, G. (1998). Reducing problem behavior through a schoolwide system of effective behavior support: Investigation of a schoolwide social skills training program and contextual variables. *School Psychology Review, 27,* 446–459.

Linn, R. L., Baker, E. L., & Betenbenner, D. W. (2002). Accountability systems: Implications of requirements of the No Child Left Behind Act of 2001. Los Angeles: Center for the Study of Evaluation, National Center for Research on Evaluation, Standards, and Student Testing, Graduate School of Education & Information Studies, University of California, Los Angeles (CSE technical report No. 567).

Lohrmann-O'Rourke, S., Knoster, T., Sabatine, K., Smith, D., Horvath, B., & Llewellyn, G. (2000). Schoolwide application of PBS in the Bangor area school district. *Journal of Positive Behavior Interventions, 2,* 238–240.

Lovitt, T., Eaton, M., Kirkwood, M., & Pelander, J. (1971). Effects of various reinforcement contingencies on oral reading rate. In E. Ramp & B. Hopkins (Eds.), *A new direction for education: Behavior analysis* (pp. 54–71). Lawrence: University of Kansas.

Mace, F. C. (1994). The significance and future of functional analysis methodologies. *Journal of Applied Behavior Analysis, 27,* 385–392.

Martens, B. (1993). A behavioral approach to consultation. In J. E. Zins & T. R. Thomas (Eds.), *Handbook of consultation services for children: Applications in educational and clinical settings.* San Francisco: Jossey-Bass.

Mash, E. J., & Terdal, L. G. (1988). Behavioral assessment of child and family disturbance. In E. J. Mash & L. G. Terdal (Eds.), *Behavioral assessment of childhood disorders* (2nd ed.), pp. 3–65. New York: The Guilford Press.

Noell, G. H., & Witt, J. C. (1999). When does consultation lead to intervention implementation? *The Journal of Special Education, 33,* 29–35.

O'Neill, R. E., Horner, R. H., Albin, R. W., Sprague, J. R., Storey, K., & Newton, J. S. (1997). *Functional assessment and program development for problem behavior: A practical handbook* (2nd ed.). Boston: Brooks/Cole.

O'Shaugnessy, T. E., Lane, K. L., Gresham, F. M., & Beebe-Frankenberger, M. E. (2002). Students with or at risk for learning and emotional-behavioral difficulties: An integrated system of prevention and intervention. In K. L. Lane, F. M. Gresham, & T. E. O'Shaugnessy (Eds.), *Interventions for children with or at risk for emotional and behavior disorders,* pp. 3–17. Boston: Allyn & Bacon.

Rowling, J. K. (1999). *Harry Potter and the chamber of secrets.* USA: Scholastic.

Scott, T. M. (2001). A schoolwide example of positive behavior support. *Journal of Positive Behavior Interventions, 3,* 88–94.

Shinn, M. R., Rosenfeld, S., & Knutson, N. (1989). Curriculum-based assessment: A comparison of models. *School Psychology Review, 18,* 229–316.

Sulzer-Azaroff, B., & Mayer, R. (1991). *Behavior analysis for lasting change.* Ft. Worth, TX: Harcourt Brace College Publishers.

Tapp, J. T., Wehby, J. H., & Ellis, D. N. (1995). A multiple option observation system for experimental studies: MOOSES. *Behavior Research Methods, Instruments and Computers, 27,* 25–31.

Taylor-Greene, S. J., & Kartub, D. T. (2000). Durable implementation of schoolwide behavior support: The high-five program. *Journal of Positive Behavior Interventions, 2,* 233–235.

Turnbull, A., Edmonson, H., Griggs, P., Wickham, D., Sailor, W., Freeman, R., Guess, D., Lassen, S., McCart, A., Park, J., Riffel, L., Turnbull, R., & Warren, J. (2002). A blueprint for schoolwide positive behavior support: Implementation of three components. *Exceptional Children, 68,* 377–402.

Umbreit, J., Ferro, J., Liaupsin, C., & Lane, K. L. (in preparation). Functional behavioral assessment and function-based interventions: An effective, practical approach.

Umbreit, J., Lane, K. L., & Dejud, C. (in press). Improving classroom behavior by modifying task difficulty: The effects of increasing the difficulty of too-easy tasks. *Journal of Positive Behavior Interventions.*

Wagner, R. K., Torgesen, J. K., & Rashotte, C. A. (1999). *Comprehensive test of phonological processes.* Austin, TX: Pro-Ed.

Walker, H. M., Block-Pedego, A., Todis, B., & Severson, H. (1991). *School archival records search.* Longmont, CO: Sopris West.

Watson, T. S., & Robinson, S. (1996). Direct behavioral consultation: An alternative to traditional behavioral consultation. *School Psychology Quarterly, 11,* 267–278.

Witt, J. & Beck, R. (1999). *One-minute academic functional assessment and interventions: 'Can't' do it...or 'won't' do it?* Longmont, CO: Sopris West.

Witt, J. C., Elliott, S. N., Daly, E. J., Gresham, F. M., & Kramer, J. J. (1998). *Assessment of at-risk and special needs children,* (2nd ed.) Boston: McGraw Hill.

Witt, J., Gresham, F. M., & Noell, G. (1996). What's behavioral about behavior consultation? *Journal of Educational and Psychological Consultation, 7,* 327–344.

Woodcock, R. W., McGrew, K. S., & Mather, N. (2001). *The Woodcock Johnson III tests of achievement.* Itasca, IL: Riverside.

# 3

## *Monitoring Changes during Intervention*

In the previous chapter we illustrated how primary, secondary, and tertiary interventions are linked to assessment information. Clearly, it is important that any intervention be designed based on data. This increases the likelihood that the intervention is directly relevant to the areas targeted for improvement, and it also increases the probability of achieving the desired intervention outcomes. Equally important to the original assessment and the corresponding intervention is *monitoring* how students respond to intervention efforts. Too often, teachers, school psychologists, and other treatment agents make the mistake of devoting so much attention to constructing the intervention itself that they inadvertently provide too little attention to identifying an appropriate tool or procedure to monitor how well students respond or change as a result of the intervention.

The goal of this chapter is four-fold. First, we will explain what it means to monitor change. Second, the importance of monitoring student progress will be established. Third, we will introduce and explain various strategies for monitoring change. Finally, we will discuss who can monitor student progress.

### What Does It Mean to Monitor Changes?

Monitoring changes during intervention is called "progress monitoring" and has also been referred to as "formative evaluation" (Fuchs & Fuchs, 1986), a process that has been shown to lead to large performance gains. Progress monitoring helps answer the following questions: (a) has there been a change in level, trend, and/or variability in performance across time? (b) have benchmark goals been met or exceeded expectations? and (c) if improvement is nonexistent or minimal, what adjustments to the intervention components are necessary, or likely, to produce the desired improvements in student performance? (Witt, Daly, & Noell, 2000).

Measurement of an academic or social skill/behavior level by relevant parameters (e.g., number correct, number completed, frequency, intensity, duration) at predetermined intervals throughout the intervention period yields the data necessary to evaluate progress (see Box 3.1). Comparisons are made across time, using pre-intervention levels as the baseline from which to judge progress (see Box 3.2).

**BOX 3.1  •  *Monitoring Changes during Intervention***

**Monitoring students in the target skill(s) provides:**
- Empirically validated method for examining the effectiveness of interventions
- Accountability by documenting student progress
- Flexibility to modify intervention components
- Motivation to continue the intervention until the goals are achieved

**BOX 3.2  •  *Measurement of Changes: Data Collection***

The "link" between assessment and intervention is using the information collected about the behavior targeted for improvement and then designing an intervention that is hypothesized to be the probable approach for reaching the desired behavior changes.

Compare data obtained prior to intervention onset to data collected during and after the intervention.  Draw conclusions about effectiveness.

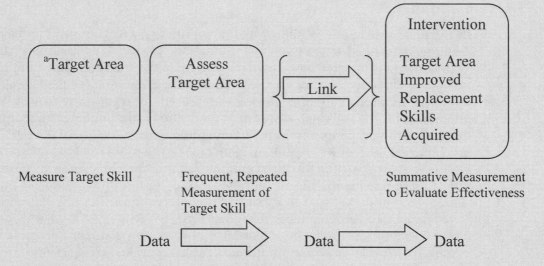

Compare data obtained prior to intervention onset to data collected during and after the intervention.  Draw conclusions about effectiveness.

*Note.* [a]Target area refers to the focus area (e.g., literacy skills) for the primary prevention and the specific skill or performance deficit identified in the secondary prevention (e.g., social skills) and tertiary prevention (e.g., academic engaged time) support.

Whether the intervention is for a student (tertiary prevention), an entire class or group (secondary prevention), or schoolwide (primary prevention), monitoring change is essential to intervention effectiveness. Measurement should be frequent, consistent, accurate, reliable, and sensitive. Reviewing the data from one measurement point to the next will assist in determining whether the student(s) is improving and helps to decide whether adjustments in the intervention are needed to facilitate improvement.

Educators are probably most familiar with monitoring student progress using statewide standardized tests. These tests are typically administered once a year and the outcomes have important implications for students and teachers alike. While these measures are one tool for monitoring student progress, they are but one tool: a tool that measures progress in the long-term. Progress measured in shorter periods of time requires instruments more sensitive to short-term changes. An example of such a tool is curriculum-based measurement procedures (CBM; Fuchs & Fuchs, 1986; Shinn, 1989).

Consider the following example of progress monitoring for a secondary prevention program: A small group of elementary students was identified through assessment as being aggressive with peers on the playground. After reviewing the teacher version of the Social Skills Rating System (SSRS; Gresham & Elliott, 1990), information obtained from the students' cumulative files (e.g., number of disciplinary contacts, number of suspensions and expulsions, and narrative comments) using the School Archival Record Search (SARS; Walker, Block-Pedego, Todis, & Severson, 1991), and direct observation of the students on the playground (A-B-C data collection; Bijou, Peterson, & Ault, 1968), it was hypothesized that the students had social skills deficits.

More specifically, the pre-intervention assessment identified the group of students as deficient in the skill of initiating peer contacts. Instead of asking peers if they can join in playground activities, the students would often use aggressive behavior as a way to initiate with peers. For example, one student always grabbed the ball away from peers, hoping to be part of the game. Pre-intervention assessment data collected on this particular student's behavior revealed zero incidences of asking to enter activities with peers and an average of nine aggressive acts per day toward peers on the playground (see Figure 3.1). The baseline data for the intervention is zero initiations with peers and nine aggressive acts while on the playground. Thus, the social skills that facilitate positive peer friendships were identified as a replacement skill to be taught using explicit instructional procedures.

Instruction in the prosocial skills would be taught during the intervention phase of the project. During this phase, trained observers would observe each student on the playground and collect data to count the frequency of initiations and aggressive acts. Although the replacement skill would be the behavior to be measured (number of peer initiations), aggressive acts would also be measured to detect whether learning and using the new replacement behavior decreases the number of aggressive acts on the playground. The intervention goal is to increase social skill with peers by stopping aggressive behavior on the playground. If the intervention proceeds as planned, initiations will increase and aggressive acts will decrease. Measuring both behaviors during intervention is monitoring for changes.

In the above example, progress is monitored by comparing student performance (initiations and aggressive acts) prior to and during the intervention. By comparing rates of behaviors in the baseline and intervention phases it is possible to assess the extent to which behaviors change. With the use of more sophisticated methodologies (e.g., multiple baseline across students or settings and reversal [ABAB] designs; Johnston & Pennypacker, 1993), it is possible to determine if a functional relationship between the intervention implementation and behavioral changes is evident. In brief, if behaviors change only when the intervention is introduced, then it is reasonable to conclude that the intervention is producing the changes in student behavior.

Progress is measured at the individual unit level (student, group, class, school) and changes are detected by comparing the same unit's original pre-intervention data to the current data. Using single case methodologies, progress is not measured by comparing the unit to other units (classmates, school norms, or nationwide

Table of Students in Social Skills Group:  Replacement Skill = # Peer Initiations

| Student | Before Intervention | Week 1 | Week 2 | Week 3 | Week 4 | Week 5 | Week 6 End Intervention | Overall Average |
|---|---|---|---|---|---|---|---|---|
| A | 0 | 0 | 0 | 1 | 3 | 2 | 3 | 1.5 |
| B | 0 | 1 | 1 | 3 | 5 | 6 | 5 | 3.5 |
| C | 0 | 0 | 0 | 0 | 2 | 4 | 3 | 1.5 |
| D | 0 | 0 | 3 | 2 | 5 | 9 | 7 | 4.3 |
| E | 0 | 2 | 4 | 3 | 7 | 10 | 9 | 5.8 |
| Average | 0 | .6 | 1.6 | 1.8 | 4.4 | 6.2 | 5.4 | 3.3 |

Table of Students Participating in Social Skills Group:  Aggressive Acts

| Student | Before Intervention | Week 1 | Week 2 | Week 3 | Week 4 | Week 5 | Week 6 End Intervention | Overall Average |
|---|---|---|---|---|---|---|---|---|
| A | 11 | 8 | 10 | 5 | 4 | 2 | 3 | 5.3 |
| B | 5 | 3 | 1 | 1 | 0 | 0 | 0 | .8 |
| C | 14 | 10 | 12 | 9 | 4 | 7 | 6 | 8.0 |
| D | 8 | 5 | 3 | 2 | 2 | 0 | 1 | 2.2 |
| E | 7 | 3 | 3 | 5 | 1 | 0 | 0 | 2.0 |
| Average | 9 | 5.8 | 5.8 | 4.4 | 2.2 | 1.8 | 2.0 | 3.7 |

**FIGURE 3.1**    *Individual Student and Social Skills Group Average Intervention Effectiveness: Example of monitoring an intervention that teaches a social skill to decrease aggressive behavior*

norms) as is the case with statewide assessments (see Chapter 2). Rather, change is measured relative to the unit of concern.

In our previous example, all of the students lack the same social skill and the group is being taught as a whole. Yet, monitoring will take place individually so that each student is evaluated for rates of change in their own behavior, not relevant to other students in the group. The intervention will be evaluated for effectiveness on both an individual student basis as well as by overall group changes. Individual student scores for the replacement social skill and aggressive acts will be analyzed using visual inspection, examination of means scores across each phase, and other procedures such as effect size calculations (Busk & Serlin, 1992; Gresham, 1998) to evaluate student performance. Group performance can be evaluated using statistical procedures (e.g., t-tests and analysis of variance) to identify significant differences between groups. In such a manner, individual and group performances are determined.

Figure 3.1 is an example of a progress monitoring data sheet for the social skills group. The first table shows the data collected for the six-week intervention on number of peer initiations on the playground, while the second table shows the data collected on number of aggressive acts on the playground for the same students. Note that both tables show information by the individual student within the social skills group as well as the average number for the social skills group per week and over the entire intervention period. For example, Student A had zero peer initiations and eleven aggressive acts in the assessment period prior to intervention. At the end of intervention, Student A made three peer initiations and committed three aggressive acts in the last week of intervention. Thus, it appears that the student acquired and performed the skill of initiating peers in playground activities in an appropriate way. It looks as if the new skill helped decrease aggressive acts for the student as well. As expected, each student varied in the rate of skill acquisition and performance. The data inform us about each student individually as well as about the overall effectiveness of the social skills training. Note that the groups as a whole increased peer initiations from 0 at pre-intervention to 5.4 at the end of week six, or an overall increase from 0 to 3.3. At the same time, the group decreased aggressive acts from a pre-intervention average group rate of nine to an average by week six of two, an overall decrease from 9 to 3.7 aggressive acts. In such a manner the interventionists are accountable by student and for the group as a whole, demonstrating intervention effectiveness in both ways. The data may support the use of future social skills groups to prevent aggressive acts on the playground.

These same procedures can be applied to primary and tertiary levels of prevention. The process (e.g., identifying the target areas; assessing performance of the target skills prior to, during, and after intervention; and making comparisons to evaluate outcomes) is parallel. However, in the case of primary prevention, additional measures such as standardized assessments (e.g., statewide assessments and teacher-completed behavior rating scales) may also be administered on a pre- and post-intervention basis as another method of monitoring student progress.

## Why Is It Important to Monitor Changes?

As previously mentioned, monitoring changes in students' academic and behavioral performance provides an empirically validated method of evaluating the effectiveness of an educational program or intervention—accountability by documenting rate of progress, flexibility to modify intervention components, and motivation to continue until goals are achieved (Box 3.1). Monitoring change by using frequent, repeated assessment procedures makes it possible to observe incremental progress toward an intervention goal. For the student who is building oral reading fluency, curriculum-based measurement procedures can be used to monitor the extent to which the student's fluency is improving.

Data also make it possible to determine whether progress is not occurring or is occurring at a minimal rate. It is important to measure the rate of change to make decisions about the ongoing effectiveness of the intervention. Data provide feedback to the student(s), interventionists, and parents regarding the extent to which the intervention should continue as planned or be modified if the progress is minimal. Thus, progress monitoring provides the flexibility, particularly in secondary and tertiary prevention programs, to modify treatment during the intervention period by refining, adding, or removing techniques, components, or even intervention goals (Sulzer-Azaroff & Mayer, 1991). Without detection of change or nonchange, intervention may fail when it could have been successful. Collecting data about skill acquisition and performance provides concrete evidence of change, thus accountability. When feedback is positive and changes are detected that signal progress toward the intervention goal (e.g., increased oral reading fluency), it provides the motivation to continue the effort by the student, teacher, parents, and others. Progress is reinforcing and helps maintain active participation by the student(s), school personnel, and parents. Moreover, monitoring what is happening during intervention may reveal unanticipated ways the environment or situation influences change.

## How Do We Monitor Changes?

### Outcome Measures

As previously discussed, it is possible to monitor students' responsiveness to primary interventions. When selecting which outcome measure to use (e.g., standardized reading measures, behavior rating scales, curriculum-based measurement, and direct observation), it is important to consider issues of reliability, sensitivity, and feasibility. The outcome measures must have demonstrated reliability so that changes on these measures can be attributed to student progress and not measurement error. Second, the outcome measures must be sensitive enough to detect changes in student performance that may be occurring in response to the intervention. Third, the outcome measures must be feasible in terms of the school's resource constraints (e.g., time, complexity, and expense). For example, consider monitoring the progress of a small group social skills intervention. If only teacher ratings of social skills (e.g., Social Skills Rating System; Gresham & Elliott, 1990) are collected, it is possible that the intervention may be determined to be ineffective. Yet there may be alternative explanations for the lack of change. It may be that (a) the measure was simply not sensitive enough to detect change and that more sensitive outcome measures such as direct observations were necessary to detect change, (b) the teachers completing the instrument were not privy to peer culture and were thus unable to observe the newly acquired social skills (Lane, 1999), or (c) the intervention was not effective. Thus, the instruments and procedures used to evaluate primary interventions need to strike a balance between being reliable, sensitive, and feasible.

We highly recommend that students be monitored from multiple perspectives. For example, we recommend including not only statewide assessments, but also district multiple measures reflective of the core curriculum, behavior rating scales (e.g., Social Skills Rating System, Gresham & Elliott, 1990; Walker-McConnell Scale of Social Competence and School Adjustment, Walker & McConnell, 1988), and information contained in the cumulative files using empirically validated tools such as SARS (Walker et al., 1991). While the district multiple measures (which include curriculum-based measures) might be administered weekly or monthly, the other measures might be administered once or twice a year with the data being analyzed using group design methodologies.

In the case of secondary and tertiary interventions, skill level changes, whether academic or behavioral, are monitored by collecting performance data relative to the newly trained skill as well as any behavior that is expected to change as a result of learning the new behavior. Data are collected frequently by measuring progress at predetermined times during the intervention period (e.g., daily, weekly) and then logged and graphed to facilitate evaluation of effects. Graphing the data provides a visual tool for evaluating the response to intervention and is essential in progress monitoring. When data is plotted on a graph, changes can easily be examined by looking for changes in the level, trend, or variability of skill performance (Baer, 1977; Gresham, 1998; Witt et al., 2000) Figure 3.2A displays what each type of change might look like, with pre-intervention data to the left of the dotted vertical lines in each graph, and data collected after intervention is implemented to the right of the dotted vertical lines. Figure 3.2A uses "mean bars" that are plotted on top of the data points. The mean bars are a visual representation of the average performance level for before intervention (left of the dotted line), and after intervention (right of the dotted line). The graph shows a change in the mean performance level of the new skill, signaling that the intervention is effectively changing performance overall. Figure 3.2B uses trend lines to detect change. In this figure, performance was stable before the intervention as indicated by the flat slope. Once the intervention began (points to the right of the dotted line), the first measurement shows performance lower than it was prior to intervention. Then, subsequent performance levels increased. When the line for overall change is superimposed over the data points, the slope changes from flat to elevating over time, indicating change in the right direction. Figure 3.2C shows how variability is examined by looking at the shape of the data. Performance before intervention was erratic and after intervention implementation remained erratic, with performance down to pre-intervention levels at two time points. Although it looks as if there may be some gradual slope change here, performance variability during intervention signals the need for modification in components that will facilitate more stable change. This might take many forms, depending on the type of intervention, but such methods as higher rates of positive reinforcement or reduced time on task could be implemented. In brief, interventions should produce changes that are maintained over time.

Progress monitoring is used to evaluate the impact of academic and behavioral interventions. Consider the following example of progress monitoring in an academic intervention: Suppose the replacement skill is regrouping in math addition. One objective, reliable, and sensitive measure is a permanent product record of the math worksheets that would provide the number or percentage of correct math addition problems attempted and correct. Permanent product records are often easily attainable because they are tangible pieces of paper that the student produces and that a teacher usually records. The difference here is that not only will the teacher record number or percentage correct in a grade book, but also both the teacher and the student will keep a graphic representation of progress. This puts the focus on measuring and being accountable for progress toward learning and achieving the benchmark and final intervention goals. Figure 3.3 is an example of how a teacher and student might graph progress toward both benchmark and final math goals. The vertical dotted lines in the figure represent benchmark goals of

A.    *Change in Level: Examine "average" by drawing "mean bars"*

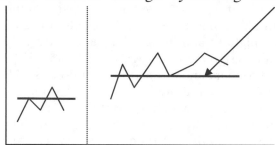

Change in level means that performance has increased overall even though performance varied every time it was measured.

B.    *Change in Trend: Examine the slope of data*

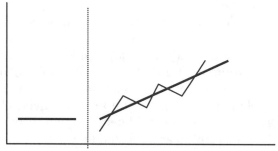

Change in slope means that there is an increasing (or decreasing if the line went down) trend in performance of the skill over the data points.

C.    *Change in Variability: Examine the shape of overall data*

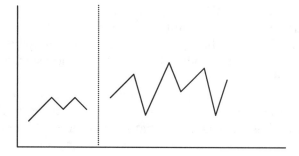

Changes are unstable, suggesting that though there is improved performance at times, the performance is not consistent. This would signal a need for modifications to the intervention with components that would support consistent and sustained increases.

**FIGURE 3.2**    *Visual Inspection of Plotted Data for Changes in Performance*

percentage of math problems correct for end of week CBA math addition tests. Note that the goal of 40 percent by the end of week two of the intervention was not quite met, while the goal of 60 percent by week four was exceeded, and so on. The final goal of 80 percent correct was exceeded by the student. We will anticipate enthusiasm on the part of the student! Notice that the student's scores were very close to the benchmarks, which indicates that these were realistic goals for the student. The benchmark goals were set as a result of the pre-intervention assessment

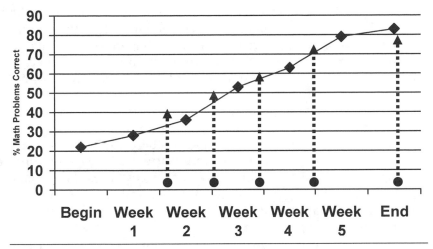

**FIGURE 3.3** *Student Permanent Product Progress-Monitoring by Graph: Math Progress*

that helped evaluate the different conditions (see Chapter 2) relevant to the requisite ability of the student and the available supports for intervention effectiveness in the learning environment and at home.

### Measurement System

A measurement system that is objective, reliable, and highly sensitive to change in skill or behavior is selected as part of the intervention design. In the previous example of the social skills group, a *frequency* count of how many times in a week the students displayed positive peer initiation behavior as well as aggressive acts was a sensitive, reliable, and objective measure for monitoring changes. Conversely, had the measure been a survey or an interview of the yard supervisors for their impressions of the students' behavior, measurement would be subjective (judgments relative to each yard supervisor's personal definition of good and bad behavior and their memory of each student's behavior: "that definitely looks intentional to me!" versus "I don't think actually he meant to give that child a nose bleed."); potentially unreliable (they could change their judgment when asked a second time, "Well, maybe he was trying to tickle rather than scratch that child."); and not sensitive to change (because reputational bias is difficult to change; Walker, Colvin, & Ramsey, 1995). Although teacher judgment may be useful in many instances, it is probably not the most sensitive indicator that can be used to monitor *incremental* student progress.

Not only should the measurement be sensitive to change, but the behaviors and/or tasks that are measured must be sensitive to change as well (Chafouleas & Martens, 2002). First, select tasks that are the most sensitive to change. For instance, the intervention goal may be to increase reading fluency, but skills/tasks targeted for intervention will be the components that comprise reading fluency (such as decoding and blending skills) that are much more sensitive to immediate change than overall reading fluency. Changes in decoding or blending skills may occur shortly after intervention implementation, whereas increased rates of reading fluency may not change until later in the intervention after the component skills have been acquired and mastered. Further, the ability of a measure to record change in the beginning acquisition phase of a skill as well as at mastery level is critical to whether the intervention is implemented and continued as designed (treatment integrity, Chapter 5). It is also pivotal for whether the learned replacement skill/behavior is applied by the student under other conditions and settings when appropriate (generalization, see Chapter 6) and that the skill/behavior becomes part of the student's repertoire (maintenance of effects, see Chapter 6). If the task is not sensitive to small changes, motivation to continue the treatment is deflated for the student, teacher, and parents.

Second, it is important to measure all relevant facets of the treatment goal whenever acquisition and mastery of more than one skill or behavior may be required to attain a goal. For example, in their studies of the effects of phonological awareness training, Chafouleas and Martens (2002) monitored acquisition and mastery of several phonological tasks as necessary components to overall reading performance. If only one skill was assessed rather than the range of phonological skills that were addressed in the intervention, it would not be possible to accurately determine the scope of intervention outcomes.

In the case of behavioral interventions when a replacement skill is being taught in an effort to provide the student with a functionally equivalent behavior (Mace, 1994) that can be used by the student instead of the problem or target behavior, be sure to assess both the target and replacement behaviors. This way, it is possible to see if increases in the replacement behavior are associated with decreases in the target behavior. Figure 3.4 displays the increase in positive peer initiations and the decrease in aggressive behaviors on the playground. The focus of training was for students to learn positive ways to initiate play with their peers. The aggressive behaviors decreased as the positive peer initiation levels increased. The new behavior most likely was reinforced (thus, increased) by naturally occurring positive peer responses.

## How Are Skills/Behaviors Measured?

As previously mentioned, primary prevention efforts can be assessed with standardized academic measures (e.g., statewide assessments), teacher rating scales, record reviews, as well as more sensitive measures such as district multiple measures, curriculum-based measures, and, for a subset of students, direct observations of behavior. When conducting secondary and tertiary interventions, academic and behavioral progress of student behaviors is most often measured with the latter types of measures. While teachers, school psychologists, administrators, and other district support personnel are typically familiar with administration procedures for the standardized measures and ratings scales, there is often a concern about how to measure various academic and behavioral skills in an objective, reliable, sensitive, and feasible method.

Monitoring skills or behavior requires that the behaviors of interest are clearly defined by (a) what they look like, (b) the dimension by which they will be measured, and (c) the measurement method. Using these three components is often termed as "operationalizing the skill" and will enable the skill/behavior to be interpretable before, during, and after intervention (Sulzer-Azaroff & Mayer, 1991).

### Define Skill/Behavior by What It Looks Like: Topography

A skill or behavior is defined by how it looks, explicitly stating every detail of what is expected to be done and seen. This is called the topography of the skill/behavior.

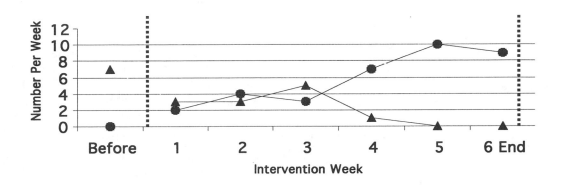

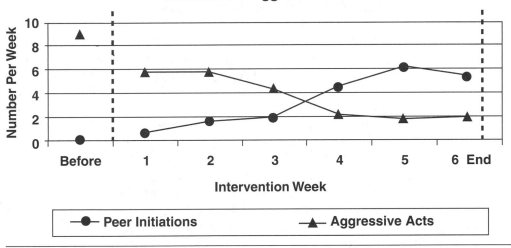

**FIGURE 3.4** *Progress-Monitoring Displayed Graphically of Intervention in Figure 3.1*

When a skill or behavior is discrete, it can be clearly described from beginning to end. Examples include number of pages read, hitting, or percentage of correct words; these are all discrete events with a distinct beginning and end. The definition of what is expected can be read by anyone, and that person will know exactly what is expected. An example of a behavioral definition is as follows:

Desired behavior:   Academic engagement
Defined as:         Academic engagement refers to the amount of time a student spends academically engaged in and working on teacher-assigned activities. Examples include (a) attending to the materials and the task (e.g., facing the board), (b) making the appropriate motoric or verbal responses (e.g., writing, computing, discussing), and (c) asking for assistance using the requested method (e.g., raising hand and waiting to be called on).

Such a definition leaves no doubt as to what is expected of the student and no doubt to an observer as to whether or not the student is academically engaged. We can say that the academic engagement behavior is discrete; it is explicitly stated, and clearly has a beginning and an end.

A second example of defining the desired replacement skill using an academic skill/behavior is as follows:

| | |
|---|---|
| Replacement skill: | Acquire and master multiplication tables through 9's |
| Defined as: | Acquire and master multiplication facts through 9's refers to performing (written and orally) multiplication problems by 1's through 9's at 75 percent accuracy. |

Again, the skill of performing multiplication tables has a discrete beginning (1 x 1) and end (9 x 9) and the definition states these will be performed both written and orally. The discrete skill has a definition that is explicit so that everyone knows what is expected.

### Define Skill/Behavior by Dimension

The most appropriate and sensitive dimension by which to measure a replacement skill/behavior must be stated so that the behavior can be effectively monitored to detect small incremental change. Dimensions of skill and behavior include (a) frequency, (b) rate, (c) intensity, (d) duration, (e) latency, and (f) accuracy (Sulzer-Azaroff & Mayer, 1991). Box 3.3 lists the dimensions and provides examples of each. In the academic skill definition for multiplication problems shown above, "at 75 percent accuracy" is the extent to which the student is expected to reach multiplication skill performance. It makes no difference whether the student is given four problems for which he will be expected to get three out of four correct, or if there are fifty problems, for which he will be expected to get at least thirty-eight correct. The definition could add the phrase "for three out of five math worksheets", which would be the *rate* at which the student would be expected to perform at the 75 percent *accuracy* level.

If one of the intervention goals is to decrease noncompliant behavior in the form of starting work on a math multiplication quiz upon teacher request, then the teacher would monitor compliance using the *latency* measure. For example, if the student initially did not begin the math quiz until three minutes after the teacher's request to begin the quiz, the teacher would measure the time it takes the student to begin the math quiz each time a quiz is presented to the student throughout the intervention phase. It may be that the student is not beginning because of poor multiplication fact skills, so that as skills increase time for compliance to the teacher request increases. However, if other factors are evaluated through assessment, such as student inattention, another component of the intervention may be to build attention skills. Although the intervention will be altered to address an attention problem, the teacher will still use *latency* to measure effectiveness of the intervention. The dimensions that best detect incremental change are selected according to the skill/behavior and then these same dimensions are measured prior to intervention, monitored during intervention, and assessed at the end of intervention. The dimensions yield the numbers that comprise the data from which accountability for intervention effectiveness is demonstrated.

**BOX 3.3** • *Dimensions of Skill/Behavior*

| Dimension | Definition | Examples |
|---|---|---|
| Frequency | Number of occurrences of the target behavior | (a) number of reports complete<br>(b) number of requests for help<br>(c) number of absences<br>(d) number of books read |
| Rate | Number of times the target behavior occurs within a specified interval or per opportunity | (a) number absences per month<br>(b) number hits per recess period<br>(c) number of correct responses out of 10 problems<br>(d) games won in football season |
| Intensity | Force with which a target behavior is demonstrated | (a) kick the ball 50 feet<br>(b) read aloud so that everyone in the class can hear<br>(c) press with the pencil so that all letters are visible |
| Duration | Amount of time that passes between when the target behavior begins and ends | (a) practice with math flashcards for 20 minutes per evening at home<br>(b) play at recess for 15 minutes without hitting<br>(c) participate in reading groups for 20 minutes |
| Latency | Amount of time that passes between a request, signal, or cue and the onset of the target behavior | (a) seconds until student response to teacher request "sit on the mat"<br>(b) days to turn in a report after teacher asks for report to be submitted |
| Accuracy | Extent to which the target behavior meets the requisite goals, standards, benchmarks, or expectations | (a) score at or above 80% on weekly spelling test<br>(b) read 90 out of 100 grade-level words correctly |

*Source:* Adapted from B. Sulzer-Azaroff and G. R. Mayer (1991), *Behavior Analysis for Lasting Change.* Fort Worth, TX: Harcourt Brace College Publishers.

## Define Monitoring Method

There are seven different monitoring *methods* for measuring change. Some of these methods focus on examining a tangible product of a behavior (e.g., permanent product), others focus on numerical dimension of the behavior (e.g., event recording, interval recording, and time sampling), and still others focus on the temporal dimension of the behavior (e.g., duration and latency; Alberto & Troutman, 1999). The dimension used to measure a behavior/skill guides selection of the appropriate recording procedure(s).

Box 3.4 outlines the names, definitions, examples, and strengths and limitations of each monitoring method. In brief, the methods are as follows: *permanent products* measure the quantity of a certain target; *event recording* measures the number of occurrences in a given length of time; *partial interval recording* measures whether or not the target behavior occurred at any point during a given time interval; *whole interval recording* measures whether or not the target behavior occurred during the entire interval; *momentary time sampling* measures whether or not the target behavior occurred at the end of the interval; *duration recording* measures the amount of time the target behavior occurs; and *latency recording* measures the amount of time between when a request or prompt is made for a specific behavior and the onset of the target behavior (Alberto & Troutman, 1999; Sulzer-Azaroff & Mayer, 1991).

### Topography, Dimension, and Method Combined

Form 3.1 is an example of a problem-solving worksheet that could be used for designing an intervention using a topographic definition of intervention components, dimension, and method of data collection. The worksheet provides the information necessary to set up the appropriate monitoring system for the intervention because it describes the replacement skill/behavior, the performance goal by level of performance accuracy expected during (benchmark goals) and at the end of intervention, and the dimension and method of measuring for progress.

Note that the initial problem skill/behavior is the first item on the worksheet. It is important to write down the exact problem or target behavior for several reasons. First, the skill or behavior that is problematic is explained fully so that all parties to the intervention understand the extent of the problem. Second, actually writing down what the problem looks like often helps with sorting through the alternatives for intervention as well as what the appropriate goals might be. Finally, there is documentation as to what the intervention specifically addresses.

A teacher or interventionist can use the worksheet as a tool when meeting with the student, parents, or other interested parties to facilitate intervention design. The form would be partially filled out with just the problem skill or behavior and recorded pre-intervention performance levels of skills or behaviors of concern. In this manner, all parties understand the problem, and brainstorming for solutions is facilitated. Moreover, the student, parents, or others may provide information about the problem that was not previously revealed during assessment, or that may need to be assessed and added as part of the problem. For example, perhaps Mr. Hanks used this worksheet to meet with Jenny's parents and discuss solutions. Mrs. Freedman may mention to Mr. Hanks that her daughter seems to have the same behaviors at home when she is supposed to be doing homework. Up until this point, the intervention would have been implemented at school. However, with the new information, a new component will be added for the parent to implement the same intervention during homework time at home. Perhaps the work preparation and stay-in-seat directions would be the same at home. However, seeking help might be done differently at home than in class, where Jenny is asked to raise her hand. In this case, the parent would monitor progress at home as well. Teachers and parents would make weekly, or even daily, comparisons of progress between school and home.

Form 3.2 displays the results of progress monitoring for the intervention during the first week of the intervention. Some goals were met while others were not.

**BOX 3.4** • *Measurement Methods for Monitoring Change*

| Measurement Type and Question | Measure Definition | Example of Measurement Use | Strengths and Limitations of Measurement |
|---|---|---|---|
| Permanent Product<br><br>How many of a certain target or 'thing'? | A tangible product that:<br>(a) Records progress toward outcome<br>(b) Records maintenance effect | (a) Number of correct words read per minute<br>(b) Number of office referrals<br>(c) Number of homework sheets completed | (a) Data easily and commonly collected<br>(b) Easy comparison<br>(c) Easy to interpret<br>(d) Limits classroom interruptions |
| Event Recording<br><br>How many occurrences in a given length of time? | An event that:<br>Records number of times the problem and replacement behavior occurs over a specific time period. | (a) Number of books read in a month<br>(b) Number of times out of seat per hour<br>(c) Number of positive peer initiations per day | (a) Easy to count (use checklist/grid, wrist or hand counter, tokens, etc.)<br>(b) Appropriate for behavior that is clearly defined and interpreted<br>( c) Cannot be used with continuous data |
| Partial Interval Recording<br><br>Does the target behavior occur at any point during the 10-second interval? | Records whether or not the target behavior occurred at any point during the interval. | (a) Profanity<br>(b) Passing note to peers | (a) Often overestimates how often the behavior occurs (too high)<br>(b) Useful for behaviors that happen quickly and briefly<br>(c) Can be used with continuous data |
| Whole Interval Recording<br><br>Does the target behavior occur during the entire 10-second interval? | Records the target behavior when it occurs throughout the entire interval. | (a) Academic engaged time<br>(b) Positive peer interactions | (a) Often underestimates how often the behavior occurs (too low)<br>(b) Useful when need to know if the behavior is not interrupted |
| Momentary Time Sampling<br><br>Does the target behavior occur at the end of the 10 minute interval? | Records behavior when it occurs at the moment the interval ends. Similar to interval recording, but intervals are in minutes rather than seconds. | (a) Out-of-seat behavior<br>(b) Repetitive hand movements | Useful for recording behaviors that tend to occur for longer lengths of time. |
| Duration Recording<br><br>How long does the target behavior occur? | Records the amount of time a behavior occurs. | (a) Length of time to complete a worksheet<br>(b) Length of time for temper tantrum | Easy to record with watch or stopwatch |
| Latency Recording<br><br>How much time elapses between when the request or prompt is made and the target behavior begins? | Records the amount of time between a request, prompt, or cue for a specific behavior and the onset of that behavior. | (a) Length of time to start the assignment<br>(b) Length of time to start cleaning up activities | Useful when you want to assess the temporal nature of the target behavior |

*Source:* (Adapted from B. Sulzer-Azaroff and G. R. Mayer (1991), *Behavior Analysis for Lasting Change.* Fort Worth, TX: Harcourt Brace College Publishers.

Problem-Solving Worksheet

Student:   Jenny Freedman                Grade: 6        Date:   10/15/02

Teacher:   Mr. Hanks

Problem Skill or Behavior (describe):

Jenny is often out-of-seat during math individual worksheet seat time.  She frequently goes to sharpen a pencil, goes to the supply box to borrow an eraser from her teacher, or leans over to whisper to another student, often interfering with other student's time to focus on math.  As a result, she rarely finishes the math problems, resulting in low math scores in spite of having good math skills. Results of a functional assessment indicated that Jenny is seeking attention from her teacher and from her peers.

Assessed Level of Performance of Problem Skill or Behavior (level/rate):

(1)     Jenny displayed out-of-seat behavior an average of 6 times during math, measured every day over 2 weeks, ranging from 2 to 13 times out-of-seat over the 2-week period.

(2)     Jenny scored an average of 53% on math over the 2 weeks, ranging from a low score of 34% to a high score of 82%.

Replacement Skill or Behavior (describe):

(1) Work Preparation:  Jenny will have 2 freshly sharpened pencils, an eraser, and scratch paper on her desk prior to beginning math worksheet time.

(2) Stay-in-seat:  Jenny will sit in an upright position at her desk with buttocks on the seat, both feet on the floor, and head and eyes directed towards the math worksheet or, when necessary, at the instructor.

(3) Raise hand for help:  Jenny will raise one arm while in the stay-in-seat position to request assistance from Mr. Hanks, the teacher, or the designated student helper.

Performance Goal at End of Intervention:

| | | |
|---|---|---|
| Work Preparation: | 5 out of 5; 100% | |
| Stay-in-seat | 90 minutes per week; 100% | |
| Raise hand for help | 100% | RESULT = Math scores   80% + |

Anticipated Length of Intervention to Goal (time):      4 weeks

Benchmark Goals (time x performance level):

| | End Week 1 | End Week 2 | End Week 3 |
|---|---|---|---|
| Work Preparation | 2 out of 5 | 3 out of 5 | 4 out of 5 |
| Stay-in-seat | 70% | 80% | 90% |
| Raise hand for help | 80% | 90% | 100% |
| Math scores | 65% | 70% | 75% |

Progress Monitored by (dimension x method):
Work Preparation = rate; # occurrences per week, event recording
Raise hand = frequency; # times, event recording
Stay-in seat = duration; how long during math worksheet time; teacher record in-seat time
Math scores = accuracy; percent correct; permanent product math worksheets

---

**FORM 3.1**   *Problem-Solving Worksheet Used for Design and Progress Monitoring*

The teacher and others review the first week results and make decisions about whether each component is producing the expected behavior by comparing the data to the benchmark goals. Notice that the decision was made to review "hand raising" with the student and then to reinforce the behavior by more verbal praise whenever she raises her hand for assistance rather than talking out. The data are used for detecting incremental changes in Jenny's behavior as well as seeing if math scores increase in accuracy when replacement behaviors are used. In brief, progress monitoring documents the response to intervention.

### What Is "Response to Intervention"?

Monitoring learning progress yields data that are interpretable as a student's response to intervention (Gresham, 2002). Whenever students are tested on curriculum, test scores measure how much students have learned. Thus, test scores measure how a student responds to the instruction. Different methods of teaching meet the needs of various student learning styles. When students test low on learning concepts, they have not responded well to the teaching to which they have been exposed. This may result from a variety of reasons from "within child" factors (e.g., neurological deficits) or to external environmental factors (e.g., family problems, poor learning environment), including too difficult or too easy curriculum or poor teaching methods. An assessment should include a variety of measures to investigate which factors contribute to the poor response to teaching. If the majority of students in a class are not responding well to instruction, the focus should be on adjusting the curriculum or the way in which it is taught. If one or only a few students respond poorly, intervention components are designed that will address the unique learning needs of the student(s) to allow for the maximum opportunity to learn.

Monitoring intervention components is monitoring the student *response to the intervention.* When an intervention component that has been implemented correctly still meets with *resistance,* change to a more intensive intervention can be considered. Continual *resistance to intervention* may signal more serious factors, such as a learning disability (Gresham, 1991, 2002), and the student may be considered for formal evaluation to receive special education support. Monitoring intervention components on a consistent basis and using sensitive measures to detect change is essential to examine student response to intervention.

## Who Monitors Intervention and How Do They Do It?

Interventions typically are monitored by whoever implements the intervention, such as the teacher, paraprofessional, or school psychologist. Interventions may be successful when only one person collects data to monitor change. However, we recommend that whenever possible the students also record and monitor their change. Whenever the intervention consists of components that are implemented in the home, parents are also asked to monitor change and are provided with easy ways to collect data. School-home notes are also recommended because they offer feedback as to how an intervention is working at school and at home.

### Teacher

The teacher, or other school professional who implements an intervention, will monitor progress toward benchmark and final goals. When using a frequency count, the

| | | | | | | |
|---|---|---|---|---|---|---|
| **Intervention Progress-Monitoring Record Sheet** | | | | | | |
| **Student:** Jenny Freedman | | | | **Activity:** In-seat math worksheet | | |
| **Teacher:** Hanks | | | | **Date:** 10/28 – 11/01/02  Week 1 | | |
| **Skill or Behavior** | **Monday** | **Tuesday** | **Wednesday** | **Thursday** | **Friday** | **Week 1 Performance** |
| Minutes of math session | 20 | 19 | 21 | 15 | 15 | Total: 90 minutes math seat work |
| Duration Stay in seat (mins) | 8 | 12 | 14 | 13 | 14 | Duration: 61 minutes 61/90 = 68% |
| Work Prepped | yes | yes | no | yes | no | 3 out of 5 |
| # Raise hand vs. talk out | 2/10 | 5/8 | 6/8 | 3/6 | 3/3 | 19/35 54% |
| % Math worksheet score | 42% | 51% | 48% | 59% | 67% | Average 53.4% |

Summary of Intervention Week 1:

| Skills/Behaviors: | Benchmark/Goal | Student Performance | Goal Met Y/N |
|---|---|---|---|
| __Work Preparation__ | (40%) 2 out of 5 days | 3/5 days | Y |
| __Stay-In Seat__ | (70%) 63 minutes | 61 mins/68% | N |
| __Raise Hand for Help__ | (80%) when need help | 54% | N |
| __Math Worksheet Score End_ | 65% accuracy | 67% | Y |

Comments:_____

Review raising hand instead of talking out; stayed in seat; almost reached goal!

Decisions:    Continue as planned, consider reinforcing raising hand for help

with additional verbal praise for attention.

**FORM 3.2**   *Progress Monitoring for Intervention Shown in Form 3.1* teacher simply makes a mark on a grid that indicates that an event, whether academic or behavioral, occurred during a predetermined period of time. For example, Form 3.3 shows how a teacher used a generic frequency count form to monitor progress for an intervention. In this example, the student was working to reduce out-of-seat behavior during independent seatwork time while increasing completing and turning in skill sheets. The goal of the five-day intervention period was to increase completed skill sheets, so this was monitored. Reducing the out-of-seat behaviors was important to monitor because this was the behavior that competed with the goal of completing skill sheets. The teacher kept a frequency count on the grid with a simple "+" mark to indicate that the event ("out-of-seat" or "completed and turned in skill sheet on time") occurred during independent seatwork activities on each of five days. On the fifth day, the student reduced out-of-seat behavior to one event and had turned in all eight skill sheets. This is summarized at the bottom of the form.

The generic form (Form 3.3) is available in the Appendix (Reproducible 3.3). It may be used for monitoring frequency of four or more skills/behaviors during any period of time a teacher chooses to monitor. There are five periods of time across the top that may be used for hours, school periods, activities, days, weeks, and so on. The teacher defines the skill/behavior below so that corresponding numbers on the left of the grid refer to the behavior. A summary at the bottom of the form is used to mark the final monitor period frequencies in order to indicate the end of the intervention frequencies of the behaviors. The use of grids to measure dimensions of skill/behavior by a selected method, whether event-recording or interval-recording, is critical for progress monitoring to demonstrate intervention effectiveness. Response to intervention is represented by the information recorded on a grid.

Graphing the collected data to visually evaluate results is essential to progress-monitoring. Figure 3.4 shows two graphs of the data for the social skills training group whose data are shown in Figure 3.1. The top graph in Figure 3.4 is the data collected for Student E, while the bottom graph displays the average changes across the five students who participated in the social skills training group. Recall that this was a secondary intervention, implemented with all five students at one time. However, data were collected on an individual basis to assess changes that were unique to each student so that modifications could be made during intervention, if necessary, for an individual student who was not responding. Had a student not made progress and was singled out for more intensive support, the next intervention for that student would be a tertiary intervention.

## *Student*

Research has repeatedly demonstrated that when students monitor their progress using visual representations such as graphs, they have a higher motivation and succeed at attaining intervention goals at a higher rate than those students who do not monitor progress (DiGangi, Maag, & Rutherford, 1991). Self-monitoring is a well-established method that is appropriate for both behavioral and academic interventions, across age and ability groups (Shapiro & Cole, 1994). Moreover, self-monitoring has been empirically demonstrated to be effective in both general and special education settings for students with diverse needs, including students with emotional and behavior disorders (Hughes, Ruhl, & Misra, 1989; Kern, Dunlap, Childs, & Clarke, 1994), developmental disabilities (Hughes, Korinek, & Gorman, 1991), learning disabilities (Dunlap & Dunlap, 1989) comorbid ADHD and learning disabilities (Shimabukuro, Prater, Jenkins, & Edelen-Smith, 1999), autism (Koegel

| Skill or Behavior | Day 1 | Day 2 | Day 3 | Day 4 | Day 5 |
|---|---|---|---|---|---|
| 1 | + + + +<br>+ + + | + + + +<br>+ | + + + | + + + | + |
| 2 | None | + + | + + + + | + + + +<br>+ + | + + + +<br>+ + + + |
| 3 | | | | | |
| 4 | | | | | |
| | | | | | |
| | | | | | |

**Skill/Behavior Key (define skill/behavior monitored):**

1. Number of times out of seat during independent seat work

2. Number of skill sheets completed on time

3. _____

4. _____

_____

**Ending Summary:**

| #1 ⬭1 | #2 ⬭8 | #3 | #4 |

**FORM 3.3**    *Sample Generic Frequency Count Form*

& Koegel, 1990), and children without special needs (Wood, Murdock, Cronin, Dawson, & Kirby, 1998).

Other studies (Cole & Bambara, 2000; Ollendick, 1995; Reynolds & Stark, 1987) have found self-monitoring to be effective for students with internalizing problems such as depression, anxiety, and phobias. This type of application requires the ability to monitor how one feels, so there may be limitations on the age or ability range for students with these types of issues (King, Ollendick, & Murphy, 1997). One of the studies (Reynolds & Stark, 1987) used self-monitoring as an intervention for students with depression. They asked students schoolwide to list five activities that make them happy and five things they like to do at school. In this manner, the researchers secured lists of events/activities that appealed to each age level of student, created by students who were not having depressive symptoms. It is often difficult for students with depression to generate events or activities that make them happy even though those activities may be going on around them. Thus, the items were compiled for each age level and were used to create self-monitoring instruments by age/grade level. Students with depression were given a self-monitoring sheet that was age-appropriate and were asked to monitor pleasant events by putting a mark next to any activity/event item that happened during a week. The study found that having students focus on positive events helped remove depressive symptoms. Form 3.4 is an example of what a self-monitoring form for pleasant events might look like for a fifth- or sixth-grade student. Forms 3.5, 3.6, and 3.7 are examples of student self-monitoring for improving academic work habits during math worksheet time (Form 3.5), for improving class participation skills (Form 3.6), and for identifying a relation-ship between "mood" and academic engagement levels (Form 3.7).

Social skills training is an important area in which self-monitoring has been used, requiring that students monitor thoughts and feelings associated with social interactions so that the most appropriate social skills are selected. Although social skills are taught explicitly using modeling, role play, and feedback techniques, once a skill is learned, self-monitoring can promote performance of the acquired skill when it is appropriate (Gumpel & Golan, 2000). For example self-monitoring was used as part of social skills training in an intervention reported by Moore, Cart-ledge, and Heckman (1995) in which boys with emotional or behavior problems tallied every time they used a newly learned technique for game-playing. The stu-dents graphed and discussed their self-monitoring of social skills, which resulted in increased appropriate game play. Self-monitoring procedures have also been used to promote independence (Trammel, Schloss, & Alper, 1994), increase self-control (Martella, Leonard, Marchand-Martella, & Agran, 1993), increase academic pro-ductivity (Shimabukuro et al., 1999), increase homework assignment completion (Trammel et al., 1994), and most commonly to increase time on task (Reid, 1996; Webber, Scheuermann, McCall, & Coleman, 1993).

Benefits of self-monitoring include that it is nonintrusive in the classroom, is easy to implement, and can be added to existing token economy point systems (e.g., Kern et al., 1994). Further, student progress monitoring facilitates communi-cation between the teacher and the student. Not only does the actual marking of progress provide a great opportunity to reinforce progress that is made, but it also provides a time to talk about the next benchmark goal. The students can talk about how they were able to reach their goals and what they think will help them con-tinue to make progress. Conversely, if progress was not made, the teacher and stu-dent can talk about why that might be and generate ideas between them about how progress could be made in the next time period. It is important that both teacher and student listen to each others' thoughts and ideas. This is a wonderful opportunity to model effective two-way communication for the student. In fact, a recent book chapter (Shapiro, Durnan, Post, & Levinson, 2002) about self-monitoring concludes from reviewing the extensive literature that it is an "extremely valuable component for impacting almost all types of behavior difficulties shown by stu-dents" and that self-monitoring "can and should be used in combination with almost all behavioral interventions" (p. 449).

As mentioned earlier in the chapter, Figure 3.3 is an example of a student graph showing progress toward a math intervention goal. Although graphing is the

**Student: Self-Monitoring of Events**

Name:_____   Week of:_____

Make a check mark next to an activity or event every time it happens in the next week. If you wish, you may write down in the blanks other things that you like when they happen.

1.   Playing volleyball in P.E.                                          _____

2.   Getting to chose a free time activity that I like to do.   _____

3.   Eating lunch with a friend.                                       _____

4.   Time during class to write a note to someone special.   _____

5.   Getting extra class points for free time at recess.       _____

6.   _____   _____

7.   _____   _____

8.   _____   _____

At the end of the week, look at your list and decide what was the best thing that happened.
Write what you think here:

_____

_____

_____

_____

Is there anything different you would want to happen next week?  If so, what is it?

_____

**FORM 3.4**   *Example of Self-Monitoring Pleasant Events for 5th–6th Grade Students with Depression*

Name:_____    _____    Date:

**Math Worksheet Check List**

Check off each item after you have done it and then turn in the checklist with your worksheet.

1.    My name is on the paper in the top right-hand corner.    ☐

2.    All the problems I completed show the work I used
to find the answer.    ☐

3.    My answers are circled.    ☐

4.    The numbers are written clearly and neatly.    ☐

5.    I went back over my work to check if everything is correct.    ☐

REMEMBER:  When you finish the checklist, put the list with your worksheet
and turn it in all together!  Good work!

**FORM 3.5**    *Self-Monitor for Neat and Complete Work Assignments*

*Source:* Adapted from E. S. Shapiro, S. L. Durnan, E. E. Post, & T. S. Levinson (2002). "Self-monitoring Procedures for Children and Adolescents." In M. R. Shinn, H. M. Walker, and G. Stoner (Eds.), *Interventions for Academic and Behavior Problems II: Preventive and Remedial Approaches.* Bethesda, MD: National Association of School Psychologists.

preferred way to demonstrate and evaluate change relative to intervention benchmark goals, there are other ways for students to keep a visual representation of progress when graphing is not possible. Some methods include (a) placing stars on a piece of paper when they reach a benchmark goal, (b) placing marbles in a jar that has been marked with lines to represent benchmark goals, so as marbles accumulate in the jar and a line is reached, the students know they met a goal, (c) accumulating paper coupons for each benchmark that later will be cashed in to receive a certificate and prize for reaching the final goal, and (d) coloring in squares on graph paper that have been marked with benchmark goals and the final goal. We recommend including the students, when appropriate, on identifying ways to monitor their progress. This increases the likelihood that whatever the method for monitoring progress toward the final goal, the student has a vested interest in learning the new skill.

### Parent

Parents often want to participate in an intervention. They can do so by monitoring the progress of their child using the same techniques discussed previously. The

**Student Self-Monitoring My Own Behavior**

Name: _____     Date: _____     Period # _____

When I hear the beep, I will make an "X" next to an item if I have done it since the last beep.

1.     Sitting in my desk seat.                                    _____

2.     Listening and paying attention to the teacher.     _____

3.     Working quietly on my assignment.                    _____

4.     Raising my hand for help.                                _____

5.     Participating in the class discussion.                 _____

**STOP** 5 minutes before the end of class, when the teacher says "you have 5 minutes to assess".

Count the check marks next to each item and place the number in the item box below.

| #1 ___ | #2 ___ | #3 ___ | #4 ___ | #5 ___ |

Turn the sheet into the teacher today as you leave the class by placing it in the box at the door. The form will be returned to you when you come to class tomorrow.
_____

Teacher Feedback:_____

_____

If after reading the teacher's feedback you want to talk about it, check the box below and give it back to your teacher immediately. The teacher will meet with you in the last 5 minutes of class.

Yes, I would like to meet with you to talk about this!     [     ]

**FORM 3.6**   *Self-Monitoring Behavior During a Class Period in Middle School*

*Source:* Adapted from E. S. Shapiro, S. L. Durnan, E. E. Post, & T. S. Levinson (2002). "Self-monitoring Procedures for Children and Adolescents." In M. R. Shinn, H. M. Walker, and G. Stoner (Eds.), *Interventions for Academic and Behavior Problems II: Preventive and Remedial Approaches.* Bethesda, MD: National Association of School Psychologists.

main point is that parents should be asked, encouraged, and shown how to monitor progress, whether by graph or data chart. Parent progress-monitoring is essential if components of the intervention are implemented in the home, as for homework completion.

## Self-Monitoring Grid

Name: _____    Date: _____

Class: _____    Period: _____    Teacher: _____

<u>55 minute class period:  Self Monitor and Record every 5 minutes for:</u>

On or Off Task (Place an X in the appropriate box)
Feeling inside:  Calm, agitated, angry (Place an X in only one box)

| 5 Minute Time Intervals | On Task | Off Task | Calm | Agitated | Angry |
|---|---|---|---|---|---|
| 5 | | | | | |
| 10 | | | | | |
| 15 | | | | | |
| 20 | | | | | |
| 25 | | | | | |
| 30 | | | | | |
| 35 | | | | | |
| 40 | | | | | |
| 45 | | | | | |
| 50 | | | | | |
| 55 | | | | | |

**FORM 3.7**   *Student Self-Monitoring Grid*

Regardless of the type of intervention, it is essential to the success of an intervention that school professionals and parents have a two-way communication during intervention to report progress toward goals (Webster-Stratton & Reid, 2002). Form 3.8, a Middle and High School Daily Progress Report, is an example of a school-home progress note (Kelley, 1990) reporting academic behavior. Each teacher in the student's scheduled day reports how the child is progressing toward displaying good academic behavior (prepared to learn, on time to class, focused). The parent is asked to respond with comments and a signature so that a counselor who receives the note back from the student can coordinate between a particular teacher and the parent if there are areas of concern. The school-home note can also be graphed over time so that there is a chart of overall progress toward goals.

Parental involvement in their child's education and school has been empirically demonstrated to support academic and social competence (Brody & Stoneman, 1992; Okagaki & Sternberg, 1993; Schaefer & Edgerton, 1985). Moreover, studies have found that direct teaching of parents on how to monitor homework, teaching the school's expectations for their children, and making parents feel respected and welcome at the school has made a difference for parents with low socioeconomic status (Alexander & Entwisle, 1996; Lareau, 1987). In the broader view, parental monitoring of children serves as a protective factor against potential risk in the environment (Patterson, DeBaryshe, & Ramsey, 1989; Reid & Patterson, 1991). The quality of parenting skills, including the ability and interest in monitoring children, mediate environmental risk factors. Lack of parental monitoring can increase risk factors within the family itself (e.g., abuse and neglect). One study (Sameroff, Bartko, Baldwin, Baldwin, & Seifer, 1998) found that only three out of twenty risk factors predicted five adolescent academic and social/behavioral outcomes. The three risk factors were all associated with parental monitoring. Clearly, parental participation in intervention is critical for a student's short- and long-term success.

## Summary

The intent of this chapter was to (a) define the meaning of monitoring change in primary, secondary, and tertiary prevention efforts, (b) establish the importance of monitoring student progress, (c) introduce and describe various strategies for monitoring change, and (d) offer suggestions as to who can monitor student progress. In the chapters to follow, we will introduce three key tools essential to the intervention process. Specifically, we will discuss social validity, treatment integrity, and generalization and maintenance as components of a core model designed to increase treatment effectiveness, foster consumer acceptability, and provide a measure of accountability.

## References

Alberto, P. A., & Troutman, A. C. (1999). *Applied behavior analysis for teachers* (5th ed.). Englewood Cliffs, NY: Merrill/Prentice Hall.

Alexander, K. L., & Entwisle, D. R. (1996). Schools and children at risk. In A. Booth & J. Dunn (Eds.), *Family-school links: How do they effect educational outcomes?* (pp. 67–88). Mahwah, NJ: Erlbaum.

Baer, D. (1977). Perhaps it would be better not to know everything. *Journal of Applied Behavior Analysis, 10,* 167–122.

Bijou, S. W., Peterson, R., F., & Ault, M. H. (1968). A method to integrate descriptive and experimental field studies at the level of data and empirical concepts. *Journal of Applied Behavior Analysis, 1,* 175–191.

Brody, G. H., & Stoneman, Z. (1992). Child competence and developmental goals among rural black families: Investigating the links. In I. E. Siegel, A. V. McGillicuddy-DeLisi, & J. J. Goodnow (Eds.), *Parental belief systems: The psychological consequences for children,* pp. 415–431. Hillsdale, NJ: Erlbaum.

Name: _____ Grade: _____ Date: _____

| Period 1 | YES | NO | N/A | Teacher Signature _____ |
|---|---|---|---|---|
| _____ | ☐ | ☐ | ☐ | Arrived on Time to Class |
| *Class* | ☐ | ☐ | ☐ | Finished His/Her Work |
| | ☐ | ☐ | ☐ | Good Student Behavior |
| | ☐ | ☐ | ☐ | Turned in Homework |
| | ☐ | ☐ | ☐ | Homework Due Tomorrow |
| | ☐ | ☐ | ☐ | Passing Class |

Comments:_____

_____

| Period 2 | YES | NO | N/A | Teacher Signature: _____ |
|---|---|---|---|---|
| _____ | ☐ | ☐ | ☐ | Arrived on Time to Class |
| *Class* | ☐ | ☐ | ☐ | Finished His/Her Work |
| | ☐ | ☐ | ☐ | Good Student Behavior |
| | ☐ | ☐ | ☐ | Turned in Homework |
| | ☐ | ☐ | ☐ | Homework Due Tomorrow |
| | ☐ | ☐ | ☐ | Passing Class |

Comments:_____

_____

| Period 3 | YES | NO | N/A | Teacher Signature: _____ |
|---|---|---|---|---|
| _____ | ☐ | ☐ | ☐ | Arrived on Time to Class |
| *Class* | ☐ | ☐ | ☐ | Finished His/Her Work |
| | ☐ | ☐ | ☐ | Good Student Behavior |
| | ☐ | ☐ | ☐ | Turned in Homework |
| | ☐ | ☐ | ☐ | Homework Due Tomorrow |
| | ☐ | ☐ | ☐ | Passing Class |

Comments:_____

_____

| Period 4 | YES | NO | N/A | Teacher Signature: _____ |
|---|---|---|---|---|
| _____ | ☐ | ☐ | ☐ | Arrived on Time to Class |
| *Class* | ☐ | ☐ | ☐ | Finished His/Her Work |
| | ☐ | ☐ | ☐ | Good Student Behavior |
| | ☐ | ☐ | ☐ | Turned in Homework |
| | ☐ | ☐ | ☐ | Homework Due Tomorrow |
| | ☐ | ☐ | ☐ | Passing Class |

Comments:_____

_____

**FORM 3.8** *School-Home Progress Note*

**Period 5**                    YES    NO    N/A    Teacher Signature: _____

_____      ☐      ☐      ☐      Arrived on Time to Class

*Class*                         ☐      ☐      ☐      Finished His/Her Work

                                ☐      ☐      ☐      Good Student Behavior

                                ☐      ☐      ☐      Turned in Homework

                                ☐      ☐      ☐      Homework Due Tomorrow

                                ☐      ☐      ☐      Passing Class

Comments:_____

_____


**Period 6**                    YES    NO    N/A    Teacher Signature: _____

_____      ☐      ☐      ☐      Arrived on Time to Class

*Class*                         ☐      ☐      ☐      Finished His/Her Work

                                ☐      ☐      ☐      Good Student Behavior

                                ☐      ☐      ☐      Turned in Homework

                                ☐      ☐      ☐      Homework Due Tomorrow

                                ☐      ☐      ☐      Passing Class

Comments:_____

_____


**Period ____**                 YES    NO    N/A    Teacher Signature: _____

_____      ☐      ☐      ☐      Arrived on Time to Class

*Class*                         ☐      ☐      ☐      Finished His/Her Work

                                ☐      ☐      ☐      Good Student Behavior

                                ☐      ☐      ☐      Turned in Homework

                                ☐      ☐      ☐      Homework Due Tomorrow

                                ☐      ☐      ☐      Passing Class

Comments:_____

_____


**Parent Comments:** _____

_____

_____

_____


**Parent Signature:** _____    Date: _____

**FORM 3.8**  *Continued*

Busk, P. L., & Serlin, R. C. (1992). Meta-analysis for single-case research. In T. Kratochwill & J. Levin (Eds.), *Single case research design and analysis*, Hillsdale, NJ: Erlbaum.

Chafouleas, S., & Martens, B. K. (2002). Accuracy-based phonological awareness tasks: Are they reliable, efficient and sensitive to growth? *School Psychology Quarterly, 17*, 128–147.

Cole, C. L., & Bambura, L. M. (2000). Self-monitoring: Theory and practice. In E. S. Shapiro & T. R. Kratochwill (Eds.), *Behavaioral assessment in schools* (2nd ed.) (pp. 202–232). New York: Guilford Press.

DiGangi, S. M., Maag, J. W., & Rutherford, R. B. (1991). Self-graphing of on-task behavior: Enhancing the reactive effects of self-monitoring on on-task behavior and academic performance. *Learning Disabilities Quarterly, 4*, 221–230.

Dunlap, L. K., & Dunlap, G. (1989). A self-monitoring package for teaching subtraction with regrouping to students with learning disabilities. *Journal of Applied Behavior Analysis, 22*, 309–314.

Fuchs, L. S., & Fuchs, D. (1986). Effects of systematic formative evaluation: A meta-analysis. *Exceptional Children, 53*, 199–208.

Gresham, F. M. (1998). Designs for evaluating behavior change: Conceptual principles of single case methodology. In T. S. Watson and F. M. Gresham (Eds.), *Handbook of child behavior therapy*, pp. 23–40. New York: Plenum Press.

Gresham, F. M. (1991). Conceptualizing behavior disorders in terms of resistance to intervention. *School Psychology Review, 20*, 1, 23–36.

Gresham, F. M. (2002). Responsiveness to intervention: An alternative approach to learning disabilities. In R. Bradley, L. Danielson, & D. Hallahan (Eds.), *Identification of learning disabilities: Research to practice*. Mahwah, NJ: Erlbaum.

Gresham, F. M., & Elliott, S. N. (1990). *Social Skills Rating System (SSRS)*. Circle Pines, MN: American Guidance Service.

Gumpel, T. P., & Golan, H. (2000). Teaching game-playing social skills using a self-monitoring treatment package. *Psychology in the Schools, 37*, 253–261.

Hughes, C. A., Korinek, L., & Gorman, J. (1991). Self-management for students with mental retardation in public school settings: A research review. *Education and Training in Mental Retardation, 26*, 271–291.

Hughes, C. A., Ruhl, K. L., & Misra, A. (1989). Self-management with behaviorally disordered students in school settings: A promise unfulfilled? *Behavioral Disorders, 14*, 250–262.

Johnston, J. M., & Pennypacker, H. S. (1993). *Strategies and tactics of behavioral research* (2nd ed.). Hillsdale, NJ: Erlbaum.

Kelley, M. (1990). School-home notes: Promoting children's classroom success. New York: Guilford Press.

Kern, L., Dunlap, G., Childs, K. E., & Clarke, S. (1994). Use of a classwide self-management program to improve the behavior of students with emotional and behavioral disorders. *Education and Treatment of Children, 17*, 445–458.

King, N. J., Ollendick, T. H., & Murphy, G. C. (1997). Assessment of childhood phobias. *Clinical Psychology Review, 17*, 667–687.

Koegel, R. L., & Koegel, L. K. (1990). Extended reductions in stereotypic behavior of students with autism through a self-management treatment package. *Journal of Applied Behavior Analysis, 23*, 119–127.

Lane, K. L. (1999). Young students at-risk for antisocial behavior: The utility of academic and social skills interventions. *Journal of Emotional and Behavioral Disorders, 7*, 211–223.

Lareau, A. (1987). Social class differences in family-school relationships: The importance of cultural capital. *Sociology of Education, 60*, 73–85.

Mace, F. C. (1994). The significance and future research of functional analysis methodologies. *Journal of Applied Behavior Analysis, 27*, 385–392.

Martella, R. C., Leonard, I. J., Marchand-Martella, N. E., & Agran, M. (1993). Self-monitoring negative statements. *Journal of Behavioral Education, 3*, 77–86.

Moore, R. J., Cartledge, G., & Heckman, K. (1995). The effects of social skill instruction and self-monitoring on game-related behaviors of adolescents with emotional or behavioral disorders. *Behavioral Disorders, 20*, 253–266.

Okagaki, L., & Sternberg, R. J. (1993). Parental beliefs and children's school performance. *Child Development, 64*, 36–56.

Ollendick, T. H. (1995). Cognitive behavioral treatment of panic disorder with agoraphobia in adolescents: A multiple baseline design analysis. *Behavior Therapy, 26*, 517–531.

Patterson, G., DeBarshye, B. D., & Ramsey, E. (1989). A developmental perspective on antisocial behavior. *American Psychologist, 44*, 329–335.

Reid, J., & Patterson, G. R. (1991). Early prevention and intervention with conduct problems: A social interaction model for the integration of research and practice. In G. Stoner, M. Shinn, & H. M. Walker (Eds.), *Interventions for achievement and behavioral problems*. Silver Spring, MD: National Association of School Psychologists.

Reid, J. B. (1996). Research in self-monitoring with students with learning disabilities: The present, the prospects, the pitfalls. *Journal of Learning Disabilities, 29*, 317–331.

Reynolds, W. M., & Stark, K. D. (1987). School-based intervention strategies for the treatment of depression in children and adolescents. *School-Based Affective and Social Interventions, 3–4*, 69–88.

Sameroff, A. J., Bartko, W. T., Baldwin, A., Baldwin, C., & Seifer, R. (1998). Family and social influences on the development of child competence. In M. Lewis, C. Feiring (Eds.), *Families, risk, and competence*. Mahwah, NJ: Erlbaum.

Schaefer, E. S., & Edgerton, M. (1985). Parent and child correlates of parental modernity. In I. E. Sigel (Ed.), *Parental belief systems: The psychological consequences for children* (pp. 287–318). Hillsdale, NJ: Erlbaum.

Shapiro, E. S., & Cole, C. L. (1994). *Behavior change in the classroom: Self-management interventions*. New York: Guilford Press.

Shapiro, E. S., Durnan, S. L., Post, E. E., & Levinson, T. S. (2002). Self-monitoring procedures for children and adolescents. In M. R. Shinn, H. M. Walker, & G. Stoner (Eds.), *Interventions for Academic and Behavior Problems II: Preventive and Remedial Approaches* (pp. 433–454). Bethesda, MD: National Association of School Psychologists.

Shimabukuro, S. M., Prater, M. A., Jenkins, A., & Edelen-Smith, P. (1999). The effects of self-monitoring of academic performance on students with learning disabilities and ADD/ADHD. *Education and Treatment of Children, 22*, 397–414.

Shinn, M. R. (1989). *Curriculum-based assessment: Assessing special children*. New York: Guilford Press.

Sulzer-Azaroff, B., & Mayer, G. R. (1991). *Behavior analysis for lasting change*. Fort Worth, TX: Harcourt Brace College Publishers.

Trammel, D. L., Schloss, P. J., & Alper, S. (1994). Using self-recording, evaluation, and graphing to increase completion of homework assignments. *Journal of Learning Disabilities, 27*, 75–81.

Walker, H. M., Block-Pedego, A., Todis, B., & Severson, H. (1991). *School archival records search*. Longmont, CO: Sopris West.

Walker, H. M., Colvin, G., & Ramsey, E. (1995). *Antisocial behavior in school: Strategies and best practices*. Albany: Brooks/Cole.

Walker, H. M., & McConnell, S. (1988). *The Walker-McConnell scale of social competence and school adjustment*. Austin, TX: PRO-ED.

Walker, H. M., & Severson, H. (2002). Developmental prevention of at-risk outcomes for vulnerable antisocial children and youth. In K. L. Lane, F. M. Gresham, & T. E. O'Shaughnessy (Eds.), *Interventions for children with or at risk for emotional and behavioral disorders* (pp. 177–194). Boston: Allyn & Bacon.

Webber, J., Scheuermann, B., McCall, C., & Coleman, M. (1993). Research on self-monitoring as a behavior management technique in special education classrooms: A descriptive review. *Remedial and Special Education, 14*, 38–56.

Webster-Stratton, C., & Reid, J. (2002). An integrated approach to prevention and management of aggressive behavior problems in preschool and elementary grade students: Schools and parent collaboration. In K. L. Lane, F. M. Gresham, & T. E. O'Shaughnessy (Eds.), *Interventions for children with or at risk for emotional and behavioral disorders* (pp. 260–278). Boston: Allyn & Bacon.

Witt, J. C., Daly, E. M., & Noell, G. (2000). *Functional assessments: A step-by-step guide to solving academic and behavior problems*. Longmont, CO: Sopris West.

Wood, S. J., Murdock, J. Y., Cronin, M. E., Dawson, N. M., & Kirby, P. C. (1998). Effects of self-monitoring on on-task behaviors of at-risk middle school students. *Journal of Behavioral Education, 8*, 263–279.

# Part II

# *Introducing the Core Components Model*

The purpose of the following chapters is to explain the key tools of our *core components model:* social validity, treatment integrity, and generalization and maintenance.

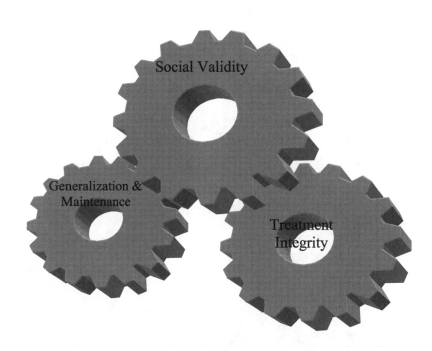

# 4

# Social Validity

## Goals, Procedures, and Outcomes

## What Do We Mean by Social Validity?

When conducting school-based intervention research, social validity refers to the assessment of the *social significance* of intervention goals, the *social acceptability* of intervention procedures to attain the goals, and the evaluation of the *social importance* of the effects resulting from an intervention (Kazdin, 1977; Wolf, 1978; see Box 4.1). Social validity in the context of intervention takes on slightly different meanings at different stages and can be best conceptualized by understanding the separate components at their respective points in the intervention cycle (see Figure 4.1, Items B, D, and H).

### Pre-Intervention: Social Validity Components

*Social significance* is the value placed on the goal of an intervention (Figure 4.1, Item A). Will achieving the goal improve the quality of life of the student participating in the intervention? Does the goal, or the consequences of it, have social value? For

**BOX 4.1 • *Social Validity Defined***

### *Social Validity*
(Wolf, 1978)

Refers to the:

- *social significance* of intervention *goals.*

- *social acceptability* of intervention *procedures.*

- *social importance* of intervention *outcomes.*

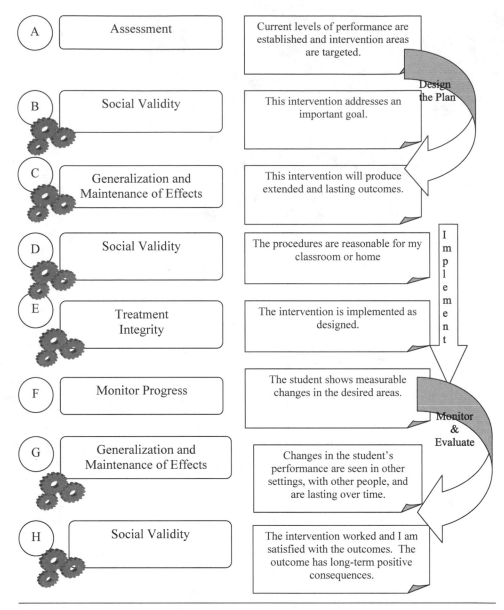

**FIGURE 4.1    *The Intervention Process***

instance, a student may not be grasping foundational math concepts and quickly falls behind his peers in math. The teacher recognizes the negative academic consequences for the student, the parents notice that their child cannot count money at the store, and the child is embarrassed about making mistakes in front of his peers. There are short- and long-term social consequences for this child, and acknowledging negative outcomes motivates an effort to change. Knowing how to do math correctly has social significance because better math grades, the ability to accurately handle money, and positive peer attention improves the student's social status. Once parties acknowledge the negative social significance of the problem behavior, goals with positive social significance can be identified and agreed upon. The important outcome of assessing the social significance of intervention goals is that participating parties (e.g., teachers and parents) agree prior to treatment implementation that the intervention addresses an important goal or keystone behavior that will solve a problem. Implicit to this agreement is that the quality of life, social status, or educational experience of the student will improve as a result of addressing the original concern. In essence, social significance of the intervention goals is established by identifying target behaviors that are meaningful, functional, and adaptive so that the student is left with a more reliable, efficient method of meeting the demands of the environment (e.g., DuPaul & Eckert, 1994; Gresham & Lopez, 1996; Lane, Beebe-Frankenberger, Lambros, & Pierson, 2001; Noell & Gresham, 1993).

*Social acceptability* of the intervention procedures (Figure 4.1, Item D) necessary to reach the intervention goals means that all parties (e.g., teacher, parents, and, in some instances, the student) agree that the intervention steps are necessary, appropriate, supportive of positive values, minimally disruptive to the environment, and worth the effort to attain the goal (Gresham, 1998; Kazdin, 1981; Reimers, Wacker, & Koeppl, 1987). Social acceptability in the consultation literature is known as *treatment acceptability.* An extensive research base identifies variables that consistently influence the acceptability of treatment based on consultant, teacher, treatment, and student factors (Witt & Elliott, 1985). Primary factors related to treatment acceptability include the type and severity of a problem, the time and cost to do the intervention, the amount of training and support available for the intervention, and the impact the procedures will have on the environment. In brief, interventions are likely to be rated as more acceptable if the severity of the problem behavior is high ("I'll do anything! Just help me to work better with this child!"), the amount of time, personal support, necessary materials, and training required to implement the intervention is minimal, and the perceived efficacy of the intervention is high (Gresham & Kendell, 1987).

Consider the previous example of the student who is not grasping math concepts. If treatment procedures depend on the parent spending three hours per night with his child on math drills, steps to get to a socially significant goal will most likely be deemed unacceptable by the parent. The expense of taking attention away from other children in the family and perhaps the parent's own low self-confidence with math concepts make this procedure toward the goal unacceptable. Thus, in spite of the fact that the parent recognizes the problem and goal as socially important, there is much less likelihood that the parent will *want* or be *able* to perform the planned procedure.

It is important to assess social acceptability of intervention procedures prior to implementing a given intervention in order to ensure that all relevant parties (e.g., teachers, parents, and other interventionists) agree that the procedures are reasonable for the classroom, home, or wherever the intervention procedures take place. Gresham and Lopez (1996) suggest that social acceptability is likely to influence treatment integrity (see Chapter 5, Treatment Integrity). Namely, if an intervention is viewed as socially acceptable, there is higher probability that it will be implemented with treatment integrity than if the intervention procedures were initially viewed to be unacceptable. In turn, higher rates of treatment integrity for carefully constructed interventions (whether primary, secondary, or tertiary in nature) are likely to yield more effective outcomes than interventions that are implemented with lower rates of fidelity (Gresham & Lopez, 1996; Lane et al., 2001).

*Social importance of the effects* refers to assessing the extent to which the treatment agents and participants view the intervention as having the potential to produce socially important outcomes. Essentially, this component involves obtaining information on the degree to which the intervention is likely to produce proximal changes directly related to participation in the intervention (e.g., improved decoding skills), intermediate or collateral effects on related behaviors (e.g., increased time spent reading), and distal outcomes (e.g., acquiring additional knowledge and an increased appreciation for literature; Fawcett, 1991).

Proximal effects are the direct outcomes of intervention; the evaluation determines whether the student(s) reached the performance goal that was targeted by the intervention. Evaluation of treatment effects is the result of monitoring intervention with data produced prior, during, and after intervention (see Chapter 3, Monitoring Changes). Intermediate/collateral and distal effects may be more difficult to measure.

A collateral effect of intervention means that there was a change in levels of an associated skill or behavior as a result of the proximal effects of intervention (see Chapter 6, Generalization and Maintenance). These may or may not be readily apparent by the end of intervention; however, they may be more likely to be recognized when post-intervention social validity assessment takes place. For a primary intervention whose target was schoolwide playground safety as demonstrated by reduced accidents, an intermediate effect might be higher rates of cooperation among students as measured by fewer referrals for not only playground fights, but also school bus area fights. As students learned new safety rules on the playground, their vigilance about safety also made them more cooperative with each other, and therefore more tolerant and less apt to fight in other settings.

Collateral effects can also be observed in secondary and tertiary interventions. For example, the proximal effect for reading fluency acquisition was met as demonstrated by students reaching the performance goal. As their reading performance increased, there was a collateral effect of decreasing rates of off-task behavior during reading (i.e., less side-talk and throwing of objects). These behaviors were reduced as a direct result of the intervention but were not the primary target of the secondary or tertiary intervention.

Finally, the distal effect of treatment refers to the long-term outcome of the change produced by attainment of the intervention goal. For instance, a tertiary intervention in which a student with antisocial behaviors learns anger management techniques to reduce conflict with peers will provide the opportunity for future prosocial friendships which may, in turn, provide peer support that prevents juvenile delinquency. Distal effects are not easily measured by observation or permanent products. Surveys about the *social importance* of effects are a way of evaluating the distal effects.

By obtaining this information, it is possible to clarify anticipated outcomes so that all parties have parallel expectations of the intervention outcomes. Further, it provides them with an opportunity to determine if the potential benefits of the intervention outweigh the costs associated with participation (e.g., time, money, and energy; Noell & Gresham, 1993). In addition to assessing social validity components at the onset of the intervention process, it is also important to assess the degree to which the intervention goals, procedures, and outcomes met expectations. This can be determined by again assessing social validity at the conclusion of the intervention.

### Post-Intervention: Social Validity Components

*Social significance* of the intervention goals is assessed at the conclusion of the intervention to establish if the goals were indeed "keystone." Moreover, did the goals produce meaningful, lasting behavior changes that led to other changes (response generalization, see Chapter 6, Generalization and Maintenance)?

For example, consider Willie who frequently roams around the classroom during literacy groups. At first glance, many people would focus on increasing in-seat behavior. However, by examining data generated to monitor the primary intervention, it is apparent that Willie is performing in the bottom quartile in reading skills. This information coupled with data obtained from a teacher-completed behavior rating scale (e.g., Social Skills Rating System; Gresham & Elliott, 1990), indicates that Willie has a skill deficit in decoding and reading comprehension skills. As such, a secondary intervention targeting both of these reading skills is designed and implemented with two other struggling readers in the class. At the end of the intervention, the parents and teacher participate in a semi-structured interview for social validation (Gresham & Lopez, 1996). According to the teacher, Willie is spending more time academically engaged in reading groups and less time wandering around the classroom. The parents report that Willie is also spending more time reading comic books at home and frequently reads to his younger sister. Thus, the information generated from the social validity interviews suggests that the intervention did target a socially significant, keystone behavior.

*Social acceptability* of intervention procedures is also assessed again after the intervention has been terminated, ideally because goals have been met to the satisfaction of all parties. It is important to confirm or disconfirm pre-intervention opinions about the treatment plan and goals. Were treatment steps to learn the new skill/behavior necessary, appropriate, supportive of positive values, and minimally disruptive to the environment? Was the treatment worth the effort to attain the goal?

Consider the example of the student who had deficient math skills. An intervention plan that included a component in which the student earned play money as a reinforcement of skill acquisition during treatment was designed and implemented in a general education classroom. The component was included in the treatment plan to address the parents' concerns about the student's inability to count money. During intervention, the student could purchase school supplies or activities by using the play money and was required to count out the appropriate amount to make purchases. Although everyone agreed prior to treatment that it was not an intrusive procedure and it targeted one of the deficit skills of the student, when the teacher was asked about treatment procedures at the end of the intervention, the component was deemed too intrusive in the classroom. Although the play money acted as an appropriate reinforcer, the student became anxious about how much money was earned and when it could be used to make purchases. The student talked about the play money almost obsessively to other students to the point where it disrupted other activities. In retrospect, the teacher would recommend a different reinforcement technique and would address the parents' concern in another manner. Thus, treatment acceptability influences the future use of the treatment for other students and situations. Asking all parties associated with the intervention (e.g., student, teacher, aide, parents) about treatment acceptability formalizes opinions by offering a structured platform for expression. Post-intervention assessment of treatment acceptability provides feedback about the specific steps toward a goal. Thus, important outcomes of social/treatment acceptability assessment during the post-intervention phase include: (a) providing a platform for participants to express their opinions about the treatment, (b) collecting feedback about specific treatment procedures and effectiveness that informs future intervention, and (c) assessing the probability that those same treatment procedures will be used again for other students in similar or other settings.

*Social importance* of the effects of an intervention establishes the practical value and social consequence of behavior change and skill acquisition after the intervention ends. Does the new behavior and/or skill improve the status of the student and heighten the probability of future success? Specifically, does the change improve the student's adaptive response to demands in the environment (Gresham & Lopez, 1996; Noell & Gresham, 1993)? The notion of *habilitative validity* (Hawkins, 1991) is an integral part of *social importance*. An intervention outcome with *habilitative validity* serves the student exponentially over time and has a long-term positive life consequence. Take, for example, the student with math problems. Perhaps initially the teacher thought the problem with math was a result of the student being off task during math instruction. Thus, the teacher set a goal of teaching the student to be quiet and stay seated. The goal has socially significant intent. Yet, if the off-task behavior was actually produced by the student to avoid math because of deficient math skills (as was the case with Willie and his out-of-seat behavior), the goal of on-task behavior does not have true habilitative value for anyone, especially for the student. A *socially significant* goal would produce on-task behavior as a side effect to the student's improved math skills. When the student is actively engaged in math instruction, inappropriate off-task behavior stops. The new goal of increasing academic engagement by improving the student's math skills has value for both the student and the teacher. Moreover, the new math skills increase the likelihood that the student will have a positive interest in learning, be reinforced naturally by better grades, receive more teacher and parent praise, and increase social status with peers. Thus, the *social importance* of the attained goal is significant and has true habilitative value. The importance of assessing social importance after the intervention is over includes (a) achieving consensus among parties regarding intervention outcomes, (b) evaluating the extent to which the goals are attained, and (c) evaluating consumer satisfaction with the immediate and potential long-term positive consequences associated with intervention outcomes.

## Why Is It Important to Assess Social Validity?

We contend that the failure of intervention to successfully teach and maintain new skills or behavior may be associated, in part, with failure to assess social validity of intervention goals, the acceptability of steps required to reach the goals, and the social value of outcomes at both the onset and conclusion of interventions (Kazdin, 1977; Lane et al., 2001; Wolf, 1978). Successful intervention is fueled by motivation to reach a skill/behavior goal that is perceived as attainable and valuable (Box 4.2 is an example of how assessing social validity prior to and after an intervention influences the entire intervention process).

It is important to assess social validity prior to and after intervention for several reasons: (a) to identify and agree on the target area for the intervention and the discrepancy between the current and desired level of performance (Bergan & Kratochwill, 1990), (b) to identify meaningful yet reasonable focus areas for primary prevention efforts, (c) to agree on appropriate, acceptable, and attainable goals and focus areas when conducting secondary and tertiary prevention, (d) to facilitate discussion among all persons germane to the student's environment while identifying environmental/cultural supports that will provide natural contingencies and reinforcement for the new skill/behavior, (e) to ensure a greater likelihood of commitment to implement and continue the treatment until the goal is attained,

**BOX 4.2** • *Practical Applications of Social Validity*

Mike is a student with moderate mental retardation enrolled as a sophomore in a special day class at the local high school. Recently he has been uncharacteristically disengaged from academic activity in the classroom, isolating himself from his friends. At home, where he normally enjoys doing chores around the house, he has started throwing tantrums when reminded to do them. His mother, Mrs. Gutierrez, noticed the changes in him first and met with his teacher, Mr. Marks, who then noted the changes at school. Mr. Marks gave a social validity survey to Mrs. Gutierrez about the problem. They decided that for the moment, the best plan of action would be to keep an eye on Mike with the expectation that his mood was only a temporary phase. Mr. Marks was starting a class-wide social skills training for teens and they decided to see if this would benefit Mike. Not long afterward, Mike had an explosive episode at school where he lashed out against his two best friends. Not only was the behavior potentially dangerous for other students, but also Mike had become so withdrawn that he had no positive interactions with peers and refused to do any schoolwork.

Mrs. Gutierrez, Mr. Marks, and the school psychologist met with Mike, who said only that everyone was against him, laughing at him, making him sad and angry. Mike's behavior was unprovoked by people in his environment. In retrospect, they realized Mike became more anxious and then depressed, when a few months ago at his Individual Educational Plan (IEP) team meeting a goal toward adult independence was set for transitioning him later in the year to vocational skills training. Everyone agreed that it is especially important for Mike to begin the vocational training that would prepare him for post-secondary school employment. They decided that Mike was fearful of being independent and was not confident that he could take care of himself. The school psychologist worked with Mrs. Gutierrez and Mr. Marks to design an intervention plan, assessing the acceptability of intense tertiary intervention procedures that would require a lot of time and effort both in school and at home. Intervention procedures required Mr. Marks and Mrs. Gutierrez to place lower demands and higher rates of praise on Mike over the next month, gradually increasing academic and home chore demands once Mike responded to behavior-shaping techniques designed to build his self-efficacy. Mrs. Gutierrez responded to the treatment acceptability survey with a "strongly disagree" rating for the item that stated "the proposed intervention is within my skill level to help." The school psychologist met with her and found that Mrs. Gutierrez was not confident about being able to use the planned response to Mike if he had a temper tantrum. The school psychologist modeled and role-played the response with Mrs. Gutierrez and they worked out ways that Mrs. Gutierrez could respond that felt more comfortable to her, but that would encourage the appropriate behavior from Mike. Another component of the intervention was to teach Mike a new skill so that he would feel successful. Mr. Marks decided to train Mike to be a class tutor in an elementary grade special day class, where he could assist younger students with disabilities with tasks that he knew well. Mrs. Gutierrez had told the school psychologist that Mike likes to help others. The intervention plan was implemented, Mike was trained, worked as the tutor in the elementary class, and he was reinforced for positive behavior both at school and at home. Six weeks later, the school psychologist met again with Mrs. Gutierrez and Mr. Marks who agreed that Mike had returned to being cheerfully engaged in social and academic activities. Postintervention social validity surveys completed by Mr. Marks, Mrs. Gutierrez, and Mike (who completed the elementary-grade-level survey) indicated that the intervention was well received and that all would do it again. Mr. Marks added the comment that he decided to train all his students to work as cross-age tutors to help build their confidence and allow them to use their skills.

and (f) to evaluate intervention outcomes and the likelihood of maintenance and use of the newly acquired skills.

Perhaps the most compelling reason for assessing social validity at each level of prevention is that lack of requisite skills for success are associated with poor short- and long-term life consequences. If school-based interventions target academic or behavioral areas that lack social validity, consumer satisfaction is likely to be low and, consequently, it is likely that adherence to treatment procedures will also be low, thereby decreasing the probability of successful intervention outcomes (Gresham & Lopez, 1996). If students are not able to participate in effective interventions or if they are subject to participation in ineffective interventions, it is likely that their academic, social, and behavioral performances will not increase at the intended rate. This is problematic given that poor academic and social performance in school is associated with negative academic outcomes as well as strained relationships with teachers and peers (Walker, Irvin, Noell, & Singer, 1992).

When students are not successful in their relationships with teachers and peers, a host of negative consequences often ensue, including academic underachievement, feelings of isolation and rejection, and antisocial behavior patterns (Walker, Colvin, & Ramsey, 1995). More specifically, when behavioral deficits and excesses become severe in the presence of social and emotional problems, outcomes can include grade retention, early school drop-out, referral to mental health agencies, contact with the juvenile justice system, substance abuse, and suspensions/expulsions from school (Elliott, Hamburg, & Williams, 1998; Hinshaw, 1992; Loeber & Farrington, 1998; Parker & Asher, 1987). Not only is impaired social adjustment associated with negative short- and long-term outcomes, but, similarly, impaired academic achievement has been empirically correlated with a number of adolescent outcomes such as teen pregnancy, alcohol and drug use and abuse, and school drop-out (Teeter, 1998). Researchers continue to study the link between academic underachievement and antisocial behavior, seeking to determine whether poor school achievement predisposes children to behavior problems, whether antisocial behavior interferes with academic achievement, or both (Coie & Krehbiel, 1984; Falk & Wehby, 2001; Hinshaw, 1992; Lane, 1999; Lane, O'Shaughnessy, Lambros, Gresham, & Beebe-Frankenberger, 2001). Clearly, antisocial behavior patterns have negative social value for a student. Thus, identifying and intervening on these behaviors is critical for future success. Constructing socially valid, effective interventions is paramount to producing academic and social gains for these youngsters.

In an effort to increase the probability of designing interventions that are likely to address goals germane to all involved parents, that consist of procedures likely to be used by the treatment agents, and that thereby lead to important social outcomes, it is important to assess social validity of the relevant parties at the onset and at the conclusion of the intervention. The discussion builds a consensus toward setting a unified target area in the case of primary prevention with reliable, feasible, sensitive outcome measures. When conducting secondary and tertiary interventions, assessing social validity essentially ensures that everyone agrees on the acquisition and performance deficits to be addressed and the positive replacement skill/behaviors to be acquired. Assessment of goal importance relative to goal setting and achievement of goals is critical to all levels of intervention.

Goal importance refers to how far the student will go to achieve a certain goal (Sideridis, 2002). The assessment captures individual differences in beliefs about if, how, and why to attain intervention goals by intervention procedures. It is important to understand that there are individual differences in goal setting and that students who are historically low achievers in an area tend to avoid or be conservative in setting goals for future achievement (Hollenbeck & Williams, 1987). Sideridis (2002) suggests that for low-achieving students, discussing the long-term importance of goals and benefits of goal attainment with the student in advance of a treatment may increase their willingness to work toward a goal.

When parties invest in designing intervention goals and procedures, there is a greater likelihood for strong commitment to implement and continue the treatment until the goal is attained. The perceived social value and acceptance of a treatment influences the probability that it will be implemented as planned and, in turn, the outcome can be demonstrated as a direct result of the planned treatment (Baer, Wolf, & Risley, 1968, 1987; Gresham & Lopez, 1996). As previously mentioned, if an intervention is acceptable, the probability of using it is likely to be high as opposed to an intervention judged to be unacceptable (Witt & Elliott, 1985). Reaching a consensus among members of an intervention team that the goal, procedures, and eventual outcomes are socially valid paves the foundation for success. In brief, social acceptability is one key to designing, implementing, and evaluating school-based interventions.

Knowledge that is essential to the generalization and maintenance of positive intervention outcomes is also derived from social validity measures. Pivotal to the intervention and its long-term success is the notion of natural contingencies and reinforcers in the environment (see Chapter 6). Once the artificial reinforcers that are often used in intervention to reshape behavior are removed, the environment must support and maintain the behavior change by natural means. Social validity assesses the proposed outcome and the degree to which it is valued by parties to the intervention. When the outcome is of value to people in the environment, then contingencies for continued appropriate skill performance and the natural reinforcement that makes it rewarding to continue performance of the skill is likely already in the student's environment.

For example, the student who had poor math skills will have positive support available in his environment for improving his math skills because he will earn higher grades, use money effectively, and gain access to desired activities and objects in the community. Natural contingencies and reinforcement provide positive behavioral/skill support and perpetuate the intervention outcome. In other words, the new positive behavior becomes a habit quickly and with very little effort on the student's part. The student's environment provides the encouragement to learn or master the skill/behavior as well as the positive reactions to prompt the student to continue doing more of the same in as many situations as possible!

Finally, assessment of the context in which a student lives and learns is also essential to successful intervention design. Teaching, parenting, student learning styles, and environmental demands vary, largely based on the social and cultural values of the individuals involved. Cultural values play a critical role in the success of an intervention. Consider, by way of illustration, a first-generation Asian-American student who is referred by his teacher for evaluation because of excessive shyness that has a significant impact on academic performance. The student does not seek help when something is not understood. The teacher is an outgoing person who encourages students to actively engage in class discussions and ask questions. Part of successful engagement in her class is making eye contact when speaking to each other. The interventionist observes the student in class and notices that when the teacher attempts to make eye contact with him, the student acts repelled, looking down or away from the teacher, which makes the teacher try even harder to make eye contact.

An intervention is designed to teach the student how to ask and receive help from his teacher. Part of the task analysis is a step requiring the student to engage with the teacher by making and holding direct eye contact while speaking. Two different cultural norms regarding personal engagement are clashing here. The problem is that the student's home environment would not support eye-contact behavior with an authority figure (teacher) because of cultural taboos about the behavior. He would not see eye-contact behavior modeled anywhere but in training, nor would there be natural reinforcers for eye contact in his family environment. In fact, his home environment may supply response costs for culturally inappropriate eye-contact behavior. The student's cultural heritage may inhibit his willingness to make eye contact, thus this particular intervention procedure would have a low probability of being mastered. Subsequently, the student may be hindered in learning how to ask for help in the way it is planned to be taught. Had the interventionist and teacher considered and evaluated the cultural heritage and social importance of eye-contact behavior for the student and his family, this particular procedure would have been discussed and either altered or eliminated from the intervention. It is critical to intervention success to assess what the social and cultural values are of *all* parties. Thus, the values of all parties are clearly articulated and incorporated into the intervention design.

## With Whom Do We Assess Social Validity and Why?

We recommend a multi-informant method of assessing social validity so that consensus is built among parties of an intervention that supports the ultimate success of the student. Specifically, the teacher, other school professionals, and especially the parent and student should be assessed for social validity measures in order to design intervention components that will ensure success. Understanding the perspective and contribution of each person involved in a school-based intervention provides the rationale for pre- and post-intervention social validity assessment. Each participant plays a different part in intervention and has different perspectives about treatment acceptability.

### Teacher

The majority of teachers, as well as other school professionals, have a basic repertoire of academic and behavioral expectations they require of students so that learning takes place in their classroom. Expectations include the ability to attend to instruction, to work independently, to use free time wisely, and to ask for help appropriately when needed (Walker et al., 1992; Walker, McConnell, & Clarke, 1985). Within these basic expectations, individual teachers have different teaching styles (Chang, 1988; Evertson & Weade, 1989), tolerance levels (Landon & Mesinger, 1989; Safran & Safran, 1984; Safran, Safran, & Barcikowski, 1985; Shinn, Tindal, & Spira, 1987), and behavioral expectations (Lane, Givner, & Pierson, in press; Kerr & Zigmond, 1986; Walker & Rankin, 1983) that influence the acceptability of intervention and thus the probability that intervention steps will be implemented as designed and sustained until goals are reached.

As alluded to earlier, specific features of the interventions (e.g., implementation time and effort, materials needed for the intervention) influence teacher ratings of acceptability (Gresham & Kendell, 1987). It is essential that intervention components fit into the teacher's schedule, are within the teacher's skill level, or that training and support is available (Lane, Mahdavi, & Borthwick-Duffy, in press), and that the teacher views the intervention as potentially effective in relation to the severity of the problem. Research conducted about teacher treatment or intervention preferences clearly suggests that the more severe a student's problem, the more acceptable *any* proposed treatment is, regardless of time or complexity (Elliott, Witt, & Kratochwill, 1996). If the student behavior is constantly interfering with the classroom learning environment, a teacher is willing to do almost anything to solve the problem. On the other hand, if the student behavior has low impact on the classroom environment (e.g., a student with selective mutism), teachers are more discriminative about what is acceptable to change in their schedule.

Other issues that directly affect teacher treatment acceptability are the time involved in the application of an intervention and whether the intervention uses positive techniques (e.g., praise) versus negative, reductive techniques (e.g., ignoring). Teachers prefer positive techniques (Gresham & Kendell, 1987). Again, the more severe the student behavior, the greater the likelihood a teacher will accept more complex, time-consuming treatment (Elliott et al., 1996). Research also suggests that there is an inverse relationship between teaching experience and acceptability; namely, the more experience a teacher has in education, the less likely *any* kind of treatment will be acceptable. However, we contend that if the experienced teacher is making a referral and is included in the pre-intervention social validity surveys, the teacher's treatment preferences will be considered and incorporated in an intervention. This involvement may, in turn, preclude any objection to classroom intervention. Finally, post-intervention social validity is important to assess with teachers because it can inform future investigations and help to design interventions that strike a balance between feasibility and effectiveness (Lane et al., 2002).

### Parent

The inclusion of a student's parent(s) in the entire school-based problem-solving model cannot be overly emphasized. We will use the term "parent," but we mean any significant adult who serves as the child's caretaker (e.g., grandparent, guardian, or foster parent). The vast majority of parents can provide vital information about their child that can enhance or impede an intervention. Parents know how their child responds to various strategies (e.g., verbal praise and token reinforcers) and what provides the greatest incentive for a child to increase or decrease a given behavior. Research has consistently found that when parents are involved in their children's education, their children tend to perform better academically than those students without parental support (Brown, Mounts, Lamborn, & Sternberg, 1993). Research also provides evidence of the strong relationship between parental beliefs about behavior and school academic and social outcomes, adolescent self-esteem, conduct disorders, and school drop-out rates (Brody & Stoneman, 1992; Okagaki & Sternberg, 1993; Reid & Patterson, 1991; Schaefer & Edgerton, 1985). Further, students with parents who support educational goals and who set behavioral boundaries tend to achieve academically and socially in school (Alexander, Entwisle, &

Dauber, 1994; Reid & Patterson, 1991; Walker, Zeller, Close, Webber, & Gresham, 1999).

As previously discussed, social validity measures of family beliefs and practices are essential to intervention design. It is often parent and/or family characteristics (e.g., culture and parenting practice) that contribute compensatory factors that mediate risk of school failure (Keogh & Weisner, 1993):

> The everyday routines and activities of the family within which the interventions must "fit" must also be understood. Too often, interventions and remedial programs are developed and "sent" by educators, psychologists, and other professionals, and are assumed to be "received" by a family. Findings from other studies suggest strongly, however, that homogeneity of family social constructions and ecocultural circumstances within a community cannot be assumed (p. 9).

For example, an intervention may be planned at school to increase a student's academic engaged time using curricular adjustments, contingency and positive reinforcement schedules, and home rewards. If interventionists fail to assess the parent/family variables, an important link to the intervention is missing. Suppose that the student's parents work nights and the child is monitored in the evening by an older brother who spends the evening on the telephone. The child will not get the home reward, will not do homework, and will go to bed late so that fatigue the next day is an issue. The parent's work schedule may not be modifiable. Had the interventionists assessed parent and family variables, the intervention design would have addressed this factor. An alternative reward system could be designed, an after-school homework club could be part of the intervention, and the parents may be able to arrange ways to monitor bedtime.

Another factor that research suggests influences parental acceptability of behavioral treatment is whether or not the parent believes the problem is related to physical or medical problems (Reimers, Wacker, Derby, & Cooper, 1995). Acceptance of behavioral treatments recommended to parents decrease as ratings of the physical attributions for their children's problems increase. The response to treatment recommendations can be mediated by parental perceptions that behavior is out of anyone's control due to a physical problem of the child. Conversely, the more a parent feels the problem behavior is within their child's ability to control, the more acceptable the treatment.

Thus, it is important for pre-intervention social validity measures to assess parents about what they believe to be the cause of inappropriate behavior and if they feel their child or they have control to change it. Even if the parent feels there is no control, the assessment brings the issue to light so that it can be discussed and parents can be informed about the importance of their support and ways they can help their child change. In this way, school professionals empower parents to facilitate and support change for their child. Consequently, it is important to encourage parental involvement in the intervention process in an effort to strengthen the home-school partnership (Webster-Stratton & Reid, 2002) to enhance intervention outcomes.

### Student

Assessing social validity from the student perspective is warranted if the child has the requisite cognitive and developmental skills to participate in the process. If the student understands how the intervention goal is desirable and reasonable, it is possible that "buy-in" will also enhance intervention outcomes. Student buy-in of an intervention is often assumed and seldom assessed. Pre-intervention social validity measures give voice to the student and provide an opportunity to discuss student concerns or misconceptions.

Central to intervention effectiveness at the secondary and tertiary levels of prevention is an evaluation of what the student seeks or avoids by performing a behavior, also referred to as the *function* of the behavior (O'Neil, Horner, Albin, Sprague, Storey, & Newton, 1997). Interventions that teach and/or reinforce a new behavior that is more efficient and effective in meeting the student's goal (getting or avoiding something) are likely to meet with greater success. Thus, the issues of function and pay-off for the student are central to the intervention process.

Moreover, it is the student who must be motivated to change. Identification of highly reinforcing pay-offs for skill acquisition or behavior change is essential. Students are often resistant to intervention because even though a deficient skill or inappropriate behavior may not be acceptable by others (parents and/or teachers), the pay-off for remaining deficient or using bad behavior more than offsets others' judgments. An example of this is the student who exhibits "learned helplessness" and cannot seem to do anything for him/herself, in spite of apparent ability. Most teachers have experienced a student like this, and it is indeed frustrating because the pay-off for the student is adult attention. Whatever the intervention, it must compete with this attention pay-off to overcome the student's unwillingness to attempt to do something without constant adult assistance. Pretreatment social validity measures used with students are particularly important because they provide information about the student's preferences that can be incorporated into the intervention plan. Thus, motivation for trying an intervention is encouraged through the use of student-identified reinforcement that competes with the pay-off of inappropriate behavior or low skill performance.

Student treatment acceptability has not been widely researched. Findings from the few studies in this area indicate that interventions are more acceptable to students when they emphasize one-on-one teacher-student interactions, group contingencies and reinforcement, and/or punishment sanctions for the misbehaving student (Elliott, Witt, Galvin, & Moe, 1986; Turco & Elliott, 1986; Witt & Elliott, 1985). Another study (Elliott, Turco, & Gresham, 1987) found that acceptability of group contingency interventions varied by gender and ethnicity. In a study of 660 ethnically diverse female students, results indicated that female students found group contingency interventions overall as less acceptable than male students did, while African-American students tended to rate group contingency interventions as more acceptable than Caucasian students rated them. It is important to be sensitive to such factors when designing treatment components. Using pretreatment social validity measures with the target student circumvents problems with treatment acceptability by asking his/her opinion about treatment and incorporating those preferences into the intervention plan.

## How Do We Assess Social Validity?

Social validity is primarily assessed using rating scales or surveys that collect self-report information (Finn & Sladeczek, 2001; Kazdin, 1977). Other methods of assessing social validity include interviews (Gresham & Lopez, 1996; Lane, 1997), direct observation and social comparisons techniques (Kazdin, 1977), and inspection of the frequency with which the interventions are repeatedly used or recommended (Gresham & Lopez, 1996) as evidence of social validity.

### Self-Report Rating Scales

Many of the instruments designed to assess social validity focus extensively on treatment acceptability (Finn & Sladeczek, 2001). The original treatment acceptability measure was the Treatment Evaluation Inventory (TEI, Kazdin, 1980a). The TEI and the Intervention Rating Profile-20 (IRP-20; Witt & Martens, 1983) are two highly used measures of treatment acceptability that have led to the development of a number of empirically validated measures (Finn & Sladeczek, 2001; Miltenberger, 1990). Currently, several instruments have been developed with roots grounded in both the TEI and the IRP-20. Some examples include the Treatment Evaluation Inventory-Short Form (TEI-SF; Kelley, Heffer, Gresham, & Elliott, 1989), the Treatment Acceptability Rating Profile-Revised (TARF-Revised; Reimers & Wacker, 1988; see Form 4.1), the Abbreviated Acceptability Rating Profile (AARP; Tarnowski & Simonian, 1992), The Intervention Rating Profile-15 (Martens, Witt, Elliott, & Darveaux, 1985; see Form 4.2), the Children's Intervention Rating Profile (CIRP; Elliott, 1988; Witt & Elliott, 1983; 1985; see Form 4.3), and the Behavior Intervention Rating Scales (BIRS; Von Brock & Elliott, 1987; see Table 4.1 for a brief description of each measure).

It is also possible to construct and use nonempirically validated measures that assess the social significance of the goals from the teacher (see Form 4.4), the parents (see Form 4.5), and the student (see Forms 4.6 through 4.8) perspectives. These rating scales address the social significance of the problem by asking questions pertaining to the cause of the problem, the ability and/or willingness to change, and how the area of concern influences the student at school, at home, or in the community. Similarly, acceptability of the treatment procedures can be assessed from multiple perspectives at the onset (see Forms 4.9 through 4.13) and the conclusion of the interventions. Treatment outcomes, in terms of the importance of intervention effects, can also be assessed by the consumers using informal rating scales (see Forms 4.14 though 4.18). These sample forms can be adapted to fit the features of any primary, secondary, or tertiary prevention program.

### Interviews

Gresham and Lopez (1996) designed a three-part semi-structured interview to be conducted with the classroom teacher (see Figure 4.2). The three sections focus on determining the social significance of the goals, establishing the social acceptability of the treatment procedures, and the social importance of effects.

Semi-structured interviews can also be conducted with children (Lane, 1997). For example, the *Children's Social Validity Interview* (CSVI; Lane, 1997) was constructed to evaluate social validity from the student perspective. The CSVI is a thirteen-item interview comprised of close-ended and open-ended items. Thirteen of the close-ended items measure acceptability of intervention components, the types of skills acquired, and the extent to which the student reportedly uses the new skills (see Form 4.19). A measure of overall use is created by combining the five items pertaining to use (Lane, 1997).

**TABLE 4.1** *Social Validity Measures*

| Instrument | Description |
|---|---|
| ***TEI-related measures*** | |
| Treatment Evaluation Inventory (TEI, Kazdin, 1980a) | The TEI is a factor analytically derived instrument comprised of 15 items that are rated on a 7-point Likert-type scale. Items pertain to fairness of an intervention, potential side effects, perceived efficacy, and appropriateness of the intervention for the given child. A composite score is computed by summing all items. Higher scores are associated with higher treatment acceptability (Kazdin, 1980a). Internal consistency reliability: .89, .97. |
| Treatment Evaluation Inventory–Short Form (TEI-SF; Kelley, Heffer, Gresham, & Elliott, 1989) | The TEI-SF is a modified version of the TEI. It was revised to include fewer items and to simplify the wording. The TEI-SF contains nine items that are rated on a 5-point Likert-type scale. Again, higher scores indicated higher acceptability. Internal consistency reliability: .85. |
| Treatment Acceptability Rating Profile (TARF; Reimers & Wacker, 1988) | The TARF was intended to refine the original TEI measure. The fifteen items constituting the TARF parallel Wolf's (1978) definition of social validity. The items are distributed across five domains: acceptability, disruption, time, effectiveness, and willingness. Each item is rated on a 7-point Likert-type scale. Internal consistency reliability: .80 to .91 (composites only). |
| Treatment Acceptability Rating Profile (TARF-Revised; Reimers & Wacker, 1988) | The TARF is a twenty-item Likert-type scale used to assess teachers' opinions about intervention acceptability. Each item is rated on a 7-point Likert-type scale. Seventeen items address acceptability, two address problem severity, and one item assesses the extent to which the intervention is understandable. Items are organized into five acceptability domains: reasonableness, effectiveness, side effects, disruptive/time, cost, and willingness. The TARF-R has strong psychometric properties and more practical value relative to the TARF. Internal consistency reliability: .69 to .95 (composites only; see Form 4.1). |
| ***IRP-Related Measures*** | |
| Intervention Rating Profile-20 (IRP-20; Witt & Martens, 1983) | The IRP-20 is comprised of twenty statements that are rated on a 6-point Likert-type scale (1 = strongly disagree; 6 = strongly agree). Items arc summed to yield an overall measure of acceptability (range: 20 to 120) with higher scores indicating higher acceptability. This instrument has been used with teachers and college students. Internal consistency reliability: .89, .85. |
| Intervention Rating Profile-15 (Martens, Witt, Elliott, & Darveaux, 1985) | The IRP-15 is a fifteen-item, factor analytically derived, teacher-completed survey designed to measure treatment acceptability and effectiveness. Each item is rated on a 6-point Likert-type scale ranging from *strongly disagree* (1) to *strongly agree* (6). The IRP-15 has been used with teachers, parents, and nurses. Total scores range from 15 to 90 with higher scores indicating higher acceptability. Internal consistency reliabilities: .88 - .98 (see Form 4.2). |
| Abbreviated Acceptability Rating Profile (AARP; Tarnowski & Simonian, 1992) | The AARP was based on the IPR-15. The AARP contains eight items, each of which are rated on a 6-point Likert-type scale. A total score is computed by adding the ratings of the eight items (range: 8 to 48). This instrument was designed for use in clinical settings with parents as raters. Internal consistency reliabilities range from .95 to .98. |
| Children's Intervention Rating Profile (CIRP; Witt & Elliott, 1985) | The CIRP is a parallel version of the IRP-15 designed for use with school-age children. Each item was written at a fifth-grade reading level. A modified version of the CIRP has also been used to evaluate social validity from younger children's perspectives (Lane, 1997). The CIRP contains seven items that are evaluated from the student perspective on a 6-point Likert-type scale ranging from *"I agree"* (6) to *"I do not agree"* (1). Total scores range from 7 to 42 points. High scores indicated high acceptability. Items assess fairness, expected effectiveness, and possible negative consequences of participation. Internal consistency reliabilities: .75 - .89 (see Form 4.3). |
| Behavior Intervention Rating Scales (BIRS; VonBrock & Elliott, 1987) | The BIRS is a twenty-four-item scale based on the IRP-15. Each item is rated on a 6-point Likert-type scale (1 = strongly disagree; 6 = strongly agree). Items are summed to produced a total acceptability score with high scores suggesting high acceptability. This scale was designed for use with teachers, parents, and psychologists. Internal consistency reliabilities: .87 - .97. |

## Semi-Structured Interview for Social Validation

Consultee's Name _____ Date _____
Consultant's Name _____ School _____

### A. Social Significance of Goals

1. What behaviors lead you to request consultation?
2. Which behaviors are the most problematic for _____ in your classroom?
3. Describe how these behaviors cause classroom problems.
4. If these problematic behaviors were decreased or eliminated, how would this affect _____ (the client)? Other students in your classroom? Your teaching in your classroom?
5. Do you see these behaviors as skill deficits? Performance deficits? What do you base this on?
6. Define each behavior as specifically as possible.
7. How do these behaviors affect other students in your classroom? Students in other classrooms?
8. How do these behaviors affect other school personnel (e.g., principal, other teachers, staff, etc.)?
9. Which behavior(s) do you think would be the most beneficial for _____ to change now? Why? Which behavior(s) would have the greatest long-term benefits for _____? Why?

### B. Social Acceptability of Procedures

10. How do you feel about the procedures we discussed to change _____'s behavior?
11. Which aspects of the intervention do you like the most? Why? Which do you like the least? Why?
12. Which aspects of this intervention would be the most difficult to implement? Why? Which aspects would be the least difficult to implement? Why?
13. Here are some ways in which we could change the intervention. Do these changes make the intervention more acceptable and easier to implement? Why? What would you recommend for the further changes?
14. What, if any, potential negative effects might this intervention have on _____? On other students in your classroom?
15. Do you think this intervention is likely to be effective in solving _____'s problem? Why? Why not? What are some ways we could determine whether or not the intervention had solved _____'s problem?

### C. Social Importance of Effects

16. Describe how well you think the intervention worked.
17. What behavior changes did you observe? Did these changes make a difference in _____'s behavior in your classroom? In other school settings (e.g., other classrooms, cafeteria, playground, etc.)?
18. Is _____'s behavior now similar to that of the average student in your classroom? If not, do you think that continued use of the intervention would accomplish this goal? Why or why not? How long do you think this might take if we continued this intervention?
19. Are you satisfied with the outcomes of this intervention? How satisfied are you? Why?
20. Do you think this intervention would work with similar problems in the future? Why or why not?
21. Would you recommend this intervention to other teachers? Why or why not? What aspects of this intervention would you change before recommending this intervention to other teachers?

---

**FIGURE 4.2**    *Semi-Structured Interview for Social Validation*

*Source:* Reprinted with permission, from F. M. Gresham & M. F. Lopez (1996), "Social Validation: A Unifying Construct for School-based Consultation Research and Practice." *School Psychology Quarterly, 11,* 204–227.

In the case of secondary and tertiary levels of support, social significance also may be assessed when the interventionist conducts the Functional Assessment Interview (FAI; see Chapter 2, Linking Assessment to Intervention). The functional assessment interviews with teachers, parents, and students provide information about the function of student behavior as well as the maintaining consequence of the targeted problem. Acknowledgment of a problem and identifying behavior triggers and consequences enables the interventionist and other parties to the intervention to suggest alternative antecedent and consequent conditions that are equally or more socially significant and desirable to the student. The FAI also helps profile the availability of natural reinforcers in the student's school and home environment for the replacement skill/behavior. Socially significant treatment goals are identified during the FAI: What would the student like to be able to do? What does the parent see the student doing by the end of treatment? What level of performance do the teachers expect as a realistically attainable goal for the student? Finally, the FAI provides the opportunity for all parties to express opinions and thoughts about the problem and offer potential solutions so that all parties have a vested interest in treatment design, implementation, and maintenance of treatment procedures until goals are reached.

### Direct Observation and Social Comparisons Techniques

Direct observation and social comparisons techniques can also be used to assess social validity. This can be accomplished by comparing the target student to a peer in the same environment who is judged to be at the target student's goal level. However, although a change may be apparent by local norms, the change may not necessarily have habilitative validity for the student. For example, the student may be on-task like the peer, but may not be getting any academic benefit from being on-task. Or, the student may be in a class where normative levels are still below developmental or grade level so that, in the big picture, the student remains deficient. To remedy the normative social comparison described by Kazdin (1977), Fawcett (1991) suggested that the interventionist establish proficiency levels for a behavior or skill (ideal, normative, or deficient) prior to intervention. In this way, intervention effectiveness can be evaluated for socially important changes by effects that move a student from a deficient range to a normative or ideal range of performance.

### Repeated Use

Another method of assessing social validity is by assessing the extent to which the intervention is used by the consumers in the future. If an intervention is used, and is used as designed, then the intervention can be determined to be socially valid. In essence, treatment use serves as a behavioral marker for acceptability (Gresham & Lopez, 1996).

## How Do We Interpret Social Validity Surveys?

The figures and forms we include in the book are rated by teachers, parents, and students using a Likert-type scale so that there are different degrees for the respondents to express their opinion about each item. In the pre-intervention problem and treatment acceptability surveys, you will look for numbers that indicate a positive response, or at least a neutral response. If items on which you would expect a "strongly agree" response are rated as "strongly disagree," then the issue rated negatively is one that the interventionist would want to probe further with the respondent. For instance, if a parent rates item number 8 on Form 4.10, "the proposed intervention will be within my skill level to help" as "strongly disagree," then you will want to probe the parent further. First, determine if they understand the intervention procedures clearly; if they do and still think they cannot help their child, then determine if they are willing to learn and try. If the parent agrees, then the interventionist would train the parent prior to implementing the intervention. This gives the parent the opportunity to learn a new skill, and their child learns that their parent is willing to help them. For other items, you may expect and desire a "strongly disagree" rating, so you would probe the item if the respondent rated the item as "strongly agree." For example, item 11 on Form 4.4, states that the student problem "is one I don't understand." If the teacher answers "strongly agree," then this means the interventionist needs to talk with the teacher about the item to address the teacher's questions or concerns.

Overall, the surveys are designed to inform the interventionist about the social validity of intervention goals, procedures, and outcomes from the perspective of all involved parties. The surveys are tools to reach consensus among parties, commitment and motivation to implement and sustain the intervention until goals are reached, and a way to affirm the positive outcomes of successful intervention.

We encourage you, when possible, to use methods other than surveys to assess social validity. For example, important information can be gleaned from interviews, social comparisons, and through examining the extent to which interventions are subsequently used. Information about social validity not only helps in forming intervention design, but it can provide important insight regarding intervention outcomes (see Lane, 1999).

The importance of establishing credibility and rapport with all parties cannot be overly stressed because of how greatly integrity influences the degree to which surveys are answered frankly. Part of the rapport comes from offering each party involved with the intervention an opportunity to express their opinions and to have those opinions be reflected in the design and implementation of the treatment.

## Summary

The intent of this chapter was to define social validity, establish the importance of assessing social validity and the onset and conclusion of intervention, identify the key parties (e.g., teachers, parents, and students) who warrant participation, and offer tools and procedures for assessing social validity. In the chapters that follow, two additional keys to designing and implementing effective school-based interventions will be presented: treatment integrity and generalization and maintenance.

## TREATMENT ACCEPTABILITY RATING FORM—REVISED (TARF-R)

Please complete the items listed below. The items should be completed by placing a check mark on the line under the question that best indicates how you feel about the psychologist's treatment recommendations.

1.  How clear is your understanding of this treatment?

    ___  ___  ___  ___  ___  ___
    Not at all                        Neutral            Very clear
    clear

2.  How acceptable do you find the treatment to be regarding your concerns about your child?

    ___  ___  ___  ___  ___  ___
    Not at all                        Neutral            Very acceptable
    acceptable

3.  How willing are you to carry out this treatment?

    ___  ___  ___  ___  ___  ___
    Not at all                        Neutral            Very willing
    willing

4.  Given your child's behavioral problems, how reasonable do you find the treatment to be?

    ___  ___  ___  ___  ___  ___
    Not at all                        Neutral            Very reasonable
    reasonable

5.  How costly will it be to carry out this treatment?

    ___  ___  ___  ___  ___  ___
    Not at all                        Neutral            Very costly
    costly

6.  To what extent do you think there might be disadvantages in following this treatment?

    ___  ___  ___  ___  ___  ___
    Not at all                        Neutral            Many are likely
    likely

7.  How likely is this treatment to make permanent improvements in your child's behavior?

    ___  ___  ___  ___  ___  ___
    Unlikely                          Neutral            Very likely

8.  How much time will be needed each day for you to carry out this treatment?

    ___  ___  ___  ___  ___  ___
    Little time                       Neutral            Much time
    will be needed                                       will be needed

---

**FORM 4.1** *Treatment Acceptability Rating Profile-Revised (TARF-Revised)*

*Source:* Reprinted with permission. T. M. Reimers and D. P. Wacker (1988). "Parents' Ratings of the Acceptability of Behavioral Treatment Recommendations Made in an Outpatient Clinic: A Preliminary Analysis of the Influence of Treatment Effectiveness." *Behavior Disorders, 14,* 7–15.

9. How confident are you that the treatment will be effective?

<u>   </u>     <u>   </u>     <u>   </u>     <u>   </u>     <u>   </u>     <u>   </u>

Not at all                            Neutral                Very confident
confident

10. Compared to other children with behavioral difficulties, how serious are your child's problems?

<u>   </u>     <u>   </u>     <u>   </u>     <u>   </u>     <u>   </u>     <u>   </u>

Not at all                            Neutral                Very serious
serious

11. How disruptive will it be to the family (in general) to carry out this treatment?

<u>   </u>     <u>   </u>     <u>   </u>     <u>   </u>     <u>   </u>     <u>   </u>

Not at all                            Neutral                Very disruptive
disruptive

12. How effective is this treatment likely to be for your child?

<u>   </u>     <u>   </u>     <u>   </u>     <u>   </u>     <u>   </u>     <u>   </u>

Not at all                            Neutral                Very effective
effective

13. How affordable is this treatment for your family?

<u>   </u>     <u>   </u>     <u>   </u>     <u>   </u>     <u>   </u>     <u>   </u>

Not at all                            Neutral                Very affordable
affordable

14. How much do you like the procedures used in the proposed treatment?

<u>   </u>     <u>   </u>     <u>   </u>     <u>   </u>     <u>   </u>     <u>   </u>

Do not like                          Neutral                Like them
them at all                                                              very much

15. How willing will other family members be to help carry out this treatment?

<u>   </u>     <u>   </u>     <u>   </u>     <u>   </u>     <u>   </u>     <u>   </u>

Not at all                            Neutral                Very willing
willing

16. To what extent are undesirable side-effects likely to result from this treatment?

<u>   </u>     <u>   </u>     <u>   </u>     <u>   </u>     <u>   </u>     <u>   </u>

No side- effects                      Neutral                Many side-effects
are likely                                                             are likely

17. How much discomfort is your child likely to experience during the course of this treatment?

<u>   </u>     <u>   </u>     <u>   </u>     <u>   </u>     <u>   </u>     <u>   </u>

No discomfort                      Neutral                Very much
at all                                                                discomfort

**FORM 4.1**  *Continued*

18.    How severe are your child's behavioral difficulties?

___    ___    ___    ___    ___    ___

Not at all                           Neutral          Very severe
severe

19.    How willing would you be to change your family routine to carry out this treatment?

___    ___    ___    ___    ___    ___

Not at all                           Neutral          Very willing
willing

20.    How well will carrying out this treatment fit into the family routine?

___    ___    ___    ___    ___    ___

Not at all                           Neutral          Very well
well

21.    To what degree are your child's behavioral problems of concern to you?

___    ___    ___    ___    ___    ___

No concern                           Neutral          Great concern
at all

**FORM 4.1    *Continued***

The purpose of this questionnaire is to obtain information that will aid in the selection of classroom interventions. These interventions will be used by teachers of children with behavior problems. Please circle the number which best describes your agreement or disagreement with each statement.

| | Strongly Disagree | Disagree | Slightly Disagree | Slightly Agree | Agree | Strongly Agree |
|---|---|---|---|---|---|---|
| 1. This would be an acceptable intervention for the child's problem behavior. | 1 | 2 | 3 | 4 | 5 | 6 |
| 2. Most teachers would find this intervention appropriate for behavior problems in addition to the one described. | 1 | 2 | 3 | 4 | 5 | 6 |
| 3. This intervention should prove effective in changing the child's problem behavior. | 1 | 2 | 3 | 4 | 5 | 6 |
| 4. I would suggest the use of this intervention to other teachers. | 1 | 2 | 3 | 4 | 5 | 6 |
| 5. The child's behavior problem is severe enough to warrant use of this intervention. | 1 | 2 | 3 | 4 | 5 | 6 |
| 6. Most teachers would find this intervention suitable for the behavior problem described. | 1 | 2 | 3 | 4 | 5 | 6 |
| 7. I would be willing to use this intervention in the classroom setting. | 1 | 2 | 3 | 4 | 5 | 6 |
| 8. This intervention would *not* result in negative side-effects for the child. | 1 | 2 | 3 | 4 | 5 | 6 |
| 9. This intervention would be appropriate for a variety of children. | 1 | 2 | 3 | 4 | 5 | 6 |
| 10. This intervention is consistent with those I have used in classroom settings. | 1 | 2 | 3 | 4 | 5 | 6 |
| 11. The intervention was a fair way to handle the child's problem behavior. | 1 | 2 | 3 | 4 | 5 | 6 |
| 12. This intervention is reasonable for the behavior problem described. | 1 | 2 | 3 | 4 | 5 | 6 |
| 13. I liked the procedures used in this intervention. | 1 | 2 | 3 | 4 | 5 | 6 |
| 14. This intervention was a good way to handle this child's behavior problem. | 1 | 2 | 3 | 4 | 5 | 6 |
| 15. Overall, this intervention would be beneficial for the child. | 1 | 2 | 3 | 4 | 5 | 6 |

**FORM 4.2    *Intervention Rating Profile-15***

*Source:* J. C. Witt and S. N. Elliott (1985). "Acceptability of Classroom Intervention Strategies." In T. R. Kratochwill (Ed.), *Advances in School Psychology*, Vol. 4 (pp. 251–288). Mahwah, NJ: Erlbaum. Reprinted with permission.

|  |  | *I agree* | *I do not agree* |
|---|---|---|---|
| 1. | The method used to deal with the behavior problem was fair. | + ---- + ---- + ---- + ---- + ---- + | |
| 2. | This child's teacher was too harsh on him. | + ---- + ---- + ---- + ---- + ---- + | |
| 3. | The method used to deal with the behavior may cause problems with this child's friend. | + ---- + ---- + ---- + ---- + ---- + | |
| 4. | There are better ways to handle this child's problem than the one described here. | + ---- + ---- + ---- + ---- + ---- + | |
| 5. | The method used by this teacher would be a good one to use with other children. | + ---- + ---- + ---- + ---- + ---- + | |
| 6. | I like the method used for this child's behavior problem. | + ---- + ---- + ---- + ---- + ---- + | |
| 7. | I think that the method used for this problem would help this child do better in school. | + ---- + ---- + ---- + ---- + ---- + | |

**FORM 4.3**   *Children's Intervention Rating Profile*

*Source:* J. C. Witt and S. N. Elliott (1985). "Acceptability of Classroom Intervention Strategies." In T. R. Katochwill (Ed.), *Advances in School Psychology,* Vol. 4 (pp. 251–288). Mahwah, NJ: Erlbaum. Reprinted with permission.

## Teacher's Child Social Validity Rating Survey

Date: _____     Teacher: _____

Student: _____

Target Behavior: _____

For each item, please circle the number that most closely represents your opinion

|  | Strongly Disagree | | | Neutral 50/50 | | | Strongly Agree |
|---|---|---|---|---|---|---|---|

The student's behavior is:

| | | | | | | | | |
|---|---|---|---|---|---|---|---|---|
| 1. just at school and not at home | 1 | 2 | 3 | 4 | 5 | 6 | 7 |
| 2. difficult for me to deal with | 1 | 2 | 3 | 4 | 5 | 6 | 7 |
| 3. caused by inherited traits | 1 | 2 | 3 | 4 | 5 | 6 | 7 |
| 4. caused by a medical condition | 1 | 2 | 3 | 4 | 5 | 6 | 7 |
| 5. going to have bad outcomes if not changed soon | 1 | 2 | 3 | 4 | 5 | 6 | 7 |
| 6. seriously hurting chances for success | 1 | 2 | 3 | 4 | 5 | 6 | 7 |
| 7. caused by family problems | 1 | 2 | 3 | 4 | 5 | 6 | 7 |
| 8. causing problems for other children | 1 | 2 | 3 | 4 | 5 | 6 | 7 |
| 9. interfering with class instruction | 1 | 2 | 3 | 4 | 5 | 6 | 7 |
| 10. beyond the student's ability to change | 1 | 2 | 3 | 4 | 5 | 6 | 7 |
| 11. something I don't understand | 1 | 2 | 3 | 4 | 5 | 6 | 7 |
| 12. something I want to help change | 1 | 2 | 3 | 4 | 5 | 6 | 7 |

Comments/Opinions: _____

_____

_____

**FORM 4.4**   *Sample Pre-Intervention Social Validity: Teacher and Problem*

## Parent's Child Social Validity Rating Survey

Date: _____     Re Your Child: _____

Parent Name: _____   Mother__ Father__ Step/Foster___ Other___

Target Behavior: _____

For each item, please circle the number that most closely represents your opinion

|  | Strongly Disagree | | | Neutral 50/50 | | | Strongly Agree |
|---|---|---|---|---|---|---|---|

The student's behavior is:

| | | | | | | | |
|---|---|---|---|---|---|---|---|
| 1. just at school and not at home | 1 | 2 | 3 | 4 | 5 | 6 | 7 |
| 2. difficult for me to deal with | 1 | 2 | 3 | 4 | 5 | 6 | 7 |
| 3. caused by inherited traits | 1 | 2 | 3 | 4 | 5 | 6 | 7 |
| 4. caused by a medical condition | 1 | 2 | 3 | 4 | 5 | 6 | 7 |
| 5. going to have bad outcomes if not changed soon | 1 | 2 | 3 | 4 | 5 | 6 | 7 |
| 6. seriously hurting chances for success | 1 | 2 | 3 | 4 | 5 | 6 | 7 |
| 7. caused by family problems | 1 | 2 | 3 | 4 | 5 | 6 | 7 |
| 8. causing problems for other children | 1 | 2 | 3 | 4 | 5 | 6 | 7 |
| 9. interfering with class instruction | 1 | 2 | 3 | 4 | 5 | 6 | 7 |
| 10. beyond the student's ability to change | 1 | 2 | 3 | 4 | 5 | 6 | 7 |
| 11. something I don't understand | 1 | 2 | 3 | 4 | 5 | 6 | 7 |
| 12. something I want to help change | 1 | 2 | 3 | 4 | 5 | 6 | 7 |

Comments/Opinions:_____

_____

_____

**FORM 4.5**   *Sample Pre-Intervention Social Validity: Parent and Problem*

## Student Self-Assessment of Social Validity (Primary Gr K-3)

Date:_____

Student Name:_____ Teacher:_____

Target Behavior:_____

Place the sheet in front of the student.  Read each item and ask the student to circle the face that best looks like how he/she feels about the item.

1.  I like school.

2.  I can learn a new way.

3.  I have friends at school.

4.  I want help with my problem.

5.  It's easy for me to ask for help.

6.  I like to try my very best.

7.  My teacher helps me learn.

8.  I like to play outside at recess.

For the remaining items, read the item and ask the student to fill in the blank.

9.  My favorite thing to do at school is _____.

10. My least favorite thing to do at school is _____.

**FORM 4.6**    *Sample Pre-Intervention Social Validity: Student and Target Behavior*

**Student Self-Assessment of Social Validity (Elementary Gr 4–6)**

Date:_____

Student Name:_____ Teacher:_____

Target Behavior:_____

For each item, please circle the number that best describes what you think.

|  | Strongly Disagree | | | Neutral 50/50 | | | Strongly Agree |
|---|---|---|---|---|---|---|---|
| The student's behavior is: | | | | | | | |
| 1. just at school and not at home | 1 | 2 | 3 | 4 | 5 | 6 | 7 |
| 2. hard for me to control | 1 | 2 | 3 | 4 | 5 | 6 | 7 |
| 3. because I was born with problems | 1 | 2 | 3 | 4 | 5 | 6 | 7 |
| 4. caused by a medical condition | 1 | 2 | 3 | 4 | 5 | 6 | 7 |
| 5. going to have bad outcomes if not changed soon | 1 | 2 | 3 | 4 | 5 | 6 | 7 |
| 6. serious and making me not successful | 1 | 2 | 3 | 4 | 5 | 6 | 7 |
| 7. caused by teacher or school | 1 | 2 | 3 | 4 | 5 | 6 | 7 |
| 8. caused by other family problems | 1 | 2 | 3 | 4 | 5 | 6 | 7 |
| 9. caused by another child/children | 1 | 2 | 3 | 4 | 5 | 6 | 7 |
| 10. needs to be corrected soon | 1 | 2 | 3 | 4 | 5 | 6 | 7 |
| 11. something I don't understand | 1 | 2 | 3 | 4 | 5 | 6 | 7 |
| 12. something I want to help change | 1 | 2 | 3 | 4 | 5 | 6 | 7 |

Fill in the blanks:

13. What I most like to do at school is _____

14. What I don't like to do at school is _____

**FORM 4.7**   *Sample Pre-Intervention Social Validity: Student and Target Behavior*

## Student Self-Assessment of Target Behavior (Secondary Gr 7–12)

Date:_____

Student Name:_____    Teacher:_____

Target Behavior:_____

For each item, please circle the number that best describes your opinion.

| | Strongly Disagree | | Neutral 50/50 | | | Strongly Agree |
|---|---|---|---|---|---|---|

My target behavior is:

| | | | | | | | |
|---|---|---|---|---|---|---|---|
| 1. just at school and not at home | 1 | 2 | 3 | 4 | 5 | 6 | 7 |
| 2. hard for me to control | 1 | 2 | 3 | 4 | 5 | 6 | 7 |
| 3. caused by inherited traits | 1 | 2 | 3 | 4 | 5 | 6 | 7 |
| 4. caused by a medical condition | 1 | 2 | 3 | 4 | 5 | 6 | 7 |
| 5. going to have bad outcomes if not changed soon | 1 | 2 | 3 | 4 | 5 | 6 | 7 |
| 6. serious and making me not successful | 1 | 2 | 3 | 4 | 5 | 6 | 7 |
| 7. caused by a teacher or school | 1 | 2 | 3 | 4 | 5 | 6 | 7 |
| 8. caused by other family problems | 1 | 2 | 3 | 4 | 5 | 6 | 7 |
| 9. making me not liked by others | 1 | 2 | 3 | 4 | 5 | 6 | 7 |
| 10. needs to be corrected soon | 1 | 2 | 3 | 4 | 5 | 6 | 7 |
| 11. something I don't understand | 1 | 2 | 3 | 4 | 5 | 6 | 7 |
| 12. something I can change | 1 | 2 | 3 | 4 | 5 | 6 | 7 |

Fill in the blanks:

13. What I most like to do at school is _____

14. What I don't like to do at school is _____

**FORM 4.8**    *Sample Pre-Intervention Social Validity: Student and Target Behavior*

### Teacher Pre-Intervention Acceptability Rating Survey

Date: _____

Student: _____ Teacher: _____

Target Behavior: _____

For each item, please circle the number that most closely represents your opinion about the proposed intervention

| | Strongly Disagree | | | Neutral 50/50 | | | Strongly Agree |
|---|---|---|---|---|---|---|---|

The proposed intervention will:

| | | | | | | | |
|---|---|---|---|---|---|---|---|
| 1. fit into my regular schedule | 1 | 2 | 3 | 4 | 5 | 6 | 7 |
| 2. not take too much time | 1 | 2 | 3 | 4 | 5 | 6 | 7 |
| 3. teach important skills | 1 | 2 | 3 | 4 | 5 | 6 | 7 |
| 4. be a fair way to handle the problem | 1 | 2 | 3 | 4 | 5 | 6 | 7 |
| 5. be appropriate given the problem | 1 | 2 | 3 | 4 | 5 | 6 | 7 |
| 6. be suitable given the classroom culture | 1 | 2 | 3 | 4 | 5 | 6 | 7 |
| 7. be easy to implement and maintain | 1 | 2 | 3 | 4 | 5 | 6 | 7 |
| 8. be within my skill level to implement | 1 | 2 | 3 | 4 | 5 | 6 | 7 |
| 9. quickly improve the student's skill | 1 | 2 | 3 | 4 | 5 | 6 | 7 |
| 10. be acceptable to other students | 1 | 2 | 3 | 4 | 5 | 6 | 7 |
| 11. have lasting positive effects | 1 | 2 | 3 | 4 | 5 | 6 | 7 |
| 12. improve student's overall performance | 1 | 2 | 3 | 4 | 5 | 6 | 7 |

Comments/Opinions:_____

_____

_____

**FORM 4.9** *Sample Pre-Intervention Social Validity Survey: Teacher and Acceptability*

## Parent Pre-Intervention Acceptability Rating Survey

Date: _____          Re Your Child: _____

Parent Name: _____  Mother__Father__ Step/Foster___Other___

Target Behavior: _____

For each item, please circle the number that most closely represents your opinion about the proposed intervention

|  | Strongly Disagree | | Neutral 50/50 | | Strongly Agree | |
|---|---|---|---|---|---|---|

The proposed intervention will:

| | | | | | | | |
|---|---|---|---|---|---|---|---|
| 1.  be easy for my child to stick with | 1 | 2 | 3 | 4 | 5 | 6 | 7 |
| 2.  be acceptable in our home | 1 | 2 | 3 | 4 | 5 | 6 | 7 |
| 3.  teach important skills | 1 | 2 | 3 | 4 | 5 | 6 | 7 |
| 4.  be a fair way to handle the_____ | 1 | 2 | 3 | 4 | 5 | 6 | 7 |
| 5.  be appropriate given the behavior | 1 | 2 | 3 | 4 | 5 | 6 | 7 |
| 6.  be suitable given our family values | 1 | 2 | 3 | 4 | 5 | 6 | 7 |
| 7.  be easy for me to assist with at home | 1 | 2 | 3 | 4 | 5 | 6 | 7 |
| 8.  be within my skill level to help | 1 | 2 | 3 | 4 | 5 | 6 | 7 |
| 9.  quickly improve my child's skill | 1 | 2 | 3 | 4 | 5 | 6 | 7 |
| 10. be encouraged at home | 1 | 2 | 3 | 4 | 5 | 6 | 7 |
| 11. have lasting positive effects | 1 | 2 | 3 | 4 | 5 | 6 | 7 |
| 12. improve my child's self-confidence | 1 | 2 | 3 | 4 | 5 | 6 | 7 |

Comments/Opinions:_____

_____

_____

**FORM 4.10**   *Sample Pre-Intervention Social Validity: Parent Acceptability*

## Student Pre-Intervention Acceptability Rating Survey (Gr. K–3)

Date: _____

Name: _____    Teacher: _____

Target Behavior: _____

Place the sheet in front of the student.  Read each item and ask the student to circle the number of stars that best tells how much he/she feels about the item.

_____

| | How much? | | | |
|---|:---:|:---:|:---:|:---:|
| | (1) | (2) | (3) | (4) |
| | * | ** | *** | **** |
| 1. I know about the steps to help me change. | | | | |
| 2. I can do the steps to change. | * | ** | *** | **** |
| 3. I like what I will earn to try my best. | * | ** | *** | **** |
| 4. I will do my best work. | * | ** | *** | **** |
| 5. The new skill I will learn will help me. | * | ** | *** | **** |
| 6. I like the plan to help me change. | * | ** | *** | **** |
| 7. I like that my parents will help me. | * | ** | *** | **** |
| 8. I like that my friends will help me. | * | ** | *** | **** |

**FORM 4.11**   *Sample Pre-Intervention Social Validity: Student and Acceptability*

## Student Pre-Intervention Acceptability Rating Survey (Gr. 4–6)

Date: _____

Name: _____  Teacher: _____

Target Behavior: _____

For each item, please circle the number that best tells what you think about the proposed intervention plan.

|  | Strongly Disagree | | | Neutral 50/50 | | | Strongly Agree |
|---|---|---|---|---|---|---|---|

The proposed intervention will:

| | | | | | | | |
|---|---|---|---|---|---|---|---|
| 1. be easy for me to stick with. | 1 | 2 | 3 | 4 | 5 | 6 | 7 |
| 2. be approved by my parents. | 1 | 2 | 3 | 4 | 5 | 6 | 7 |
| 3. teach me important skills. | 1 | 2 | 3 | 4 | 5 | 6 | 7 |
| 4. be fair to me. | 1 | 2 | 3 | 4 | 5 | 6 | 7 |
| 5. help me change in important ways. | 1 | 2 | 3 | 4 | 5 | 6 | 7 |
| 6. help me make more friends. | 1 | 2 | 3 | 4 | 5 | 6 | 7 |
| 7. be easy for me to ask for help. | 1 | 2 | 3 | 4 | 5 | 6 | 7 |
| 8. quickly improve my skill | 1 | 2 | 3 | 4 | 5 | 6 | 7 |
| 9. make a difference in my grades. | 1 | 2 | 3 | 4 | 5 | 6 | 7 |
| 10. help me feel better about myself. | 1 | 2 | 3 | 4 | 5 | 6 | 7 |
| 11. give me things I like to earn. | 1 | 2 | 3 | 4 | 5 | 6 | 7 |
| 12. help me do better in school overall. | 1 | 2 | 3 | 4 | 5 | 6 | 7 |

What else do you think?

_____

_____

**FORM 4.12**   *Sample Pre-Intervention Social Validity: Student and Acceptability*

## Student Pre-Intervention Acceptability Rating Survey (Gr. 7–12)

Date: _____

Name: _____ Teacher: _____

Target Behavior: _____

For each item, please circle the number that best tells what you think about the proposed intervention plan.

| | Strongly Disagree | | | Neutral 50/50 | | | Strongly Agree |
|---|---|---|---|---|---|---|---|

The proposed intervention will:

| | | | | | | | | |
|---|---|---|---|---|---|---|---|---|
| 1. | be easy for me to stick with. | 1 | 2 | 3 | 4 | 5 | 6 | 7 |
| 2. | be approved by my parents. | 1 | 2 | 3 | 4 | 5 | 6 | 7 |
| 3. | teach me important skills. | 1 | 2 | 3 | 4 | 5 | 6 | 7 |
| 4. | be fair to me. | 1 | 2 | 3 | 4 | 5 | 6 | 7 |
| 5. | help me change in important ways. | 1 | 2 | 3 | 4 | 5 | 6 | 7 |
| 6. | help me make more friends. | 1 | 2 | 3 | 4 | 5 | 6 | 7 |
| 7. | be easy for me to ask for help. | 1 | 2 | 3 | 4 | 5 | 6 | 7 |
| 8. | quickly improve my skill | 1 | 2 | 3 | 4 | 5 | 6 | 7 |
| 9. | make a difference in my grades. | 1 | 2 | 3 | 4 | 5 | 6 | 7 |
| 10. | help me feel better about myself. | 1 | 2 | 3 | 4 | 5 | 6 | 7 |
| 11. | help me stay in school to graduate. | 1 | 2 | 3 | 4 | 5 | 6 | 7 |
| 12. | help me learn skills to help in life. | 1 | 2 | 3 | 4 | 5 | 6 | 7 |

What else do you think?

_____

_____

**FORM 4.13** *Sample Pre-Intervention Social Validity: Student and Acceptability*

## Teacher Post-Intervention Acceptability and Importance of Effects Survey

Date: _____

Name: _____    Teacher: _____

Intervention Goals reached: _____

For each item, please circle the number that most closely represents your opinion about the intervention

|  | Strongly Disagree | | Neutral 50/50 | | | Strongly Agree | |
|---|---|---|---|---|---|---|---|

The intervention:

| | | | | | | | |
|---|---|---|---|---|---|---|---|
| 1. fit into my regular schedule | 1 | 2 | 3 | 4 | 5 | 6 | 7 |
| 2. did not take too much time | 1 | 2 | 3 | 4 | 5 | 6 | 7 |
| 3. taught important skills | 1 | 2 | 3 | 4 | 5 | 6 | 7 |
| 4. was a fair way to handle the behavior | 1 | 2 | 3 | 4 | 5 | 6 | 7 |
| 5. was appropriate given the behavior | 1 | 2 | 3 | 4 | 5 | 6 | 7 |
| 6. was suitable given the classroom culture | 1 | 2 | 3 | 4 | 5 | 6 | 7 |
| 7. was easy to implement and maintain | 1 | 2 | 3 | 4 | 5 | 6 | 7 |
| 8. was within my skill level to implement | 1 | 2 | 3 | 4 | 5 | 6 | 7 |
| 9. quickly improved the student's skill | 1 | 2 | 3 | 4 | 5 | 6 | 7 |
| 10. was acceptable to other students | 1 | 2 | 3 | 4 | 5 | 6 | 7 |
| 11. will have lasting positive effects | 1 | 2 | 3 | 4 | 5 | 6 | 7 |
| 12. improved student's overall performance | 1 | 2 | 3 | 4 | 5 | 6 | 7 |
| 13. is one I will use again when needed | 1 | 2 | 3 | 4 | 5 | 6 | 7 |
| 14. is one I will recommend to others | 1 | 2 | 3 | 4 | 5 | 6 | 7 |

Comments/Opinions:_____

_____

**FORM 4.14**    *Sample Post-Treatment Acceptability and Importance of Effects Teacher Survey*

**Parent Post-Intervention Acceptability and Importance of Effects Survey**

Date: _____     Re Your Child: _____

Parent Name: _____  Mother__Father__ Step/Foster__Other__

Intervention ended (date):_____ Goals were reached: ___Yes ___No___Some

For each item, please circle the number that most closely represents your opinion about the intervention for your child's problem.

| | Strongly Disagree | | | Neutral 50/50 | | | Strongly Agree |
|---|---|---|---|---|---|---|---|

The intervention:

1. was easy for my child to stick with  1  2  3  4  5  6  7
2. was acceptable in our home  1  2  3  4  5  6  7
3. taught important skills  1  2  3  4  5  6  7
4. was a fair way to handle the behavior  1  2  3  4  5  6  7
5. was appropriate given the behavior  1  2  3  4  5  6  7
6. was suitable given our family values  1  2  3  4  5  6  7
7. was easy for me to assist with at home  1  2  3  4  5  6  7
8. was within my skill level to help  1  2  3  4  5  6  7
9. quickly improved my child's skill  1  2  3  4  5  6  7
10. was easy to encourage at home  1  2  3  4  5  6  7
11. will have lasting positive effects  1  2  3  4  5  6  7
12. improved my child's self-confidence  1  2  3  4  5  6  7
13. is one I would recommend to others  1  2  3  4  5  6  7

Comments/Opinions:_____

_____

**FORM 4.15**  *Sample Post-Intervention Social Validity: Parent and Acceptability*

### Student Post-Intervention Acceptability and Importance of Effects Survey (Gr. K–3)

Date: _____

Name: _____ Teacher: _____

I reached my goal:_____Yes    _____No    _____Some

Place the sheet in front of the student. Read each item and ask the student to circle the number of stars that best tells how much he/she feels about the item.

_____

|  | How much? | | | |
|---|:---:|:---:|:---:|:---:|
|  | (1) | (2) | (3) | (4) |
|  | * | ** | *** | **** |
| 1. I did all the steps to help me change. | * | ** | *** | **** |
| 2. It was easy to do the steps to change. | * | ** | *** | **** |
| 3. I like what I earned to try my best. | * | ** | *** | **** |
| 4. I did my best work. | * | ** | *** | **** |
| 5. The new skill I learned helps me. | * | ** | *** | **** |
| 6. I liked the plan that helped me learn. | * | ** | *** | **** |
| 7. I liked that my parents helped me learn. | * | ** | *** | **** |
| 8. I liked that my friends helped me. | * | ** | *** | **** |

_____

**FORM 4.16**    *Sample Post-Intervention Social Validity: Student and Acceptability*

**Student Post-Intervention Acceptability and Importance of Effects Survey (Gr. 4–6)**

Date: _____

Name: _____ Teacher: _____

I reached my goal:____Yes ____No ____Some

For each item, please circle the number that best tells what you think about the intervention that you just finished.

|  | Strongly Disagree | | | Neutral 50/50 | | | Strongly Agree |
|---|---|---|---|---|---|---|---|

The intervention:

1. was easy for me to stick with — 1 2 3 4 5 6 7
2. was approved by my parents — 1 2 3 4 5 6 7
3. taught me important skills — 1 2 3 4 5 6 7
4. was fair to me — 1 2 3 4 5 6 7
5. helped me change in important ways — 1 2 3 4 5 6 7
6. helped me make more friends — 1 2 3 4 5 6 7
7. made it easy for me to ask for help — 1 2 3 4 5 6 7
8. quickly improved my skill — 1 2 3 4 5 6 7
9. made a difference in my grades — 1 2 3 4 5 6 7
10. helped me feel better about myself — 1 2 3 4 5 6 7
11. gave me things I liked to earn — 1 2 3 4 5 6 7
12. helped me do better in school overall — 1 2 3 4 5 6 7
13. is one I would tell other kids about — 1 2 3 4 5 6 7
14. is one I would do over again if I had to — 1 2 3 4 5 6 7

What else do you think?

_____

**FORM 4.17** *Sample Post-Intervention Social Validity: Student and Acceptability*

**Student Post-Intervention Acceptability and Importance of Effects Survey (Gr. 7–12)**

Date: _____

Name: _____ Teacher: _____

I reached my goal:____Yes ____No ____Some

For each item, please circle the number that best tells what you think about the intervention that you just finished.

|  | Strongly Disagree | | Neutral 50/50 | | Strongly Agree | |
|---|---|---|---|---|---|---|
| The intervention: | | | | | | |
| 1. was easy for me to stick with | 1 2 3 4 5 6 7 |
| 2. was approved by my parents | 1 2 3 4 5 6 7 |
| 3. taught me important skills | 1 2 3 4 5 6 7 |
| 4. was fair to me | 1 2 3 4 5 6 7 |
| 5. helped me change in important ways | 1 2 3 4 5 6 7 |
| 6. helped me make more friends | 1 2 3 4 5 6 7 |
| 7. made it easy for me to ask for help | 1 2 3 4 5 6 7 |
| 8. quickly improved my skill | 1 2 3 4 5 6 7 |
| 9. made a difference in my grades | 1 2 3 4 5 6 7 |
| 10. helped me feel better about myself | 1 2 3 4 5 6 7 |
| 11. helped me want to stay in school | 1 2 3 4 5 6 7 |
| 12. helped me learn skills to help in life | 1 2 3 4 5 6 7 |
| 13. is one I would recommend to friends | 1 2 3 4 5 6 7 |
| 14. is one I would do again, if necessary | 1 2 3 4 5 6 7 |

What else do you think?

_____

_____

**FORM 4.18** *Sample Post-Intervention Social Validity: Student and Acceptability*

## Student Participant Interview

Student Participant: _____     Interventionist: _____

Interviewer: _____     Date: _____

1.  Did you like being in this special program?     _____Yes    _____No

2.  What did you like best about the special program?

_____

3.  Did you like…

| | Not Much | A Little | A Lot |
|---|---|---|---|
| being out of class? | * | ** | *** |
| spending time with the group leader? | * | ** | *** |
| earning prizes? | * | ** | *** |
| learning new skills? | * | ** | *** |

4.  Do you feel you learned important things?     _____Yes    _____No

If yes, What is/are the most important thing(s) you learned?

_____

5.  Did you learn things that will

| | Not Much | A Little | A Lot |
|---|---|---|---|
| help you do better work in school? | * | ** | *** |
| help you get along with other kids? | * | ** | *** |
| help you make good choices? | * | ** | *** |
| help you at home? | * | ** | *** |

6.  Do you use the skills that you learned in our special program? ____Yes ____No

If yes, where do you use these skills?

| | Not Much | A Little | A Lot |
|---|---|---|---|
| in class? | * | ** | *** |
| with your teacher? | * | ** | *** |

**FORM 4.19**   *Children's Social Validity Interview (CSVI)*

*Source:* Adapted from K. L. Lane (1997), *Students At-risk for Antisocial Behavior: The Utility of Academic and Social Skills Interventions*. Doctoral dissertation.

| | | | |
|---|---|---|---|
| with your friends? | * | ** | *** |
| with other kids? | * | ** | *** |
| at home? | * | ** | *** |

7. Do you wish our special program could have lasted longer? (Clarify...meet for more time, like for another week?)     _____Yes     _____No

If yes, how much longer would you like to have met? _____

8.   Is there anything else you would like to tell me about our special program?

_____

_____

_____

**FORM 4.19**   *Continued*

*References* _____

Alexander, K., Entwisle, D., & Dauber, S. (1994). *On the success of failure: A measurement of the effects of primary grade retention.* New York: Cambridge University Press.

Baer, D. M., Wolf, M. M., & Risley, T. R. (1968). Some current dimensions of applied behavior analysis. *Journal of Applied Behavior Analysis, 1,* 91–97.

Baer, D. M., Wolf, M. M., & Risley, T. R. (1987). Some still-current dimensions of applied behavior analysis. *Journal of Applied Behavior Analysis, 20,* 313–327.

Bergan, J., & Kratochwill, T. (1990). *Behavioral consultation and therapy.* New York: Plenum Press.

Brody, G. H., & Stoneman, Z. (1992). Child competence and developmental goals among rural black families: Investigating the links. In I. E. Siegel, A. V. McGillicuddy-DeLisi, & J. J. Goodnow (Eds.), *Parental belief systems: The psychological consequences for children* (pp. 415–431). Hillsdale, NJ: Erlbaum.

Brown, B. B., Mounts, N., Lamborn, S. D., & Steinberg, L. (1993). Parenting practices and peer group affiliation in adolescence. *Child Development, 64,* 467–482.

Chang, C. (1988). Matching teaching styles and learning styles and verification of students' learning adaptation model. *Bulletin of Educational Psychology,* 113–172.

Coie, J., & Krehbiel, G. (1984). Effects of academic tutoring on the social status of low-achieving, socially rejected children. *Child Development, 55,* 1465–1478.

DuPaul, G., & Eckert, T. (1994). The effects of social skills curricula: Now you see them, now you don't. *School Psychology Quarterly, 9,* 113–132.

Elliott, D., Hamburg, B. A., & Williams, K. (1998). *Violence in American schools: A new perspective.* New York: Cambridge University Press.

Elliott, S.N. (1988). Acceptability of behavioral treatments in educational settings. In J. Witt, S. Elliott, & F. Gresham (Eds.), *Handbook of behavior therapy in education,* (pp. 121–150). New York: Plenum Press.

Elliott, S. N., Turco, T. L., & Gresham, F. M. (1987). Consumers' and clients' pretreatment acceptability ratings of classroom-based group contingencies. *Journal of School Psychology, 25,* 145–154.

Elliott, S. N., Witt, J. D., Galvin, G. A., & Moe, G. L. (1986). Children's involvement in intervention selection: Acceptability of interventions for misbehaving peers. *Professional Psychology: Research and Practice, 17,* 235–241.

Elliott, S. N., Witt, J. D., & Kratochwill, T. R. (1996). Selecting, implementing, and evaluating classroom interventions. In G. Stoner, M. R. Shinn, & H. M. Walker (Eds.), *Interventions for Achievement and Behavior Problems* (2nd ed.), (pp. 99–135). Bethesda, MD: National Association of School Psychologists.

Evertson, C. M., & Weade, R. (1989). Classroom management and teaching style: Instructional stability and variability in two junior high English classrooms. *Elementary School Journal, 89,* 379–393.

Falk, K. B., & Wehby, J. H. (2001). The effects of peer-assisted learning strategies on the beginning reading skills of young children with emotional or behavioral disorders. *Behavioral Disorders, 26,* 344–359.

Fawcett, S. (1991). Social validity: A note on methodology. *Journal of Applied Behavior Analysis, 24,* 235–239.

Finn, C. A., & Sladeczek, I. E. (2001). Assessing the social validity of behavior interventions: A review of treatment acceptability measures. *School Psychology Quarterly, 16,* 176–206.

Gresham, F. M. (1998). Designs for evaluating behavioral change: Conceptual principles of single case methodology. In T. Watson & F. Gresham (Eds.), *Handbook of child behavior therapy.* New York, Plenum Press.

Gresham, F. M., & Elliott, S. N. (1990). *Social Skills Rating System (SSRS).* Circle Pines, MN: American Guidance Service.

Gresham, F. M., & Kendell, G. K. (1987). School consultation research: Methodological critique and future directions. *School Psychology Review, 16,* 306–316.

Gresham, F. M., & Lopez, M. F. (1996). Social validation: A unifying construct for school-based consultation research and practice. *School Psychology Quarterly, 11,* 204–227.

Hawkins, R. (1991). Is social validity what we are interested in? Argument for a functional approach. *Journal of Applied Behavior Analysis, 24,* 205–213.

Hinshaw, S. P. (1992). Externalizing behavior problems and academic underachievement in childhood and adolescence: Causal relationships and underlying mechanisms. *Psychological Bulletin, 111,* 127–155.

Hollenbeck, J. R., & Williams, C. R. (1987). Goal importance, self-focus, and the goal-setting process. *Journal of Applied Psychology, 72*, 204–211.

Kazdin, A. E. (1977). Assessing the clinical or applied significance of behavior change through social validation. *Behavior Modification, 1*, 427–452.

Kazdin, A. E. (1980a). Acceptability of alternative treatments for deviant child behavior. *Journal of Applied Behavior Analysis, 13*, 259–273.

Kazdin, A. E. (1981). Acceptability of child treatment techniques: The influence of treatment efficacy and adverse side effects. *Behavior Therapy, 12*, 493–506.

Kelley, M. J., Heffer, R. W., Gresham, F. M., & Elliott, S. N. (1989). Development of a modified Treatment Evaluation Inventory. *Journal of Psychopathology & Behavioral Assessment, 11*, 235–247.

Keogh, B. K., & Weisner, T. (1993). An ecocultural perspective on risk and protective factors in children's development: Implications for learning disabilities. *Learning Disabilities Research & Practice, 8*, 3–10.

Kerr, M. M., & Zigmond, N. (1986). What do high school teachers want? A study of expectations and standards. *Education and Treatment of Children, 9*, 239–249.

Landon, T., & Mesinger, J. F. (1989). Teacher tolerance ratings on problem behaviors. *Behavioral Disorders, 14*, 236–249.

Lane, K. L. (1997). *Students at-risk for antisocial behavior: The utility of academic and social skills interventions.* Doctoral dissertation.

Lane, K. L. (1999). Young students at risk for antisocial behavior: The utility of academic and social skills interventions. *Journal of Emotional and Behavioral Disorders, 7*, 211–223.

Lane, K. L., Beebe-Frankenberger, M. E., Lambros, K. L., & M. E., Pierson (2001). Designing effective interventions for children at-risk for antisocial behavior: An integrated model of components necessary for making valid inferences. *Psychology in the Schools, 38*, 365–379.

Lane, K. L., Givner, C. C., & Pierson, M. R. (in press). Teacher expectations of student behavior: Social skills necessary for success in elementary school classrooms. *Journal of Special Education.*

Lane, K. L., Mahdavi, J. N., & Borthwick-Duffy, S. A. (in press). Teacher perceptions of the pre-referral intervention process: A call for assistance with school-based interventions. *Preventing School Failure.*

Lane, K. L., O'Shaughnessy, T., Lambros, K. M., Gresham, F. M., & Beebe-Frankenberger, M. (2001). The efficacy of phonological awareness training with students who have externalizing and hyperactive-inattentive behavior problems. *Journal of Emotional and Behavioral Disorders, 9*, 219–231.

Loeber, R., & Farrington, D. (Eds.) (1998). *Serious and violent juvenile offenders: Risk factors and successful interventions.* Thousand Oaks, CA: Sage.

Martens, B. K., Witt, J. C., Elliott, S. N., & Darveaux, D. (1985). Teacher judgments concerning the acceptability of school-based interventions. *Professional Psychology: Research and Practice, 16*, 191–198.

Miltenberger, R. G. (1990). Assessment of treatment acceptability: A review of the literature. *Topics in Early Childhood Special Education, 10*, 24–38.

Noell, G. H., & Gresham, F. M. (1993). Functional outcome analysis: Do the benefits of consultation and prereferral interventions justify the costs? *School Psychology Quarterly, 8*, 200–226.

Okagaki, L., & Sternberg, R. J. (1993). Parental beliefs and children's school performance. *Child Development, 64*, 36–56.

O'Neill, R. E., Horner, R. H., Albin, R. W., Sprague, J. R., Storey, K., & Newton, J. S. (1997). *Functional assessment and program development for problem behavior: A practical handbook* (2nd ed.). Boston: Brooks/Cole.

Parker, J., & Asher, S. (1987). Peer relations and later personal adjustment. *Psychological Bulletin, 102*, 357–389.

Reid, J. B., & Patterson, G. R. (1991). Early prevention and intervention with conduct problems: A social interactional model for the integration of research and practice. In G. Stoner, M. R. Shinn, & H. M. Walker (Eds.), *Interventions for achievement and behavior problems* (pp. 715–739). Silver Springs, MD: National Association of School Psychologists.

Reimers, T. M., & Wacker, D. P. (1988). Parents' ratings of the acceptability of behavioral treatment recommendations made in an outpatient clinic: A preliminary analysis of the influence of treatment effectiveness. *Behavior Disorders, 14*, 7–15.

Reimers, T. M., Wacker, D. P., Derby, K. M., & Cooper, L. J. (1995). Relation between parental attributions and the acceptability of behavioral treatments for their child's behavior problems. *Behavioral Disorders, 20,* 171–178.

Reimers, T. M., Wacker, D. P., & Koeppl, G. (1987). Acceptability of behavioral treatments: A review of the literature. *School Psychology Review, 15,* 212–227.

Safran, S. P., & Safran, J. S. (1984). Elementary teachers' tolerance of problem behaviors. *Elementary School Journal, 85,* 237–243.

Safran, S. P., Safran, J. S., & Barcikowski, R. S. (1985). Differences in teacher tolerance: An illusory phenomena? *Behavioral Disorders, 11,* 11–16.

Schaefer, E. S., & Edgerton, M. (1985). Parent and child correlates of parental modernity. In I. E. Sigel (Ed.), *Parental belief systems: The psychological consequences for children,* (pp. 287–318). Hillsdale, NJ: Erlbaum.

Shinn, M. R., Tindal, G. A., & Spira, D. A. (1987). Special education referrals as an index of teacher tolerance: Are teachers imperfect tests? *Exceptional Children, 54,* 32–40.

Sideridis, G. D. (2002). Goal importance and students at risk of having language difficulties: An underexplored aspect of student motivation. *Journal of Learning Disabilities, 35,* 343–356.

Tarnowski, K. J., & Simonian, S. J. (1992). Assessing treatment acceptance: The Abbreviated Acceptability Rating Profile. *Journal of Behavioral Therapy and Experimental Psychiatry, 23,* 101–106.

Teeter, P. A. (1998). *Interventions for ADHD: Treatment in developmental context.* New York: Guilford Press.

Turco, T. L., & Elliott, S. N. (1986). Student's acceptability ratings of interventions for classroom misbehaviors: A study of well-behaving and misbehaving youth. *Journal of Psychoeducational Assessment, 4,* 281–289.

VonBrock, M., & Elliott, S. N. (1987). The influence of treatment effectiveness information on the acceptability of classroom interventions. *Journal of School Psychology, 25,* 131–144.

Walker, H. M., Colvin, G., & Ramsey, E. (1995). *Antisocial behavior in school: Strategies and best practices.* Pacific Grove, CA: Brooks/Cole.

Walker, H. M., Irvin, L. K., Noell, G, H., & Singer, G. H. (1992). A constructive score approach to the assessment of social competence: Rationale, technological considerations, and anticipated outcomes. *Behavior Modification, 16,* 448–474.

Walker, H. M., McConnell, S., & Clarke, J. Y. (1985). Social skills training in school settings: A model for the social integration of handicapped children into less restrictive settings. In R. McMahon & R. D. Peters (Eds.), *Childhood disorders: Behavior-developmental approaches* (pp. 140–168). New York: Brunner/Mazel.

Walker, H. M., & Rankin, R. (1983). Assessing the behavioral expectations and demands of less restrictive settings. *School Psychology Review, 12,* 274–284.

Walker, H. M., Zeller, R. W., Close, D. W., Webber, J., & Gresham, F. (1999). The present unwrapped: Change and challenge in the field of behavior disorders. *Behavior Disorders, 24,* 293–304.

Webster-Stratton, C., & Reid, J. (2002). An integrated approach to prevention and management of aggressive behavior problems in preschool and elementary grade students: Schools and parent collaboration. In K. L. Lane, F. M. Gresham, & T. E. O'Shaughnessy (Eds.), *Interventions for children with or at risk for emotional and behavioral disorders* (pp. 260–278). Boston: Allyn & Bacon.

Witt, J. C., & Elliott, S. N. (1983, August). *Assessing the acceptability of behavioral interventions.* Paper presented at the annual meeting of the American Psychological Association, Anaheim, CA.

Witt, J. C., & Elliott, S. N. (1985). Acceptability of classroom intervention strategies. In T. R. Kratochwill (Ed.), *Advances in school psychology* (Vol. 4). Mahwah, NJ: Erlbaum.

Witt, J. C., & Martens, B. (1983). Assessing the acceptability of behavioral interventions used in classrooms. *Psychology in the Schools, 20,* 510–517.

Wolf, M. M. (1978). Social validity: The case for subjective measurement or how applied behavior analysis is finding its heart. *Journal of Applied Behavior Analysis, 11,* 203–214.

# 5

## *Treatment Integrity*

### *Is the Intervention Really Happening?*

### *What Do We Mean by Treatment Integrity?*

Treatment integrity, also known as treatment fidelity or reliability of the independent variable, refers to the degree to which the intervention plan was put into place as originally designed (Gresham, 1989, 1998; Yeaton & Sechrest, 1981; also see Box 5.1). In other words, was the intervention implemented as intended (see Figure 5.1, item E)?

School-based interventions, whether primary, secondary, or tertiary (see Chapter 1), are all designed with the goal of achieving a change in academic, social, or behavioral performance. For example, when a school faculty decides to implement a schoolwide discipline plan, the goal is to implement an intervention for all students attending the school in order to prevent the misbehavior (e.g., noncompliance, talking without permission) and promote those behaviors (e.g., following directions, task completion) that facilitate the learning process (Lane, Givner, & Pierson, in press; Walker, Irvin, Noell, & Singer, 1992). Similarly, when an Individualized Educational Plan (IEP) team decides to design and implement a positive behavioral support program to address the concern of physical aggression toward peers (e.g., hitting students to get a toy), the goal is to provide an intervention program that will decrease either the frequency or intensity of aggressive episodes and at the same time increase the frequency of a functionally equivalent replacement behavior (e.g., asking the student to borrow a toy). In this case, the intervention is designed to decrease a specific problem behavior and increase a prosocial behavior. In both of these examples, the treatment agents (faculty and IEP team) design interventions based on empirically validated practices with the intent of preventing (primary interventions) or remediating (tertiary interventions) problem behaviors (see Box 5.2). However, if steps are not taken to monitor the degree to which each intervention step is implemented as originally designed, it is difficult to draw accurate conclusions about the extent to which the intervention worked or was effective.

**BOX 5.1 • *Treatment Integrity Defined***

> ***Treatment Integrity***
>
> (Gresham, 1989, 1998; Yeaton & Sechrest, 1989)
>
> Treatment integrity refers to the degree to which a specific intervention plan is put in place (implemented) as designed.

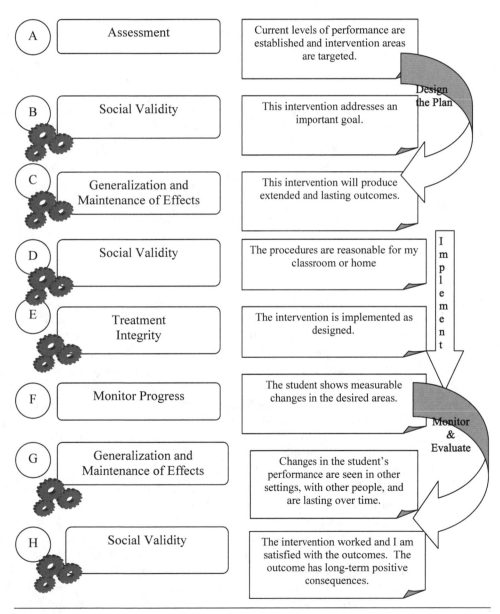

**FIGURE 5.1    *The Intervention Process***

**BOX 5.2 • *Practical Applications of Treatment Integrity***

Jennifer is a first-grade, general education student who has become increasingly aggressive and noncompliant with her teacher, Mrs. Beasley. At the beginning of the school year, Jennifer often refused to participate in the literacy activities stating that they were too hard. Over the past four months, Jennifer's behavior has become more challenging to manage. In addition to using inappropriate words in the classroom and yelling at Mrs. Beasley, Jennifer has become physically aggressive (i.e., hitting, pushing, and pinching) with her peers. Jennifer does not yet know all of the letters in the alphabet but has awareness of the individual sounds that constitute words. She has become even more resistant to participating in literacy activities; however, she does enjoy listening to stories and doing science activites. Her mother, Mrs. Anderson, has expressed concern about Jennifer "pitching a fit" when asked to do homework. Ultimately, the mother winds up doing the homework for her.

Mrs. Beasley and Mrs. Anderson held a conference with the principal and counselor. They decided to implement a secondary intervention in the classroom and a tertiary home-school intervention. The secondary intervention will focus on improving Jennifer's phonemic awareness skills so that she will be better prepared to participate in the literacy skills during class time. Mrs. Beasley suggested involving three other students in the class to also participate in this small group intervention. The intervention will be conducted by a student teacher during centers time. The group will meet four days a week for twenty minutes. Mrs. Beasley will monitor treatment integrity of the intervention process with the use of a treatment integrity checklist once a week. Jennifer will also be asked to self-evaluate treatment integrity by completing the treatment integrity checklists. However, Jennifer will be asked to complete the checklists on a daily basis immediately following each lesson. The tertiary intervention will involve a school-home note system (see Forms 5.6 and 5.7). The goal of the school-home note system is to increase the number of activities and assignments that Jennifer attempts. Treatment integrity of the tertiary intervention will be evaluated using permanent products.

## Why Is It Important to Monitor Treatment Integrity?

If we do not assess treatment integrity, then we do not know if the intervention simply did not produce the desired change or if the intervention was altered in some way that might have influenced the outcomes (e.g., adding two servings of chocolate fudge cake to the diet plan of the week; hmmm . . . I wonder why I gained 2 lbs? I have been dieting all week!). Conversely, what if the intervention produces results that are consistent with the original goals but you did not monitor treatment integrity? In this situation, you cannot be certain that it was the intervention that was responsible for the change. It is possible that the person implementing the intervention (e.g., classroom teacher or school psychologist) might have altered the intervention by adding, deleting, or modifying some of the components and it was actually the modified intervention that resulted in the desired outcomes. For example, consider the case of an intervention designed to improve a class's problem-solving skills in mathematics. The original intervention design required one or two students to come to the board to solve problems. However, the teacher, recognizing that students are likely to benefit from increased opportunities to respond (Rosenberg, 1986; Sindelar, Rosenberg, Wilson, & Bursuck, 1984; Skinner & Shapiro, 1989; Skinner, Turco, Beatty, & Rasavage, 1989; Sutherland, Wehby, & Yoder, 2002), modified the intervention during the third week of implementation. Instead of one or two students coming to the board, Mrs. Schumaker

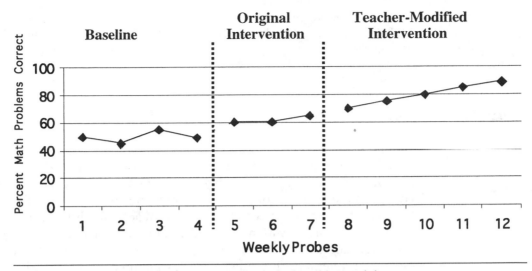

**FIGURE 5.2**    *Classwide Progress on Mathematical Problem-Solving*

gave each student a small chalk board and asked everyone in the class to attempt each problem. This modification dramatically increased each student's opportunity to respond. In graphing the data (see Figure 5.2), it is evident that problem-solving skills accuracy showed marked improvement with the introduction of this modification. Had treatment integrity data not been collected, it would not have been possible to explain the increased performance that occurred during the third week of the intervention. In this case, the modification was associated with improved outcomes. In other cases, alterations might not prove as effective. In order to draw valid, accurate conclusions about intervention outcomes, it is imperative that treatment integrity be evaluated (Gresham, 1998).

Unless it can be clearly shown that the student's behavior changed only when the intervention was introduced, you cannot state with certainty that intervention prompted the change. In research terminology, the absence of treatment integrity poses a major threat to the internal validity of study. Further, if we cannot be sure of the relationship between the intervention or treatment procedure and the target behavior (internal validity), then we cannot say with confidence that this type of intervention should be effective with other students with similar types of problems (external validity). In other words, if treatment integrity is not assessed then it is not possible to generalize the findings of this particular intervention to other students, treatment agents, and other settings (see Figure 5.1, items E–G). It also makes it difficult for other people to use the same intervention technique if the details are not specified and the necessity of each component verified (Lane, Beebe-Frankenberger, Lambros, & Pierson, 2001). Sometimes minor adjustments to the intervention plan can result in major differences in the outcomes (e.g., omitting sour cream and adding cream cheese to a beef stroganoff recipe).

Given the importance of treatment integrity as it relates to internal validity and external validity, it is surprising that treatment integrity is seldom monitored in both the research and teaching communities (Gresham, Gansle, & Noell, 1993). A great deal of attention has been devoted to defining and measuring student behaviors (dependent variables) as they participate in various interventions; yet, little attention has been given to defining and measuring the precision with which the intervention (independent variable) is put in place. This circumstance has been referred to a "curious double standard" (Peterson, Homer, & Wonderlich, 1982; Gresham, MacMillan, Beebe-Frankenberger, & Bocian, 2000; Lane, Bocian, MacMillan, & Gresham, 2003).

## Why Aren't Interventions Implemented with Integrity?

When an intervention is altered in some manner, treatment integrity is compromised. Yet teachers and other professionals, also referred to as treatment agents, are typically not making these changes in a random fashion. We contend that when a change is made to the original treatment, the change, at least in part, may reflect the treatment agents' views about the social acceptability of the intervention procedures (see Figure 5.1, items D and E). In other words, if the treatment agents view the intervention as socially valid (see Chapter 4, Social Validity), then they are likely to implement the intervention as planned (high integrity). However, if the intervention is not seen as socially valid, then they are likely to modify the intervention in minor (moderate integrity) or major (low integrity) ways.

Thus, treatment integrity can be thought of as a mediating link between treatment acceptability and the use of interventions (Gresham et al., 2000; Gresham, McIntyre, Olson-Tinker, Dolstra, McLaughlin, & Van, 2000; Witt & Elliott, 1985; Yeaton & Sechrest, 1981). If the treatment agent views the intervention goals as significant and the intervention procedures as acceptable (Kazdin, 1977; Wolf, 1978), then the intervention will most likely be implemented with greater fidelity (high treatment integrity) as compared to those interventions viewed as targeting insignificant goals and requiring unacceptable procedures (low treatment integrity; Gresham, MacMillan et al., 2000). Interventions implemented with high treatment integrity are, consequently, likely to produce the desired goals (e.g., improved student performance). In brief, socially valid interventions are likely to be implemented with greater integrity and, therefore, are likely to meet with positive outcomes. So, why are not all interventions implemented with integrity?

Research suggests that a number of factors are believed to be related to treatment integrity (Gresham, 1989). These factors include intervention complexity, implementation time, materials required, views about effectiveness, and motivation of the person responsible for the intervention. In brief, if the intervention appears to be overly complex and time consuming, it is less likely to be implemented as planned (Yeaton & Sechrest, 1981). If the intervention requires additional resources or materials that are typically unavailable in a general education classroom, it is unlikely that the interventions will be implemented with integrity. Poor treatment integrity is also likely when more than one adult or treatment agent is necessary to implement the intervention. As mentioned earlier, perceptions of social acceptability also influence implementation. If the person responsible for conducting the intervention views the intervention to be potentially effective, he/she is more likely to implement the intervention with a high level of integrity than if he/she viewed the intervention as potentially ineffective. Lastly, motivation of the treatment agent also plays a role. If the teacher feels that he or she cannot meet the student's needs in the general education classroom, it is possible that the teacher may not implement an intervention with a high level of accuracy if the intervention is designed to keep the student in his or her classroom (Witt & Martens, 1983). If the teacher feels the child would be better served in an alternate setting and the goal is not to identify a way to better serve the student in the general education setting (Ysseldyke, Christenson, Pianta, & Algozzine, 1983), then poor treatment integrity is likely to follow.

## How Do We Assess Treatment Integrity?

Given that treatment integrity is a necessary component of designing and evaluating intervention outcomes, it is essential to understand how treatment integrity can be assessed. A number of strategies that range from direct to indirect approaches are available for monitoring treatment integrity including direct observation procedures, behavior rating scales, self-reporting strategies, permanent products, and manualized treatments (Elliott & Busse, 1993; Gresham, MacMillan et al., 2000; Lane et al., 2003).

### Direct Observation Procedures

Treatment integrity can be assessed using direct observation procedures. A trained observer can either watch the intervention as it occurs in the classroom or watch a video of the intervention at a later date to code treatment integrity. Direct observation of treatment integrity involves three steps (Gresham, MacMillan et al., 2000). First, a detailed list of each treatment component (also referred to as a task analysis) is developed (see Form 5.1). Each component must be defined in operational terms in order to limit the amount of inference necessary to determine whether or not the component was present. To the extent possible, the definitions should be defined along verbal, spatial, temporal, and physical parameters. However, it is important that the definitions not be so precise and the tasks so specific that the list becomes cumbersome for the observer to complete (Gresham, MacMillan et al., 2000). Second, the observer records whether or not each treatment component occurred. Third, the level of integrity by session and by component is computed.

For example, in Form 5.1 you will see that the intervention, Phonological Awareness Training for Reading (PATR; Torgeson & Bryant, 1994), contains nine components. According to the observer, the intervention leader successfully implemented eight out of the nine components. Apparently, the picture cards were not presented so that each of the four students in the group could see the cards. As such, the session integrity rating for lesson 24 is 89.9%. Session integrity is computed by dividing the number of components present by the total number of components in the intervention (eight divided by nine) and then multiplying by 100.

$$\text{Percentage (\%)} = (\text{number of components present} \div \text{total number of components}) \times 100$$

It is also possible to compute component integrity by looking at all of the treatment integrity ratings across several lessons (see Form 5.2). In this example, you see the same components included in Form 5.1; however, this time space is provided to evaluate treatment integrity over five consecutive lessons. When completing this form, the person observing or conducting the lesson will write a "1" if the component was addressed and a "0" if the component was not present. Then, session integrity is computed as explained in the previous paragraph for each of the five sessions (labeled A through E). Component integrity is computed by dividing the number of times the component was present over a fixed set of lessons (in this

# Phonological Awareness Training for Reading (PATR)
## Torgeson & Bryant (1994)
### Treatment Integrity Checklist

Intervention Leader:  <u>Mr. Hemsely</u>                               Date: <u>1/5/02</u>

Lesson #: <u>24</u>          Students Present: <u>Katie, Nathan, Ryan, Bryce,</u>

Intervention Level: __ Primary      ✓ Secondary          __ Tertiary

| Component | Present? | |
|---|---|---|
| | Yes | No |
| 1. Explained each activity correctly and clearly. | X | |
| 2. Pronounced individual word sounds correctly. | X | |
| 3. Presented picture cards in correct sequence. | X | |
| 4. Placed picture cards so that every student could see. | | X |
| 5. Modeled each activity before asking students to perform the activity. | X | |
| 6. Provided each student an opportunity to respond. | X | |
| 7. Provided corrective feedback for incorrect answers. | X | |
| 8. Provided positive reinforcement for correct answers (e.g., praise). | X | |
| 9. Maintained appropriate, quick pacing throughout the lesson. | X | |
| Total | 8 | 1 |

**FORM 5.1**   *Sample Treatment Integrity Protocol for PATR*

Adapted from K. L. Lane, T. Fletcher, J. DeLorenzo, & V. McLaughlin (in preparation). "Improving Early Literacy Skills of Young Children At-risk for Antisocial Behavior: Collateral Effects on Behavior.

case five lessons) and then dividing by the total number of times it was possible for that component to be presented.

Percentage (%)  =  (number of times the component was present ÷
total number of times the component could be present) × 100

For example, consider component 1. In Form 5.2 you will see that component 1 was present in four out of the five lessons being evaluated. Component integrity

Phonological Awareness Training for Reading (PATR)
Torgeson & Bryant (1994)
Weekly Treatment Integrity Checklist

Intervention Leader:    Mr. Hemsley          Week: 1/5/02          Lesson #: 24-28

Students Present:  Katie, Nathan, Ryan, Bryce,

Intervention Level:  __ Primary    ✓ Secondary    __ Tertiary

Phonological Awareness Training: Treatment Integrity Checklist

| Component | Monday | Tuesday | Wednesday | Thursday | Friday | Component Integrity |
|---|---|---|---|---|---|---|
| | Present | Present | Present | Present | Present | |
| 1. Explained each activity correctly and clearly. | 1 | 1 | 0 | 1 | 1 | F 80% |
| 2. Pronounced individual word sounds correctly. | 1 | 1 | 1 | 1 | 1 | G 100% |
| 3. Presented picture cards in correct sequence. | 1 | 1 | 1 | 1 | 1 | H 100% |
| 4. Placed picture cards so that every student could see. | 1 | 1 | 1 | 1 | 1 | I 100% |
| 5. Modeled each activity. | 1 | 1 | 1 | 0 | 1 | J 80% |
| 6. Provided each student an opportunity to respond. | 1 | 1 | 1 | 1 | 1 | K 100% |
| 7. Provided corrective feedback for incorrect answers. | 1 | 1 | 1 | 1 | 1 | L 100% |
| 8. Provided positive reinforcement for correct answers (praise). | 1 | 1 | 1 | 1 | 1 | M 100% |
| 9. Maintained appropriate, quick pacing throughout the lesson. | 0 | 0 | 1 | 1 | 1 | N 60% |
| Total | A | B | C | D | E 100% | OVERALL MEAN |

FORM 5.2  *Weekly Treatment Integrity: PATR*

*Note:* If the component is present, write '1'; if the component is not present, write '0'.

Adapted from F. M. Gresham (1989). "Assessment of Treatment Integrity in School Consultation and Prereferral Intervention." *School Psychology Review, 18,* 37–50.

is computed by dividing the number of times the component was present by the total number of times the component could be present over five lessons (four divided by five) and then multiplying by 100. As such, the component integrity for component 1 is 80 percent during this week of the intervention. The process is repeated for components 2 through 9 (labeled G through N).

A number of researchers have used component checklists. Vaughn, Hughes, Schumm, and Klingner (1998) conducted an intervention to improve instruction of reading and writing skills of students being taught in an inclusive program. They used an intervention validity checklist (IVC) to monitor the extent to which the teacher implemented each element of the intervention. In this study, both the teacher and an outside observer completed the IVC, which assessed both the integrity and frequency of implementation of each component. Lane and colleagues used this method to monitor treatment integrity of secondary interventions focused on improving the phonological awareness skills of general education, at-risk first-grade students (Lane, O'Shaughnessy, Lambros, Gresham, & Beebe-Frankenberger, 2001; Lane, Wehby, Menzies, Gregg, Doukas, & Munton, 2002). In the Lane et al. (2002) study, an outside observer and the interventionist both collected treatment integrity data to look at the accuracy, or reliability, of independent observers. The interventionist indicated that the treatment integrity forms were useful in helping her to ensure that each step was implemented. Results indicated that the observer and the interventionist had highly similar ratings.

One of the benefits of collecting treatment integrity data using direct observation procedures is that it can be graphed along with student outcome data. This allows the teacher and other treatment agents to see the relationship between the intervention (independent variable) and the student behavior (e.g., oral reading fluency, phonemic awareness, and raising one's hand; dependent variable) as it relates to treatment integrity.

For example, in Figure 5.3 you see graph of oral reading fluency and treatment integrity. After collecting baseline data for four weeks on the number of

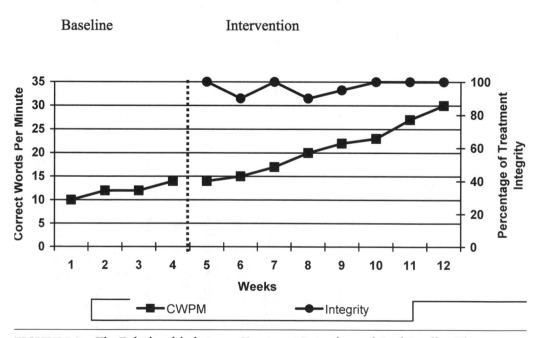

**FIGURE 5.3** *The Relationship between Treatment Integrity and Oral Reading Fluency*

words Jennifer, a first-grade student struggling in the area of reading, can read correctly in one minute, her teacher implemented a secondary, small-group intervention to develop Jennifer's phonological awareness skills. The program, Phonological Awareness Training for Reading (PATR; Torgesen & Bryant, 1994), was implemented by a student teacher four days a week with three other students in class who also had limited early literacy skills. Weekly data were collected to monitor Jennifer's progress in oral reading fluency (see the squares and solid dark line for correct words per minute, CWPM). Weekly treatment integrity data (overall session integrity ratings that were converted to percentages as described above) was plotted on the same graph to determine the relationship between treatment integrity and intervention outcomes (oral reading fluency). The graph indicates that intervention, which was implemented with very high rates of integrity, was associated with improvements in oral reading fluency. Notice how Jennifer's oral reading fluency was low and stable during the baseline phase and that her oral reading fluency showed improvement only when the intervention was introduced.

A more empirically sound design would include a withdrawal phase in which the intervention is withdrawn and data are collected to see if oral reading fluency either decreases or maintains. Using the withdrawal design, it is possible to identify functional relationships between independent variables (PATR) and dependent variables (CWPM). Namely, if the fluency measure (CWPM) increased only during those phases when the intervention (PATR) was being implemented, then one can concluded that the intervention (PATR) and not other, extraneous variables was responsible for the changes in student performance.

A drawback of using an outside observer to assess treatment integrity is that it can be difficult to obtain additional resources in light of budgetary constraints facing many schools. Another concern is the notion of observer reactivity. Namely, it is possible that the intervention may be implemented differently when the observer is present than when the observer is not present (Jones, Wickstrom, & Friman, 1997).

### Behavior Rating Scales

It is also possible to assess treatment integrity in a less direct method using behavior rating scales. This strategy requires an observer to view the entire treatment session and then complete a behavior rating scale (see Forms 5.3, 5.4, and 5.5). Rather than rating the presence or absence of each component during the intervention session, the ratings are based on observation of the entire treatment (Gresham, 1989; Gresham, MacMillan et al., 2000). A variety of scales could be used; we recommend using a four-point Likert type scale that ranges from *low integrity to high integrity* (see Form 5.3) or a four-point Likert type scale based on percentages (see Form 5.4).

### Self-Reporting Strategies

Self-reporting strategies, an indirect approach to assessment, can also be used to monitor treatment integrity. For example, the person conducting the intervention, usually the classroom teacher, can rate the degree to which he or she implemented each intervention component on a Likert-type scale (Gresham, MacMillan et al., 2000; also see Form 5.5). Self-reports are easy to complete and may actually serve

Corrective Reading: Decoding
Treatment Integrity Rating Scale

Teacher: _____   Date: _____   Grade Level: _____

Lesson #: _____   Number of Students Present: _____

Intervention Level: __ Primary   __ Secondary   __ Tertiary

| COMPONENT | | Low Integrity | | | High Integrity |
|---|---|---|---|---|---|
| 1. | Classroom is organized per program guidelines (assigned permanent seats & lower performing students in front). | 1 | 2 | 3 | 4 |
| 2. | Teacher uses scripted lesson during instruction. | 1 | 2 | 3 | 4 |
| 3. | Teacher used appropriate correction procedures (part firming). | 1 | 2 | 3 | 4 |
| 4. | Teacher maintained even, quick pace for exercises. | 1 | 2 | 3 | 4 |
| 5. | Teacher used signals per program guidelines. | 1 | 2 | 3 | 4 |
| 6. | Each student was offered multiple opportunities to participate. | 1 | 2 | 3 | 4 |
| 7. | Teacher provided positive reinforcement in the form of behavior specific verbal praise for correct responses. | 1 | 2 | 3 | 4 |
| 8. | Provided positive reinforcement by allocating points as specified in the program's point system. | 1 | 2 | 3 | 4 |
| 9. | Teacher brought students to 100% accuracy criterion on every task. | 1 | 2 | 3 | 4 |

**FORM 5.3**   *Treatment Integrity Rating Scale: Reading Intervention*

as a prompt to implement the intervention as designed. These rating scales can be completed midway through the intervention. Further, self-reports can be completed independently or as a supplement to direct observation methods.

In actuality, treatment integrity has most often been assessed by teacher report (Witt, Gresham, & Noell, 1996). Although this method is rather popular because it does not require the participation of a trained observer, self-report strategies may not be as objective as more direct procedures. Wickstrom (1995) stated

Corrective Reading: Decoding Treatment Integrity Rating Scale

Teacher: _____     Date: _____     Grade Level: _____

Lesson #: _____     Number of Students Present: _____

Intervention Level: __ Primary        __ Secondary        __ Tertiary

| COMPONENT | Absent (0) | Present 11-25% (1) | Present 26-50% (2) | Present 51-75% (3) | Present 76-100% (4) |
|---|---|---|---|---|---|
| 1. Classroom is organized per program guidelines (seat assignments & lower performing students in front). | 0 | 1 | 2 | 3 | 4 |
| 2. Teacher uses scripted lesson during instruction. | 0 | 1 | 2 | 3 | 4 |
| 3. Teacher used correction procedures (part firming) correctly. | 0 | 1 | 2 | 3 | 4 |
| 4. Teacher maintained even, quick pace for exercises. | 0 | 1 | 2 | 3 | 4 |
| 5. Teacher used signals correctly. | 0 | 1 | 2 | 3 | 4 |
| 6. Each student was offered multiple opportunities to participate. | 0 | 1 | 2 | 3 | 4 |
| 7. Teacher provided positive reinforcement (e.g., specific verbal praise) for correct responses. | 0 | 1 | 2 | 3 | 4 |
| 8. Provided positive reinforcement by allocating points as specified in the program's point system. | 0 | 1 | 2 | 3 | 4 |
| 9. Teacher brought students to 100% accuracy criterion on every task. | 0 | 1 | 2 | 3 | 4 |
| Total Score (sum of all ratings) | | | | | |
| Average Score (Average of all items) | | | | | |

**FORM 5.4**  *Treatment Integrity Rating Scale*

*Note:* For descriptions of specific components, see *SRA Corrective Reading Series Guide,* pp. 22–31, Teaching Techniques.

# Independent Group Contingency Plan with a Response Cost Component

Teacher: _____    Date: _____    Grade Level: _____

Lesson #: _____    Number of Students Present: _____

Intervention Level: ___ Primary    ___ Secondary    ___ Tertiary

| Components | Low Integrity | | | High Integrity |
|---|---|---|---|---|
| 1. I clearly stated and explained the rules and expectations to the students. | 1 | 2 | 3 | 4 |
| 2. I distributed a 4 x 6 index card to each student or taped the card on their desk. | 1 | 2 | 3 | 4 |
| 3. I allocated points by placing a tally mark on the student's index card. | 1 | 2 | 3 | 4 |
| 4. I took away points by crossing out a tally mark if student refused to participate or exhibited negative behavior (e.g., shouting or derogatory comments). Note. This should be rarely done and students should NEVER earn negative points for the week. | 1 | 2 | 3 | 4 |
| 5. At the end of the week, students who met the prespecified point criteria (e.g., 25 points week 1; 30 points week 2) traded in their points for a tangible reinforcer (e.g., pencil or eraser). Students with the most points chose first. | 1 | 2 | 3 | 4 |
| Total (sum of all points) Average (average of all items) | | | | |

**FORM 5.5**  *Independent Group Contingency Plan with a Response Cost*

that treatment integrity data collected using teacher self-report produced higher levels of treatment integrity in comparison to treatment integrity data collected using direct observation. It is possible that self-reports may be less accurate relative to direct measures, as the treatment agents may intentionally, or unintentionally, present their efforts in a more favorable light than actual practices due to social desirability effects (Gresham, MacMillan et al., 2000). However, as previously described, it is possible to assess treatment integrity from multiple perspectives (Lane et al., 2002; Vaughn et al., 1998), which may increase accuracy of responding.

### Permanent Products

Permanent products assessment is a more recent strategy used to assess treatment integrity. In brief, permanent product assessment involves specifying a permanent product for each intervention component. For example, if the teacher is to award a table group a point for all team members completing homework (a dependent group contingency plan), then the corresponding permanent product could be the hash mark indicated on the table's point card. If the table with the most points at the end of the day is to receive positive reinforcement in the form of an extrinsic reward (e.g., sticker or stamp), then the corresponding permanent product could be the sticker or stamp on the student's daily behavior chart. See Forms 5.6 and 5.7 for examples of how to monitor an independent group contingency plan with a response cost component using a permanent products approach.

### Manualized Interventions

Some interventions (e.g., SRA Corrective Reading Program) come with treatment manuals that contain explicit step-by-step guidelines for implementing the intervention. One of the benefits of using an empirically validated, manualized intervention is that the person (e.g., interventionist, teacher, paraprofessional, or parent volunteer) responsible for conducting the intervention has very specific guidelines for implementing it. The manual can be used when training the interventionist and when working with the students. However, one concern with presuming that manualized interventions will lead to higher treatment integrity ratings is that the treatment integrity information is not collected—it is assumed (and we all remember what our high school teachers said about making assumptions!).

Like the volumes of exercise books resting (in dust) on our bookshelves, treatment manuals can be viewed as a necessary—but not sufficient—method of ensuring that interventions are implemented as designed (Gresham, MacMillan et al., 2000). As such, it would be wise to use manualized treatments in conjunction with direct observation (see Forms 5.1 and 5.2), behavior rating scales (see Forms 5.3 and 5.4), self-reports (see Form 5.5), or permanent product methods (see Forms 5.6 and 5.7) of evaluating treatment integrity.

## Which Methods Should I Choose?

We have discussed a wide variety of approaches for monitoring treatment integrity, so how does one decide on which approach to use? What criteria should we use? Ease? Rigor?

At times this difference in treatment integrity ratings using different assessment approaches can be quite striking. To illustrate this point, consider the study conducted by Wickstrom, Jones, LaFleur, and Witt (1998). The purpose of this

School-Home Notes Guidelines

Intervention Leader: _____     Date : _____     Student: _____

Intervention Level: ___ Primary   ___ Secondary   ___ Tertiary

### Guidelines for Designing School-Home Notes

| Guideline | Permanent Product |
| --- | --- |
| Schedule a meeting with the teacher, the parent, and student to discuss the goals of the school-home notes (e.g., to increase the number of assignments Jennifer attempts at home and at school). | Notes from meeting |
| At this conference, define specific target behaviors that will be listed on the school-home note. (e.g., Jennifer will attempt to participate in every activity or complete each assignment). | Target behaviors defined |
| Include the following information on the notes: student's name, date, teacher's signature, parent signature, and space for the teacher to record whether or not the behavior occurred (see Form 7). | Note cards created |
| Establish the responsibilities of each party: | Collect and review weekly notes |
| Parents will (a) sign or initial the note daily, (b) give the note to their child every day before school; and (c) allocate reinforcers and consequences based on the child's daily performance as indicated on the card. | |
| The child will (a) take the note to school daily, (b) obtain the teacher's signature or initial each day, and (c) Bring the note home from school each day. | |
| The teacher will (a) evaluate each target behavior, (b) sign or initial the note daily, and (c) give the note to the student every day before going home. | |
| At the conference, delineate specific criteria for a "good" day based on points earned. | Create point system |
| At the conference, list reinforcers and consequences for "good" and "not good" days. Emphasize the importance of not scolding the child; just implement the system and provide praise as appropriate. At the conference, discuss the importance of consistency and follow through. | Lists created |
| Once the goals are being met, begin to fade the program (e.g., move from daily to weekly notes). However, do not stop the intervention immediately. | Collect and review weekly notes |

**FORM 5.6**   *Treatment Integrity: Permanent Product Evaluation*

*Source:* Adapted from S. Elliott & F. M. Gresham (1991). *Social Skills Intervention Guide.* Circle Pines, MN: American Guidance Service.

142

School-Home Note

Intervention Leader: _____ Date : _____ Student: _____

Intervention Level: ___ Primary ___ Secondary ___ Tertiary

| Behavior | Monday | Tuesday | Wednesday | Thursday | Friday |
|---|---|---|---|---|---|
| Participated in morning activities | | | | | |
| Attempted morning assignments | | | | | |
| Participated in afternoon activities | | | | | |
| Attempted morning assignments | | | | | |
| Attempted homework assignments | | | | | |
| Teacher's Initials | | | | | |
| Parent's Initials | | | | | |

Evaluation:  4 = outstanding
             3 = satisfactory
             2 = poor
             1 = unacceptable

Teacher Comments: _____

Parent Comments: _____

_____          _____
Teacher's Signature            Parent's Signature

FORM 5.7  *School-Home Note Card*

*Source:* Adapted from H. M. Walker, G. Colvin, & E. Ramsey (1995). *Antisocial Behavior in School: Strategies and Best Practices.* Albany, NY: Brooks/Cole.

study was to examine the relationship between independent variables, or intervention procedures, and three methods of assessing treatment integrity: use of intervention stimulus products across teachers, teacher self-report, and direct observation. Findings revealed tremendous differences in treatment integrity rates with respective treatment integrity scores of 62 percent for use of intervention stimulus produced across teachers, 54 percent for teacher self-report, and only 4 percent for direct observation of actual intervention use (Wickstrom et al., 1998). This result illustrates a concern that needs to be considered when selecting a method of assessing treatment integrity: at times there is a discrepancy between what people say they do and what they actually do (Bergan & Kratochwill, 1990).

## Summary

In the best of all situations, treatment integrity would be monitored from different perspectives: direct observations, behavior rating scales, and self-reports. This information would allow people to check the accuracy of their perceptions relative to an outside observer. Further, the information gleaned from multiple perspectives could also help to identify which components are indeed essential. It may be that omitting a certain step does not negatively influence intervention outcomes. Therefore, that component may not be necessary, and a more parsimonious intervention can be created.

However, it is not always feasible to assess treatment integrity from multiple perspectives. Therefore, we recommend that you select a method for evaluating treatment integrity that is as direct as possible, but one that is reasonable given your time and resource constraints. If monitoring integrity becomes too cumbersome, then it is less likely to be monitored for the duration of the intervention. If accurate conclusions are to be drawn about intervention outcomes, then treatment integrity must be assessed. As shown in Figure 5.1 item E, treatment integrity is a essential step when designing and implementing effective interventions. In addition, treatment integrity can lend support to achieving generalization and maintenance of new skills.

## References

Bergan, J., & Kratochwill, T. (1990). *Behavioral consultation and therapy.* New York: Plenum Press.

Elliott, S. N., & Busse, R. (1993). Effective treatments with behavioral consultation. In J. Zins, T. Kratochwill, & S. Elliott (Eds.), *Handbooks of consultation service for children* (pp.179–203). San Francisco: Jossey-Bass.

Gresham, F. M. (1989). Assessment of treatment integrity in school consultation and prereferral intervention. *School Psychology Review, 18,* 37–50.

Gresham, F. M. (1998). Designs for evaluating behavioral change: Conceptual principles of single case methodology. In T. Watson & F. Gresham (Eds.), *Handbook of child behavior therapy.* New York, Plenum Press.

Gresham, F. M., Gansle, K. A., & Noell, G. H. (1993). Treatment integrity in applied behavior analysis with children. *Journal of Applied Behavior Analysis, 26,* 257–263.

Gresham, F. M., & Lopez, M. F. (1996). Social validation: A unifying construct for school-based consultation research and practice. *School Psychology Quarterly, 11,* 204–227.

Gresham, F. M., MacMillan, D. L., Beebe-Frankenberger, M. E., & Bocian, K. M. (2000). Treatment integrity in learning disabilities intervention research: Do we really know how treatments are implemented? *Learning Disabilities Research & Practice, 15,* 198–205.

Gresham, F. M., McIntyre, L., Olson-Tinker, H., Dolstra, L., McLaughlin, V., & Van, M. (2000, March). Treatment integrity: Necessary, but not sufficient for treatment-based interventions.

Symposium conducted at the meeting of the National Association of School Psychologists, New Orleans, LA.

Jones, K. M., Wickstrom, K. F., & Friman, P. C. (1997). The effects of observational feedback on treatment integrity in school-based behavioral consultation. *School Psychology Quarterly, 12,* 316–326.

Kazdin, A. (1977). Assessing the clinical or applied importance of behavior change through social validation. *Behavior Modification, 1,* 427–452.

Lane, K. L., Beebe-Frankenberger, Lambros, K. L., & M. E., Pierson. (2001). Designing effective interventions for children at-risk for antisocial behavior: An integrated model of components necessary for making valid inferences. *Psychology in the Schools, 38,* 365–379.

Lane, K. L., Bocian, K. M., MacMillan, D. M., & Gresham, F. M. (2003). Treatment integrity: An essential—but often forgotten—component of school-based interventions. Unpublished manuscript.

Lane, K. L., Givner, C. C., & Pierson, M. R. (in press). Teacher expectations of student behavior: Social skills necessary for success in elementary school classrooms. *Journal of Special Education.*

Lane, K. L., O'Shaughnessy, T., Lambros, K. M., Gresham, F. M., & Beebe-Frankenberger, M. E. (2001). The efficacy of phonological awareness training with first-grade students who have behavior problems and reading difficulties. *Journal of Emotional and Behavioral Disorders, 9,* 219–231.

Lane, K. L., Wehby, J. H., Menzies, H. M., Gregg, R. M., Doukas, G. L., & Munton, S. M. (2002). Early literacy instruction for first-grade students at-risk for antisocial behavior. *Education and Treatment of Children, 25,* 438–458.

Peterson, L., Homer, A., & Wonderlich, S. (1982). The integrity of independent variables in behavior analysis. *Journal of Applied Behavior Analysis, 15,* 477–192.

Rosenberg, M. S. (1986). Maximizing the effectiveness of structured classroom management programs: Implementing rule-review procedures with disruptive and distractible students. *Behavioral Disorders, 11,* 239–248.

Sindelar, P. T., Rosenberg, M. S., Wilson, R. J., & Bursuck, W. D. (1984). The effects of group size and instructional method on the acquisition of mathematical concepts by fourth grade students. *Journal of Educational Research, 77,* 178–183.

Skinner, C. H., & Shapiro, E. S. (1989). A comparison of taped-words and drill interventions on reading fluency in adolescents with behavior disorders. *Education and Treatment of Children, 12,* 123–133.

Skinner, C. H., Turco, T. L., Beatty, K. L., & Rasavage, C. (1989). Cover, copy, and compare: A method for increasing multiplication performance. *School Psychology Review, 18,* 412–420.

Sutherland, K. S., Wehby, J. H., & Yoder, P. J. (2002). Examination of the relationship between teacher praise and opportunities for students with EBD to respond to academic requests. *Journal of Emotional and Behavioral Disorders, 10,* 5–13.

Torgesen, J. K., & Bryant, B. R. (1994). *Phonological awareness training for reading.* Austin, TX: ProEd.

Vaughn, S., Hughes, M., Schumm, J., & Klingner, J. (1998). A collaborative effort to enhance reading and writing instruction in inclusive classrooms. *Learning Disability Quarterly, 21,* 57–74.

Walker, H. M., Irvin, L. K., Noell, J., & Singer, G. H. (1992). A constructive score approach to the assessment of social competence: Rationale, technological considerations, and anticipated outcomes. *Behavior Modification, 16,* 448–474.

Wickstrom, K. (1995). *A study of the relationship among teacher, process and outcome variables with school-based consultation.* Unpublished doctoral dissertation, Louisiana State University, Baton Rouge.

Wickstrom, K., Jones, K., LaFleur, L., & Witt, J. (1998). An analysis of treatment integrity in school-based behavioral consultation. *School Psychology Quarterly, 13,* 141–154.

Witt, J. C., & Elliott, S. N. (1985). Acceptability of classroom intervention strategies. In T. R. Kratochwill (Ed.), *Advances in school psychology* (Vol. 4., pp. 251–288). Hillsdale, NJ: Erlbaum.

Witt, J. C., Gresham, F. M., & Noell, G. H. (1996). What's behavioral about behavioral consultation? *Journal of Educational and Psychological Consultation, 7,* 327–344.

Witt, J. C., & Martens, B. (1983). Assessing the acceptability of behavioral interventions used in classrooms. *Psychology in the Schools, 20,* 510–517.

Wolf, M. M. (1978). Social validity: The case for subjective measurement or how applied behavior analysis is finding its heart. *Journal of Applied Behavior Analysis, 11,* 203–214.

Yeaton, W., & Sechrest, L. (1981). Critical dimensions in the choice and maintenance of successful treatments: Strength, integrity, and effectiveness. *Journal of Consulting and Clinical Psychology, 49,* 156–167.

Ysseldyke, J. E., Christenson, S., Pianta, B., & Algozzine, B. (1983). An analysis of teachers' reasons and desired outcomes for students referred for psychoeducational assessment. *Journal of Psychoeducational Assessment, 1,* 73–83.

# 6

## *Generalization and Maintenance of Treatment Outcomes: Making It Last?*

### *What Is Generalization and Maintenance?*

When designing any type of intervention, there is the expectation that a student will learn new skills such as how to decode multisyllabic words, subtract across zeros with regrouping, manage anger using words rather than physical contact, and develop new friendships. Further, there is an expectation that the behavioral changes will represent meaningful, important changes (see Chapter 4, Social Validity) that will ultimately lead to significant lifestyle changes (e.g., improved reading skills or improved social interactions) for the students involved in the intervention (Baer, Wolf, & Risley, 1968; Dunlap, 1993; Horner, Dunlap, & Koegel, 1988). On one hand, interventions are designed with great detail in hopes of teaching explicit skills that are executed with precision. On the other hand, interventions are also designed with the goal of producing lasting changes with skills that can be easily adapted for use in novel learning conditions and with a variety of people. Thus, effective interventions must address a balance between two key concerns: discrimination and generalization (Gresham, 1994; Lane, Beebe-Frankenberger, Lambros, & Pierson, 2001; Stokes, 1992).

The first concern is discrimination. When discrimination is present, a given behavior or response will occur when a specific stimulus is present and will not occur when a different stimulus is present (Sulzer-Azaroff & Mayer, 1991). Consider a student who is being taught how to deliver a compliment in a social skills training group. If the student says to a friend in the social skills training session, "I like your Chicago Bulls jacket" and the friend is wearing a Chicago Bulls jacket, then stimulus control is evident. Namely, the student has learned how to discriminate when the compliment should be given. More technically, the response (e.g., giving a compliment) is said to be under stimulus control. Stimulus control refers to "systematic influence of an antecedent stimuli (or set of stimuli) on the probability of occurrence of a response" (Sulzer-Azaroff & Mayer, 1991, p. 598). However, if that same compliment is delivered to a friend who is wearing a Hornets jacket, then discrimination skills are less than refined and stimulus control is incomplete.

The second concern pertains to generalization. *Generalization* refers to the presence of the target behavior beyond the training session. For example, if the student delivers a compliment to other friends, in other settings, and for other behaviors, then generalization is occurring. More explicitly, generalization is traditionally defined as "the occurrence of relevant behavior under different, nontraining conditions (i.e., across subjects, settings, people, behaviors, and/or time) without the scheduling of the same events in those conditions as had been scheduled in the training conditions" (Stokes & Baer, 1977, p. 350). *Maintenance*, a term often heard in conjunction with the term generalization, refers to the presence of the target behavior over time (Stokes & Baer, 1977; Stokes & Osnes, 1989) even after the intervention has concluded (Lane et al., 2001; also see Box 6.1). Thus, generalization, in conjunction with maintenance, can be conceptualized as expanding stimulus control. Moreover, generalization can be also viewed as "an effective discriminative stimulus exert[ing] control over a targeted response in a nontraining setting" (Dunlap, 1993, p. 272).

Given that we conduct interventions with the goal of teaching students new, socially significant skills that will lead to *lasting* important social outcomes (see Figure 6.1, items C and G, and Chapter 4, Social Validity), it is important that the notions of generalization and maintenance be addressed prior to implementing an intervention.

## Why Is It Important to Consider Generalization and Maintenance?

When we think about altering a behavior, it is essential to recognize that both discrimination and generalization are necessary components of the intervention program. Think about these two concepts being on a continuum, with discrimination on one end and generalization on the other (Edelstein, 1989; also see Figure 6.2). When new skills (e.g., sound symbol relationships) are being taught, it is important

**BOX 6.1 •** *Generalization Defined*

### Generalization

(Stokes & Baer, 1977, p. 350)
- ". . . the occurrence of relevant behavior under different, nontraining conditions (i.e., across subjects, settings, people, behaviors, and/or time) without the scheduling of the same events in those conditions as had been scheduled in the training conditions"
- the broadening of stimulus control (Dunlap, 1993)

### Maintenance

(Lane et al., 2001)
- Maintenance refers to the extent to which behavior change continues over time after a given intervention has concluded.

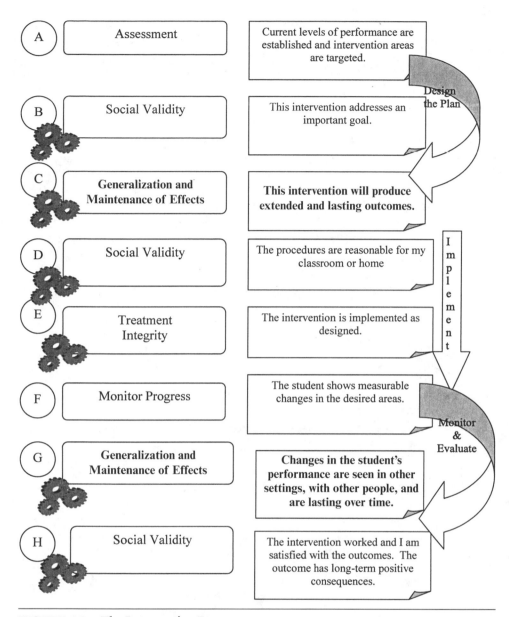

**FIGURE 6.1** *The Intervention Process*

**FIGURE 6.2** *A Continuum of Discrimination and Generalization*

that they be taught succinctly enough that the students clearly understand the skills and can perform them precisely. Then, once mastery is achieved, they need to be taught how to broaden the use and form of the skill (Rutherford & Nelson, 1988). As such, both discrimination and generalization skills are essential for altering and acquiring skills and for being able to use these new skills competently, both in and beyond the school walls.

Unfortunately, too often issues of generality are not attended to when designing school-based interventions (Lane, Umbreit, & Beebe-Frankenberger, 1999; Rutherford & Nelson, 1988). Instead, many interventionists assume the "train and hope" stance (Stokes & Baer, 1977). If attention is not devoted to ensuring that the newly acquired behaviors can occur in nonprogrammed settings, in the presence of varying stimuli (stimulus generalization), in varying forms (response generalization), and continue over time once the intervention has concluded (maintenance), then the new behaviors have little functional utility (Rutherford & Nelson, 1988). Accordingly, the new behaviors will most likely cease to occur or will only occur in settings that closely approximate the training conditions (see Box 6.2). Therefore, rather than "train and hope," we recommend that you program, observe, and evaluate.

**BOX 6.2 • *The Importance of Programming for Generalization***

As a second-year special education teacher, I had a student named Mike. Mike was certified as having a learning disability and was receiving services in a resource program at the middle school level. Mike was the brightest student in my class—above average intelligence, average academic performance on standardized tests, adequate writing skills, and highly verbal. However, he had poor work habits that interfered with his ability to complete work. Further, he had exceedingly poor social skills that impeded not only his relationships with teachers but also his relationships with peers. Over the course of the year, Mike's work habits and social skills improved in my classroom. We used a variety of approaches (e.g., homework assignment sheets, positive postcards mailed home, and programmed instruction) to develop improved work habits. By March, Mike rarely missed a class or homework assignment, he attended school more regularly, and he frequently participated in classroom discussion. His vocabulary had become significantly less colorful. Mike actually became someone I could call on to help others with their work during class time. He was my model student.

One day, I was on my way to another classroom to observe a different student in a general education classroom when I passed by Mike's fifth-period class—general education science. Out of the corner of my eye I saw Mike—hat on backwards, pants sagging with six inches of underwear showing, his arms up in the air flashing a well-known sign, and shouting "YO, DUDE!!!" in the science teacher's face. I couldn't believe what I was seeing.

I took one step into the classroom door and, although I didn't say a word, Mike saw me. In front of 32 other students, he immediately said, "Sorry Mrs. Lane," turned his hat around, pulled up his pants, walked to his desk, took out a pencil, and started the assignment.

It hit me like a ton of bricks. I read about it in school, heard lectures about the importance of it, but I failed to do it. I hadn't programmed for generalization. Mike's wonderful behavioral changes had only been taught, exhibited, and evidenced in my class, and consequently, the changes were not observed beyond my classroom walls.

## How Do We Program for Generalization and Maintenance?

There are two main approaches used to program for generalization and maintenance: topographical generalization and functional generalization (Gresham, 2002). Topographical, which is the most often used approach, focuses on what the behavior looks like. In contrast, functional generalization focuses on why the behavior occurs (Gresham, 1994; Gresham, 2002).

### Topographical Approaches

Topographical generalization is defined as the presence of the target behavior (e.g., giving a compliment, reading a book, calming oneself down) in settings other than the training conditions (Stokes & Baer, 1977; Stokes & Osnes, 1989). The target behavior can be demonstrated over time (e.g., six weeks after the social skills training concluded), in novel environments (e.g., general education teacher's classroom), with other people (e.g., at the request of the general education teacher), and using a slightly varied method (e.g., saying "yes, Ma'am," instead of saying "yeah sure," Gresham, 1994). Topographic generalization provides evidence that the trained behaviors are still occurring; however, it does not explain why the behavior generalized. Topographical generalization allows you to answer the question "Did the newly trained skills occur outside of the training conditions?" But, it does not afford a justification as to *why* this new behavior or skill is continuing to occur beyond the training circumstances.

Stokes and Osnes (1989) developed a topographical system of programming for generalization within the intervention designed. In brief, this system is comprised of three broad principles: *using functional contingencies, training broadly,* and *incorporating functional mediators* (see Form 6.1; see Stokes & Osnes for a detailed discussion).

***Incorporating functional contingencies.*** This principle includes a variety of methods for tapping into contingencies that occur naturally in day-to-day life. Namely, this principle is based on identifying and then capitalizing on antecedents, responses, and consequences that influence the target behavior with respect to intensity, frequency, or duration (Stokes & Osnes, 1989). Antecedents refer to events that happen before the behavior occurs and consequences are events that occur after the behavior occurs (see Figure 6.3). Incorporation of functional contingencies includes

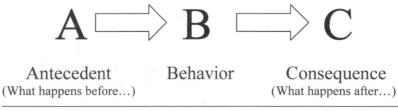

FIGURE 6.3 *Behavioral Chain*

| Principles & Tactics | Selected Approaches | Completed √ |
|---|---|---|
| **Exploit Functional Contingencies** | | |
| Contact natural consequences. | | |
| Recruit natural consequences. | | |
| Modify maladaptive consequences. | | |
| Reinforce occurrences of generalization. | | |
| | | |
| **Train Diversely** | | |
| Use sufficient stimulus exemplars. | | |
| Use sufficient response exemplars. | | |
| Make antecedents less discriminable. | | |
| Make consequences less discriminable. | | |
| | | |
| **Incorporate Functional Mediators** | | |
| Incorporate common salient physical stimuli. | | |
| Incorporate common salient social stimuli. | | |
| Incorporate self-mediated physical stimuli. | | |
| Incorporate self-mediated verbal and covert stimuli. | | |

**FORM 6.1    *Programming for Generalization: Topographical Approaches***

*Source:* Reprinted with permission from T. F. Stokes & P. G. Osnes (1989). "An Operant Pursuit of Generalization." *Behavior Therapy, 20,* 337–355 (Page 340).

tactics such as (a) contacting and recruiting consequences that occur naturally in the environment, (b) modifying maladaptive or undesirable consequences, and (c) providing reinforcement when the target behavior does generalize.

*Contacting and recruiting consequences that occur naturally* is often more efficient and more effective than having the interventionist program artificial consequences.

For example, consider a social skills lesson in which a student is being taught to initiate a social interaction with a same-age peer. Rather than taking away a point or a token if the student fails to smile and greet a peer at recess, build on the natural consequence—missing an opportunity to play with a peer. It is helpful if the target behavior(e.g., smiling and saying hello) is part of the chain that leads to the reinforcer (e.g., the peer saying hello in response).

If reinforcement is not readily available in the environment, it can be difficult for students to obtain enough reinforcement to maintain the new skill. In these instances, students can be taught to *recruit the desired natural consequences.* Consider the following example: A teacher is busy working with a group of students on a comprehension activity while the other students are silently reading. One of the students engaged in silent reading uses his/her newly acquired decoding skills to decipher a novel word. That student can be taught to solicit reinforcement from the teacher by raising his/her hand, demonstrating his/her decoding skills to the teacher, and then cuing the teacher to respond (e.g., "How was that?"). Ideally, the teacher would respond with verbal praise to encourage the continued use of this new skill. The use of infrequent cuing statements can be used to prompt positive attention from teachers and peers.

Another approach to exploiting functional contingencies involves *altering the existing maladaptive consequences* that are reinforcing the behavior. For example, children with antisocial behavior problems will frequently make lewd, hostile, or negative comments during instructional activities. Their peers will often respond with laughter or snickering, which serves as a reinforcer. If the comments are viewed to be a skills deficit, meaning that the child simply does not have more prosocial skills in his/her repertoire, social skills training may serve as an effective intervention (see Box 6.2). However, social skills interventions often suffer from poor generalization. In order to improve generalization of the use of prosocial comments, one strategy is to eliminate reinforcement for the maladaptive behavior (rude comments). Although this task becomes more challenging as children increase in age, it is possible to instruct the classmates to not respond to the inappropriate talk and to only respond when the child makes more appropriate comments. By eliminating the reinforcement the child receives for the *problem* behavior, he/she will be more likely to use the more *adaptive, replacement* behavior.

Another method of capitalizing on functional contingencies involves *delivering reinforcement when the target behavior occurs beyond the training setting.* For example, if the student is participating in a program to improve decoding skills and is seen using the strategy during another literacy activity (e.g., during partner reading), then provide behavior-specific praise to reinforce the use of the decoding strategy. Similarly, when you see a student raising his hand and waiting to be called on as taught during a social skills intervention, you can encourage generalization by reinforcing that behavior (e.g., calling on the student as quickly as possible).

Each of these tactics—contacting and recruiting consequences that naturally occur, modifying maladaptive consequences, and reinforcing instances of generalization—represent specific methods of taking advantage of existing functional contingencies. These tactics represent feasible, effective methods that require minimal effort and resources.

***Training broadly.*** When training procedures and environments are exceedingly focused, the outcomes are also more focused (Stokes & Osnes, 1989). If one of the goals is to achieve broad, outreaching outcomes, the training conditions must also be broad. When training "broadly" or "diversely," specific controlled variations in the training procedures (e.g., training settings, intervention leaders, and acceptable responses) must be systematically incorporated into the intervention procedures *prior* to beginning the intervention program. To this end, this principle includes using sufficient stimulus and response exemplars, and making antecedents and consequences less discriminable as compared to the training conditions.

Using *sufficient stimuli exemplars* refers to incorporating variations of the training circumstances for which you wish to achieve generalization. For example, if a goal of social skills training is to promote the use of the acquired skills in other settings (e.g., cafeteria, homeroom, math class, and on the bus) and with other individuals (e.g., other teachers, peers, and members of the community), then it is important to vary these components of the training procedures (e.g., intervention setting and leader, respectively).

Similarly, *using sufficient response exemplars* is another method of training broadly. For example, if your goal is to teach students a range of acceptable methods for greeting another person, then the intervention must be designed to teach and accept a range of acceptable greetings (e.g., hello, hey there, hi, and what's up). The key is providing sufficient examples and nonexamples of circumstances under which to use the various greetings (e.g., saying "what's up, girlfriend" to your great-grandmother may not be as acceptable as saying it to your seventh-grade peer!).

Another tactic used to train broadly is to make *antecedents less discriminable*. Many interventions call for highly precise implementation under highly controlled conditions. Although this may be useful for teaching a target behavior, this level of precision does not lend itself to generalization of effects. On the contrary, if the goal includes behaviors that occur under a variety of circumstances, then it is important to make the antecedents less discriminable. In other words, the training format should be somewhat varied so that the students will not associate the desired behavior with a narrowly defined set of circumstances. For example, if you are teaching children with low cognitive abilities how to determine when it is time to sit down and begin their work, it is important that the training condition include a variety of antecedents (e.g., teacher requests) that should prompt the same response (e.g., sit down and begin work; see Figure 6.4). These methods can be thought of as broadening stimulus control, meaning that more than one stimulus (e.g., division problems presented in various ways) will set the stage for the desired behavior (e.g., correct numerical response).

*Making consequences less discriminable* refers to altering the predictability of the consequences that follow the target behavior as taught in the training conditions. Specific strategies for making consequences less discriminable include providing intermittent reinforcement when the target behavior is demonstrated, delaying the time between observing the target behavior and delivering the consequence, and varying the presence of the treatment agent (Stokes & Osnes, 1989). For example, rather than providing verbal praise or awarding points every time a student raises his hand *and* waits to be called on, reinforce students on a more variable schedule to promote maintenance of effects. Similarly, rather than reinforcing children for using "inside voices" in the school cafeteria at the end of every lunch period, distribute slips as part of a lottery system (see Figure 6.5). Indicate on the slip the specific schoolwide behavioral expectation that was demonstrated, the date of occurrence, location of the occurrence, the student's name, and the observer's name (e.g., teacher, volunteer, paraprofessional, custodian, secretary, or administrator). Students can turn these slips in to the main office, and the administrator or designee can randomly select a slip once a week. The "winner's" name is displayed

**Stimuli**                                                **Response**

**Example #1:**

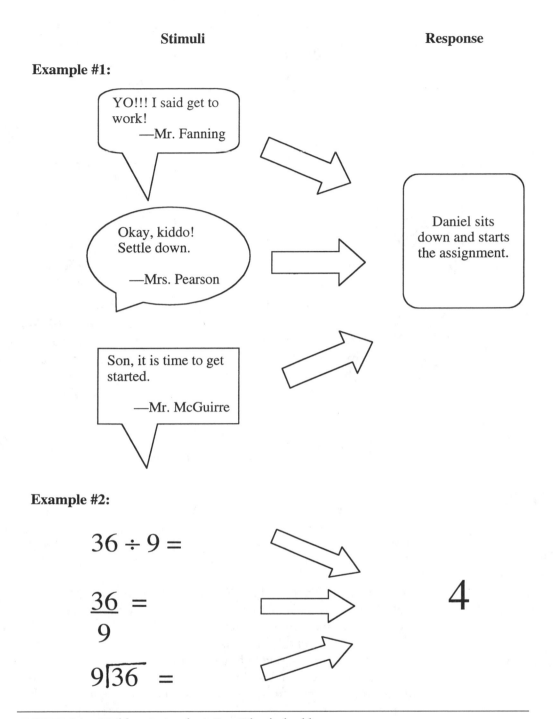

**Example #2:**

**FIGURE 6.4** *Making Antecedents Less Discriminable*

on a bulletin board and a token reinforcer is awarded to the selected student as part of the schoolwide discipline plan. These slips provide intermittant and delayed reinforcement, given that not every child will receive reinforcement (slip) at the end of every lunch period (intermittent reinforcement), and students will have to wait to see if they are selected for a larger reinforcement (delayed reinforcement). A more common example of delayed reinforcement is the use of table points. For

| **Caught Being Good** | **Caught Being Good** |
|---|---|
| Student: _____ | Student: _____ |
| Observer: _____ | Observer: _____ |
| Date: _____ | Date: _____ |
| Location: _____ | Location: _____ |
| √ You followed directions the first time.<br>√ You asked for help in an acceptable way.<br>√ You resolved a conflict using your words.<br>√ You finished your work in a timely manner.<br>√ You invited a friend to work/play with you. | √ You followed directions the first time.<br>√ You asked for help in an acceptable way.<br>√ You resolved a conflict using your words.<br>√ You finished your work in a timely manner.<br>√ You invited a friend to work/play with you. |

**FIGURE 6.5**    *Schoolwide Intervention: Social Skills*

example, if students are arranged in small groups for a cooperative learning activity, it is possible to allocate points for positive participation as part of a secondary, classwide intervention. These points can be traded in for small tangible rewards at the end of the week to program for maintenance.

***Incorporating functional mediators.*** A mediator, also referred to as a discriminative stimulus, is a stimulus that sets the stage for the occurrence of the academic or social behavior taught during an intervention; the mediator is evident between the training condition and generalization instance in such a manner that it prompts the occurrence of the trained behavior (Stokes & Osnes, 1989). There are several tactics for incorporating functional mediators, such as building in common physical stimuli, common social stimuli, self-mediated physical stimuli, and self-mediated verbal and overt stimuli.

*Building in common physical stimuli* refers to incorporating the same or similar physical object (e.g., rules posted in the training environment and in the general education classroom) in both the training and generalization setting. For example, if at-risk students are involved in a study skills class and the topic is homework completion, one strategy to promote generalization between the skills taught in the study skills class and the regular education English class is to use common homework forms. If the entire school is using homework reminder sheets (a weekly homework form, see Figure 6.6), then one way to program for generalization is to use the binder reminder form in the study skills class. The form serves as a common

# Homework Reminder Sheet

|  | Assignment | Completed √ | Parent Signature |
|---|---|---|---|
| Monday | | | |
| Reading | | | |
| Math | | | |
| Science | | | |
| Social Studies | | | |
| PE | | | |
| Elective | | | |
| | | | |
| Tuesday | | | |
| Reading | | | |
| Math | | | |
| Science | | | |
| Social Studies | | | |
| PE | | | |
| Elective | | | |
| | | | |
| Wednesday | | | |
| Reading | | | |
| Math | | | |
| Science | | | |
| Social Studies | | | |
| PE | | | |
| Elective | | | |
| | | | |
| Thursday | | | |
| Reading | | | |
| Math | | | |
| Science | | | |
| Social Studies | | | |
| PE | | | |
| Elective | | | |
| | | | |
| Friday | | | |
| Reading | | | |
| Math | | | |
| Science | | | |
| Social Studies | | | |
| PE | | | |
| Elective | | | |

**FIGURE 6.6**  *Homework Reminder Form*

salient physical stimulus (Stokes & Osnes, 1989) that is present in both the training and generalization settings.

Another tactic for incorporating functional mediators is to build in *common social stimuli*. One method is to design your intervention so that the intervention leader or member is also present in the generalization setting. Although it is not always possible, one approach is to take steps to ensure that the intervention leader is occasionally present in the desired generalization setting. For example, if the school counselor is leading a social skills group, then one method of incorporating functional mediators to program for generalization is to arrange for the counselor to drop in to the students' classroom. In these instances, the counselor's presence serves as the discriminative stimulus that prompts the desired behavior (e.g., following directions the first time, giving other students a compliment). Given that time is a precious commodity (which is why my 3½-year-old clings to me like Velcro when I am home in the evenings) it may not be possible for the trainer to make appearances beyond the training sessions. In these cases, it may be appropriate to build in peer confederates or peer models. By inviting other, non-at-risk students to be a part of the intervention groups, the nontargeted students can benefit from the intervention, act as role models during the intervention session, serve as discriminative stimuli, or prompt for the target behavior in the generalization settings (see Lane, Wehby, Menzies, Doukas, Munton, & Gregg, in press).

*Including self-mediated physical stimuli* is another tactic used to build in functional mediators. Essentially, a self-mediated physical stimulus is an object or stimulus that is carried between the training and generalization environments. For example, if the study skills class attempts to teach time management with the use of a day planner, then generalization can be programmed by teaching the student to bring the day planner to all classrooms throughout the day and keep track of requisite assignments. Similarly, if a student who tends to be withdrawn during classroom discussion is participating in an intervention designed to increase classroom participation, one strategy for monitoring participation can be as simple as a paper clip intervention. During the intervention sessions, the child can be taught to self-monitor participation by moving paper clips from his or her left pocket to the right one. The same child could be sent back to the general education classroom with a left pocket full of paper clips and told to move a paper clip to the right pocket every time she makes a contribution to a classroom discussion. Thus, the key is to have the student be responsible for transporting the physical stimuli between settings. Of course, it will be important for the intervention leader to inform essential personnel (e.g., classroom teacher, paraprofessionals, or parent volunteers) of the intervention so that they do not suspect the child of hoarding paper clips!

Finally, another tactic for building in functional mediators is to involve *self-mediated verbal and overt stimuli* (Stokes & Osnes, 1989). This approach involves teaching the students to overtly (say aloud) or covertly (think about) perform the procedures and steps taught in the training sessions. This can prove to be a challenging strategy to measure and may also require prompting from an adult in the generalization setting (e.g., Peter, please use your "self talk" to help you stay focused on your work) to use this generalization strategy (Guevremont, Osnes, & Stokes, 1988).

These three categories—exploiting functional contingencies, training diversely, and incorporating functional mediators—are topographic approaches to generalization derived from correlational evidence. In other words, the expectation is that the strategies constituting these three categories will facilitate generalization. This has been referred to as the "train and hope" approach to generalization. Gresham (2002) suggests that while these form-based approaches have met with varying degrees of success, generalization efforts rooted in a functional orientation may prove to be more effective.

## *Functional Approaches*

As previously mentioned, a functional approach to generalization focuses on why (function) the behavior occurs, as opposed to topographical generalization, which focuses on how (form) behavior occurs. The basic question asked from a functional perspective is "What are the functional variables that set the stage for generalization to occur?" (Gresham, 1994; Lane et al., 2001) The fundamental question being asked in functional generalization is "What are the functional variables that account for generalization?"

If you subscribe to a functional approach to generalization, there are two likely outcomes: *stimulus generalization* and *response generalization*. Stimulus generalization refers to the presence of the target behavior under different variations of the original stimulus. For example, stimulus generalization is said to have occurred when the child has exhibited self-control when teased on the playground and when frustrated in mathematics class after having participated in an anger management intervention. Response generalization refers to variations of the responses (which are said to part of the same functional response class) following presentation of the same stimulus. For example, response generalization is said to have occurred when the student demonstrates higher rates of academic engaged time during literacy instruction and shows decreases in disruptive classroom behavior (e.g., out of seat, noncompliance, and provoking peers) after having participated in an explicit reading intervention. Higher rates of academic engaged time is a direct outcome of the intervention, whereas the changes in disruptive behavior patterns is a collateral effect or response generalization (Lane, O'Shaughnessy, Lambros, Gresham, & Beebe-Frankenberger, 2001).

Yet, generalization errors occur, and are particularly evident in social skills intervention research. Namely, there is a tendency for the newly acquired skills to not generalize beyond the training condition (Gresham, 1998). This is a classic example of a stimulus generalization error. The students are taught via explicit instruction in protective settings (e.g., small groups that meet outside of the classroom) to use specific skills in the classroom (e.g., raising their hands *and* waiting to be called on by the teacher). Despite performing the skills as taught in the training setting during the intervention, the skills seem to be absent beyond the training setting.

There are a number of explanations as to why social skills interventions have demonstrated poor generalization of treatment outcomes (see Gresham, 1998). One explanation is the lack of correspondence between the training and naturally occurring, proposed generalization settings. It may be that (a) the natural reinforcers present in the natural settings are not explicitly linked with the target behavior response class, (b) the newly acquired skills are simply not prompted with the appropriate discriminative stimulus, (c) the discriminative stimulus is overshadowed by a competing stimulus in the proposed generalization setting, (d) another stimulus in the proposed generalization environment is prompting a response that competes with the target response, or (e) the behavior is simply not reinforced in the natural setting (Dunlap, 1993; Gresham, 1994).

For example, a student, Germaine, is placed into a secondary, small group intervention for social skills training to better meet teacher expectations for student behavior. Germaine is taught numerous skills such has raising his hand and waiting to be called on, using free time in an acceptable manner, and making his assistance needs known without disrupting others. He practices the skill with the trainer until he is able to perform all necessary steps delineated in the task analysis. When Germaine returns to his homeroom class it is time to participate in a class discussion. He attempts to use the new skill by raising his hand and waiting to be called on (despite the fact that Germaine is now losing circulation in his right arm) by the teacher. The teacher does not call on Germaine; instead, she responds to Robert, who shouted out the response. Thus, the teacher's reaction does not coincide with the trainer's reaction. Consequently, Germaine reverts to his previous, seemingly maladaptive behavior (e.g., yelling out) because it works. Essentially, the skill (raising hand and waiting) was not trained sufficiently in the sense that it was not trained across different stimuli conditions, the training circumstances were too different from the naturally occurring conditions, and arrangements had not been made to ensure that the target behavior would be adequately reinforced by adults and peers in the natural environment. As a result of these training problems, stimulus generalization did not occur.

In addition to stimulus generalization errors, there are also response generalization errors. A response generalization error is evident when the target skill is not a member of the desired functional response class (Gresham, 1994; Lane, Beebe-Frankenberger et al., 2001). Consider the following example: Youngsters will often engage in a range of less than desirable behaviors (e.g., being out of seat, making rude or distracting comments to the teacher, provoking their peers) when confronted with tasks that are either too easy (e.g., doing fifty long division problems for the fifth consecutive day) or too difficult (e.g., asking a fifth-grade child with poor reading skills to silently read and summarize the first chapter in *Harry Potter and the Chamber of Secrets* (Rowling, 1999). In the latter example, if the intervention focuses on the acquisition deficit (see Chapter 1; poor reading skills) rather than the escape-motivated, disruptive behaviors, the student is likely to acquire a functional response to the instructional activity—reading to learn. However, if the intervention focuses, as is often the case, on the nonfunctional, associated disruptive behavior (e.g., strategies to decrease talking out behavior and/or increase in-seat behavior), positive outcomes are less likely. Although it is possible to use strategies such as differential reinforcement of lower rates of behavior (see Elliott & Gresham, 1991), other problem behaviors (e.g., throwing objects, cursing, or somatic complaints) are likely to materialize. Why? Because the prescribed intervention did not address the function of the target behavior. If the student is engaging in disruptive or problematic behaviors because he or she does not have the skills to successfully engage in the activity, then the intervention needs to provide the student with a *functionally equivalent behavior*.

In this sense, generalization failures can be explained in terms of the *reliability* and *efficiency* of the competing behaviors (Horner & Billingsley, 1988). Moreover, if you want the new behavior (e.g., raising the hand and waiting to be called on by the teacher) to be used beyond the training situation in other environments and in the presence of teachers other than the social skills trainer, then the new behavior must work better than the previous, problematic behavior (e.g., shouting out questions without teacher permission). This is referred to as *functional generalization.*

For example, few educators would disagree with the statement that verbal aggression such as caustic, coercive, and threatening verbalizations are not appropriate in the school setting. This being the case, why do such behaviors continue even in the face of empirically validated social skills training efforts (see Gresham, 1998; Zaragoza, Vaughn, & McIntosh, 1991)? One explanation is that the skills taught in the social skills training programs are not as reliable and efficient as the former, aberrant behavior. For example, asking a peer for $1.00 to buy a soda may simply not consistently result in the desired outcome—receiving the dollar and subsequently buying the soda. Yet, threatening a peer (e.g., "Give me the money or I'm going to kick your _____ [insert desired body part here]) may result in the desired outcome more often and with less time spent negotiating the demand. In this example, the trained skill of seeking assistance from a peer does not generalize across time, setting, or persons because the former behavior (verbal aggression) is more efficient and more reliable than the trained replacement behavior. This is another reason why it is imperative that problem behaviors such as verbal and physical aggression be dealt with early in a child's educational career, when students are more amenable to intervention efforts (Kazdin, 1987, 1993) and before the problem behaviors become an increasingly stable part of the student's behavioral repertoire (Walker, Colvin, & Ramsey, 1995). Put more simply, intervention needs to occur as early as possible before students become really good at behaving poorly. If we, as school personnel, wait too long to begin intervening with children at-risk for behavior problems, it becomes more and more challenging to identify and teach replacement behaviors that are more efficient and reliable than the former problem behavior (DuPaul & Eckert, 1994; Horner & Billingsley, 1988; Lane, Beebe-Frankenberger et al., 2001).

## Did the Intervention Outcomes Last?

So, how do we determine if the new behaviors have maintained or generalized? This is a question that can be answered most precisely with the use of frequent, repeated assessment (typically using direct observation and curriculum-based measures) after the training has occurred. Further, maintenance and generalization can also be evaluated indirectly via teacher and student report.

### Data-Based Decision Making

A direct approach to assessing the extent to which intervention outcomes lasted (maintained) and expanded (generalized) is to continue with data collection (see Chapter 3, Monitoring Progress) after completing the intervention phase. Maintenance questions (e.g., Now that instruction in self-monitoring has concluded, is Shawna continuing to turn in her homework in my math class?) can be answered by collecting data (e.g., number of homework assignments turned in per week in math class) under the same conditions specified in the baseline and intervention phases. Generalization questions (e.g., Now that the intervention in self-monitoring is finished, is Shawna now turning in more homework assignments in other classes?) can be answered by collecting data (e.g., number of homework assignments turned in per week in language arts and science classes) in new, untrained circumstances.

For example, if you have designed a socially valid intervention based on the function of the behavior and the intervention plan was implemented with a high degree of treatment integrity, it is likely that the intervention will produce the desired outcomes. The treatment outcomes (e.g., turning in homework assignments) are likely to maintain over time under the training circumstances (e.g., in the math class under the direction of the math teacher) and generalize to new circumstances (e.g., in the language arts class under the direction of the special education teacher). If Shawna's homework-completion rates *in math* are high and homework-missed rates are low, then maintenance of intervention outcomes is evident. Similarly, if her homework-completion rates in other classes (e.g., language arts and science) improve after the intervention concludes and the rates of missed homework assignments are low, then generalization of treatment effects is said to have occurred (Lane, Beebe-Frankenberger et al., 2001).

## *Programming for Generalization: Comprehensive Guidelines*

If the hallmarks of effective interventions, whether primary, secondary, or tertiary levels of support (Walker & Severson, 2002), are meaningful behavioral changes that are sustained over time (response maintenance), are exhibited in a variety of environments (stimulus generalization), and extend to a wide range of associated behaviors (response generalization; Baer et al., 1968; Rutherford & Nelson, 1988), then programming for and assessment of generalization is an absolute priority. The question remains, how do we program for generalization? With topographical approaches? With functional approaches? With a combination of approaches?

Dunlap (1993) offers seven guidelines for addressing generalization that are comprised of techniques for circumventing programs and programming of contingencies (see Table 6.1).

*1. Plan for generalization when you are designing your intervention.* Generalization should be considered at the beginning of the process. Whether you are developing prereferral intervention plans, individualized educational programs (IEP), individualized transition plans (ITP), or behavior intervention plans (BIP), generalization needs to be addressed explicitly. Each plan should include a precise statement about the specific contexts in which change is anticipated and expected to occur. Include the specific target behavior you expect to see, any response generalizations that are anticipated, the locations and social contexts in which these responses should occur, and which individuals will be present. Think back to your

**TABLE 6.1**    *Generalization Guidelines*

### *Guidelines*
- Plan for generalization when you are designing your intervention.
- Examine stimulus and reinforcement conditions in the environment.
- Conduct interventions in relevant environments under naturally occurring conditions.
- Incorporate the current generalization technology.
- Examine issues of stimulus control when there are concerns about stimulus generalization.
- Examine issues of reinforcement when there are concerns about response maintenance.
- Examine generalization of functional alternatives for concerns about generalized response suppression.

*Source:* Adapted from G. Dunlap (1993). "Promoting Generalization: Current Status and Functional Considerations." In R. V. Houten & S. Axelrod (Eds.), *Behavior Analysis and Treatment.* New York: Plenum Press.

fifth-grade book reports (Thank you, Mrs. Whitton!) to encourage you to report what, where, when, and with whom (Dunlap, 1993). If you have incorporated a functional approach, you will already know the why.

**2. *Examine stimulus and reinforcement conditions in the environment.*** Be sure to carefully examine the targeted contexts before implementing the intervention. More specifically, think about where you would like generalization to occur (e.g., in other classrooms, on the playground, or at home) and then observe in these settings before you start implementing the intervention. Some questions to ask yourself are the following: What are the controlling antecedent conditions in this environment? What are the contextual factors and setting events in this environment? What types of reinforcement contingencies are available?

For example, if you are working with a child with severe disabilities on hand-washing skills, there are several assessments that need to be made: What types of sinks are in the proposed generalization settings (controlling antecedent conditions)? Do they have turn knobs? Are they touch-activated spouts? If the classroom sink has turn knobs and the public restrooms have touch-activated spouts, then the training conditions should include practice with both types of sinks in order to facilitate generalization. Similarly, observations in the proposed generalization environments can provide important information about how to design or modify the training conditions. For example, if your observations indicate that the public restrooms typically have multiple sinks or have a higher noise level (contextual factors and setting events), this provides the intervention trainer with important factors that need to be considered when designing and conducting the intervention. Likewise, it is important to consider the reinforcement contingencies that are present in the proposed generalization context. Do some of the classrooms use tangible reinforcement systems to encourage hand washing? Such schedules are typically not likely to occur naturally in public settings. (However, it would be a lot easier to ensure that my children washed their hands if a chocolate dispenser was linked to the faucet. Maybe ten seconds of running water leads to two chocolate squares being dispensed—what do you think?). Here again, knowing what type of reinforcement is available can provide important information about how best to proceed in the training condition.

**3. *Conduct interventions, when possible, in the relevant environments.*** Ideally, training should be conducted in the settings where you would like the behavior to occur once the training has concluded. In addition, the probability of achieving generalization is increased by delivering intervention under naturally occurring conditions. For example, when possible, it is best to conduct early literacy interventions (see Lane, Wehby, Menzies, Gregg, Doukas, & Munton, 2002) and social skills interventions (Lane, Wehby, & Miller, in preparation) in the classroom during the course of the traditional school day. Frequently, it is not possible to conduct interventions in every desired generalization setting. In these instances, identify the context to which generalization is most imperative (Dunlap, 1993). Then, make every effort to promote generalization using topographical and functional generalization approaches.

**4. *Incorporate the current generalization technology.*** Review the guidelines presented in this text on topographical generalization as contained in Stokes and Osnes's (1989) generalization principles (see Form 6.1). Review each of these tactics and determine which of these approaches are appropriate to your proposed intervention. Again, let us remind you, this step needs to occur before beginning any intervention. Too often, generalization is an afterthought, which is often why treatments do not produce lasting change.

**5. *Examine issues of stimulus control when there are concerns about stimulus generalization.*** Research in applied behavior analysis has clearly established the A-B-C (Antecedent-Behavior/Response-Consequence) relationship. It is the antecedent stimulus conditions that prompt the occurrence or nonoccurrence of a given behavior. As such, interventions need to clearly identify and modify the specific stimuli that are intended to bring about the target behavior. To the extent that this process is executed in a pristine fashion, the probability of generalization is improved (Dunlap, 1993). Therefore, be sure that the proposed intervention clearly reflects specifications as to the antecedent stimuli that will prompt the presence or absence of the target behavior.

**6. *Examine issues of reinforcement when there are concerns about response maintenance.*** Maintenance and reinforcement are inextricably linked in the sense that a response will only continue to occur if the said behavior continues to be reinforced beyond the training conditions. Therefore, an adequate schedule of reinforcement is necessary to maintain stimulus control. When designing an intervention, therefore, be sure to examine the targeted generalization settings to determine that (a) adequate reinforcement is naturally available or (b) the environment can be altered to provide systematic reinforcement in order to maintain the desired behavior (Dunlap, 1993).

**7. *Examine generalization of functional alternatives for concerns about generalized response suppression.*** Problem behaviors, although often referred to as maladaptive behaviors, are far from maladaptive. Problem behaviors such as verbal aggression and physical aggression are developed, maintained, and generalized because they are adaptive in the sense that they bring about the desired outcomes. In this respect, if you are concerned about making sure that problem behaviors (e.g., yelling out, biting, hitting, cursing) continue to be suppressed beyond the training environment, then make sure that your intervention focuses on teaching functionally equivalent behaviors that are more reliable and efficient than problem behaviors (Lane, Beebe-Frankenberger et al., 2001). Ask yourself if the intervention allows for new, reliable, efficient, functionally equivalent behaviors to be acquired. In other words, determine if the student is learning a new way of getting what he wants.

Collectively, these seven guidelines offer techniques for increasing the probability of generalization. Included in these guidelines are practical recommendations for circumventing generalization errors and for "programming of stimuli and reinforcement contingencies" (Dunlap, 1993, p. 287).

## Summary

This chapter has introduced a variety of technical concepts and procedures for ensuring that the newly acquired skills continue to occur over time, in the presence of a variety of people, under a range of circumstances, and in varying forms. These procedures represent traditional, topographical approaches (Stokes, 1977; Stokes & Osnes, 1989) as well as more functional approaches (Dunlap, 1993). Collectively, the guidelines offered here (Dunlap, 1993) are intended to take the mystery out of generalization. Intervention outcomes are likely to meet the intended purpose of bringing about meaningful changes that have important effects for the student participants (Baer et al., 1968; Dunlap, 1993; Horner et al., 1988) if generalization is given attention before the intervention occurs, and not as an afterthought (e.g., Geez! This worked. Now how can I make this last?)

## References

Baer, D. M., Wolf, M. M., & Risley, T. R. (1968). Some current dimensions of applied behavior analysis. *Journal of Applied Behavior Analysis, 1,* 91–97.

Dunlap, G. (1993). Promoting generalization: Current status and functional considerations. In R. V. Houten, & S. Axelrod (Eds.), *Behavior analysis and treatment.* New York: Plenum Press.

DuPaul, G., & Eckert, T. (1994). The effects of social skills curricula: Now you see them, now you don't. *School Psychology Quarterly, 9,* 113–132.

Edelstein, B. (1989). Generalization: Terminological, methodological and conceptual issues. *Behavior Therapy, 20,* 311–324.

Elliott, S., & Gresham, F. M. (1991). *Social skills intervention guide.* Circle Pines, MN: American Guidance Service.

Gresham, F. M. (1994). Generalization of social skills: Risks of choosing form over function. *School Psychology Quarterly, 9,* 142–144.

Gresham, F. M. (1998). Social skills training: Should we raze, remodel, or rebuild? *Behavioral Disorders, 24,* 19–25.

Gresham, F. M. (2002). Treatment of social skills and problem behaviors. Unpublished manuscript.

Guevremont, D. C., Osnes, P. G., & Stokes, T. F. (1988). The functional role of preschoolers' verbalizations in the generalization of self-instruction training. *Journal of Applied Behavioral Analysis, 21,* 45–55.

Horner, R. H., & Billingsley, F. F. (1988). The effect of competing behavior on the generalization and maintenance of adaptive behavior in applied settings. In R. H. Horner, G. Dunlap, & R. L. Koegel (Eds.), *Generalization and maintenance: Lifestyle changes in applied settings.* Baltimore, MD: Paul H. Brookes.

Horner, R., H., Dunlap, G., & Koegel, R. L. (Eds.) (1988). *Generalization and maintenance: Lifestyle changes in applied settings.* Baltimore, MD: Paul H. Brookes.

Kazdin, A. E. (1987). Treatment of antisocial behavior in children: Current status and future directions. *Psychological Bulletin, 102,* 187–203.

Kazdin, A. E. (1993). Treatment of conduct disorders: Progress and directions in psychotherapy research. *Development and Psychopathology, 5,* 277–310.

Lane, K. L., Beebe-Frankenberger, Lambros, K. L., & M. E., Pierson (2001). Designing effective interventions for children at-risk for antisocial behavior: An integrated model of components necessary for making valid inferences. *Psychology in the Schools, 38,* 365–379.

Lane, K. L., O'Shaughnessy, T., Lambros, K. M., Gresham, F. M., & Beebe-Frankenberger, M. E. (2001). The efficacy of phonological awareness training with first-grade students who have behavior problems and reading difficulties. *Journal of Emotional and Behavioral Disorders, 9,* 219–231.

Lane, K. L., Umbreit, J., & Beebe-Frankenberger, M. (1999). A review of functional assessment research with students with or at-risk for emotional and behavioral disorders. *Journal of Positive Behavioral Interventions, 1,* 101–111.

Lane, K. L., Wehby, J., Menzies, H., Doukas, G., Munton, S., & Gregg, R. (submitted 2002) Social skills training for students at-risk for antisocial behavior: The effects of small group instruction. *Behavioral Disorders.*

Lane, K. L., Wehby, J. H., Menzies, H. M., Gregg, R. M., Doukas, G. L., & Munton, S. M. (2002). Early literacy instruction for first-grade students at-risk for antisocial behavior. *Education and Treatment of Children, 25,* 438–458.

Lane, K. L., Wehby, J., & Miller, M. J. (submitted). Social skills instruction for students with high incidence disabilities: An effective, efficient approach for addressing acquisition deficits. Manuscript submitted for publication.

Rowling, J. K. (1999). *Harry Potter and the chamber of secrets.* USA: Scholastic.

Rutherford Jr., R. B., & Nelson, C. M. (1988). Generalization and maintenance of treatment effects. In J. C. Witt, S. N. Elliott, and F. M. Gresham (Eds), *Handbook of behavior therapy in education* (pp. 277-324). New York: Plenum Press.

Stokes, T., (1992). Discrimination and generalization. *Journal of Applied Behavior Analysis, 25,* 429–432.

Stokes, T., & Baer, D. M. (1977). An implicit technology of generalization. *Journal of Applied Behavior Analysis, 10,* 349–367.

Stokes, T., & Osnes, P. G. (1989). An operant pursuit of generalization. *Behavior Therapy, 20,* 337–355.

Sulzer-Azaroff, B., & Mayer, G. R. (1991). *Behavior analysis for lasting change.* Fort Worth, TX: Holt, Rinehart, & Winston.

Walker, H. M., Colvin, G., & Ramsey, E. (1995). *Antisocial behavior in school: Strategies and best practices.* Albany, NY: Brooks/Cole.

Walker, H. M., & Severson, H. (2002). Developmental prevention of at-risk outcomes for vulnerable antisocial children and youth. In K. L. Lane, F. M. Gresham, & T. E. O'Shaughnessy (Eds.), *Interventions for children with or at risk for emotional and behavioral disorders* (pp. 177–194). Boston: Allyn & Bacon.

Zaragoza, N., Vaughn, S., & McIntosh, R. (1991). Social skill intervention and children with behavior problems: A review. *Behavioral Disorders, 16,* 260–275.

# III

# A Summative Example

The purpose of the final chapter is to review and illustrate the intervention process in light of the key tools of the core components model.

# 7

## *Putting It All Together*

As we said at the onset of this book, teachers, administrators, parents, and the students themselves begin school each year with the expectation that students will acquire a vast array of knowledge, experiences, and skills that will ultimately prepare them to be successful both within and beyond the school setting (O'Shaughnessy, Lane, Gresham, & Beebe-Frankenberger, 2002). In addition to achieving competence in academic areas, schools are now expected to create safe learning environments in which students also develop social skills and behavioral competencies that will allow them to become life-long learners and contributing members of society. These increasingly rigorous expectations also coincide with a call for academic excellence in the form of standards-based education (The Leave No Child Behind Act of 2001, Fournier, AP), a demand for safer schools, (Public Law 103-882, October 20, 1994), a shift toward proactive rather than reactive services for students (Lane & Wehby, 2002), and a trend toward inclusive programming for students with exceptionalities (Fuchs & Fuchs, 1994; MacMillan, Gresham, & Forness, 1996). Given the magnitude of this charge, it is imperative that school systems design, implement, and evaluate comprehensive, progressive layers of support to better serve an increasingly diverse set of learners (Nelson, Rutherford, Center, & Walker, 1991; Walker & Severson, 2002).

As you recall, primary prevention efforts focus on preventing harm by providing every student with a particular intervention (e.g., schoolwide literacy programs, *Second Step Violence Prevention Curriculum*, Committee for Children, 1992; Walker & Severson, 2002). Secondary prevention efforts focus on reversing harm by providing more intensive, focused interventions (e.g., social skills, anger management, reading comprehension groups) for students who are either nonresponsive to more global intervention efforts or who are identified as at risk for learning and behavior problems. Tertiary prevention efforts focus on reducing harm by providing individualized, intensive programs (e.g., functional assessment-based interventions and one-to-one reading programs) for students exposed to multiple risk factors. These students are typically nonresponsive to primary and secondary prevention efforts and are often viewed to be at high risk for learning and behavior problems. Collectively, these three levels of prevention allow schools to provide systematic, graduated support with appropriate levels of intensity and scope to better serve all learners.

When schools make the commitment to provide these layers of support, they are confronted with a number of questions such as the following: How can we implement these levels of support in a coordinated fashion? How can we determine how well these interventions are working? How do we decide which students need more intensive levels of support? How do we know if these interventions produce lasting outcomes? How do teachers, parents, and students feel about the results of these interventions?

In this book, we discussed specific tools that, if incorporated into school-based interventions, have the potential to enhance intervention outcomes of primary, secondary, and tertiary levels of prevention. More specifically, we established the importance of and strategies for linking interventions to assessment information, evaluating student performance, assessing social validity, monitoring treatment integrity, and attending to issues of generalization and maintenance (Lane, Beebe-Frankenberger, Lambros, & Pierson, 2001; also see Figure 7.1).

In this chapter, we will briefly reiterate these key tools and then provide an example of a school-based intervention with primary, secondary, and tertiary levels of prevention.

## Key Tools

First, before implementing any intervention (primary, secondary, or tertiary) it is important to *link interventions to assessment information*. For example, if the district is offering training in the *Second Step Violence Prevention Curriculum* (Committee for Children, 1992) the process begins by examining available information to determine if such a program is warranted. This can be done by reviewing both the frequency and the nature of disciplinary contacts, suspensions, and expulsions. Is there a need great enough to justify the cost of implementing a schoolwide primary intervention? Are there high rates of verbal or physical aggression amongst the student body as a whole? Is there a subset of students who are being frequently suspended due to hostile interactions with peers or adults? If the scope of the problem is widespread across the student body, then a primary prevention program is warranted. If assessment results indicate that a small core of students is initiating hostile actions, a secondary intervention may be warranted.

Second, in order to determine how well the intervention is working, it is important to *monitor student progress*. In order to evaluate the extent to which the interventions are producing the desired changes, it is important to have some initial measures of student performance and then monitor student progress along the way to see how students respond over time. For example, in order to evaluate the effectiveness of the Second Step Violence Prevention Plan, a faculty member might decide to have the vice principal monitor average weekly disciplinary contacts and attendance rates for all students. The specific outcome measures selected for monitoring are related to the goals of the intervention.

Third, prior to implementing intervention and at the conclusion of the intervention, *assess social validity* (Kazdin, 1977; Lane et al., 2001; Wolf, 1978). Social validity refers to the extent to which all people involved with a given intervention (teachers, parents, and students) view the intervention goals as significant, the intervention procedures as acceptable, and the outcomes as important. This is an important step in the intervention process because it allows people an opportunity to identify common goals, come to a consensus about the reasonableness of the specific steps, and assess the likelihood of (onset) and actual (end) intervention outcomes. Moreover, the process of establishing social validity from multiple

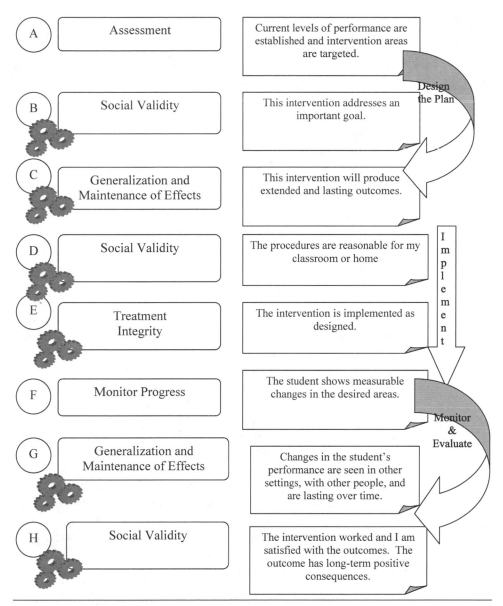

**FIGURE 7.1** *The Intervention Process*

perspectives promotes ownership of the intervention and outcomes by all parties, thereby increasing the likelihood that the intervention will be implemented as planned.

Fourth, it is important to monitor *treatment integrity* (Gresham, 1989; Yeaton & Sechrest, 1981). As you recall, treatment integrity refers to the degree to which each step in the intervention plan was put in place as originally designed. This information allows people to draw more accurate conclusions about treatment effectiveness. Given that many schools have limited resources, it is important that schools invest their resources in only those interventions that clearly achieve their intended goals. Treatment integrity also assesses the strength of the contribution of each intervention component to the outcome so that future interventions can be tailored to include only those components deemed necessary to achieving the desired outcomes.

Fifth, because the ultimate goal of interventions is to produce meaningful, lasting changes that continue long after the formal intervention concludes, it is also important to pay attention to *generalization and maintenance* issues before interventions are implemented (Horner & Billingsley, 1988). Often, school-based interventions are implemented and the intended goals (e.g., increased reading comprehension skill, high levels of academic engaged time, and improved social interactions on the playground) are reached. Unfortunately, shortly thereafter, the effects seem to fade away. This occurs, in part, because the intervention was not designed to encourage generalization.

Finally, it is important that professionals have a precise, concise method of *presenting intervention outcomes*. Given the call for increased emphasis on student performance as it relates to district-level and state-level standards, school personnel must have a defensible, data-based method for documenting both the intervention efforts attempted and the corresponding student outcomes. In brief, there is a need to demonstrate accountability. These reports need to clearly state (a) the intervention goals and objectives, (b) a justification of these goals and objectives, (c) a detailed description of the intervention including training and implementation procedures, (d) information on treatment integrity of the intervention procedures, (e) information on social validity of key persons at the onset and conclusion of the intervention, (f) data on student performance before, throughout, and beyond the intervention that includes information about the reliability of the data collected, and (g) recommendations for future interventions.

The pages that follow will demonstrate a method of documenting student progress for each level of prevention. In order to clearly illustrate this reporting procedure, an example of a school-based intervention with primary (see Box 7.1, Forms 7.1 and 7.2), secondary (see Box 7.2, Forms 7.3 to 7.6), and tertiary (see Box 7.3, Forms 7.7 and 7.8) levels of prevention loosely based on actual interventions conducted by Lane and Menzies (2002), Lane, Wehby, Menzies, Doukas, Munton, and Gregg (in press), and Lane, Wehby, Menzies, Gregg, Doukas, and Munton (2002) will be presented in narrative and in a brief report form. The narrative presentation will describe each level of intervention in light of the above-mentioned key features. Forms 7.1 through 7.6 will present the same information in a more concise format appropriate for documenting outcomes at the school site. Finally, a brief summary and conclusion will be presented.

## A Three-Tiered Model of Prevention: A Hypothetical Sample

### Primary Intervention

A newly hired principal at a small suburban elementary school, Serenity Lane Elementary School, was asked by the superintendent to identify a better method of serving all students at an at-risk school. Specifically, the superintendent was concerned about the reading performance and high rates of disciplinary contacts at the school. Although many of the seventeen teachers had been working at this school for a number of years, the superintendent had trouble finding a principal who was willing to work at this school. Previous principals had complained about resistant teachers, poor reading skills of the students, high levels of aggression in the classroom and on the playground, low levels of parental involvement, and the high poverty characteristic of the community (80 percent of the 300 students were receiving free/reduced lunch services).

**BOX 7.1 • *Primary Intervention Planning Guide***

**Planning Guide for
a Primary Intervention**

I. **The Target Area for Intervention is:**
II. **Pre-Intervention Evaluation/Assessment of the Target Area:**
   A. What is present level of functioning?
   B. Statement of need to increase functioning
III. **Convene Intervention Advisory Panels:**
   A. School personnel (administrator, teachers, yard supervisors, nurse, psychologist)
   B. Parent (representative of school population by culture)
   C. Community (when intervention may impact the community-at-large; e.g., representatives from a mental heath organization, youth sport activities, service organizations, etc.)
IV. **Intervention Planning Activities:**
   A. Social Validity; evaluate the following components:
     a. Social significance
       i. Will achieving the goal improve the quality of life for students as a result of participating in the intervention?
       ii. Does the goal, or the consequences of it, have social value?
       iii. What would be the outcomes if intervention was not implemented?
     b. Treatment acceptability of the intervention components are (ask teachers and parent advisory committees):
       i. Necessary
       ii. Appropriate
       iii. Supportive of positive values
       iv. Minimally disruptive to the environment
       v. Worth the effort to attain the goal
     c. Social importance of the intervention goal; extent to which intervention goals are viewed as having socially important outcomes by:
       i. Intervention implementers
       ii. Parents
       iii. Students
   B. Task Analysis
     a. List essential components of intervention
     b. Determine intensity and duration of intervention
   C. Methods to Monitor Intervention
     a. How will progress be monitored?
     b. How frequently will data be collected?
     c. Who will evaluate progress?
     d. Who will determine if intervention needs adjustment?
   D. Methods for Treatment Integrity
     a. Type(s) (e.g., permanent product, observation, checklists)
     b. Who will collect and evaluate?
   E. Methods for Generalization and Maintenance
     a. Programming discrimination opportunities
       i. Contingency planning
       ii. Reinforcement, response-cost
     b. Programming for generalization
       i. Alternative settings to provide opportunities to demonstrate skill
       ii. Natural or planned reinforcers in other settings
V. **Intervention Implementation**
   A. Collect Treatment Integrity Information
   B. Collect Assessment Monitoring Data
   C. Provide Generalization and Maintenance Components

**BOX 7.1 • *Continued***

D.  Review Progress
E.  Make Adjustments to Intervention as Result of Progress Monitoring Information
**VI.  Terminate Intervention**
A.  Measure/Evaluate Strength of Intervention Outcomes Using Data
   a.  How much change?
   b.  Were goals met, exceeded, not met?
B.  Evaluation of Intervention Outcomes (How did we do?) by:
   a.  Degree of treatment integrity
      i.   How closely was the intervention implemented as planned?
      ii.  Did any components change during intervention?
   b.  Degree of generalization and maintenance (follow-up)
      i.   Measure new skill/behavior in other settings
      ii.  Measure use of new skill/behavior several weeks/months after intervention ends.
   c.  Social validity by observation and by measure (advisory committees)
      i.   Social significance of the intervention goals
         1.  Were goals "keystone"?
         2.  Did goals produce meaningful, lasting behavior changes that led to other changes?
      ii.  Social acceptability of intervention procedures; were treatment steps to learn the new skill/behavior:
         1.  Necessary?
         2.  Appropriate?
         3.  Supportive of positive values?
         4.  Minimally disruptive to the environment?
         5.  Worth the effort to attain the goal?
      iii. Social importance of the effects:
         1.  Does the new behavior and/or skill improve the status of students?
         2.  Do outcomes heighten the probability of future success?
         3.  Would you recommend the intervention to others or use it again at another time or place?

### *Identifying the Intervention Target Areas: Pre-Intervention Assessment*

Given the limited amount of school site resources, the principal and the school site literacy coordinator contacted the local university and set a meeting with a professor interested in schoolwide interventions. Together, they reviewed Serenity Lane's test scores, attendance rates, and disciplinary contact rates from the previous two years. State test scores had not shown much improvement over the last two school years with over 50 percent of the students performing in the lower two quadrants. Attendance rates were of concern, with a schoolwide attendance rate of 80 percent and a transciency rate of 60 percent. Disciplinary contacts were quite high with approximately 10 percent of the students seeing the vice-principal two or more times a week (see Forms 7.1 and 7.2).

### *Intervention Planning Activities*

In order to get input from the teachers and parents, the principal sent a brief *social validity questionnaire* to all teachers and parents to get their opinions about how the

## IAP Primary Intervention Worksheet

IAP Members:                                                    Date Convened:  8/5/01

Attach list of teacher, administrative personnel, other school professionals, parents, students, and community representatives that will serve on the IAP for the term of the intervention period.

Skill or Behavior of Concern (describe):

| |
|---|
| (1) low statewide test scores, (2) poor attendance, (3) high disciplinary referrals |

Assessed Level of Performance of Skill or Behavior of Concern (State level/rate):

| Skill/Behavior | Assessment Level of Performance |
|---|---|
| Low test scores on statewide testing | $20\% < 10^{th}\%$, $30\% < 25^{th}\%$, $2\% > 60^{th}\%$ |
| Social Skills (SSRS-T baseline September) | Mean Standard Score 86 |
| Disciplinary Contacts | 10% students; >2 times per week |
| Attendance Levels | 80% |

Replacement Skill or Behavior (describe):

| |
|---|
| Literacy Skills:  Reading Comprehension<br>Social Skills |

Performance Goal at End of Intervention:

| Skill/Behavior | Intervention Goal Level of Performance |
|---|---|
| Reading Literacy (District, CBM, May 02 and Statewide Testing, April 02) | Mean Reading Comprehension District: SS 95-105; CBM within grade level; $20\% < 25^{th}$ percentile and $10\% > 60^{th}$ percentile |
| Social Skills (SSRS-T rating May 02) | Mean Standard Score 95-105 |
| Disciplinary Contacts (# per month, May 02) | <2% students, 2 times per month |
| Attendance Rates  (% days attended May 02) | 95% |

Program Generalization Methods:

    (1) Issue "Caught being good" slips (classroom & playground) using 10 social skills

    (2) Once a month "lottery" of slips for selected prizes (choice for:  attention & tangibles)

Anticipated Length of Intervention to Goal (time, e.g. days, weeks): Nov 2001 – May 2002

Progress Monitored by (dimension x method):

| Skill/Behavior | Dimension | Monitoring Method |
|---|---|---|
| Reading Skills: | Reading Comprehension | Once per month:  CBM & District standards testing |
| Social skills | Self-control, Cooperation, Problem Behavior | SSRS-Teacher rated Sept, Dec, May |
| Attendance | # days present | Monthly review school record |
| Disciplinary contacts | #referrals; #suspensions | Review monthly # |

Benchmark Goals (time x performance level):

| Skill/Behavior | Benchmark Date | Expected Performance by Dimension |
|---|---|---|
| (1) Read, (2) Soc Skill (3) Attend (4) Discipline | Dec 31, 02 | (1&2) SS 86-92; (3) 85%; (4) 7% |
| (1) Read, (2) Soc Skill (3) Attend (4) Discipline | March 15, 02 | (1&2) SS 90-95; (3) 90%; (4) 4% |
| (1) Read, (2) Soc Skill (3) Attend (4) Discipline | May 30, 02 | (1&2) SS 92-105; (3) 95%; (4) 2% |

**FORM 7.1**   *Intervention Advisory Panel (IAP) Primary Intervention Worksheet*

# Primary Intervention
## A Planning Guide and Checklist

I.    The Target Area of Primary Intervention is:

A.  **Describe main concern:**  Serenity Lane Elementary School:  CHRONIC Schoolwide:

    (1) Low reading performance scores

    (2) High number of disciplinary referrals for detention, suspension

    (3) High absenteeism rates

    (4)

B.  **List factors contributing to target area of concern:**

    (1) "Resistant" teachers

    (2) Poor student reading skills

    (3) High levels of aggression on playground and in classroom

    (4) Low level of parental involvement

    (5) Low SES; families with limited resources; 80% students eligible for free/reduced lunch

II. Pre-Intervention Evaluation/Assessment of Target Area:

A.  **What is the present level of functioning for the contributing factors listed above?**

    (1) Statewide testing:  more than 50% students scoring in lower 2 quadrants

    (2) Schoolwide attendance rate low at 80% of school days

    (3) Mobility (transciency rate) at 60%

    (4) 10% of students receive disciplinary referrals to Vice Principal, 2+ times per week

B.  **Statement of need to promote the new skill/behavior (s) schoolwide;**
    **this will become the "Mission Statement" of the primary intervention.**

Serenity Lane Elementary School will be proactive by raising expectations for success. We will actively promote and support proficient levels of academic and social performance schoolwide by (1) increasing student reading skill levels, (2) teaching social skills, and (3) implementing anti-violence prevention methods. Our goal is excellence for students, teachers, and parents.

---

**FORM 7.2**    *Example of Primary Intervention Guide and List*

III.    Use the checklist below to guide the intervention process AND as an overall intervention treatment integrity measure! Use relevant forms to document procedures to validate intervention outcomes and accountability.

| Check (√) When Done | Date(s) Complete | Task | Form # | Intervention Phase Component |
|---|---|---|---|---|
| √ | 8/01/01 | **Distribute brief** *social validity surveys* to all teachers, other school professionals, and parents to query appropriate goals given area of concern and current functioning. | 4.4 (T) 4.5 (P) 4.6, 4.7 (S) | **Pre-Intervention Planning** |
| √ | 8/05/01 | **Convene Intervention Advisory Panel (IAP)**, comprised of school, student, parent, & community representatives. | 7.1 | |
| √ | 8/15/01 | **IAP outline critical intervention targets and goals** based on results of social validity surveys. | 7.1 | |
| √ | 8/15/01 | **Decide strategy to address each goal** by (1) adopting a prepackaged evidenced-based intervention OR (2) design intervention. | | |
| √ √ | 8/15/01 8/30/01 | **Operationally define** each skill/behavior to be taught to achieve each goal. 7.1 List (1) essential components to attain each goal (2) intervention intensity and duration (3) benchmark goals, (4) methods to program contingencies for *generalization and maintenance,* (5) responsible parties. | 7.1 and "Being good" lottery | **Intervention Design** |
| √ | 8/30/01 | **Decide methods** and intervals to (1) *monitor progress* and (2) *monitor treatment integrity* during intervention. | 7.1, 7.2 | |
| √ | 9/5/01 | **Distribute** *treatment acceptability* **survey** to teachers and parents; provide description of intervention goals and procedures. | 4.9 (T) 4.10 (P) 4.11/12(S) | |
| √ | 9/10/01 | **Revise** any goals or procedures deemed as not acceptable by a majority of surveys. | | |
| √ | 9/12/01 | **Train intervention implementers** (2-day training to 98% reliability). | Observe Measure | |
| √ | Began 9/15/01 End 5/15/02 | **Implementation of intervention components** as designed. District Literacy Plan (DLP) Schoolwide Behavior Plan, Canter's (SBP) Social Skills Plan (SSP). | | **Intervention Phase** |
| √ | Began 9/30/01 thru end 5/30/02 | **Collect** *treatment integrity* measures at predetermined intervals. Collect measures bi-monthly; immediately evaluate and gave feedback to teachers. | 5.4 | |

**FORM 7.2**    *Continued*

| Check (√) when Done | Date(s) Complete | Task | Form # | Intervention Phase Component |
|---|---|---|---|---|
| √ | 9/15/01 thru end | **Collect data to monitor progress** at predetermined intervals. | | Intervention Phase |
| √ | Dec 01 Feb 02 April 02 | **Assess *generalization*** of skills/behaviors across settings (playground/classroom/home). | Observation Parent Report | |
| √ | 10/15/01 12/10/01 1/31/02 2/28/02 3/31/02 4/30/02 | Convene IAP to evaluate progress and treatment integrity data at regular intervals. IAP makes decision to adjust procedures if data provide evidence for need of change. | | |
| √ | Duration | Implementation of changes as needed. | | |
| √ | Duration 12/10/01 2/15/02 | Evaluate students resistant to intervention as indicated by no or low progress in comparison to peers. Evaluate students for secondary 12/01. Evaluate students tertiary by 1/31/02. | See 7.3, 7.5 See 7.7, 7.8 | |
| √ | End 5/30/02 | **Terminate intervention** when goals are attained or at predetermined time. | | Post-Intervention Assessment |
| √ | Statewide Test 4/02 5/30/02 | **Assess post-intervention levels** of newly trained skills/behaviors. Assess post intervention levels of any skills/behaviors targeted for decrease. | DLP;CBM SSRS-T School Records | |
| √ | May 02 | **Assess *generalization*** of skills/behaviors across settings (playground/classroom/home). | Observation Reports | |
| √ | 6/1/02 | **Distribute *social validity* surveys** to IAP, teachers, and randomly selected sample of students and parents to assess (1) ***treatment acceptability*** and (2) ***social significance*** of intervention outcomes. | 4.14 (T) 4.15 (P) 4.16 (S) 4.17 (S) | |
| √ | 6/15/02 | **IAP prepare and report intervention outcomes** to students, teachers, parents, and community. | 7.2 | |
| √ | 6/15/02 | **Assess *maintenance* of treatment outcomes** after a reasonable time interval assuring effects are sustained or continuing to progress. | Observation SSRS-T CBM Records | |
| √ | 9/15/02 (Begin new year) | **Booster sessions** to reteach relevance of components assessed as not maintaining, or consider reimplementation. | | |

**FORM 7.2**   *Continued*

IV.     Final Report by IAP of Intervention Process and Outcomes

A.      List components/procedures of intervention that were *not as successful* as planned; indicate those that were adjusted during intervention:

Literacy procedures did not help 4-6th graders boost reading skills immediately, by December. However, as the year continued, reading comprehension levels started increasing. The SBP (behavior) was more difficult to implement all components consistently across classes/settings.

B.      List components/procedures of intervention that were *more successful* than planned:

Literacy procedures for K-3rd graders boosted reading skills immediately and continued throughout the year. Social skills lessons, taught as "social skill of the month" across all grade levels were easy to incorporate into class and playground activities; easily reinforced. The "caught being good" slips were fun and easy to do and got a great response from students.

C.      Summarize intervention outcomes by answering the following questions:

Question 1. *To what extent did the primary intervention help students improve academically?*

In terms of the district designed comprehension tests, 4th through 6th grade students did not improve significantly over the first three months of the school year. However, K-3rd grade students did show significant improvement. In terms of the CBM, scores in December were significantly higher than scores in September for both primary and upper-grade students. Statewide testing in April 2002 provided evidence of increased reading literacy skills.

Question 2. *To what extent did the primary intervention help students improve behavioral and social competence?*

Results indicated that average disciplinary contacts were dropped to approximately 1.3 per month per student. Suspension and expulsion rates were lower between September and December when compared to the previous year. Social skills scores, as measured by the Social Skills Rating System, did show some improvement. Students appeared to have higher levels of cooperation, yet there was not significant growth in terms of self-control skills. Attendance rates also improved to 85%.

Question 3: *Did the primary intervention differentially influence students? If so, how?* Primary-grade students improved faster on reading and social skills than did students in grades 4-6. Seventeen (17) students resisted change with the primary intervention and were assessed and then referred for secondary interventions.

Question 4: *If yes to #3, what decisions were made to implement secondary or tertiary interventions for students who did not make progress during the primary intervention?*

Seventeen students, 10 primary grade (K-3) and 7 elementary grade (4-6), participated in small group secondary intervention that targeted specific deficits in social skills and reading skills. One student with particular difficulty was assessed and received tertiary-level treatment using functional-based assessment and analysis procedures to set goals and monitor progress.

Question 5: *To what extent were intervention components implemented with integrity? List percent of integrity by intervention component.*

(1)     District Literacy Program (DLP); mean integrity = 90%

(2)     Canter's Behavioral Program (BP); mean integrity = 80%

(3)     Social Skills Program (SSP); mean integrity = 92%

(4)

**FORM 7.2**   *Continued*

**Question 6:** *To what extent was treatment procedure judged overall as acceptable prior to intervention by the following groups of people?*

| | |
|---|---|
| Teachers: | Pre-training acceptability 65%; post-training acceptability 80% |
| Other school professionals: | 95% acceptability (principal, RSP teacher, psychologist) |
| Students: | 80% agreed needed help and wanted help |
| Parents: | 82% agreed needed students help and they would use home-school note |
| Community representatives: | N/A |

**Question 7:** *To what extent was treatment procedure judged overall as acceptable after intervention by the following groups of people?*

| | |
|---|---|
| Teachers: | 95% of teachers judged the DLP literacy, SSP social skills & SBP acceptable |
| Other school professionals: | 100% DLP, 95% SSP, 100% SBP (SBP was more difficult) |
| Students: | 92% thought steps were necessary and, though sometimes difficult, helped them |
| Parents: | 89% parents said procedure for home-school note & literacy at home were good |
| Community representatives: | N/A |

**Question 8:** *To what extent did intervention agents/consumers/beneficiaries judge intervention outcomes as socially important?*

| | |
|---|---|
| Teachers: | High:  92% literacy; 90% lowered discipline contacts; 95% improved attendance |
| Other school professionals: | High: 98% literacy and attendance, 92% discipline |
| Students: | Liked all the interventions:  High rating = 92%;  Low rating = 4% |
| Parents: | 92% of parents rated students improved in reading and school attitudes |
| Community representatives: | N/A |

**Question 9:** *To what extent did intervention outcomes generalize to other settings, people?*

Students were measured by observational techniques to demonstrate social skills taught in class on the playground, at the bus stops, and, by parent reports (SSRS-Parent), at home.  The exception was those students who were targeted for secondary and tertiary intervention.  High level of generalization across settings.

**Question 10:** *To what extent did outcome effects maintain after intervention was terminated?*

Measures for maintenance of effects that were taken in September 02 indicated:  reading skills (CBM, district standards testing) slightly increased for 1-3 graders; maintained for 4-6 graders;  social skills stable across grades (SSRS-T), attendance and discipline referral rates stable at acceptable rates measured in May 02.

D.    Rate the success of the intervention process overall.

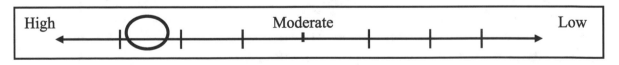

FORM 7.2    *Continued*

school needed to proceed in terms of identifying *socially significant goals*. While waiting for the questionnaires to be returned, the principal assembled an advisory panel that consisted of one general education teacher, one special education teacher, a parent member of the Parent-Teacher Association, the literacy coordinator, a researcher, and the principal herself. Based on the survey, the advisory panel identified two target areas as critical: *literacy skills* and *disruptive classroom behavior*. Next, the advisory panel identified the following *goals* based on current levels of performance: (a) improve reading comprehension skills as evidenced by fewer than 40 percent of the students placing in the first two quadrants on the state exam, (b) improve attendance rates to 95 percent, and (c) reduce disciplinary contacts to no more than one per month per student throughout the school year. They decided to implement a comprehensive, *three-tiered model of prevention* with both literacy and behavioral features. All 300 students attending Serenity Elementary School were to participate in this program.

Further, they decided to include a variety of assessment tools and procedures to *monitor student progress*. They decided that they would need to collect curriculum-based measures and teacher report data on all students. In order to determine the extent to which students were at risk for antisocial behavior problems in general, the advisory panel decided to use the Student Risk Screening Scale (SRSS; Drummond, 1994). The SRSS is a universal screening tool containing seven items (steals; lies, cheats, sneaks; behavior problems; peer rejection; low achievement; negative attitude; and aggressive behavior). Each item is rated by the classroom teacher on a four-point Likert-type scale (*never* = 0, *occasionally* = 1, *sometimes* = 2, *frequently* =3). Scores are totaled (0 to 21) and then students are classified into three levels of risk: Low Risk (0 to 3), Moderate Risk (4 to 8), and High Risk (9 or more). The SRSS is an effective, efficient method for identifying students who do and do not display early behaviors characteristic of antisocial behavior (Drummond, Eddy, & Reid, 1998a, 1998b).

According to the SRSS, approximately 10 percent of the students at Serenity Lane Elementary School were at high risk for antisocial behavior, 20 percent were at moderate risk, and the remainder of the student population fell into the low-risk range.

## The Primary Intervention Plan: Design, Preparation, and Implementation

The *primary intervention* contained three components: a district literacy plan component, a behavioral plan, and a social skills plan. Features of each component including training procedures and treatment integrity information are provided below.

***District Literacy Plan (DLP).*** The DLP is a system-wide plan developed by the district. It includes three categories of instruction: whole group, small group, and individual work. During whole group instruction, literary pieces, empirically validated reading strategies, and elements of literature are introduced. Small groups are developed based on common skill strengths and deficits. Teachers are required to meet with each small group twice a week to target specific skills. Students engage in extensive individual reading practice at their independent reading level. Lesson plans are required to be linked to the district standards and benchmarks that were developed from the state framework.

Teachers participated in a two-day workshop prior to the onset of the school year to review the plan and to familiarize the teachers with each instructional component. Specific attention was given to delineating the specific empirically validated strategies for small group instruction (e.g., guided reading, phonics instruction, and repeated readings). Teachers were also given scoring rubrics and anchor papers.

The literacy coach met with the teachers on a monthly basis during the team meetings to develop plans for small group instruction. Each teacher was allocated a support staff member to assist for thirty minutes a day during small group instruction. The literacy coach conducted demonstration lessons and coached teachers on their implementation of the plan. Feedback was provided individually during brief after-school meetings.

***Schoolwide Behavior Plan (SBP).*** The principal and staff adopted Lee Canter's Assertive Discipline Plan (Canter, 1990; Canter & Canter, 1992) as the primary intervention plan. The goal of Assertive Discipline is to enable teachers to effectively manage their classrooms by creating an environment in which individual student needs are addressed, behavior is dealt with respectfully, and learning takes place as intended by the teachers. This is accomplished by (a) developing positively phrased classroom rules, specific consequences, and incentives for adhering to rules, (b) specifying behavioral expectations by directly teaching the expectations to the students, (c) giving students consistently high rates of positive attention, (d) helping students who exhibit problematic behaviors, and (e) enforcing the classroom rules by providing consequences and incentives as specified in the plan (Charles, 1996).

The researcher and literacy coach conducted a half-day workshop prior to the onset of the school year to introduce this plan and give each teacher a copy of Canter's textbook. During this workshop, teachers developed rules, consequences, and incentives for their classrooms. Classroom plans were shared with the other staff members to ensure continuity across classrooms in order to promote *generalization* of the desired behaviors across classrooms. Three additional staff meetings were used to clarify how to develop classroom routines, refine transitions, and ensure consistent implementation. The literacy coach and vice-principal visited each classroom monthly to provide teachers with coaching and feedback about the implementation of their management plan.

***Social Skills Plan (SSP).*** The social skills program involved each teacher teaching a "skill of the month." Prior to the beginning of the school year, teachers read a list of the thirty social skills listed in the Social Skills Rating System (SSRS; Gresham & Elliott, 1990). Teachers rated the importance of each item on a Likert-type scale: *not important* = 0, *important* = 1, *critical* = 2. These thirty items represent three domains of social skills: *assertion* (e.g., initiates conversations with peers and joins ongoing activities), *self-control* (e.g., controls temper with peers and receives criticism well), and *cooperation* (e.g., attends to instructions and produces correct school work). The top ten social skills determined by teacher ratings were taught to every student in the school using the lesson plans provided in Elliott and Gresham's (1991) Social Skills Intervention Guide. The lessons use explicit instructional procedures that include the following phases: introduce, tell, show, do, follow-through and practice, and *generalization*. The later two phases involved teachers, staff, and noon duty supervisors giving slips to students "caught being good" either in the classroom or on the playground. Specifically, slips containing a list of the ten social skills to be taught during the school year were distributed to students who demonstrated a given skill (which were marked by the adult by circling the skill displayed). Students who received these slips turned them in to a box located in the main office. Once a month, five students' names were drawn from the box and read over the loudspeaker. Each student received the choice of a "front of the lunch line" pass for their class or a small tangible reward (e.g., pencil, eraser). This was done to recognize and reinforce the desired behaviors using peer attention and tangible rewards. By selecting skills that were most important to the teachers, it was anticipated that the skills would be more likely to be reinforced by the teacher as opposed to a prepackaged social skills program. If the skills were more likely to prompt reinforcement, then it was likely that the skills would *generalize* beyond the training sessions and would continue to occur over time, or *maintain*.

***Treatment integrity.*** In order to make sure that each component of the primary intervention plan was taking place as designed, behavioral checklists containing important steps of each component of the district literacy plan (DLP), the school-wide behavior plan (SBP), and the social skills plan (SSP) were developed by the advisory panel and used to monitor treatment integrity. Each teacher was observed twice a month throughout the school year by the literacy coach, vice-principal, principal, and researchers. Each component on the checklists was rated on a three-point Likert-type scale (0 = *no opportunity to observe during the session;* 1 = *not observed;* 2 = *observed*). Session integrity ratings were computed. The mean session integrity for the DLP was 90 percent ($SD = 27.99$); SBP was 80 percent ($SD = 30.25$); and SSP was 92 percent ($SD = 28.34$).

***Social validity.*** Prior to implementing the primary intervention, a summary of each intervention component and the *treatment integrity checklists* were sent to all teachers and staff as well as to a randomly selected group of fifty parents and their children to get their opinions about the appropriateness of the goals, the acceptability of the procedures, and the likelihood of effective outcomes. Results suggested that all parties were in favor of the intervention plans, although the teachers were concerned about having the time to devote to small group instruction in the literacy component. In order to address this concern, the demonstration lessons were added to that component.

Social validity was again assessed at the conclusion of the school year. Again, the results were favorable, with all parties (teachers, staff, parents, and students) stating that the intervention was fair, reasonable, and effective.

## Monitoring Student Progress

In order to evaluate how students were responding to the program, information (data) was collected over the course of the school year and from a variety of sources. Reading skills were assessed using district-designed reading comprehension measures and curriculum-based measures of reading comprehension, which were administered once a month beginning in September and ending in May. Both measures require students in second through sixth grade to silently read a passage and then answer five reading comprehension questions. Students in kindergarten and first grade listened to a passage read aloud by their teachers and then answered five reading comprehension questions, which were also read aloud to them. Reading skills were also assessed using the statewide assessment, which was administered once a year in April.

Behavioral performance was assessed by examining monthly rates of disciplinary contacts, suspensions, and expulsions. Monthly rates of attendance were also computed for each student. Monthly averages were computed based on the number of instructional days per month. Behavioral performance, or more specifically, risk status, was measured three times a year (September, December, and May) using the Student Risk Screening Scale (Drummond, 1994).

Social skills were assessed by having the teachers complete the thirty social skills items on the Social Skills Rating System (SSRS; Gresham & Elliott, 1990) for each student in their class. This was done three times a year (September, December, and May).

## Results

With the help of the researcher, student performance was evaluated using statistical procedures. The first set of questions involved looking at how all students responded between September and December.

***Question 1: To what extent did the primary intervention program help upper and lower elementary school students improve academically?*** In terms of the district-designed comprehension tests, upper elementary students (fourth through sixth grade) did not improve significantly over the first three months of the school year. However, primary elementary students (grades kindergarten through third grade) did show significant improvement. In terms of the curriculum-based measures, scores in December were significantly higher than scores in September for both primary and upper grade students.

***Question 2: To what extent did the primary intervention program help upper and lower elementary school students improve behaviorally and socially?*** Results indicated that average disciplinary contacts were dropped to approximately 1.3 per month per student. Suspension and expulsion rates were lower between September and December during this year as compared to the previous year. In terms of Student Risk Screening Scale scores, there were not significant differences between primary and upper elementary grade students. Further, the scores did not change significantly between September and December. Social skills scores, as measured by the Social Skills Rating System, did, however, show some improvement. Students appeared to have higher levels of cooperation, yet there was not significant growth in terms of self-control skills. Attendance rates also improved to 85 percent.

***Question 3: Did the primary intervention program differentially influence students with low-, moderate-, and high-risk status as measured by the Student Risk Screening Scale?*** Results showed that all students, regardless of risk status, showed improvement in the area of reading according to district-designed comprehension scores and curriculum-based measurement scores. Thus, the reading program was effective for the majority of the students.

***Question 4: To what extent was risk status impacted by the universal intervention during the first three months of the school year?*** Results showed that sixteen students were at high risk for antisocial behavior in September and seventeen students were at high risk in December. Thirty-one students were at moderate risk for antisocial behavior in September, whereas only twenty-seven students were at moderate risk in December. In brief, there was some improvement for moderate-risk students. Similarly, there was improvement in the low-risk category. The remaining students fell into the low-risk category at both time points.

***Summary.*** Results of the first three months of implementation suggest that a primary intervention, when implemented with a high level of treatment integrity, can improve the academic performance of a relatively large number of students. In brief, this comprehensive primary intervention helped to improve students' reading comprehension and social performance across the school. However, student risk scores did not improve significantly over time. Although the majority of the students remained consistent in their risk status, there was some improvement in the lower risk categories. Regardless of risk status, students continued to make academic progress in reading comprehension. This finding is particularly encouraging given that the research indicates that students with higher levels of antisocial behavior tend to become less responsive to intervention efforts as they get older (Kazdin, 1987, 1993; Walker, Colvin, & Ramsey, 1995; Walker & Severson, 2002).

### *Identifying Nonresponsive Students to Participate in Secondary Prevention Efforts*

After carefully examining the above findings, the advisory panel felt that the seventeen students at high risk for antisocial behavior were in need of extra assistance. Therefore, they reviewed all of the data for these seventeen youngsters. Seven of the students were first-grade students who showed limited growth on the district-designed measure and the curriculum-based measures of reading comprehension. Although their social skills fell within the average range, their teachers reported that they were starting to see some acting-out behaviors when asked to participate in the literacy instructional block. The remaining ten students, who ranged from third to sixth grades, were identified as having higher than average disciplinary contacts and fewer than average self-control skills on the Social Skills Rating System (Gresham & Elliott, 1990). Therefore, it was decided that two secondary interventions were warranted: one targeting the academic deficits of the first-grade students and a second targeting the social skills deficits of the other ten youngsters.

## *Secondary Intervention: Academic Target*

### *Identifying the Intervention Target Areas: Pre-Intervention Assessment*

The purpose of this secondary intervention was to assist the first-grade students identified as *nonresponsive to the primary intervention*. Students were selected for this intervention based on their scores on the Student Risk Screening Scale (Drummond, 1994) as well as on the district-designed reading comprehension measures and the curriculum-based measures of reading comprehension as explained above(see Box 7.2; Forms 7.3 and 7.4).

In order to obtain a more complete picture of their *present levels of functioning,* students were assessed from multiple perspectives using psychometrically sound measures. Specifically, the following instruments were used: the Comprehensive Test of Phonological Processes (CTOPP; Wagner, Torgesen, & Rashotte, 1999) to

**BOX 7.2 • *Secondary Intervention Planning Guide***

**Planning Guide for
a Secondary Intervention**

I.   **The Target Area for Intervention is:**
II.  **Nomination of students for participation in the intervention:**
   A.   Method of nomination
   B.   Actual nomination of student participants
   C.   Parent notification of student as participant
III. **Pre-Intervention Evaluation/Assessment of the Target Area:**
   A.   What is present level of functioning?
      a.   By participant
      b.   By group
   B.   Statement of need to increase functioning
      a.   By participant
      b.   By group
IV.  **Convene Intervention Advisory Panel:**
   A.   School personnel (administrator, teachers, yard supervisors, nurse, psychologist)
   B.   Community (when intervention may impact the community-at-large; e.g., representatives from a mental heath organization, youth sport activities, service organizations, etc.)
V.   **Intervention Planning Activities:**
   A.   Social Validity; evaluate the following components; interview implementer(s), parents, and student participants:
      c.   Social significance
         i.    Will achieving the goal improve the quality of life for students as a result of participating in the intervention?
         ii.   Does the goal, or the consequences of it, have social value?
         iii.  What would be the outcomes if intervention was not implemented?
      d.   Treatment acceptability of the intervention components are (ask teachers and parent advisory committees):
         i.    Necessary?
         ii.   Appropriate?
         iii.  Supportive of positive values?
         iv.   Minimally disruptive to the environment?
         v.    Worth the effort to attain the goal?
      e.   Social importance of the intervention goal; extent to which intervention goals are viewed as having socially important outcomes by:
         i.    Intervention implementers
         ii.   Parents
         iii.  Students
   B.   Intervention Design and Task Analysis
      a.   Design (by group, by sub-groups?)
      b.   List essential components of intervention
      c.   Determine intensity and duration of intervention
   C.   Methods to Monitor Intervention
      a.   How will progress be monitored?
         i.    By implementer
         ii.   By student
         iii.  By parent
      b.   How frequently will data be collected?
      c.   Who will evaluate progress?
      d.   Who will determine if intervention needs adjustment?

**BOX 7.2 • *Continued***

    D.   Methods for Treatment Integrity
        a.   Type(s) (e.g., permanent product, observation, checklists)
        b.   Who will collect and evaluate?
    E.   Methods for Generalization and Maintenance
        a.   Programming discrimination opportunities
            i.   Contingency planning
            ii.   Reinforcement, response-cost
        b.   Programming for generalization
            i.   Alternative settings to provide opportunities to demonstrate skill
            ii.   Natural or planned reinforcers in other settings

**VI.   Intervention Implementation**
    A.   Collect Treatment Integrity Information
    B.   Provide generalization and maintenance components
    C.   Collect Assessment Monitoring Data
    D.   Review Progress
    E.   Make adjustments to intervention as result of progress monitoring information

**VII.   Terminate Intervention**
    A.   Measure/Evaluate Strength of Intervention Outcomes Using Data
        a.   How much change?
        b.   Were goals met, exceeded, not met?
    B.   Evaluation of Intervention Outcomes (How did we do?) by:
        a.   Degree of treatment integrity
            i.   How closely was the intervention implemented as planned?
            ii.   Did any components change during intervention?
        b.   Degree of generalization and maintenance (follow-up)
            i.   Measure new skill/behavior in other settings
            ii.   Measure use of new skill/behavior several weeks/months after intervention ends
        c.   Social validity by observation and by measure (advisory committees)
            i.   Social significance of the intervention goals
               1.   Were goals "keystone"?
               2.   Did goals produce meaningful, lasting behavior changes that led to other changes?
            ii.   Social acceptability of intervention procedures; were treatment steps to learn the new skill/behavior:
               1.   Necessary?
               2.   Appropriate?
               3.   Supportive of positive values?
               4.   Minimally disruptive to the environment?
               5.   Worth the effort to attain the goal?
           iii.   Social importance of the effects:
               1.   Does the new behavior and/or skill improve the status of students?
               2.   Do outcomes heighten the probability of future success?
               3.   Would you recommend the intervention to others or use it again at another time or place?

Secondary Intervention IAP Worksheet

IAP Members:                                    Date Convened: _____1/5/02__
Attach list of teacher, administrative personnel, other school professionals, parents, students, and community representatives that will serve on the IAP for the term of the intervention period.
Targeted Skill or Behavior (describe):

| Group of 7 first-grade students: |
|---|
| (1) no progress in reading comprehension during primary intervention |
| (2) teachers observing increased acting-out behaviors in classroom |

Assessed Level of Performance of Skill or Behavior of Concern (State level/rate):

| Skill/Behavior | Assessment Level of Performance |
|---|---|
| Reading comprehension, CTOPP | Group Mean 82 standard score; Decoding skills, mean score 78 (very low) |
| Social skills, problem beh., academics, SSRS-T | SS mn 92; PB mn 110; AC mn 90 |
| High intensity/low frequency behaviors, CEI | Raw score 2.5 items (3=concern level) |
| Cum folder review for historical info, SARS | Absenteeism; negative academic comments |

Replacement Skill or Behavior (describe):

| Improve phonetic skills to acceptable level to boost overall reading ability |
|---|
| Use phonic-based chapter books |

Performance Goal at End of Intervention:

| Skill/Behavior | Intervention Goal Level of Performance |
|---|---|
| Reading comprehension, fluency | Group mn 90-102 standard score DLP |
| Behavior: classroom disruptive and playground negative social interactions | Absence of problem behaviors |

Program Generalization Methods:
    Group reading lessons conducted in classroom during "centers" time.

Anticipated Length of Intervention to Goal (time, e.g. days, weeks):_____
Progress Monitored by (dimension x method):

| Skill/Behavior | Dimension | Monitoring Method |
|---|---|---|
| Decoding Skills | 30 hrs group sessions: 30 min session; 3-4 per week; over 9 weeks | CBM CWPM probes DIBELS NWF probes |
| Playground: Neg Soc Interact (NSI) | Duration record 10 min | Observation |
| Classroom: Ttl Disrupt Beh (TDB) | Duration record 10 min | Observation |
| Treatment Integrity | Scripted lessons | Observation; Checklists |

Benchmark Goals (time x performance level):

| Skill/Behavior | Benchmark Date | Expected Performance by Dimension |
|---|---|---|
| (1)CWPM (2) NWF (3) NSI (4) TDB | 1/31/02 | (1) 35 (2) 10 (3) 20%  (4) 20% |
| (1)CWPM (2) NWF (3) NSI (4) TDB | 2/15/02 | (1) 45 (2) 20 (3) 10%  (4) 10% |
| (1)CWPM (2) NWF (3) NSI (4) TDB | 3/1/02 | (1) 60 (2) 30 (3) 0  (4) 0 |
| Read Comprehension DLP and CBM | 3/15/02 | Group Mn 90-102 SS |

**FORM 7.3** *Intervention Advisory Panel (IAP) Academic Secondary Intervention*

## Secondary Intervention
### A Planning Guide and Checklist

I.  The Target Area of Secondary Intervention is:

A.  Describe main concern:  7 first-grade students

  (1) Academic deficits; limited growth during primary intervention for reading comprehension as measured by district standards and CBM

  (2) Acting-out behaviors in first-grade classroom

B.  List appropriate replacement skills/behaviors to remediate areas of concern:

  (1) Improve decoding skills (assessment identified decoding as deficit area of reading that impedes comprehension)

  (2) Anticipated that externalizing behaviors will decrease as reading skill increases.

II.  Pre-Intervention Evaluation/Assessment of Target Area:

A.  What is the present level of functioning for skills/behaviors listed above?

  (1) Decoding Skills measured by:  CBM correct words per minute (CWPM) = 12 out of 100 in 1-minute probe time

  (2) Decoding skills measured by:  DIBELS nonsense word fluency (NWF) = 2 in 1 minute

  (3) SSRS-T:  Social Skills group mean = 92; Problem Behavior group mean = 110; Academic Competence group mean = 90

  (4) CEI:  group mean = 2.5 high impact, low frequency behaviors

  (5) SARS:  cumulative folder review shows history of high absenteeism and average of 3 negative academic comments in kindergarten and first part of 1$^{st}$ grade

B.  Statement of need to promote the new skill/behavior(s) for the small group of students; list levels deemed as proficient for each new skill/behavior component as well as normative levels for each skill/behavior that will decrease as a result

The 7 first-grade students who showed little progress during schoolwide literacy intervention will comprise a small group of students who will work to improve reading decoding skills.  The group of students will decrease acting-out, externalizing behaviors as they improve reading skill.

**FORM 7.4**   *Example of Academic Secondary Intervention: Guide and Checklist*

III.    Use the checklist below to guide the intervention process AND as an overall intervention treatment integrity measure!  Use relevant forms to document procedures to validate intervention outcomes and accountability.

| Check (√) When Done | Date(s) Complete | Task | Form # | Intervention Phase Component |
|---|---|---|---|---|
| √ | 1/3/02 | Distribute brief *social validity surveys* to teachers, other school professionals and parents to query appropriate goals given area of concern and current functioning. | 4.4 (T) 4.5 (P) 4.6, 4.7 (S) | Pre-Intervention Planning |
| √ | 1/5/02 | Convene Intervention Advisory Panel (IAP), comprised of school, student, parent, & community representatives. | 7.3 | |
| √ | 1/5/02 | IAP outline critical intervention targets and goals based on results of social validity surveys. | 7.3 | |
| √ | 1/5/02 | Decide strategy to address each goal by (1) adopting a pre-packaged evidenced-based intervention OR (2) design intervention. | | |
| √ | 1/5/02 | Operationally define each skill/behavior to be taught to achieve each goal | 7.3 | Intervention Design |
| √ | 1/7/02 | List (1) essential components to attain each goal, (2) intervention intensity and duration (3), benchmark goals, (4) methods to program contingencies for *generalization and maintenance*, & (5) responsible parties. | 7.3  and reading sessions in classroom | |
| √ | 1/7/02 | Decide methods and intervals to (1) *monitor progress* and (2) *monitor treatment integrity* during intervention. | 7.3 | |
| √ | 1/8/02 | Distribute *treatment acceptability* survey to teachers and parents; provide description of intervention goals and procedures. | 4.9 (T) 4.10 (P) 4.11/12(S) | |
| √ | 1/10/02 | Revise any goals or procedures deemed as not acceptable by a majority of surveys. | | |
| √ | 1/15/02 | Implementation of intervention components as designed. | Observe Measure | Intervention Phase |
| √ | Began 1/20/02 End 3/15/02 | Collect *treatment integrity* measures at predetermined intervals. Observe sessions bimonthly. Collect teacher checklists weekly. | 5.3 5.4 | |
| √ | 1/15/02 | Collect data to monitor progress  at predetermined intervals (see 7.4); graph. | See Graphs | |

FORM 7.4    *Continued*

| √ | Date(s) Complete | Task | Observation Parent Report | Intervention Phase Component |
|---|---|---|---|---|
| √ | | Convene IAP to evaluate progress and treatment integrity data at regular intervals. IAP makes decision to adjust procedures if data provides evidence for need of change. Implementation of changes as needed. | | |
| √ | Ongoing with progress monitoring | Evaluate students resistant to intervention as indicated by no or low progress in comparison to peers. Consider for tertiary interventions, one-on-one intense treatment. | CBM; ORF, NWF; Observe NSI, TDB | Intervention Phase |
| √ | 3/15/02 | Terminate intervention when goals are attained or at predetermined time. | | Post-Intervention Assessment |
| √ | 3/15/02 to 3/20/02 | Assess post-intervention levels of newly trained skills/behaviors. Assess post-intervention levels of any skills/behaviors targeted for decrease. | See 7.3 | |
| √ | 3/20/02 | Assess *generalization* of skills/behaviors. | Observed | |
| √ | 3/20/02 | Distribute *social validity* surveys to IAP, teacher(s), students, and parents to assess (1) *treatment acceptability* and (2) *social significance* of intervention outcomes. | 4.2 (T) 4.15 (P) 4.3 (S) 4.16 (S) | |
| √ | 3/31/02 | IAP report intervention outcomes to students, teachers, parents. | 7.4 | |
| √ | 5/31/02 | Assess *maintenance* of treatment outcomes after a reasonable time interval assuring effects are sustained or continuing to progress. | Observation SSRS-T CBM Records | |
| √ | 9/15/02 | Booster sessions of components assessed as not maintaining; consider tertiary intervention. | Observation SSRS-T CBM Records | |

IV.    Final Report by IAP of Intervention Process and Outcomes

A.    List components/procedures of intervention that were *not as successful* as planned; indicate those that were adjusted during intervention:

One student said intervention was "too hard" (CIRP interview). Two other students withdrew from the intervention early (one moved, the other was expelled). One teacher felt the intervention was not broad enough to address students' concerns.

**FORM 7.4** *Continued*

B.     List components/procedures of intervention that were *more successful* than planned

Teachers did not implement the interventions, and this was a particularly important factor because teachers did not have to take time away from other students.  Intervention in the classroom prompted generalization of skills.  Increasing reading skills clearly decreased negative and disruptive behaviors in classroom and on the playground.  Thus, intervention produced change with relatively few extra costs.

C.     Summarize intervention outcomes by answering the following questions.

Question 1: *To what extent did the secondary intervention help students improve academic performance?*

The 5 students who completed the intervention  made substantial growth in decoding skills, which improved reading comprehension.

Question 2: *To what extent did the secondary intervention help students improve behavioral performance and social competence?*

Teaching and increasing reading skill decreased disruptive behavior in the classroom and negative social interactions with peers on the playground

Question 3: *Did the secondary intervention differentially influence students?   If so, how?*

Some students made higher gains than others.  One student required a tertiary intervention to address inattentive behaviors and difficulty completing work.

Question 4: *If yes to #3, what decisions were made to implement more intense, tertiary interventions on a one-to-one basis for students who did not make progress?*

One student, who made some progress, continued to exhibit inattentive behaviors in class (daydreaming) and continued to not complete class work.  Thus a more intensive, tertiary intervention, was designed and implemented as designed to address these additional areas of concern.

Question 5: *To what extent were intervention components implemented with integrity? List percent of integrity by intervention component.*

(1)    Behavioral scripted literacy lessons; observed by literacy coordinator; mn integrity = 98%

(2)    10% Behavioral scripted literacy lessons; observed by researcher; mn integrity = 100%

Question 6: *To what extent was treatment procedure judged overall as acceptable prior to intervention by the following people?*

Teacher(s):    70% acceptable (reluctant about reading decreasing behavior)

Other school professionals:    N/A

**FORM 7.4** *Continued*

Students:        60% (worried might be too hard)

Parents:        100% (want help for their children)

Question 7: *To what extent was treatment procedure judged overall as acceptable after intervention by the following groups of people?*

Teacher(s):        90% acceptable (liked that another person implemented, but in the classroom)

Other school professionals:    N/A

Students:        80% (1 out of 5 students still thought it was too hard)

Parents:        80% (1 student still having problems)

Question 8: *To what extent did intervention agents/consumers/beneficiaries judge intervention outcomes as socially important?*

Teachers:        High importance = 100%

Other school professionals:    N/A

Students:        Very important = 80%

Parents:        High importance = 100% (reading and behaving in school)

Question 9: *To what extent did intervention outcomes generalize to other settings, times, people?*

High generalization of reading skills and collateral effect of decreasing disruptive behavior in the classroom and negative interactions to peers on the playground.

Question 10: *To what extent did outcome effects maintain after intervention was terminated?*

For the students who completed the intervention, the gains were maintained over time once the intervention concluded despite the low social validity ratings given by one student, who went on to a tertiary intervention.

D.        Rate the success of the intervention process overall.

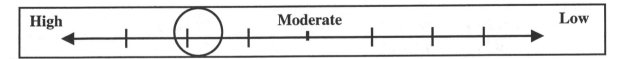

assess specific phonetic skills', the complete version of the Social Skills Rating System (SSRS; Gresham & Elliott, 1990) to evaluate academic performance, problem behaviors, and social skills; the Critical Events Index (CEI; Walker & Severson, 1992) to measure high intensity and low frequency behaviors (i.e., steals and physically assaults an adult); and the School Archival Record Search (SARS; Walker, Block-Pedago, Todis, & Severson, 1991), used to extract information from the cumulative file (e.g., demographics, attendance, achievement test information, school failure, disciplinary contacts, within-school referrals, certification for special education, placement out of regular classrooms, receiving Chapter 1 services, out-of-school referrals, and negative narrative comments).

## Intervention Planning Activities

After reviewing the information presented by the literacy coordinator and the researcher, the advisory panel determined that the students had limited phonetic skills and higher than average rates of acting out or externalizing behaviors. Thus, the *goal* of the program was to improve their phonetic skills. It was hypothesized that the students might have been acting out because they did not have the necessary skills to participate in the formal reading program. Therefore, it was decided that the *replacement skill* should focus on improving decoding skills. An early literacy program, John Shefelbine's Phonics Chapter Books (Shefelbine, 1998), was selected as a supplemental program for first-grade students identified by their teachers as at-risk for antisocial behavior who were unresponsive to a schoolwide literacy and behavior intervention. *Social validity* was assessed from the teacher, parent, and student perspectives via semi-structured interviews (Gresham & Lopez, 1996; Lane, 1997) that were completed with each of the students, their parents, and their teachers. Everyone interviewed felt that the intervention was appropriate given the difficulty their child/student was having in reading. Two students from the same first-grade classroom did, however, indicate that they would feel most comfortable if they could stay in a classroom for the intervention groups. Consequently, it was planned that the group sessions would take place in their classroom.

## The Secondary Intervention Plan: Design, Preparation, and Implementation

*Intervention and assessment procedures.* The seven students were randomly assigned to one of two intervention groups, both of which were to be led by the school literacy coach. The experimental design was a multiple baseline (Johnston & Pennypacker, 1993) across intervention groups study. This means that baseline would be collected for both groups; however, when the intervention was started for one group, the second group would continue to remain in the baseline phase for additional time. Once the first group started to show changes in the behaviors being monitored, then the second group would begin the intervention phase. If the behaviors changed only when the intervention was introduced, then it could be concluded that the changes were due to the intervention and not some other situation (e.g., maturing or weather changes).

Each intervention group participated in a total of thirty lessons (thirty minutes in length). Lessons were conducted three or four times a week over a nine-week period of time resulting in fifteen hours of intervention. Based on the information gleaned from the *social validity interviews* and in an effort to *promote generalization* of the newly acquired skills, lessons were conducted in a general education classroom during regularly scheduled center times.

***Academic intervention.*** John Shefelbine's Phonics Chapter Books (Shefelbine, 1998) were selected as the intervention for this secondary intervention. This phonics-based program is comprised of six books that contain four components: practice phonemic awareness strategies, connect sound-symbol relationships and introduce high-frequency words, read the chapter aloud, and dictate and write.

Prior to conducting the intervention sessions, the literacy coordinator, who had a masters degree in education, reviewed the instructional materials in the kit and practiced conducting the intervention with one of her other students. Total training time was approximately five hours.

***Treatment integrity.*** In order to ensure that the lessons were implemented as intended, behavioral scripts were developed that contained each of the following components: rereading the previous chapter, participating in oral blending activities, introducing new sounds, reviewing previously taught sounds, blending words, introducing high-frequency words, reviewing high-frequency words, reading the new chapter aloud, and writing a dictated sentence. Treatment integrity data were collected during each session by the literacy coordinator and for 10 percent of the sessions by the research person on the parent advisory panel. Session integrity ratings were computed: 98 percent according to the literacy coordinator and 100 percent according to the researcher.

### Monitoring Student Progress

In order to evaluate the effects of this program, the advisory panel decided to use curriculum-based measures of oral reading fluency as well as direct observations of classroom and playground behavior. Three graduate students in school psychology received two hours of formal training by the researcher in curriculum-based assessment and direct observation procedures. The specific reading measures included curriculum-based measures of oral reading fluency (ORF) measured in terms of correct words read per minute (Shinn, 1989) and the nonsense word fluency (NWF) subtest of Dynamic Indicators of Basic Early Literacy Skills (DIBELS; Kaminki & Good, 1996). Grade-level passages were developed from highly decodable texts. Each student was asked to orally read a passage containing approximately 100 words. Each passage was scored for the number of words read correctly, number of words attempted, and errors (substitutions, hesitations, mispronunciations, or omissions). Nonsense word fluency was assessed using the twenty, one-minute probes provided. These probes contained nonwords (e.g., wuf, zim), and each passage was scored for the number of correct phonemes per minute.

The graduate students also learned how to observe and score total disruptive behavior (TDB) in the classroom setting and negative social interactions (NSI) occurring in the playground setting using videotaped segments of students in classrooms (Walker & Severson, 1992). Duration recording procedures were used for both TDB and NSI to determine the percentage of time spent engaged in disruptive behavior in the classroom (TDB) and the percentage of time spent engaged in negative social interactions on the playground. More specifically, total disruptive behavior (TDB) refers to behaviors that disturb the classroom environment and interfere with instruction. Examples include being out-of-seat without teacher permission, taking other people's property, hitting or pestering other students, and making any audible noise that is not part of the instructional activity. Negative social interaction (NSI) refers to behaviors that disrupt ongoing play activities and include any formal aggression (physical or verbal). Examples include name-calling, demeaning statements, possessive statements, threats, taunts, rough body contact, physical pestering, and rough contact with objects (Walker & Severson, 1992). TDB and NSI data were collected during academic instructional periods using a stopwatch. Students were observed for ten minutes; the stopwatch was started when the student was engaged in the target behavior and stopped when the student stopped performing the target behavior. TDB and NSI were then converted to a percentage by dividing the amount of time lapsed on the stop watch by the total amount of time observed and then multiplying the quantity by 100 (Range: 0 percent to 100 percent; see Lane, O'Shaughnessy, Lambros, Gresham, & Beebe-Frankenberger, 2001). Interobserver scores were high: NWF 97 percent (SD = 5.0); ORF 96 percent (SD = 4.74); TDB 97 percent (SD = 6.61); and NSI 96 percent (SD = 13.55).

*Social validity.* Social validity was assessed by the teacher using the Intervention Rating Profile (IRP-15; Martens, Witt, Elliott, & Darveaux, 1985). Students' views of social validity were assessed using a modified version of the Children's Intervention Rating Profile (CIRP; Witt & Elliott, 1985; Lane, 1997, 1999; Lane et al., 2001) and a semi-structured interview (Lane, 1997).

## Results

As mentioned earlier, a multiple baseline across intervention groups was used to evaluate the outcomes. Data were collected prior to beginning the intervention (baseline), during the intervention, immediately following the intervention (post), as well as three months later (follow-up). The last two phases (post and follow-up) were included to assess *maintenance* of skills. Each of the four variables mentioned above (NWF, ORF, TDB, and NSI) were assessed once a week for each student.

Data were graphed and analyzed with the help of the researcher. Two students in the second group did not finish the intervention (one moved and one was expelled). Visual inspection of the graphs for group 1 (see Fig 7.2) showed that all students who completed the intervention made growth in their decoding skills as measured by NWF probes, and in ORF skills as measured by correct words per minute. Total TDB decreased to 0 during post-intervention for all students who finished the intervention. Similarly, negative social interactions, although low to begin with, fell over the course of the intervention.

*Social validity.* Four of the five students who completed the intervention viewed the intervention favorably according to responses on the modified version of the CIRP. However, one student, Jimmy, rated the intervention unfavorably. The semi-structured interview revealed that he thought the intervention was too hard. This child was the only student in group 2 who finished intervention. Thus, it is possible that the attrition influenced his acceptability ratings.

Although the first-grade teachers did not lead the intervention, they were asked to complete the IRP-15. Ratings were somewhat mixed. One teacher viewed

Secondary Intervention IAP Worksheet

IAP Members:                                        Date Convened: _____1/5/02_
Attach list of teachers, administrative personnel, other school professionals, parents, students, and community representatives who will serve on the IAP for the term of the intervention period.
Targeted Skill or Behavior (describe):

| |
|---|
| Group of 10 3rd-6th grade students: |
| (1) High disciplinary contacts |
| (2) Teachers observing increased acting-out behaviors in classroom and on playground. |
| (3) Low academic engagement in classroom |

Assessed Level of Performance of Skill or Behavior of Concern (State level/rate):

| Skill/Behavior | Assessment Level of Performance |
|---|---|
| Social skills, problem beh, academics, SSRS-T | SS mn 82; PB mn 115; AC mn 88 |
| High intensity/low frequency behaviors, CEI | Raw score 3.2 items (3 = concern level) |
| Cum folder review for historical info, SARS | (1)Absenteeism mn = 8 days per month; (2)Negative behavior comments mn=5 |

Replacement Skill or Behavior (describe):

| |
|---|
| Teach self-control behaviors to mediate for acquisition deficits. Use scripted lessons. |

Performance Goal at End of Intervention:

| Skill/Behavior | Intervention Goal Level of Performance |
|---|---|
| Social Skills (rated by teacher) | Group mn 90-102 standard score |
| Behavior: classroom disruptive and playground negative social interactions | None |
| Number of discipline contacts per month | 0 - 1 |
| Days absent per month | 0 - 2 |

Program Generalization Methods:
Training groups will contain typical students as peer models for target students. Typical students naturally serve as stimuli (visual prompts) for appropriate self-control social skills in other than training conditions.

Anticipated Length of Intervention to Goal (time, e.g. days, weeks):_____10 weeks_
Progress Monitored by (dimension x method):

| Skill/Behavior | Dimension | Monitoring Method |
|---|---|---|
| Self-Control Social Skills Training Lessons Scripted | 30 sessions: 30 min session; over 10 weeks | Treatment Integrity: (1) Trainer checklist (2) Observation |
| Playground: Neg Soc Interact (NSI) | Duration record 10 min | Observation |
| Classroom: Ttl Disrupt Beh (TDB) | Duration record 10 min | Observation |
| Academic Engage(AE)/Unengaged(AUE) | Duration record 10 min | Observation |

Benchmark Goals (time x performance level):

| Skill/Behavior | Benchmark Date | Expected Performance by Dimension |
|---|---|---|
| (1) AE (2) AUE (3) NSI (4) TDB | 1/31/02 | (1)65% (2) 35% (3) 20% (4) 20% |
| (1) AE (2) AUE (3) NSI (4) TDB | 2/15/02 | (1) 75% (2)25% (3)10% (4) 10% |
| (1) AE (2) AUE (3) NSI (4) TDB | 3/1/02 | (1) 85% (2)15% (3) 0 (4) 0 |

**FORM 7.5** *Intervention Advisory Panel (IAP) Social Secondary Intervention Worksheet*

# Secondary Intervention
## A Planning Guide and Checklist

I.    The Target Area of Secondary Intervention is:

A.    Describe main concern:_____10 students (grades 3 to 6)_____

    (1) High number of disciplinary contacts_____

    (2) Significantly fewer than average self-control social skills_____

    _____

B.    List appropriate replacement skills/behaviors to remediate areas of concern:

    (1) Improve social skills that support self-control behaviors._____

    (2) Anticipated that externalizing behaviors will decrease as self-control skill increases.____

    _____

II.  Pre-Intervention Evaluation/Assessment of Target Area:

A.  What is the present level of functioning for skills/behaviors listed above?

    (1) SSRS-T; Social skills acquisition deficits for self-control behaviors____

    (2) SSRS-T; Problem behaviors, undercontrolled aggressive behaviors____

    (4) CEI: group mean = 3.2 high impact, low frequency behaviors_____

    (5) SARS: cumulative folder review shows history of high absenteeism, group average 8____

    days per month, and an average of 5 negative behavioral comments in the previous school

    year_____

B.    Statement of need to promote the new skill/behavior(s) for the small group of students;
       list levels deemed as proficient for each new skill/behavior component as well as
       normative levels for each skill/behavior that will decrease as a result

The 10 students who showed little progress during schoolwide literacy intervention will_____

comprise a small group of students who will work to improve self-control social skills.  The____

group of students will decrease acting-out, externalizing behaviors as they improve self-control.

_____

_____

**FORM 7.6**    *Example of Social Secondary Intervention: Guide and Checklist*

III.    Use the checklist below to guide the intervention process AND as an overall intervention treatment integrity measure!  Use relevant forms to document procedures to validate intervention outcomes and accountability.

| Check (√) when Done | Date(s) Complete | Task | Form # | Intervention Phase Component |
|---|---|---|---|---|
| √ | 1/3/02 | Distribute brief *social validity surveys* to teachers, other school professionals, and parents to query appropriate goals given area of concern and current functioning. | 4.4 (T) 4.5 (P) 4.6, 4.7 (S) | Pre-Intervention Planning |
| √ | 1/5/02 | Convene Intervention Advisory Panel (IAP), comprised of school, student, parent, & community representatives. | 7.5 | |
| √ | 1/5/02 | IAP outline critical intervention targets and goals; based on results of social validity surveys. | 7.5 | |
| √ | 1/5/02 | Decide strategy to address each goal by (1) adopting a pre-packaged evidenced-based intervention OR (2) design intervention. | | |
| √ | 1/5/02 | Operationally define each skill/behavior to be taught to achieve each goal | 7.5 | Intervention Design |
| √ | 1/7/02 | List (1) essential components to attain each goal, (2) intervention intensity and duration (3), benchmark goals, (4) methods to program contingencies for *generalization and maintenance*, (5) responsible parties. | 7.5 and train in class using peers as models | |
| √ | 1/7/02 | Decide methods and intervals to (1) *monitor progress* and (2) *monitor treatment integrity* during intervention. | 7.5 | |
| √ | 1/8/02 | Distribute *treatment acceptability* survey to teachers and parents; provide description of intervention goals and procedures. | 4.9 (T) 4.10 (P) 4.11/12(S) | |
| √ | 1/10/02 | Revise any goals or procedures deemed as not acceptable by a majority of surveys. | | |
| √ | 1/15/02 | Implementation of intervention components as designed. | Observe Measure | Intervention Phase |
| √ | Began 1/20/02 End 3/15/02 | Collect *treatment integrity* measures at predetermined intervals. Observe sessions bi-monthly. Collect teacher checklists weekly. | 5.3 5.4 | |
| √ √ | 1/15/02 | Collect data to monitor progress at predetermined intervals (see 7.4); graph. Convene IAP to evaluate progress and treatment integrity data at regular intervals. IA: makes decision to adjust procedures if data provides evidence for need of change. | See Graphs | |
| √ | | Implementation of changes as needed. | | |

**FORM 7.6**  *Continued*

| √ | Date(s) Complete | Task | Observation Parent Report | Intervention Phase Component |
|---|---|---|---|---|
| √ | On going with progress monitoring | **Evaluate students resistant to intervention** as indicated by no or low progress in comparison to peers.  **Consider for tertiary interventions,** one-on-one intense treatment. | Observe NSI, TDB Playground Observe AET Class | Intervention Phase |
| √ | 3/15/02 | **Terminate intervention** when goals are attained or at predetermined time. | | Post-Intervention Assessment |
| √ | 3/15/02 to 3/20/02 | **Assess post intervention levels** of newly trained skills/behaviors.  Assess post-intervention levels of any skills/behaviors targeted for decrease. | See 7.6 | |
| √ | 3/20/02 | **Assess *generalization*** of skills/behaviors. | Observed | |
| √ | 3/20/02 | **Distribute *social validity*** surveys to IAP, teacher(s), students, and parents to assess (1) ***treatment acceptability*** and (2) ***social significance*** of intervention outcomes. | 4.2 (T) 4.15 (P) 4.3 (S) | |
| √ | 3/31/02 | **IAP report intervention outcomes** to students, teachers, parents | 7.8 | |
| √ | 5/31/02 | **Assess *maintenance*** of treatment outcomes after a reasonable time interval assuring effects are sustained or continuing to progress. | Observation SSRS-T # Discipline Contacts | |
| √ | 9/15/02 | **Booster sessions** of components assessed as not maintaining; consider tertiary intervention. | Observation SSRS-T # Discipline Contacts | |

IV.    **Final Report by IAP of Intervention Process and Outcomes**

A.    List components/procedures of intervention that were *not as successful* as planned; indicate those that were adjusted during intervention:

Teachers felt the intervention overall "worked better for some students than others."

B.    List components/procedures of intervention that were *more successful* than planned

Both teachers and students rated the intervention procedures favorably.  All students wished the intervention could have lasted longer (another week, the whole school year).

**FORM 7.6**    *Continued*

C.  Summarize intervention outcomes by answering the following questions.

Question 1. *To what extent did the secondary intervention help students improve academic performance?*

The 10 students made substantial growth in academic engaged time.  As a result academic work completion and accuracy increased.

Question 2. *To what extent did the secondary intervention help students improve behavioral performance and social competence?*

Teaching and increasing self-control social skill decreased disruptive behavior in the classroom and negative social interactions with peers on the playground

Question 3: *Did the secondary intervention differentially influence students?  If so, how?*

Some students were able to learn and generalize self-control skills better than others.  Although this intervention targeted acquisition of self-control skills and planned for generalization by training in the classroom with peer models, some students did not receive powerful enough reinforcers, in relation to the competing antisocial behavior, to shape self-control.

Question 4: *If yes to #3, what decisions were made to implement more intense, tertiary interventions on a one-to-one basis for students who did not make progress?*

Plans were made for a tertiary intervention to target specific replacement behaviors with rich schedules of high reinforcers that will compete with reinforcers maintaining antisocial behavior.

Question 5: *To what extent were intervention components implemented with integrity? List percent of integrity by intervention component.*

(1)   Behavioral scripted social skills lessons; observed by trained observers; group 1 = 92% (SD 2.30); group 2 = 89% (SD=5.30), group 3= 91% (SD=3.71).

(2)   Social skills trainers component checklist;  permanent product collected weekly

(3)

(4)

**FORM 7.6** *Continued*

**Question 6:** *To what extent was treatment procedure judged overall as acceptable prior to intervention by the following people?*

Teacher(s):     90% acceptable (teachers wanted behaviors to improve at all costs!)

Other school professionals:   N/A

Students:     75%  (Some students didn't want to be singled out)

Parents:     100% (want help for their children)

**Question 7:** *To what extent was treatment procedure judged overall as acceptable after intervention by the following groups of people?*

Teacher(s):     100% acceptable (liked that another person implemented, but in the classroom)

Other school professionals:   N/A

Students:     95%  (Students wanted the intervention to last longer=attention motivated)

Parents:     90% (2 students still having problems)

**Question 8:** *To what extent did intervention agents/consumers/beneficiaries judge intervention outcomes as socially important?*

Teachers:     High importance = 100%

Other school professionals:   N/A

Students:     Very important = 90%

Parents:     High importance = 100% (reading and behaving in school)

**Question 9:** *To what extent did intervention outcomes generalize to other settings, times, people?*

High generalization of self-control skills and collateral effects of increasing academic engaged time in the classroom, decreasing disruptive behavior in the classroom, and negative interactions with peers on the playground.

**Question 10:** *To what extent did outcome effects maintain after intervention was terminated?*

Gains were maintained over time once the intervention concluded despite the lower social validity ratings given by one student, who went on to a tertiary intervention.

D.     Rate the success of the intervention process overall.

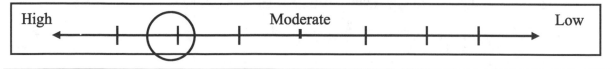

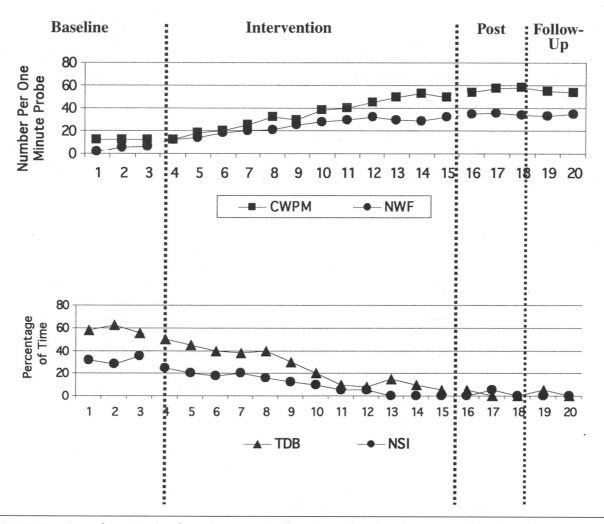

**FIGURE 7.2** *Secondary Intervention to Improve Reading Comprehension: Group 1 Students Mean Score Changes*

the intervention as favorable; however, the other teacher did not feel the intervention was broad enough to address her student's concerns. However, results of the direct observation and reading data suggest that the student did show progress.

***Summary.*** The results of the academic intervention suggested that improved early literacy skills were associated with decreases in disruptive behavior in the general education setting. Further, for the students who completed the intervention, the gains were maintained over time once the intervention concluded despite the low social validity ratings given by Jimmy.

## Secondary Intervention: Social Skills Target

### Identifying the Intervention Target Areas: Pre-Intervention Assessment

The purpose of this secondary intervention was to assist the ten students (third through sixth grade) *identified as nonresponsive to the primary intervention.* Students were selected for this intervention based on their scores on the Student Risk

Screening Scale as well as their self-control skills on the Social Skills Rating System (Gresham & Elliott, 1990; also see Forms 7.5 and 7.6).

In order to obtain a more complete picture of their *present levels of functioning*, students were assessed from multiple perspectives using psychometrically sound measures. Specifically, teachers completed the entire Social Skills Rating System (SSRS; Gresham & Elliott, 1990) to evaluate academic performance, problem behaviors, and social skills, and the Critical Events Index (CEI; Walker & Severson, 1992) to measure high-intensity and low-frequency behaviors (i.e., steals, physically assaults an adult). Further, the School Archival Record Search (SARS; Walker et al., 1991) was designed to extract information from the cumulative file.

## Intervention Planning Activities

After reviewing the information presented by the researcher, the advisory panel determined that the students had *skill deficits* in the areas of self-control according to the SSRS. Thus, the goal of the program was to improve students' self-control skills in an effort to decrease disruptive classroom behavior, decrease negative interactions on the playground, and increase academic engaged time in the classroom. Given that the students had skill deficits, as opposed to performance deficits, it was decided that the students would need formal instruction in social skills. *Social validity* was assessed from the teacher, parent, and student perspectives via semi-structured interviews. It was agreed by all parties that improvements in self-control were necessary and that formal instruction in a small group format was acceptable and likely to be effective. However, the majority of the students (eight) said they would feel embarrassed if the interventions took place in their classroom. Therefore, the advisory panel decided to have the intervention groups meet in various locations around the school (conference rooms and empty classrooms) to accommodate the students' requests and to promote *generalization*.

## The Secondary Intervention Plan: Design, Preparation, and Implementation

*Intervention and assessment procedures.* The ten target students and six typical students were randomly assigned to one of three intervention groups, each of which would be led by a paraprofessional trained in the intervention procedures by the school counselor and the researcher. The typical students were in the low-risk category according to the Student Risk Screening Scale. These students were included to serve as appropriate models for the target students and to *promote generalization* by prompting appropriate social behavior beyond the training environment.

Each of the three intervention groups participated in a total of thirty lessons (thirty minutes in length). Lessons were conducted twice a week over a ten-week period. Based on information obtained from the social validity interviews, the interventions were to be conducted outside the general education classroom.

*Social skills intervention.* The specific social skills lessons selected were based on student skill areas. A list of skill deficits of students in each group were developed based on the results of the Social Skills Rating System. Skill deficits referred to those skills rated as never occurring and critical to the classroom teacher (frequency score = 0; importance score = 2). These skills were the curricular content for each group. Formal lesson plans for each skill were found in Elliott and Gresham's (1991) *Social Skills Intervention Guide: Practical Strategies for Social Skills Training*. Three lessons were used as review sessions. Each lesson is based on a direct instruction paradigm and uses a role-play format to move through each of the five stages (tell, show, do, follow-through and practice, and generalization). Students were given generalization activities to do beyond the training sessions.

***Intervention training.*** The paraprofessional received four hours of formal training in social skills instruction prior to starting the groups. Specific topics included recommended practices in social skills instruction, direct instruction techniques, behavior management strategies, and issues of generalization. Weekly meetings were held with the counselor, researcher, and paraprofessional to provide ongoing training and support.

***Treatment integrity.*** Behavioral component checklists were developed for the social skills lessons in order for the paraprofessional to monitor treatment integrity. One form was completed at the end of each session. Session integrity ratings were quite high (group 1 = 92 percent, *SD* = 2.30; group 2 = 89 percent, *SD* = 5.30; and group 3 = 91 percent, *SD* = 3.71).

### Monitoring Student Progress

In order to evaluate the effects of this program, the advisory panel decided to directly assess classroom and playground behavior. The same graduates were again trained in *direct observation* procedures during two two-hour training sessions. The specific behavioral measures included total disruptive behavior (TDB) and negative social interactions (NSI) as previously defined. In addition, academic engaged time was also assessed using *duration recording procedures*. Academic Engaged Time (AET) refers to the participation in instructional activities specified by the teacher. Examples include attending to the instructional materials, participating in the teacher-assigned motor activity (e.g., writing, cutting, discussing), listening to the teacher speak, and requesting assistance as specified by the teacher (Walker & Severson, 1992). Interobserver scores were as follows: AET 99 percent (*SD* = 0.59); TDB 96 percent (*SD* = 2.61); and NSI 98 percent (*SD* = 13.78).

***Social validity.*** Social validity was assessed from the teacher using the Intervention Rating Profile (IRP-15; Martens et al., 1985) and from the student perspective using a semi-structured interview (Lane, 1997).

### Results

Data were collected prior to the intervention (baseline), during the intervention, immediately following the intervention (post), as well as three months later (follow-up). The last two phases (post and follow-up) were again included to assess *maintenance* of skills. Each of the three variables—TDB, NSI, and AET—were assessed once a week for each student.

Data were graphed (see Fig. 7.3) and analyzed with the help of the researcher. Each group showed decreases in disruptive behavior (TDB) from baseline to post-intervention phases. Each group also showed immediate decreases in disruptive behavior once the intervention started. Despite the noteworthy differences in social behavior between the groups, each group showed decreases in the rates of negative social interactions on the playground between baseline and post-intervention phases. All students showed increases in academic engaged time once the intervention started. These increases were maintained into the follow-up phases. Given that all direct observation data were collected in the general education classroom and

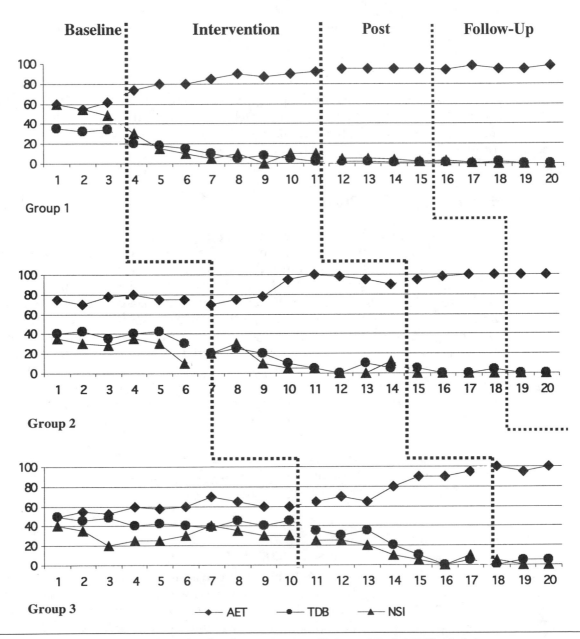

**FIGURE 7.3**   *Secondary Intervention in Three Groups: Self-Control Social Skills Training*

not during the training sessions, this suggests that the newly acquired skills *generalized to other settings* and was associated with increased rates of academic engagement.

***Social validity.*** Both the teachers and the students rated the intervention procedures favorably. All students wished the intervention could have lasted longer (another week, the whole school year). Teachers did note, however, that the intervention worked better for some students than for others.

***Summary.*** In brief, in this small group, customized intervention produced the desired outcomes. Results indicated that the students showed improved social competences as illustrated by fewer problem behaviors in the classroom and improved social interactions on the playground. Given the immediate changes in rates of disruptive behavior, it may be that students were responding to the type of instruction provided rather than the skills acquired during the intervention. Nonetheless, the changes in problem behaviors were lasting. It is hopeful that the increases in academic engaged time will later lead to increased academic performance.

### Identifying Nonresponsive Students to Participate in Tertiary Prevention Efforts

After carefully reviewing the group and individual data from both secondary interventions, the advisory panel determined that the interventions had been largely successful for most of the students. On closer inspection of the teachers' social validity ratings, however, Jimmy's teacher registered concern about his behavior during individual work time. Specifically, although participation in the secondary academic prevention program was associated with improved reading skills and decreased disruptive behavior, she was concerned that Jimmy seldom completed his work during the literacy block. He appeared to spend time daydreaming and occasionally talking to his peers without permission. Thus, the advisory panel decided that a tertiary prevention program was warranted.

## Tertiary Intervention: Functional Assessment-Based Intervention

### Identifying the Intervention Target Areas: Pre-Intervention Assessment

The goal of this tertiary intervention was to increase the amount of work completed by Jimmy, a first-grade student identified as *partially nonresponsive to the secondary intervention.* Jimmy was selected for this intervention by the advisory panel based on teacher concerns regarding work completion and engaging in instructional activities during the assigned work time. According to the teacher, over the past two months, Jimmy's work completion rates had fallen to 60 percent. The quality of his work was good; however, the amount of work completed during the assigned work time was unacceptable. The advisory panel felt that improving

## BOX 7.3 • *Tertiary Intervention Planning Guide*

**Planning Guide for
a Tertiary Intervention**

I.   **Referral problem:**
   A.   Define problem
   B.   Identify parties to intervention
   C.   Hypothesize function of problem behavior

II.   **Select replacement skill/behavior:**
   A.   Type skill/behavior
   B.   Determine proficiency level that will make student successful

III.   **Pre-Intervention Evaluation/Assessment of the Target Area:**
   A.   What is present level of functioning?
   B.   Conduct functional assessment interviews (teacher, parents, student)
   C.   Statement of need to increase functioning

IV.   **Convene Intervention Committee:**
   A.   School personnel (administrator, teachers, yard supervisors, nurse, psychologist)
   B.   Parents
   C.   Student

V.   **Intervention Planning Activities**
   A.   Social Validity; evaluate the following components; interview implementer(s), parents, and student:
      a.   Social significance
         i.   *Will achieving the goal improve the quality of life for the student as a result of participating in the intervention?*
         ii.   *Does the goal, or the consequences of it, have social value?*
         iii.   *What would be the outcomes if intervention was not implemented?*
      b.   Treatment acceptability of the intervention components are (teacher, parents, students):
         i.   *Necessary*
         ii.   *Appropriate*
         iii.   *Supportive of positive values*
         iv.   *Minimally disruptive to the environment*
         v.   *Worth the effort to attain the goal*
      c.   Social importance of the intervention goal; extent to which intervention goals are viewed as having socially important outcomes by:
         i.   *Intervention implementers*
         ii.   *Parents*
         iii.   *Student*
   B.   Intervention Design and Task Analysis
      a.   Design (where, when, how?)
      b.   List essential components of intervention
      c.   Determine intensity and duration of intervention
   C.   Methods to Monitor Intervention
      a.   How will progress be monitored?
         i.   By implementer
         ii.   By student
         iii.   By parent
      b.   How frequently will data be collected?
      c.   Who will evaluate progress?
      d.   Who will determine if intervention needs adjustment?
   D.   Methods for Treatment Integrity
      a.   Type(s) (e.g., permanent product, observation, checklists)
      b.   Who will collect and evaluate?

**BOX 7.3 • *Continued***

    E.    Methods for Generalization and Maintenance
        a.   Programming discrimination opportunities
            i.    Contingency planning
            ii.   Reinforcement, response-cost
        b.   Programming for generalization
            i.    Alternative settings to provide opportunities to demonstrate skill
            ii.   Natural or planned reinforcers in other settings

**VI.  Intervention Implementation**
    A.   Collect Treatment Integrity Information
    B.   Provide Generalization and Maintenance Components
    C.   Collect Assessment Monitoring Data
    D.   Review Progress
    E.   Make Adjustments to Intervention as Result of Progress Monitoring Information

**VII.  Terminate Intervention**
    A.   Measure/Evaluate Strength of Intervention Outcomes using data
        a.   How much change?
        b.   Were goals met, exceeded, not met?
    B.   Evaluation of Intervention Outcomes (How did we do?) by:
        a.   Degree of treatment integrity
            i.    How closely was the intervention implemented as planned?
            ii.   Did any components change during intervention?
        b.   Degree of generalization and maintenance (follow-up)
            i.    Measure new skill/behavior in other settings.
            ii.   Measure use of new skill/behavior several weeks/months after intervention ends.
        c.   Social validity by observation and by measure (teacher, parents, student participants, peers, significant persons in community)
            i.    Social significance of the intervention goals:
                1.  *Were goals "keystone"?*
                2.  *Did goals produce meaningful, lasting behavior changes that led to other changes?*
            ii.   Social acceptability of intervention procedures; were treatment steps to learn the new skill/behavior:
                1.  *Necessary?*
                2.  *Appropriate?*
                3.  *Supportive of positive values?*
                4.  *Minimally disruptive to the environment?*
                5.  *Worth the effort to attain the goal?*
           iii.  Social importance of the effects:
                1.  *Does the new behavior and/or skill improve the status of students?*
                2.  *Do outcomes heighten the probability of future success?*
                3.  *Would you recommend the intervention to other, or use it again at another time or place?*

## Tertiary Intervention IT Committee Worksheet

Student: _____ Jimmy _____ Date: _2/10/02_____

Literacy Coordinator:_____ Ms. Jackson _____

Teacher(s)_____ Mrs. Smitty _____ Parent(s):_____ Jimmy's Parents _____

**Targeted Skill or Behavior (describe):**

| |
|---|
| Poor Work Completion<br>Inattention during independent seatwork time<br>Side-talking with peers during independent seatwork time. |

**Assessed Level of Performance of Skill or Behavior of Concern (State level/rate):**

| Skill/Behavior | Assessment Level of Performance |
|---|---|
| Work completion | 60% |
| Academic Engaged Time | 50% |
| | |
| | |

**Replacement Skill or Behavior (describe):**

| |
|---|
| Receive teacher attention by completing work during independent seatwork time. |

**Performance Goal at End of Intervention:**

| Skill/Behavior | Intervention Goal Level of Performance |
|---|---|
| Work completion during independent work | 100% |
| Academic engaged time (AET) | 100% |
| | |
| | |

**Anticipated Length of Intervention to Goal (time, e.g. days, weeks):_____ 30 days  (6 wks) _____**

**Progress Monitored by (dimension x method):**

| Skill/Behavior | Dimension | Monitoring Method |
|---|---|---|
| AET | 10 min.duration 2-3 times per week | Observation |
| Work completion | % work completed | Permanent Product (work) |
| | | |
| | | |

**Program Generalization & Maintenance:**

      Parents structure homework time and place at home.

      Jimmy receive teacher attention at circle time (another activity)

**Benchmark Goals (time x performance level):**

| Skill/Behavior | Benchmark Date | Expected Performance by Dimension |
|---|---|---|
| (1) AET (2) work completion | 2/20/02 | (1) 70% (2) 80% |
| (1) AET (2) work completion | 3/05/02 | (1) 80% (2) 85% |
| (1) AET (2) work completion | 3/15/02 | (1) 90% (2) 90% |
| (1) AET (2) work completion | 3/31/02 | (1)100%  (2) 100% |

**FORM 7.7**   *Tertiary Intervention IT (Intervention Team) Committee Worksheet*

# Tertiary Intervention*
## A Planning Guide and Checklist

I.    Target Area of Tertiary Intervention  Student:_____Jimmy_____

List problematic skill/behavior(s):

(1)    Low rate of work completion

(2)    Daydreams during independent seatwork

(3)    Side-talking with peers during independent seatwork

(4)

II.    Pre-Intervention Evaluation/Assessment of Target Area:

A.    Conduct and evaluate assessment for following:

- Present level of functioning for skills/behaviors listed above:

(1)    60% rate of work completion previous 2 months.  (quantity poor)

(2)    Grade level performance on WJ-III   (quality good)

(3)

- Nature of skill/behavior deficits (acquisition, performance, or fluency):

(1)    Performance deficit (won't do)

(2)

- Function of behavior:

(1)    Teacher attention

(2)

B.    List appropriate replacement skills/behaviors:

(1)    Teach new way to attain teacher attention:  raise hand when work complete;  receive praise for work completion.

(2)    Increase Academic Engaged Time (AET);   initially reduce time for task and gradually increase as able to attend to and complete task

(3)

C.    List levels deemed as proficient for each new skill/behavior component as well as normative levels for each skill/behavior that will decrease as a result.

(1)    100% Academic Engaged Time (AET) during independent seatwork

(2)    100% work completion of independent seatwork tasks

---

**FORM 7.8**   *Example of Tertiary Intervention: Guide and Checklist*

Use the checklist below to guide the intervention process AND as an overall intervention treatment integrity measure!  Use relevant forms to document procedures to validate intervention outcomes and accountability.

| Check (√) when Done | Date(s) Complete | Task | Form # | Intervention Phase Component |
|---|---|---|---|---|
| √ | 2/05/02 | Conduct and evaluate **skills-based assessment** with student.  Review records. | | Pre-Intervention Assessment and Planning |
| √ | 2/05/02 | Conduct observational assessments: (1) A-B-C Event, (2) Reinforcement, (3) Environment. | 2.4, 2.5, 2.6 | |
| √ | 2/06/02 | Conduct and evaluate **Functional Assessment Interviews** (FAI) with teacher(s), student, parents, other relevant people. | 2.1 (T, P) 2.2 (S) | |
| √ | 2/06/02 | Assess *social validity* with teacher, student, and parents to query understanding of problem and appropriate goals given area of concern, current functioning, and potential functions. | 4.4 (T) 4.5 (P) 4.6-4.8 (S) | |
| √ | 2/10/02 | **Convene Intervention Team (IT)** comprised of teacher(s), administrator, psychologist, parents and student.  **Discuss & decide** (1) critical intervention targets and goals. (2) strategy to address each goal. | 7.7 | |
| √ | 2/11/02 | **Interventionist:  Operationally define** each skills/behaviors to be taught to achieve goals. | 3.1 | Intervention Design |
| √ | 2/11/02 | **List** (1) essential components to attain each goal, (2) intervention intensity and duration, (3) benchmark goals, (4) methods to program contingencies for *generalization and maintenance*, & (5) responsible parties. | 3.1 6.1 | |
| √ | 2/11/02 | **Decide methods** and intervals to (1) *monitor progress* and (2) *monitor treatment integrity* during intervention. | 3.1 3.2-3.7 5.1-5.7 (as appropriate) | |
| √ | 2/12/02 | Assess *treatment acceptability* information by survey with teachers and parents; provide description of intervention goals and procedures. | 4.9 (T) 4.10 (P) 4.11, 12, 4.13(S) | |
| √ | 2/13/02 | **Revise** any goals or procedures deemed as not acceptable by a majority of surveys. | | |
| √ | 2/13/02 | **Explain, train** teacher(s) , student, and parents on components they will implement, monitor, and graph. | 3.2 3.3 | |

**FORM 7.8**    *Continued*

| Check (√) when Done | Date(s) Complete | Task | Form # | Intervention Phase Component |
|---|---|---|---|---|
| √ | 2/15/02 | Implementation of intervention components as designed. | | Intervention Phase |
| √ | 2/15/02 to End | Collect *treatment integrity* measures at predetermined intervals. | 5.3, 5.4 | |
| √ | 2/15/02 3/31/02 | Collect data to monitor progress at predetermined intervals. | | |
| √ | Weekly | Graph data about progress. | | |
| √ | 2/20/02 2/28/02 3/10/02 3/20/02 | Convene IT to evaluate progress and treatment integrity data at regular intervals. IT makes decision to adjust procedures if data provides evidence for need of change. | 7.7 | |
| √ | 2/28/02 | Implementation of changes as needed. | | |
| √ | N/A Good response | Evaluate students resistant to intervention as indicated by no or low progress towards goals. Consider for formal evaluation for special education supports. | | |
| √ | 3/31/02 | Terminate intervention when goals are attained or at predetermined time. | | |
| √ | 3/31/02 | Assess post-intervention levels of newly trained skills/behaviors. Assess and graph post-intervention levels of any skills/behaviors targeted for decrease. | | Post-Intervention Assessment |
| √ | 4/5/02 | Assess *generalization* of skills/behaviors to other settings, people, situations. | Observed | |
| √ | 4/5/02 | Assess *social validity* of intervention outcomes with teacher(s), student, parents; (1) *treatment acceptability* and (2) *social significance* of intervention outcomes. | 4.2 (T) 4.3 (S) Interview (P) | |
| √ | 4/10/02 | IT meets for report of intervention outcomes. | 7.8 | |
| √ | 5/01/02 6/15/02 | Assess *maintenance* of treatment outcomes after a reasonable time interval, assuring effects are sustained or continuing to progress. | Observe % work complete | |
| | N/A | Booster sessions of components assessed as not maintaining; consider formal evaluation for special education supports. | | |

**FORM 7.8** *Continued*

IV.    Final Report by IT of Intervention Process and Outcomes

A.    List components/procedures of intervention that were *not as successful* as planned; indicate those that were adjusted during intervention:

_____ None _____

_____

B .    List components/procedures of intervention that were *more successful* than planned:

_____ Self-monitoring and home chart for work completion.  Parents' cooperation produced _____ meaningful results for them and their child; parents learned how to promote work completion in the home (provide space and time to do work); parents felt efficacious on behalf of their child. _____

C.    Summarize intervention outcomes by answering the following questions.

Question 1.  *To what extent did the tertiary intervention help the student improve academic performance?* Compare pre-intervention to post-intervention levels.

_____ 100% improvement;  100% work completion during seatwork time _____

_____ Pre-intervention = 60% work complete; Post-intervention = 100% work complete _____

_____

Question 2.  *To what extent did the tertiary intervention help the student improve behavioral performance and social competence?* Compare pre-intervention to post-intervention levels.

_____ 100% AET improvement during independent seatwork.  Learned to seek teacher _____ attention by raising hand when work was completed. _____

_____

Question 3:  *Did the intervention differentially influence the student?* (change vs. no change)

_____ No.  Student changed work completion and attention to task to same criterion (100%).  Correct _____ function was targeted (teacher attention). _____

Question 4:  *If yes to #3, what decisions were made to implement with more intensity, increase duration of the tertiary intervention, or consider for formal evaluation for special education?*

_____ N/A _____

Question 5:  *To what extent were intervention components implemented with integrity? List percent of integrity by intervention component.*

(1)    Teacher check list = 98% _____

(2)    Student self-monitor = 93% _____

(3)    _____

**FORM 7.8**  *Continued*

Question 6: *To what extent was treatment procedure judged overall as acceptable prior to intervention by the following people?*

Teacher(s):     Very sure procedures reasonable; goals relevant

Other school professionals:          N/A

Student:  Not acceptable;  work completion not important; "could finish during detention"

Parents:  Very sure procedures reasonable in light of son's lack of work completion

Question 7: *To what extent was treatment procedure judged overall as acceptable after intervention by the following groups of people?*

Teacher(s):     100%; resulted in less time to attend to student, more time for others

Other school professionals:          N/A

Student:  Liked the new way for attention; parents were happy with him; earned treats at home

Parents:   100% satisfied;  will continue with chart at home for chores

Question 8: *To what extent did intervention agents/consumers/beneficiaries judge intervention outcomes as socially important?*

Teachers:       High social importance; work completion pivotal to future successes.

Other school professionals:          N/A

Student:        Important to finish work and "totally liked" teacher attention.

Parents:        High social, long-term importance for their son.

Question 9: *To what extent did intervention outcomes generalize to other settings, times, people?*

Academic engaged time generalized to all work.

Question 10: *To what extent did outcome effects maintain after intervention was terminated?*

100% maintenance at 2-, 6- and 10-week follow-up observations AET and work completion

D.     Rate the success of the intervention process overall.

High                         Moderate                         Low

**FORM 7.8**   *Continued*

Jimmy's *work completion* and *academic engaged time* were appropriate goals (see Box 7.3; Forms 7.7 and 7.8).

In order to determine Jimmy's present level of functioning academically and behaviorally, current assessment information was reviewed. After reviewing the academic competence subscale on the Social Skills Rating System (SSRS; Gresham & Elliott, 1990), the results of the Comprehensive Test of Phonological Processing (Wagner et al., 1999), and talking informally to the teachers, it was hypothesized that Jimmy had the necessary skills to complete the requisite task, and the low rates of work completion were the result of a *performance deficit* (a "won't do" problem). According to the School Archival Records Search, Jimmy had high attendance rates but was frequently given after-school detentions due to lack of work completion. To verify this hypothesis, one additional test was administered, the Woodcock Johnson III Tests of Achievement (Woodcock, McGrew, & Mather, 2001). Results indicated that Jimmy was performing at grade level.

The advisory panel decided that a functional assessment was necessary to identify the reason Jimmy was not completing the required tasks during the literacy block. The teacher, parents, a classroom aide, and Jimmy himself were invited to participate in the functional assessment process by being part of the functional assessment team.

The teacher, Mrs. Smitty, was a bright, organized, and attractive general education teacher who had been teaching for five years. Her classroom was highly structured and the twenty-four students were, for the most part, very well behaved. The literacy block began with thirty minutes of whole group instruction followed by twenty minutes of small groups and then twenty-minute blocks of independent seatwork. During seatwork, students were asked to work on their tasks independent of peer or teacher input. Jimmy participated in both the whole group and small group activities; it was during the independent seatwork that he had trouble staying engaged and completing assignments in the allotted time.

*Social validity* was assessed from the teacher, parent, and student perspectives via rating scales designed to assess the significance of the goals. Results indicated that both the teacher and parents felt that the goals were relevant. Jimmy, however, did not see a reason to increase the amount of assignments he finished. He said that he "could just finish them during detention."

## Intervention Planning Activities

**Target and replacement behaviors.** *Work completion behavior* was defined as attempting all problems or activities as specified by the teacher. This was assessed via permanent product recording. Each product was assessed to determine the percentage of assignments completed. The teacher simply counted the number of problems attempted during each independent assignment, divided that number by the total number of problems, and then multiplied the quantity by 100 (e.g., two completed out of five = (2/5) X 100 = 40 percent).

Academically unengaged (AUE) behavior was defined as any behavior other than working on the teacher-assigned task. Examples of academically unengaged behavior included gazing around the classroom, talking with other students about topics not related to the task, leaving his seat without permission, and engaging in noninstructional tasks. This was measured with duration recording procedures as previously described (number of minutes unengaged divided by the total time observed and multiplying the quantity by 100; range: 0 to 100 percent).

*Academically engaged behavior* (AE) was defined as any verbal or motor behavior related to the instructional objective. Examples of academically engaged behavior included gazing at the teacher or instructional materials as requested by the teacher, any motor (e.g., cutting or writing) or verbal (e.g., discussing) behavior related to the instructional task, looking at the materials or teacher, as requested, or listening to the teacher. This behavior was also measured with duration recording procedures (number of minutes engaged divided by the total time observed and multiplying the quantity by 100; range: 0 to 100 percent).

***Functional assessment tools.*** A variety of functional assessment procedures were used to identify why Jimmy was not completing his assignments during independent seatwork time. Functional assessment interviews were conducted with the teacher, parents, and Jimmy. The *Preliminary Functional Assessment Survey* (Dunlap et al., 1993; Dunlap, Kern-Dunlap, Clarke, & Robbins, 1991) was used with both the parents and teachers, and the *Student-Assisted Functional Assessment Interview* (Kern, Dunlap, Clarke, & Childs, 1994) was used with Jimmy. The teacher and parents agreed that work completion was the primary concern for Jimmy given that failure to complete his assignments would ultimately lead to decreases in academic performance. The parents, who had previously been very pleased with the improved early reading skills that stemmed from the secondary intervention, were concerned that Jimmy's progress would "backslide" if work completion did not increase. The parents, the teacher, and Jimmy himself mentioned that the work eventually was completed during detention, given that "most work was easy"; yet, this took an inordinate amount of time on the part of the teacher to sit with Jimmy after school.

In addition to the functional assessment interventions, data were also collected through direct observation using the A-B-C (Bijou, Peterson, & Ault, 1968) data observation system. A-B-C data were collected during five thirty-minute observations during one week. Observations were conducted during the literacy block. The observers recorded the antecedent conditions that occurred prior to the occurrence of the target behaviors and the consequences that followed each instance of academic unengaged behavior and absence of work completion. After reviewing the data collected during five thirty-minute observation sessions, it appeared that when Jimmy daydreamed or spoke to other students, the teacher, Mrs. Smitty, would redirect Jimmy and stand by him while he started the next portion of the assignment. However, as soon as she walked away, Jimmy would cease working. After two or three attempts to encourage Jimmy to complete the task, Mrs. Smitty would assign Jimmy detention. During detention, the work was completed, without assistance, in approximately fifteen to twenty minutes.

The teacher was asked to complete the Motivation Assessment Scale (MAS; Durand & Crimmins, 1988) as another method of identifying the function. Results of the MAS confirmed the findings of both the interviews and the direct observation data. Jimmy did not complete the assignments in an effort to spend more time with his teacher, Mrs. Smitty. Thus, it was hypothesized that low rates of work completion were being maintained by teacher attention.

More specifically, the results of the interviews, direct observational data, and MAS indicated that Jimmy's academic unengaged time and low levels of work completion occurred during independent work time (antecedent condition) and was maintained by obtaining teacher attention (consequence). Thus, the goal of the intervention plan was to teach Jimmy a new method of obtaining teacher attention that would allow him to complete assignments during the allotted time for independent seatwork.

### The Tertiary Intervention Plan: Design, Preparation, and Implementation

***Intervention and assessment procedures.***  Prior to beginning the intervention, baseline data were collected on work completion, academically unengaged behavior, and academically engaged behavior using the definitions and recording procedures above. In order to evaluate intervention outcomes, a withdrawal design was used (Johnston & Pennypacker, 1993). This involves taking baseline data (phase A) until the rates of behavior appear stable and then beginning the intervention (phase B). Once the rates of behavior show steady change, the intervention is removed and the baseline conditions are resumed (phase A). Once stability is again achieved, the intervention is reintroduced (phase B). If the rates of behavior only increase (or decrease) when the intervention is introduced, then it can be concluded that the behavioral changes were due to the intervention and not some other variable.

The goal of the intervention was to increase Jimmy's rates of academic engaged time and percentage of problems attempted and to teach him a functionally equivalent method of obtaining teacher attention. The functional assessment team decided to conduct an antecedent-based intervention by making a curricular adjustment that would be clarified in a behavioral contract. Specifically, the contract included the following components: When the teacher distributed the independent activity, she was instructed to (a) present the task, (b) check for understanding with a brief question-and-answer session, (c) call on Jimmy at least once while checking for understanding, and (d) mark a stopping point on Jimmy's paper with a highlighter.

Once Jimmy attempted the problems up to the indicated mark, he was asked to raise his hand to solicit teacher attention in the form of checking work and providing verbal praise. The process was repeated by having the teacher mark the next stopping point after having delivered the proper attention and reinforcement for work completion. This process was repeated throughout the independent seatwork time. If the assignments were not completed, they were to be sent home and returned the next day. Mrs. Smitty would again provide attention in the form of checking the work and delivering verbal praise when Jimmy turned in the completed assignment. Over time, the amount of problems required until the next stopping point was increased to eventually shape Jimmy to not require reinforcement until the end of the twenty-minute lesson.

The parents were asked to provide a quiet place for Jimmy to work at home, to be available for questions during the fifteen- to twenty-minute activity, to verify that each problem was attempted, and to make sure that the homework assignment was placed in Jimmy's backpack. Staying after school was no longer a consequence for low rates of work completion. A bonus clause was included in the contract: If Jimmy attempted all problems for five consecutive days, he could sit by Mrs. Smitty during circle time. In order to promote Jimmy's involvement in this process and teach him new skills that could generalize to other task demand situations, Jimmy would be asked to monitor each intervention step (0 = *it did not hap-*

*pen;* 1 = *it did happen*) for which he was responsible. At the end of the day, the percentage of components was computed and graphed.

In order to assess social validity, the intervention components were delineated on a form (to serve later as a treatment integrity checklist) and delivered to each member of the functional assessment team. Each step was rated on a three-point Likert-type scale ranging from 0 = *unacceptable,* 1 = *somewhat acceptable,* to 2 = *acceptable.* The parents, teacher, and Jimmy viewed each step as acceptable. Jimmy indicated that he "totally liked" being able to sit next to Mrs. Smitty during circle time.

***Treatment integrity.*** Jimmy's self-monitoring recording was used to assess treatment integrity of his components. The teacher used the treatment integrity checklists of all parties' responsibilities to track student progress. According to both sources, the intervention was implemented with fidelity (Jimmy's ratings: 93 percent, *SD* = 4.10; teacher's ratings: 98 percent, *SD* = 3.94)

## Monitoring Student Progress

In order to evaluate the effects of this tertiary intervention, the teacher collected data on work completion on a daily basis. A paraprofessional was trained in the direct observation procedures during two two-hour training sessions to learn how to collect academic unengaged and academic engaged behaviors using duration recording procedures. Once he reached a 95 percent criterion, baseline data were collected. One of the graduate students collected data alongside the paraprofessional for 20 percent of the sessions. Interobserver scores were as follows: AUE = 98 percent (*SD* = 2.61) and AE 99 percent (*SD* = 0.59). Direct observation measures were observed in ten-minute blocks of time, two to three days a week. AUE and AE were collected in separate ten-minute intervals.

***Social validity.*** At the conclusion of the study, social validity was assessed from the teacher perspective using the Intervention Rating Profile (IRP-15; Martens et al., 1985) and from the student and parent perspectives using a semi-structured interview (Gresham & Lopez, 1996; Lane, 1997).

## Results

Results indicated that the intervention was highly effective in increasing work completion rates (see Figure 7.4) and improving academic engagement. Given that the behaviors returned to baseline rates during the withdrawal phase (see the second Phase A) and again increased when the introduction was reintroduced (see the second Phase B), the changes in the behavior can be attributed to the intervention.

All parties indicated that they viewed the intervention as fair and effective. Jimmy's parents were pleased with the intervention and stated that Jimmy has asked if they could "do the chart thing" to help remind him to complete his assigned chores at home.

***Summary.*** Although not being academically engaged may not be a serious problem, most people would agree that if students do not participate in the assigned

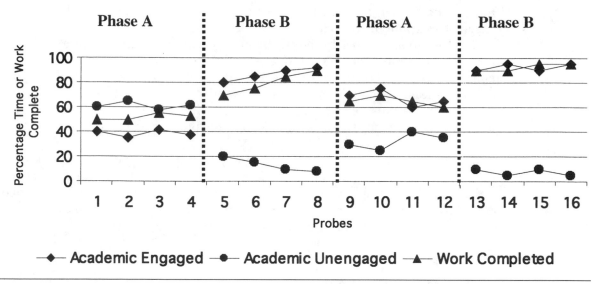

**FIGURE 7.4**    *Tertiary Intervention: Increase in Work Completion Maintained by Teacher Attention*

tasks, they are less likely to learn the necessary skills and gain meaningful experiences (Umbreit, Lane, & Dejud, in press). Findings of this intervention reveal an effective, feasible method of increasing both productivity and academic engagement of a student whose poor work habits were maintained by teacher attention.

## Multilevel Intervention: Summative Findings

After collecting the final data in May, the advisory panel, with the help of the researcher, again evaluated student performance using statistical procedures. This set of questions looked at how all students responded between September and May. This allowed the advisory panel to determine how the three-tiered model of intervention *as a whole* (meaning the combined effects of primary, secondary, and tertiary levels of support) influenced student performance.

*Question 1: To what extent did the three-tiered model of intervention help upper and lower elementary school students improve academically?* In terms of the district-designed comprehension tests, upper elementary students (fourth through sixth grade) showed significant improvement by the end of the year. Similar gains were also made on the curriculum-based measures. For the school as a whole, students improved on the reading component of the statewide assessment, with approximately 38 percent of the students falling in the first two quadrants on the state exam.

*Question 2: To what extent did the three-tiered model of intervention help upper and lower elementary school students improve behaviorally and socially?* Results indicated that average disciplinary contacts were approximately .67 per month per student by May. Suspension and expulsion rates were lower between September and May during this year as compared to the previous year. Attendance rates were up to 92 percent, exceeding the original goal. In terms of Student Risk Screening Scale scores, there were significant improvements, with total risk scores decreasing substantially. Social Skills scores, as measured by the Social Skills Rating System, also showed improvement in both cooperation and self-control skills.

***Question 3: Did the three-tiered model of intervention differentially influence students with low-, moderate-, and high-risk status as measured by the Student Risk Screening Scale?*** Results showed that all students, regardless of risk status, continued to show improvement in the area of reading according to district-designed comprehension scores and curriculum-based measurement scores. Thus, the reading program was effective for the majority of the students.

***Question 4: To what extent was risk status impacted by the three-tiered model of intervention during the school year?*** Results showed that none of the students who started and ended the year at Serenity Lane Elementary School were at high risk for antisocial behavior in September. Forty-two students were at moderate risk for antisocial behavior in May whereas, the remaining students were in the low-risk category.

***Summary.*** Results of data collected by *carefully monitoring student progress* using reliable, feasible measures indicate that a *three-tiered model of intervention linked to assessment results* and implemented with attention to *social validity, treatment integrity,* and *generalization and maintenance* issues can be effective in addressing the academic, social, and behavioral needs of a wide range of learners.

## Summary and Conclusions

As you know, there are numerous interventions implemented in schools today. These interventions include (a) *tertiary prevention efforts:* highly individualized interventions designed and implemented by the prereferral intervention team, the special education teachers, school psychologists, and behavior specialists, (b) *secondary prevention efforts:* small group interventions targeting specific areas of concern such as social skills, anger management, and conflict resolution, which are implemented by trained professionals such as the school counselors and program specialists, and (c) *primary intervention efforts:* more comprehensive, broad-based interventions such as schoolwide positive behaviors and violence prevention programs, which are implemented by an entire faculty. These intervention plans can be improved and the outcomes enhanced by addressing key features such as linking interventions to assessment results, monitoring student progress over the course of the intervention, and incorporating the essential tools (social validity, treatment integrity, and generalization/maintenance; see Figure 7.5) necessary to draw accurate conclusions about intervention acceptability and effectiveness.

In addition to refining the design, implementation, and evaluation of school-based interventions, incorporating these key tools into school-based programs will enable school site personnel to document outcomes that will ultimately drive decisions about students' learning. Furthermore, educators will be able to comply with legal mandates set by the federal government (Individuals with Disabilities Education Act, IDEA, 1997), including establishing a student's responsiveness to instruction (Fuchs, Fuchs, & Speece, 2002) and documenting a student's resistance to intervention (Gresham, 1991, 2002). More specifically, incorporating these key features will allow you to acquire the data necessary to document your efforts and to demonstrate accountability for results. In sum, this comprehensive approach to school-based interventions provides the necessary tools to offer comprehensive, progressively intensive support, which collectively provides successful educational experiences for *all* learners.

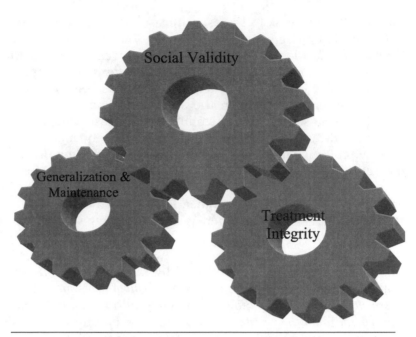

**FIGURE 7.5**   *The Core Component Model: Key Tools for Designing, Implementing, and Evaluating Multilevel-Based Interventions*

## References

Bijou, S. W., Peterson, R., F., & Ault, M. H. (1968) A method to integrate descriptive and experimental field studies at the level of data and empirical concepts. *Journal of Applied Behavior Analysis, 1,* 175–191.

Canter, L. (1990). *Lee Canter's back to school with assertive discipline.* Santa Monica, CA: Canter & Associates.

Canter, L., & Canter, M. (1992). *Lee Canter's assertive discipline.* Santa Monica, CA: Canter & Associates.

Charles, C. M. (1996). *Building classroom discipline* (5th ed.). White Plains, NY: Longman.

Committee for Children. (1992). *Second Step: Violence prevention curriculum for preschool–grade 9.* Seattle, WA: Author.

Drummond, T. (1994). *The Student Risk Screening Scale (SRSS).* Grants Pass, OR: Josephine County Mental Health Program.

Drummond, T., Eddy, J. M., & Reid, J. B. (1998a). *Follow-Up Study #3; Risk Screening Scale: Prediction of Negative Outcomes by 10th Grade from 2nd Grade Screening.* Unpublished technical report. Eugene: Oregon Social Learning Center.

Drummond, T., Eddy, J. M., & Reid, J. B. (1998b). *Follow-Up Study #4; Risk Screening Scale: Prediction of Negative Outcomes in Two Longitudinal Samples.* Unpublished technical report. Eugene: Oregon Social Learning Center.

Dunlap, G., Kern, L., dePerczel, M., Clarke, S., Wilson, D., Childs, K. E., White, R., & Falk, G. D. (1993). Functional analysis of classroom variables for students with emotional and behavioral challenges. *Behavioral Disorders, 18,* 275–291.

Dunlap, G., Kern-Dunlap, L., Clarke, S., & Robbins, F. R. (1991). Functional assessment, curricular revision, and severe behavior problems. *Journal of Applied Behavior Analysis, 24,* 387–397.

Durand, M., & Crimmins, D. (1988). *Motivation Assessment Scale.* Topeka, KS: Monaco.

Elliott, S., & Gresham, F. M. (1991). *Social skills intervention guide.* Circle Pines, MN: American Guidance Service.

Fournier, R. (2002, January 9). Education overhaul signed. *The Associated Press syndicated article in The Riverside Press Enterprise,* pp. Al, A9.

Fuchs, D., & Fuchs, L. S. (1994). Inclusive schools movement and the radicalization of special education reform. *Exceptional Children, 60,* 294–309.

Fuchs, L. S., Fuchs, D., & Speece, D. L. (2002). Treatment validity as a unifying construct for identifying learning disabilities. *Learning Disability Quarterly, 25,* 33–45.

Gresham, F. M. (1989). Assessment of treatment integrity in school consultation and prereferral intervention. *School Psychology Review, 18,* 37–50.

Gresham, F. M. (1991). Conceptualizing behavior disorders in terms of resistance to intervention. *School Psychology Review, 20,* 1, 23–36.

Gresham, F. M. (2002). Responsiveness to intervention: An alternative approach to learning disabilities. In R. Bradley, L. Danielson, & D. Hallahan (Eds.), *Identification of learning disabilities: Research to practice.* Mahwah, NJ: Erlbaum.

Gresham, F. M., & Elliott, S. N. (1990). *Social Skills Rating System (SSRS).* Circle Pines, MN: American Guidance Service.

Gresham, F. M., & Lopez, M. F. (1996). Social validation: A unifying construct for school-based consultation research and practice. *School Psychology Quarterly, 11,* 204–227.

Horner, R., & Billingsley, F. (1988). The effect of competing behavior on the generalization and maintenance of adaptive behavior in applied settings. In R. Horner, G., Dunlap, & R. Koegel (Eds.), *Generalization and maintenance: Lifestyle changes in applied settings* (pp. 197-220). Baltimore: Paul H. Brookes.

*Individuals with Disabilities Education Act Amendments of 1997.* Pub. L. No. 105-17, Section 20, 111 Stat. 37 (1997). Washington, DC: U.S. Government Printing Office.

Johnston, J. M., & Pennypacker, H. S. (1993). *Strategies and tactics of behavioral research* (2nd ed.). Hillsdale, NJ: Erlbaum.

Kaminski, R. A., & Good, R. H. (1996). Toward a technology for assessing basic early literacy skills. *School Psychology Review, 25,* 215–227.

Kazdin, A. E. (1977). Assessing the clinical or applied significance of behavior change through social validation. *Behavior Modification, 1,* 427–452.

Kazdin, A. E., (1987). Treatment of antisocial behavior in children: Current status and future directions. *Psychological Bulletin, 102,* 187–203.

Kazdin, A. E. (1993). Treatment of conduct disorders: Progress and directions in psychotherapy research. *Development and Psychopathology, 5,*277–310.

Kern, L., Dunlap, G., Clarke, S., & Childs, K. E. (1994). Student-assisted functional assessment interview. *Diagnostic, 19,* 20–39.

Lane, K. L. (1997). Students at-risk for antisocial behavior: The utility of academic and social skills interventions. Doctoral dissertation.

Lane, K. L. (1999). Young students at-risk for antisocial behavior: The utility of academic and social skills interventions. *Journal of Emotional and Behavioral Disorders, 7,* 211–223.

Lane, K. L., Beebe-Frankenberger, M. E., Lambros, K. L., & M. E., Pierson (2001). Designing effective interventions for children at-risk for antisocial behavior: An integrated model of components necessary for making valid inferences. *Psychology in the Schools, 38,* 365–379.

Lane, K. L., & Menzies, H. M. (2002). Promoting achievement and minimizing risk—phase I: The impact of a school-based primary intervention program. *Preventing School Failure, 47,* 26–32.

Lane, K. L., O'Shaughnessy, T., Lambros, K. M., Gresham, F. M., & Beebe-Frankenberger, M. E. (2001). The efficacy of phonological awareness training with first-grade students who have behavior problems and reading difficulties. *Journal of Emotional and Behavioral Disorders, 9,* 219–231.

Lane, K. L., Umbreit, J., & Beebe-Frankenberger, M. (1999). A review of functional assessment research with students with or at-risk for emotional and behavioral disorders. *Journal of Positive Behavioral Interventions, 1,* 101–111.

Lane, K. L., & Wehby, J. (2002). Addressing antisocial behavior in the schools: A call for action. *Academic Exchange Quarterly, 6,* 4–9.

Lane, K. L., Wehby, J., Menzies, H., Doukas, G., Munton, S., & Gregg, R. (in press). Social skills training for students at-risk for antisocial behavior: The effects of small group instruction.

Lane, K. L., Wehby, J. H., Menzies, H. M., Gregg, R. M., Doukas, G. L., & Munton, S. M. (2002). Early literacy instruction for first-grade students at-risk for antisocial behavior. *Education and Treatment of Children, 25,* 438–458.

MacMillan, D., Gresham, F., & Forness, S. (1996). Full inclusion: An empirical perspective. *Behavioral Disorders, 21,* 145–159.

Martens, B. K., Witt, J. C., Elliott, S. N., & Darveaux, D. (1985). Teacher judgments concerning the acceptability of school-based interventions. *Professional Psychology: Research and Practice, 16,* 191–198.

Nelson, C. M., Rutherford, R. B., Center, D. B., & Walker, H. M. (1991). Do public schools have an obligation to serve troubled children and youth? *Exceptional Children, 57,* 406–415.

O'Shaughnessy, T., Lane, K. L., Gresham, F. M., & Beebe-Frankenberger, M. E. (2002). Students with or at-risk for learning and emotional behavioral difficulties: An integrated system of prevention and intervention. In K. L. Lane, F. M. Gresham, and T. E. O'Shaughnessy (Eds.), *Interventions for children with or at risk for emotional and behavioral disorders* (pp. 3-17). Boston: Allyn & Bacon.

Public Law 103-882 (October 20. 1994). Appendix A—The Gun-Free Schools Act of 1994 20 USC 8921.

Shefelbine, J. (1998). *Phonics chapters books 1–6: Teachers guide.* New York: Scholastic.

Shinn, M. R. (1989). *Curriculum-based assessment: Assessing special children.* NY: Guilford.

Umbreit, J., Lane, K. L., & Dejud, C. (*in press*). Improving classroom behavior by modifying task Difficulty: The effect of increasing the difficulty of too-easy tasks. *Journal of Positive Behavior Interventions.*

Wagner, R. K., Torgesen, J. K., & Rashotte, C. A. (1999). *Comprehensive test of phonological processes.* Austin, TX: Pro-Ed.

Walker, H. M., Block-Pedego, A., Todis, B., & Severson, H. (1991). *School archival records search.* Longmont, CO: Sopris West.

Walker, H. M., Colvin, G., & Ramsey, E. (1995). *Antisocial behavior in school: Strategies and best practices.* Albany: Brooks/Cole.

Walker, H. M., & Severson, H. H. (1992). *Systematic Screening for Behavior Disorders* (SSDB): User's guide and technical manual. Longmont, CO: Sopris West.

Walker, H. M., & Severson, H. H. (2002). Developmental prevention of at-risk outcomes for vulnerable antisocial children and youth. In K. L. Lane, F. M. Gresham, & T. E. O'Shaughnessy (Eds.), *Interventions for children with or at risk for emotional and behavioral disorders.* (pp. 177-194). Boston: Allyn & Bacon.

Witt, J. C., & Elliott, S. N. (1985). Acceptability of classroom intervention strategies. In T. R. Kratochwill (Ed.), *Advances in school psychology,* Vol. 4. (pp. 251-288). Hillsdale, NJ: Erlbaum.

Wolf, M. M. (1978). Social validity: The case for subjective measurement or how applied behavior analysis is finding its heart. *Journal of Applied Behavior Analysis, 11,* 203–214.

Woodcock, R. W., McGrew, K. S., & Mather, N. (2001). *The Woodcock Johnson III Tests of Achievement.* Itasca, IL: Riverside.

Yeaton, W., & Sechrest, L. (1981). Critical dimensions in the choice and maintenance of successful treatments: Strength, integrity, and effectiveness. *Journal of Consulting and Clinical Psychology, 49,* 156–167.

# *Appendix*

## *Reproducibles*

This section contains some of the forms introduced and reprinted in this text.

*Positive Behavioral Support*
...for Children
and Their Families

TIME STARTED: _____

PRELIMINARY FUNCTIONAL ASSESSMENT SURVEY

Instructions to PBS Staff:  The following interview should be conducted with the student's teacher. Prior to the interview, ask the teacher whether or not the Classroom Aide should participate. If yes, indicate both respondents' names. In addition, in instances where divergent information is provided, note the sources attributed to specific information.

Student: _____   Subject #: _____

Age: _____   Sex:  M _____   F _____

Interviewer: _____   Date: _____

Respondent(s): _____

1.  List and describe behavior(s) of concern.

    a.

    b.

    c.

    d.

    e.

2.  Prioritize these behaviors (which is the most important?)

    a.

    b.

    c.

    d.

    e.

3.  What procedures have you followed when the behaviors first occurred?

    a.

    b.

    c.

    d.

    e.

---

**REPRODUCIBLE 2.1**   *Preliminary Functional Assessment Interview*

Reprinted with permission from Glen Dunlap. Interview was referred to in G. Dunlap, L. Kern, M. dePerczel, S. Clarke, D. Wilson, K. E. Childs, R. White, & G. D. Falk. (1993). "Functional Analysis of Classroom Variables for Students with Emotional and Behavioral Challenges." *Behavioral Disorders, 18,* 275-291.

4. What do you think causes (or motivates) the behavior?

    a.

    b.

    c.

    d.

    e.

5. When do these behaviors occur?

    a.

    b.

    c.

    d.

    e.

6. How often do these behaviors occur?

    a.

    b.

    c.

    d.

    e.

7. How long has this/these behavior(s) been occurring?

    a.

    b.

    c.

    d.

    e.

8. Is there any circumstance under which the behavior does not occur?

    a.

    b.

    c.

    d.

    e.

9. Is there any circumstances under which the behavior always occurs?

    a.

    b.

    c.

    d.

    e.

**REPRODUCIBLE 2.1** *Continued*

10. Does the behavior occur more often during certain times of the day?

    a.

    b.

    c.

    d.

    e.

11. Does the behavior occur in response to the number of people in the immediate environment?

    a.

    b.

    c.

    d.

    e.

12. Does the behavior occur only with certain people?

    a.

    b.

    c.

    d.

    e.

13. Does the behavior occur only during certain subjects?

    a.

    b.

    c.

    d.

    e.

14. Could the behavior be related to any skills deficit?

    a.

    b.

    c.

    d.

    e.

15. What are the identified reinforcers for this student?

    a.

    b.

    c.

    d.

    e.

**REPRODUCIBLE 2.1** *Continued*

16. Is the student taking any medication that might affect his/her behavior?

    a.

    b.

    c.

    d.

    e.

17. Could the student's behavior be signaling some deprivation condition (e.g. thirst, hunger, lack of rest, etc.)?

    a.

    b.

    c.

    d.

    e.

18. Could the behavior be the result of any form of discomfort (e.g., headaches, stomachaches, blurred vision, ear infection, etc.)?

    a.

    b.

    c.

    d.

    e.

19. Could the behavior be caused by allergies (e.g., food, materials in the environment, etc.)?

    a.

    b.

    c.

    d.

    e.

20. Do any other behaviors occur along with this behavior?

    a.

    b.

    c.

    d.

    e.

21. Are there any observable events that signal the behavior of concern is about to occur?

    a.

    b.

    c.

    d.

    e.

---

**REPRODUCIBLE 2.1** *Continued*

22. What are the consequences when the behavior(s) occur?

a.

b.

c.

d.

e.

TIME COMPLETED:_____

TOTAL TIME:_____

COMMENTS

## STUDENT ASSESSMENT

Student: _____

Date: _____          Administration Time: _____

Target Behavior: _____

_____

1. When do you think you have the fewest problems with _____(target behavior) in school?



    Why do you not have problems during this/these time(s)?



2. When do you think you have the most problems with _____(target behavior) in school?



    Why do you have problems during this/these time(s)?



3. What causes you to have problems with _____(target behavior)?



4. What changes could be made so you would have fewer problems with _____ (target behavior)?



5. What kind of rewards would you like to earn for good behavior or good schoolwork?

---

**REPRODUCIBLE 2.2**    *Student Functional Assessment Interview*

*Source:* Reprinted with permission. L. Kern, G. Dunlap, S. Clarke, & K. E. Childs (1994). "Student-Assisted Functional Assessment Interview." *Diagnostic, 19*, 20-39.

**231**

Rate how much you like the following subjects:

| | Don't like at all | | Fair | | Like very much |
|---|---|---|---|---|---|
| Reading | 1 | 2 | 3 | 4 | 5 |
| Math | 1 | 2 | 3 | 4 | 5 |
| Spelling | 1 | 2 | 3 | 4 | 5 |
| Handwriting | 1 | 2 | 3 | 4 | 5 |
| Science | 1 | 2 | 3 | 4 | 5 |
| Social Studies | 1 | 2 | 3 | 4 | 5 |
| English | 1 | 2 | 3 | 4 | 5 |
| Music | 1 | 2 | 3 | 4 | 5 |
| P.E. | 1 | 2 | 3 | 4 | 5 |
| Art | 1 | 2 | 3 | 4 | 5 |

What do you like about _____?

What do you like about _____?

What do you like about _____?

What do you like about _____?

What do you like about _____?

What do you like about _____?

What do you like about _____?

**REPRODUCIBLE 2.2**   *Continued*

What could be done to improve _____?

What do you like about _____?

What do you like about _____?

What do you like about _____?

What do you like about _____?

Is there any type of _____ you have ever done that you've liked?

What could be done to improve _____?

What do you like about _____?

What do you like about _____?

What do you like about _____?

What do you like about _____?

What don't you like about _____?

Is there any type of _____ you have ever done that you've liked?

What could be done to improve _____?

---

**REPRODUCIBLE 2.2** *Continued*

## STUDENT ASSESSMENT

Student: _____ Date: _____

Interviewer: _____

| | | | |
|---|---|---|---|
| 1. In general, is your work too hard for you? | always | sometimes | never |
| 2. In general, is your work too easy for you? | always | sometimes | never |
| 3. When you ask for help appropriately, do you get it? | always | sometimes | never |
| 4. Do you think work periods for each subject are too long? | always | sometimes | never |
| 5. Do you think work periods for each subject are too short? | always | sometimes | never |
| 6. When you do seatwork, do you do better when someone works with you? | always | sometimes | never |
| 7. Do you think people notice when you do a good job? | always | sometimes | never |
| 8. Do you think you get the points or rewards you deserve when you do good work? | always | sometimes | never |
| 9. Do you think you would do better in school if you received more rewards? | always | sometimes | never |
| 10. In general, do you find your work interesting? | always | sometimes | never |
| 11. Are there things in the classroom that distract you? | always | sometimes | never |
| 12. Is your work challenging enough for you? | always | sometimes | never |

**REPRODUCIBLE 2.2** *Continued*

# ABC EVENT RECORD

Student:_____

Date:_____ Start Time:_____

Observer:_____ School:_____

Grade:_____ Intervals:_____

| Time H:min | ANTECEDENT and SETTING What happened *before* the behavior? | OFF-TASK BEHAVIOR (check) | | | | | CONSEQUENCE(S) What happened *after* the behavior? |
|---|---|---|---|---|---|---|---|
| | | Side Talk | Out of Seat | Stare Off | Head on Desk | Other | |
| | | | | | | | |
| | | | | | | | |
| | | | | | | | |
| | | | | | | | |
| | | | | | | | |
| | | | | | | | |
| | | | | | | | |
| | | | | | | | |
| | | | | | | | |
| | | | | | | | |
| | | | | | | | |
| | | | | | | | |
| | | | | | | | |
| | | | | | | | |

**REPRODUCIBLE 2.3**   *Sample Observational Assessment of Student Inappropriate Behavioral Events*

REINFORCEMENT ASSESSMENT

Positive Reinforcement: _____ Yes _____ No    Frequency: _____ per _____

       Types in Use:

       Praise_____ Close Proximity ____ Tokens _____ Points _____

       Other: _____

       _____


Negative Reinforcement: _____ Yes _____ No    Frequency: _____ per _____

       Types in Use:

       Ignore____ Activity Withdrawal ____ Tokens ____ Points ____

       Other: _____

       _____


Punishers:          _____ Yes _____ No    Frequency: _____ per _____

       Types in Use:

       Time-Out _____ Detention _____ Office _____ Parent _____

       Other: _____

       _____


Frequency count positive/negative teacher/aide statements in classroom:

Duration of recording:_____    Time of day:_____

|  | Target Child | All Others |
|---|---|---|
| Positive |  |  |
| Negative |  |  |

**REPRODUCIBLE 2.4**  *Observation Measure of the Learning Environment: Schedules of Reinforcement*

# LEARNING ENVIRONMENT ASSESSMENT

**Physical Setting:**

Number of Students _____    Teacher/Aides: _____    Size of Room: _____

Furnished with (desks, tables, bookcases, bean bag chairs, toys, etc.): _____

_____

_____

Student Location (where does student normally sit in the class relative to peers and teacher?):

_____

Lighting (good, fair, poor?): _____    Number of Doors: _____    Number of Windows: __

Class Rules Posted: _____ Y _____ N    Rules are (list): _____

_____

_____

Schedule Posted: _____ Y _____ N    Schedule is (list): _____

_____

_____

Student Work Displayed: _____ Y _____ N

Definitive Areas: _____ Y _____ N    Briefly describe or sketch (e.g. play area, reading area):

_____

_____

Time Out Area: _____ Y _____ N
If yes, where . . . describe (location relative to teacher & peers): _____

_____

Point System Displayed?: Group _____ Individual _____ Description of point system: _____

_____

_____

**Social Setting:**

Supervision for peer interaction? _____ Y _____ N

Classroom conducive to social interaction? _____ Y _____ N

Interaction facilitated by teacher/aide? _____ Y _____ N

**REPRODUCIBLE 2.5**    *Sample Observational Assessment of Classroom Learning Environment*

# Problem-Solving Worksheet

Student: _____ Grade: _____ Date: _____

Teacher: _____

Problem Skill or Behavior (describe):

|  |
|--|
|  |

Assessed Level of Performance of Problem Skill or Behavior (State level/rate):

| Skill/Behavior | Assessment Level of Performance |
|----------------|----------------------------------|
|  |  |
|  |  |
|  |  |
|  |  |

Replacement Skill or Behavior (describe):

|  |
|--|
|  |

Performance Goal at End of Intervention:

| Skill/Behavior | Intervention Goal Level of Performance |
|----------------|-----------------------------------------|
|  |  |
|  |  |
|  |  |
|  |  |

Anticipated Length of Intervention to Goal (time, e.g., days, weeks): _____

Benchmark Goals (time x performance level):

| Skill/Behavior | Benchmark Date | Expected Performance by Dimension |
|----------------|----------------|------------------------------------|
|  |  |  |
|  |  |  |
|  |  |  |
|  |  |  |

Progress Monitored by (dimension x method):

| Skill/Behavior | Dimension | Monitoring Method |
|----------------|-----------|-------------------|
|  |  |  |
|  |  |  |
|  |  |  |
|  |  |  |

**REPRODUCIBLE 3.1**   *Problem-Solving Worksheet*

| Intervention Progress-Monitoring Record Sheet | | | | | | |
|---|---|---|---|---|---|---|
| Student: | | | | Activity: | | |
| Teacher: | | | | Date: | | |
| Skill or Behavior | Monday | Tuesday | Wednesday | Thursday | Friday | Week ____ Performance |
| | | | | | | |
| | | | | | | |
| | | | | | | |
| | | | | | | |
| | | | | | | |

**Summary of Intervention Week ___:**

| Skills/Behaviors: | Benchmark/Goal | Student Performance | Goal Met Y/N |
|---|---|---|---|
| _____ | _____ | _____ | ____ |
| _____ | _____ | _____ | ____ |
| _____ | _____ | _____ | ____ |
| _____ | _____ | _____ | ____ |

Comments: _____

_____

_____

Decisions: _____

_____

_____

REPRODUCIBLE 3.2    *Weekly Summary Intervention Monitoring*

| Skill or Behavior | 1 | 2 | 3 | 4 | 5 |
|---|---|---|---|---|---|
| 1 | | | | | |
| 2 | | | | | |
| 3 | | | | | |
| 4 | | | | | |
| | | | | | |
| | | | | | |

Skill/Behavior Key (define skill/behavior monitored):

1. _____

2. _____

3. _____

4. _____

_____

_____

Ending Summary:

| #1 | #2 | #3 | #4 |
|---|---|---|---|

**REPRODUCIBLE 3.3**   *Generic Frequency Count Form*

Student Self-Monitoring of Events

Name:_____ Week of:_____

Make a check mark next to an activity or event every time it happens in the next week.
If you wish, you may write down in the blanks other things that you like when they

happen.

1.  Playing volleyball in P.E.                                    _____

2.  Getting to chose a free time activity that I like to do.      _____

3.  Eating lunch with a friend.                                   _____

4.  Time during class to write a note to someone special.        _____

5.  Getting extra class points for free time at recess.          _____

6.  _____                     _____

7.  _____                     _____

8.  _____                     _____


At the end of the week, look at your list and decide what was the best thing that
happened.
Write what you think here:

_____

_____

_____

_____

Is there anything different you would want to happen next week?  If so, what is it?

_____

**REPRODUCIBLE 3.4**   *Self-Monitoring Pleasant Events*

Name:_____        _____        Date:

**Math Worksheet Check List**

Check off each item after you have done it and then turn in the checklist with your worksheet.

1.    My name is on the paper in the top right-hand corner.        ☐

2.    All the problems I completed show the work I used
      to find the answer.        ☐

3.    My answers are circled.        ☐

4.    The numbers are written clearly and neatly.        ☐

5.    I went back over my work to check if everything is correct.        ☐

REMEMBER:  When you finish the checklist, put the list with your worksheet
and turn it in all together!  Good work!

---

**REPRODUCIBLE 3.5**    *Self-Monitoring for Neat and Complete Work Assignments*

*Source:* Adapted from E. S. Shapiro, S. L. Durnan, E. E. Post, & T. S. Levinson (2002). "Self-monitoring Procedures for Children and Adolescents." In M. R. Shinn, H. M. Walker, and G. Stoner (Eds.) *Interventions for Academic and Behavior Problems II: Preventive and Remedial Approaches.* Bethesda, MD: National Association of School Psychologists.

**Student Self-Monitoring My Own Behavior**

Name: _____ Date: _____ Period # _____

When I hear the beep, I will make an "X" next to an item if I have done it since the last beep.

1.  Sitting in my desk seat.                              _____

2.  Listening and paying attention to the teacher.      _____

3.  Working quietly on my assignment.                   _____

4.  Raising my hand for help.                           _____

5.  Participating in the class discussion.              _____

**STOP** 5 minutes before the end of class, when the teacher says "you have 5 minutes to assess".

Count the check marks next to each item and place the number in the item box below.

| #1 ___ | #2 ___ | #3 ___ | #4 ___ | #5 ___ |

Turn the sheet into the teacher today as you leave the class by placing it in the box at the door. The form will be returned to you when you come to class tomorrow.

_____

Teacher Feedback:_____

_____

If after reading the teacher's feedback you want to talk about it, check the box below and give it back to your teacher immediately. The teacher will meet with you in the last 5 minutes of class.

Yes, I would like to meet with you to talk about this!     [    ]

---

**REPRODUCIBLE 3.6**   *Self-Monitoring Behavior during a Class Period in Middle School*

*Source:* Adapted from E. S. Shapiro, S. L. Durnan, E. E. Post, & T. S. Levinson (2002). "Self-monitoring Procedures for Children and Adolescents." In M. R. Shinn, H. M. Walker, and G. Stoner (Eds.) *Interventions for Academic and Behavior Problems II: Preventive and Remedial Approaches.* Bethesda, MD: National Association of School Psychologists.

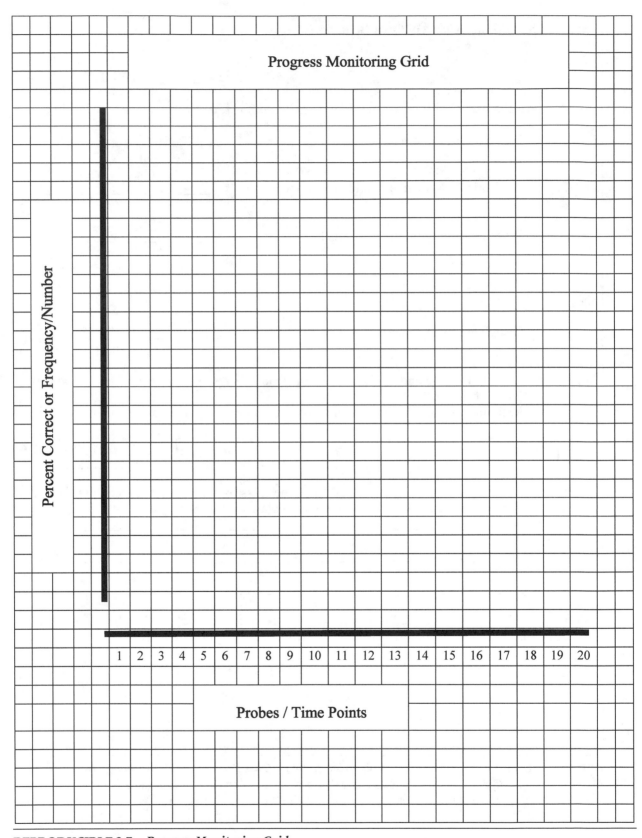

**REPRODUCIBLE 3.7** *Progress Monitoring Grid*

Name: _____ Grade: _____ Date: _____

| Period 1 | YES | NO | N/A | Teacher Signature _____ |
|---|---|---|---|---|
| _____ | ☐ | ☐ | ☐ | Arrived on Time to Class |
| *Class* | ☐ | ☐ | ☐ | Finished His/Her Work |
| | ☐ | ☐ | ☐ | Good Student Behavior |
| | ☐ | ☐ | ☐ | Turned in Homework |
| | ☐ | ☐ | ☐ | Homework Due Tomorrow |
| | ☐ | ☐ | ☐ | Passing Class |

Comments:_____

| Period 2 | YES | NO | N/A | Teacher Signature: _____ |
|---|---|---|---|---|
| _____ | ☐ | ☐ | ☐ | Arrived on Time to Class |
| *Class* | ☐ | ☐ | ☐ | Finished His/Her Work |
| | ☐ | ☐ | ☐ | Good Student Behavior |
| | ☐ | ☐ | ☐ | Turned in Homework |
| | ☐ | ☐ | ☐ | Homework Due Tomorrow |
| | ☐ | ☐ | ☐ | Passing Class |

Comments:_____

| Period 3 | YES | NO | N/A | Teacher Signature: _____ |
|---|---|---|---|---|
| _____ | ☐ | ☐ | ☐ | Arrived on Time to Class |
| *Class* | ☐ | ☐ | ☐ | Finished His/Her Work |
| | ☐ | ☐ | ☐ | Good Student Behavior |
| | ☐ | ☐ | ☐ | Turned in Homework |
| | ☐ | ☐ | ☐ | Homework Due Tomorrow |
| | ☐ | ☐ | ☐ | Passing Class |

Comments:_____

| Period 4 | YES | NO | N/A | Teacher Signature: _____ |
|---|---|---|---|---|
| _____ | ☐ | ☐ | ☐ | Arrived on Time to Class |
| *Class* | ☐ | ☐ | ☐ | Finished His/Her Work |
| | ☐ | ☐ | ☐ | Good Student Behavior |
| | ☐ | ☐ | ☐ | Turned in Homework |
| | ☐ | ☐ | ☐ | Homework Due Tomorrow |
| | ☐ | ☐ | ☐ | Passing Class |

Comments:_____

**REPRODUCIBLE 3.8**   *School-Home Progress Note*

| Period 5 | YES | NO | N/A | Teacher Signature: _____ |
|----------|-----|----|----|-----------------------------------------------|
| _____ | ☐ | ☐ | ☐ | Arrived on Time to Class |
| *Class* | ☐ | ☐ | ☐ | Finished His/Her Work |
| | ☐ | ☐ | ☐ | Good Student Behavior |
| | ☐ | ☐ | ☐ | Turned in Homework |
| | ☐ | ☐ | ☐ | Homework Due Tomorrow |
| | ☐ | ☐ | ☐ | Passing Class |

Comments:_____

_____

| Period 6 | YES | NO | N/A | Teacher Signature: _____ |
|----------|-----|----|----|-----------------------------------------------|
| _____ | ☐ | ☐ | ☐ | Arrived on Time to Class |
| *Class* | ☐ | ☐ | ☐ | Finished His/Her Work |
| | ☐ | ☐ | ☐ | Good Student Behavior |
| | ☐ | ☐ | ☐ | Turned in Homework |
| | ☐ | ☐ | ☐ | Homework Due Tomorrow |
| | ☐ | ☐ | ☐ | Passing Class |

Comments:_____

_____

| Period ____ | YES | NO | N/A | Teacher Signature: _____ |
|----------|-----|----|----|-----------------------------------------------|
| _____ | ☐ | ☐ | ☐ | Arrived on Time to Class |
| *Class* | ☐ | ☐ | ☐ | Finished His/Her Work |
| | ☐ | ☐ | ☐ | Good Student Behavior |
| | ☐ | ☐ | ☐ | Turned in Homework |
| | ☐ | ☐ | ☐ | Homework Due Tomorrow |
| | ☐ | ☐ | ☐ | Passing Class |

Comments:_____

_____

Parent Comments: _____

_____

_____

_____

Parent Signature: _____ Date: _____

**REPRODUCIBLE 3.8**   *Continued*

# TREATMENT ACCEPTABILITY RATING FORM—REVISED (TARF-R)

Please complete the items listed below. The items should be completed by placing a check mark on the line under the question that best indicates how you feel about the psychologist's treatment recommendations.

1.  How clear is your understanding of this treatment?

    ___      ___      ___      ___      ___
    Not at all                      Neutral        Very clear
    clear

2.  How acceptable do you find the treatment to be regarding your concerns about your child?

    ___      ___      ___      ___      ___
    Not at all                      Neutral        Very acceptable
    acceptable

3.  How willing are you to carry out this treatment?

    ___      ___      ___      ___      ___
    Not at all                      Neutral        Very willing
    willing

4.  Given your child's behavioral problems, how reasonable do you find the treatment to be?

    ___      ___      ___      ___      ___
    Not at all                      Neutral        Very reasonable
    reasonable

5.  How costly will it be to carry out this treatment?

    ___      ___      ___      ___      ___
    Not at all                      Neutral        Very costly
    costly

6.  To what extent do you think there might be disadvantages in following this treatment?

    ___      ___      ___      ___      ___
    Not at all                      Neutral        Many are likely
    likely

7.  How likely is this treatment to make permanent improvements in your child's behavior?

    ___      ___      ___      ___      ___
    Unlikely                      Neutral        Very likely

8.  How much time will be needed each day for you to carry out this treatment?

    ___      ___      ___      ___      ___
    Little time                      Neutral        Much time
    will be needed                                      will be needed

---

**REPRODUCIBLE 4.1**    *Treatment Acceptability Rating Profile-Revised (TARF-Revised)*

Reprinted with permission. T. M. Reimers, and D. P. Wacker (1988). "Parents' Ratings of the Acceptability of Behavioral Treatment Recommendations Made in an Outpatient Clinic: A Preliminary Analysis of the Influence of Treatment Effectiveness." *Behavior Disorders,* *14,* 7–15.

    

9. How confident are you that the treatment will be effective?

___    ___    ___    ___    ___    ___

Not at all                            Neutral            Very confident
confident

10. Compared to other children with behavioral difficulties, how serious are your child's problems?

___    ___    ___    ___    ___    ___

Not at all                            Neutral            Very serious
serious

11. How disruptive will it be to the family (in general) to carry out this treatment?

___    ___    ___    ___    ___    ___

Not at all                            Neutral            Very disruptive
disruptive

12. How effective is this treatment likely to be for your child?

___    ___    ___    ___    ___    ___

Not at all                            Neutral            Very effective
effective

13. How affordable is this treatment for your family?

___    ___    ___    ___    ___    ___

Not at all                            Neutral            Very affordable
affordable

14. How much do you like the procedures used in the proposed treatment?

___    ___    ___    ___    ___    ___

Do not like                         Neutral            Like them
them at all                                                       very much

15. How willing will other family members be to help carry out this treatment?

___    ___    ___    ___    ___    ___

Not at all                            Neutral            Very willing
willing

16. To what extent are undesirable side-effects likely to result from this treatment?

___    ___    ___    ___    ___    ___

No side- effects                        Neutral            Many side-effects
are likely                                                    are likely

17. How much discomfort is your child likely to experience during the course of this treatment?

___    ___    ___    ___    ___    ___

No discomfort                        Neutral            Very much
at all                                                     discomfort

**REPRODUCIBLE 4.1** *Continued*

18.     How severe are your child's behavioral difficulties?

___        ___        ___                ___        ___
Not at all                              Neutral              Very severe
severe

19.     How willing would you be to change your family routine to carry out this treatment?

___        ___        ___                ___        ___
Not at all                              Neutral              Very willing
willing

20.     How well will carrying out this treatment fit into the family routine?

___        ___        ___                ___        ___
Not at all                              Neutral              Very well
well

21.     To what degree are your child's behavioral problems of concern to you?

___        ___        ___                ___        ___
No concern                              Neutral              Great concern
at all

**REPRODUCIBLE 4.1**   *Continued*

The purpose of this questionnaire is to obtain information that will aid in the selection of classroom interventions. These interventions will be used by teachers of children with behavior problems. Please circle the number which best describes your agreement or disagreement with each statement.

| | Strongly Disagree | Disagree | Slightly Disagree | Slightly Agree | Agree | Strongly Agree |
|---|---|---|---|---|---|---|
| 1. This would be an acceptable intervention for the child's problem behavior. | 1 | 2 | 3 | 4 | 5 | 6 |
| 2. Most teachers would find this intervention appropriate for behavior problems in addition to the one described. | 1 | 2 | 3 | 4 | 5 | 6 |
| 3. This intervention should prove effective in changing the child's problem behavior. | 1 | 2 | 3 | 4 | 5 | 6 |
| 4. I would suggest the use of this intervention to other teachers. | 1 | 2 | 3 | 4 | 5 | 6 |
| 5. The child's behavior problem is severe enough to warrant use of this intervention. | 1 | 2 | 3 | 4 | 5 | 6 |
| 6. Most teachers would find this intervention suitable for the behavior problem described. | 1 | 2 | 3 | 4 | 5 | 6 |
| 7. I would be willing to use this intervention in the classroom setting. | 1 | 2 | 3 | 4 | 5 | 6 |
| 8. This intervention would *not* result in negative side-effects for the child. | 1 | 2 | 3 | 4 | 5 | 6 |
| 9. This intervention would be appropriate for a variety of children. | 1 | 2 | 3 | 4 | 5 | 6 |
| 10. This intervention is consistent with those I have used in classroom settings. | 1 | 2 | 3 | 4 | 5 | 6 |
| 11. The intervention was a fair way to handle the child's problem behavior. | 1 | 2 | 3 | 4 | 5 | 6 |
| 12. This intervention is reasonable for the behavior problem described. | 1 | 2 | 3 | 4 | 5 | 6 |
| 13. I liked the procedures used in this intervention. | 1 | 2 | 3 | 4 | 5 | 6 |
| 14. This intervention was a good way to handle this child's behavior problem. | 1 | 2 | 3 | 4 | 5 | 6 |
| 15. Overall, this intervention would be beneficial for the child. | 1 | 2 | 3 | 4 | 5 | 6 |

**REPRODUCIBLE 4.2** *Intervention Rating Profile-15*

*Source:* J. C. Witt and S. N. Elliott (1985). "Acceptability of Classroom Intervention Strategies." In T. R. Kratochwill (Ed.), *Advances in School Psychology,* Vol. 4, pp. 251–288. Mahwah, NJ: Erlbaum. Reprinted with permission.

|   | | I agree | | | | | I do not agree |
|---|---|---|---|---|---|---|---|

1. The method used to deal with the behavior problem was fair.

+ ---- + ---- + ---- + ---- + ---- +

2. This child's teacher was too harsh on him.

+ ---- + ---- + ---- + ---- + ---- +

3. The method used to deal with the behavior may cause problems with this child's friend.

+ ---- + ---- + ---- + ---- + ---- +

4. There are better ways to handle this child's problem than the one described here.

+ ---- + ---- + ---- + ---- + ---- +

5. The method used by this teacher would be a good one to use with other children.

+ ---- + ---- + ---- + ---- + ---- +

6. I like the method used for this child's behavior problem.

+ ---- + ---- + ---- + ---- + ---- +

7. I think that the method used for this problem would help this child do better in school.

+ ---- + ---- + ---- + ---- + ---- +

**REPRODUCIBLE 4.3**   *Children's Intervention Rating Profile (CIRP)*

*Source:* J. C. Witt and S. N. Elliott (1985). "Acceptability of Classroom Intervention Strategies." In T. R. Kratochwill (Ed.), *Advances in School Psychology,* Vol. 4., 251–288. Mahwah, NJ: Erlbaum. Reprinted with permission.

# Phonological Awareness Training for Reading (PATR)

## Treatment Integrity Checklist

Intervention Leader: _____ Date: _____

Lesson #: _____ Students Present: _____

Intervention Level: ___ Primary       ___ Secondary       ___ Tertiary

| Component | Present? | |
|---|---|---|
| | Yes | No |
| 1. Explained each activity correctly and clearly. | | |
| 2. Pronounced individual word sounds correctly. | | |
| 3. Presented picture cards in correct sequence. | | |
| 4. Placed picture cards so that every student could see. | | |
| 5. Modeled each activity before asking students to perform the activity. | | |
| 6. Provided each student an opportunity to respond. | | |
| 7. Provided corrective feedback for incorrect answers. | | |
| 8. Provided positive reinforcement for correct answers (e.g., praise). | | |
| 9. Maintained appropriate, quick pacing throughout the lesson. | | |
| Total | | |

Percentage of Components Present _____ ( / 9 =      %)

---

**REPRODUCIBLE 5.1**   *Sample Treatment Integrity Protocol: PATR*

*Source:* Adapted from K. L. Lane, T. Fletcher, J. DeLorenzo, & V. McLaughlin (in preparation). "Improving Early Literacy Skills of Young Children at-risk for Antisocial Behavior: Collateral Effects on Behavior." Unpublished.

## Phonological Awareness Training for Reading (PATR)
### Weekly Treatment Integrity Checklist

Intervention Leader: _____    Week: _____    Lesson #: _____

Students Present: _____

Intervention Level: _____ Primary    _____ Secondary    _____ Tertiary

### Phonological Awareness Training: Treatment Integrity Checklist

| Component | Monday | Tuesday | Wednesday | Thursday | Friday | Component Integrity |
|---|---|---|---|---|---|---|
| | Present | Present | Present | Present | Present | |
| 1. Explained each activity correctly and clearly. | | | | | | |
| 2. Pronounced individual word sounds correctly. | | | | | | |
| 3. Presented picture cards in correct sequence. | | | | | | |
| 4. Placed picture cards so that every student could see. | | | | | | |
| 5. Modeled each activity. | | | | | | |
| 6. Provided each student an opportunity to respond. | | | | | | |
| 7. Provided corrective feedback for incorrect answers. | | | | | | |
| 8. Provided positive reinforcement for correct answers (praise). | | | | | | |
| 9. Maintained appropriate, quick pacing throughout the lesson. | | | | | | |
| Session Percentages | | | | | | |

**REPRODUCIBLE 5.2** *Weekly Treatment Integrity: PATR*

*Note:* If the component is present, write '1'; if the component is not present, write '0'.

*Source:* Adapted from F. M. Gresham (1989). "Assessment of Treatment Integrity in School Consultation and Prereferral Intervention." *School Psychology Review, 18,* 37–50.

Intervention _____

Teacher: _____ Date: _____ Grade Level: _____

Intervention Level: __ Primary        __ Secondary ☐__ Tertiary

| COMPONENT | Low Integrity | | | High Integrity |
|---|---|---|---|---|
| 1. | 1 | 2 | 3 | 4 |
| 2. | 1 | 2 | 3 | 4 |
| 3. | 1 | 2 | 3 | 4 |
| 4. | 1 | 2 | 3 | 4 |
| 5. | 1 | 2 | 3 | 4 |
| 6. | 1 | 2 | 3 | 4 |
| 7. | 1 | 2 | 3 | 4 |
| 8. | 1 | 2 | 3 | 4 |
|  |  |  |  |  |

**REPRODUCIBLE 5.3**  *Behavior Rating and Self-Evaluation Scale*

Intervention _____

Teacher: _____ Date: _____ Grade Level: _____

Intervention Level: __ Primary        __ Secondary        __ Tertiary

| COMPONENT | Absent (0) | Present 11-25% (1) | Present 26-50% (2) | Present 51-75% (3) | Present 76-100% (4) |
|---|---|---|---|---|---|
| 1. | 0 | 1 | 2 | 3 | 4 |
| 2. | 0 | 1 | 2 | 3 | 4 |
| 3. | 0 | 1 | 2 | 3 | 4 |
| 4. | 0 | 1 | 2 | 3 | 4 |
| 5. | 0 | 1 | 2 | 3 | 4 |
| 6. | 0 | 1 | 2 | 3 | 4 |
| 7. | 0 | 1 | 2 | 3 | 4 |
| 8. | 0 | 1 | 2 | 3 | 4 |
| 9. | 0 | 1 | 2 | 3 | 4 |
| Total Score (sum of all ratings) | | | | | |
| Average Score (Average of all items) | | | | | |

REPRODUCIBLE 5.4    *Treatment Integrity Rating Scale: Percentages*

# Independent Group Contingency Plan with a Response Cost Component

Teacher: _____     Date: _____     Grade Level: _____

Lesson #: _____     Number of Students Present: _____

Intervention Level: ___ Primary     ___ Secondary     ___ Tertiary

| Components | Low Integrity | | | High Integrity |
|---|---|---|---|---|
| 1.  I clearly stated and explained the rules and expectations to the students. | 1 | 2 | 3 | 4 |
| 2.  I distributed a 4 x 6 index card to each student or taped the card on their desk. | 1 | 2 | 3 | 4 |
| 3.  I allocated points by placing a tally mark on the student's index card. | 1 | 2 | 3 | 4 |
| 4.  I took away points by crossing out a tally mark if student refused to participate or exhibited negative behavior (e.g., shouting or derogatory comments). Note. This should be rarely done and students should NEVER earn negative points for the week. | 1 | 2 | 3 | 4 |
| 5.  At the end of the week, students who met the prespecified point criteria (e.g., 25 points week 1; 30 points week 2) traded in their points for a tangible reinforcer (e.g., pencil or eraser).  Students with the most points chose first. | 1 | 2 | 3 | 4 |
| Total (sum of all points) <br> Average (average of all items) | | | | |

REPRODUCIBLE 5.5   *Independent Group Contingency Plan with a Response Cost*

School-Home Notes Guidelines

Intervention Leader: _____   Date : _____   Student: _____

Intervention Level: ___ Primary  ___ Secondary  ___ Tertiary

## Guidelines for Designing School-Home Notes

| Guideline | Permanent Product |
|---|---|
| Schedule a meeting with the teacher, the parent, and student to discuss the goals of the school-home notes (e.g., to increase the number of assignments Jennifer attempts at home and at school). | Notes from meeting |
| At this conference, define specific target behaviors that will be listed on the school-home note.  (e.g., Jennifer will attempt to participate in every activity or complete each assignment). | Target behaviors defined |
| Include the following information on the notes: student's name, date, teacher's signature, parent signature, and space for the teacher to record whether or not the behavior occurred (see Form 7). | Note cards created |
| Establish the responsibilities of each party: | Collect and review weekly notes |
| Parents will (a) sign or initial the note daily, (b) give the note to their child every day before school; and (c) allocate reinforcers and consequences based on the child's daily performance as indicated on the card. |  |
| The child will (a) take the note to school daily, (b) obtain the teacher's signature or initial each day, and (c) Bring the note home from school each day. |  |
| The teacher will (a) evaluate each target behavior, (b) sign or initial the note daily, and (c) give the note to the student every day before going home. |  |
| At the conference, delineate specific criteria for a "good" day based on points earned. | Create point system |
| At the conference, list reinforcers and consequences for "good" and "not good" days. Emphasize the importance of not scolding the child; just implement the system and provide praise as appropriate. At the conference, discuss the importance of consistency and follow through. | Lists created |
| Once the goals are being met, begin to fade the program (e.g., move from daily to weekly notes).  However, do not stop the intervention immediately. | Collect and review weekly notes |

**REPRODUCIBLE 5.6**  *Treatment Integrity: Permanent Product Evaluation*

*Source:* Adapted from S. Elliott, & F. M. Gresham (1991). *Social Skills Intervention Guide.* Circle Pines, MN: American Guidance Service.

# School-Home Note

Intervention Leader: _____  Date : _____  Student: _____

Intervention Level: ___ Primary  ___ Secondary  ___ Tertiary

| Behavior | Monday | Tuesday | Wednesday | Thursday | Friday |
|---|---|---|---|---|---|
| Participated in morning activities | | | | | |
| Attempted morning assignments | | | | | |
| Participated in afternoon activities | | | | | |
| Attempted morning assignments | | | | | |
| Attempted homework assignments | | | | | |
| Teacher's Initials | | | | | |
| Parent's Initials | | | | | |

Evaluation:  4 = outstanding
3 = satisfactory
2 = poor
1 = unacceptable

Teacher Comments:

Parent Comments:

_____  _____
Teacher's Signature          Parent's Signature

**REPRODUCIBLE 5.7**  *School-Home Note*

*Source:* Adapted from H. M. Walker, G. Colvin, & E. Ramsey (1995). *Antisocial Behavior in School: Strategies and Best Practices.* Albany, NY: Brooks/Cole.

| Principles & Tactics | Selected Approaches | Completed √ |
|---|---|---|
| Exploit Functional Contingencies | | |
| Contact natural consequences. | | |
| Recruit natural consequences. | | |
| Modify maladaptive consequences. | | |
| Reinforce occurrences of generalization. | | |
| | | |
| Train Diversely | | |
| Use sufficient stimulus exemplars. | | |
| Use sufficient response exemplars. | | |
| Make antecedents less discriminable. | | |
| Make consequences less discriminable. | | |
| | | |
| Incorporate Functional Mediators | | |
| Incorporate common salient physical stimuli. | | |
| Incorporate common salient social stimuli. | | |
| Incorporate self-mediated physical stimuli. | | |
| Incorporate self-mediated verbal and covert stimuli. | | |

**REPRODUCIBLE 6.1** *Programming for Generalization: Topographical Approaches*

*Source:* Reprinted with permission from T. F. Stokes & P. G. Osnes (1989). "An Operant Pursuit of Generalization." *Behavior Therapy, 20,* 337–355 (Page 340).

**259**

| Guidelines | Completed |
|---|---|
| • Plan for generalization when you are designing your intervention. | _____ |
| • Examine stimulus and reinforcement conditions in the environment. | _____ |
| • Conduct interventions in relevant environments under naturally occurring conditions. | _____ |
| • Incorporate the current generalization technology. | _____ |
| • Examine issues of stimulus control when there are concerns about stimulus generalization. | _____ |
| • Examine issues of reinforcement when there are concerns about response maintenance. | _____ |
| • Examine generalization of functional alternatives for concerns about generalized response suppression | _____ |

**REPRODUCIBLE 6.2**    *Generalization Guidelines*

*Source:* Adapted from G. Dunlap. (1993). "Promoting Generalization: Current Status and Functional Considerations." In R. V. Houten, & S. Axelrod. *Behavior Analysis and Treatment.* New York: Plenum Press.

| Caught Being Good | Caught Being Good |
|---|---|
| Student: _____ | Student: _____ |
| Observer: _____ | Observer: _____ |
| Date: _____ | Date: _____ |
| Location: _____ | Location: _____ |
| √ You followed directions the first time. | √ You followed directions the first time. |
| √ You asked for help in an acceptable way. | √ You asked for help in an acceptable way. |
| √ You resolved a conflict using your words. | √ You resolved a conflict using your words. |
| √ You finished your work in a timely manner. | √ You finished your work in a timely manner. |
| √ You invited a friend to work/play with you. | √ You invited a friend to work/play with you. |

**REPRODUCIBLE 6.3**  *Schoolwide Intervention: Social Skills*

# Homework Reminder Sheet

|  | Assignment | Completed √ | Parent Signature |
|---|---|---|---|
| Monday |  |  |  |
| Reading |  |  |  |
| Math |  |  |  |
| Science |  |  |  |
| Social Studies |  |  |  |
| PE |  |  |  |
| Elective |  |  |  |
|  |  |  |  |
| Tuesday |  |  |  |
| Reading |  |  |  |
| Math |  |  |  |
| Science |  |  |  |
| Social Studies |  |  |  |
| PE |  |  |  |
| Elective |  |  |  |
|  |  |  |  |
| Wednesday |  |  |  |
| Reading |  |  |  |
| Math |  |  |  |
| Science |  |  |  |
| Social Studies |  |  |  |
| PE |  |  |  |
| Elective |  |  |  |
|  |  |  |  |
| Thursday |  |  |  |
| Reading |  |  |  |
| Math |  |  |  |
| Science |  |  |  |
| Social Studies |  |  |  |
| PE |  |  |  |
| Elective |  |  |  |
|  |  |  |  |
| Friday |  |  |  |
| Reading |  |  |  |
| Math |  |  |  |
| Science |  |  |  |
| Social Studies |  |  |  |
| PE |  |  |  |
| Elective |  |  |  |

**REPRODUCIBLE 6.4**   *Homework Reminder Form*

## Primary Intervention
### A Planning Guide & Checklist

I.     The Target Area of Primary Intervention is:

A.     Describe main concern:_____

_____

_____

_____

B.     List factors contributing to target area of concern:

(1) _____

(2) _____

(3) _____

(4) _____

II.     Pre-Intervention Evaluation/Assessment of Target Area:

A.     What is the present level of functioning for the contributing factors listed above?

(1) _____

(2) _____

(3) _____

(4) _____

B.     Statement of need to promote the new skill/behavior (s) schoolwide;
this will become the "Mission Statement" of the Primary Intervention.

_____

_____

_____

_____

_____

_____

_____

**REPRODUCIBLE 7.1**   *Primary Intervention Planning Guide and Checklist*

III.  Use the checklist below to guide the intervention process AND as an overall intervention treatment integrity measure!  Use relevant forms to document procedures to validate intervention outcomes and accountability.

| Check (√) when Done | Date(s) Complete | Task | Form # | Intervention Phase Component |
|---|---|---|---|---|
| | | Distribute brief *social validity surveys* to all teachers, other school professionals and parents to query appropriate goals given area of concern and current functioning | | Pre-Intervention Planning |
| | | Convene Intervention Advisory Panel (IAP), comprised of school, student, parent & community representatives | | |
| | | IAP outline **critical intervention targets and goals;** based upon results of social validity surveys | | |
| | | **Decide strategy to address each goal** by (1) adopting a pre-packaged evidenced-based intervention OR (2) design intervention | | |
| | | **Operationally define** each skill/behavior to be taught to achieve each goal | | Intervention Design |
| | | **List** (1) essential components to attain each goal (2) intervention intensity and duration (3) benchmark goals, (4) methods to program contingencies for *generalization and maintenance* (5) responsible parties | | |
| | | **Decide methods** and intervals to (1) *monitor progress* and (2*) monitor treatment integrity* during intervention | | |
| | | Distribute *treatment acceptability* survey to teachers and parents; provide description of intervention goals and procedures. | | |
| | | **Revise** any goals or procedures deemed as not acceptable by a majority of surveys | | |
| | | **Implementation of intervention components** as designed. | | Intervention Phase |
| | | Collect *treatment integrity* measures at predetermined intervals. | | |
| | | **Collect data to monitor progress** at predetermined intervals. | | |
| | | **Convene IAP to evaluate progress and treatment integrity data** at regular intervals. IAP makes decision to adjust procedures if data provides evidence for need of change. | | |
| | | **Implementation of changes as needed.** | | |

---

**REPRODUCIBLE 7.1**   *Continued*

| Check (√) when Done | Date(s) Complete | Task | Form # | Intervention Phase Component |
|---|---|---|---|---|
| | | Evaluate students resistant to intervention as indicated by no or low progress in comparison to peers. **Consider for secondary or tertiary interventions.** | | Intervention Phase |
| | | **Terminate intervention** when goals are attained or at predetermined time. | | Post Intervention Assessment |
| | | **Assess post intervention levels** of newly trained skills/behaviors. Assess post intervention levels of any skills/behaviors targeted for decrease. | | |
| | | **Assess** *generalization* of skills/behaviors | | |
| | | **Distribute** *social validity* surveys to IAP, teachers and randomly selected sample of students and parents to assess (1) *treatment acceptability* and (2) *social significance* of intervention outcomes | | |
| | | **IAP report intervention outcomes** to students, teachers, parents and community | | |
| | | **Assess** *maintenance* of treatment outcomes after a reasonable time interval assuring effects are sustained or continuing to progress | | |
| | | **Booster sessions** of components assessed as not maintaining or consider re-implementation. | | |

IV.    Final Report by IAP of Intervention Process and Outcomes

A.    List components/procedures of intervention that were *not as successful* as planned; indicate those that were adjusted during intervention:

_____

_____

_____

_____

B.    List components/procedures of intervention that were *more successful* than planned

_____

_____

_____

_____

**REPRODUCIBLE 7.1**    *Continued*

C.　　Summarize intervention outcomes by answering the following questions.

**Question 1.**  *To what extent did the primary intervention help students improve academic performance?*

_____

_____

_____

_____

**Question 2.**  *To what extent did the primary intervention help students improve behavioral performance and social competence?*

_____

_____

_____

_____

**Question 3:**  *Did the primary intervention differentially influence students?  If so, how?*

_____

_____

_____

_____

**Question 4:**  *If yes to #3, what decisions were made to implement secondary or tertiary interventions for students who did not make progress during the primary intervention?*

_____

_____

_____

_____

**Question 5:**  *To what extent were intervention components implemented with integrity? List percent of integrity by intervention component.*

(1) _____

(2) _____

(3) _____

(4) _____

**REPRODUCIBLE 7.1**  *Continued*

**Question 6:** *To what extent was treatment procedure judged overall as acceptable **prior** to intervention by the following groups of people?*

Teachers: _____

Other school professionals: _____

Students: _____

Parents: _____

Community representatives: _____

**Question 7:** *To what extent was treatment procedure judged overall as acceptable **after** intervention by the following groups of people?*

Teachers: _____

Other school professionals: _____

Students: _____

Parents: _____

Community representatives: _____

**Question 8:** *To what extent did intervention agents/consumers/beneficiaries judge intervention outcomes as socially important?*

Teachers: _____

Other school professionals: _____

Students: _____

Parents: _____

Community representatives: _____

**Question 9:** *To what extent did intervention outcomes generalize to other settings, times, people?*

_____

_____

_____

**Question 10:** *To what extent did outcome effects maintain after intervention was terminated?*

_____

_____

_____

**D.** Rate the success of the intervention process overall.

| High | | | | Moderate | | | | Low |
|------|--|--|--|----------|--|--|--|-----|

REPRODUCIBLE 7.1    *Continued*

# Secondary Intervention
## A Planning Guide & Checklist

I.      The Target Area of Secondary Intervention is:

A.      Describe main concern:_____

_____

_____

_____


B.      List appropriate replacement skills/behaviors to remediate areas of concern:

(1)_____

(2)_____

(3)_____

(4)_____


II.     Pre-Intervention Evaluation/Assessment of Target Area:

A.      What is the present level of functioning for skills/behaviors listed above?

(1)_____

(2)_____

(3)_____

(4)_____


B.      Statement of need to promote the new skill/behavior(s) for the small group of students;
        list levels deemed as proficient for each new skill/behavior component as well as
        normative levels for each skill/behavior that will decrease as a result

_____

_____

_____

_____

_____

_____

_____

_____

**REPRODUCIBLE 7.2**   *Secondary Intervention Planning Guide and Checklist*

III. Use the checklist below to guide the intervention process AND as an overall intervention treatment integrity measure! Use relevant forms to document procedures to validate intervention outcomes and accountability.

| Check (√) when Done | Date(s) Complete | Task | Form # | Intervention Phase Component |
|---|---|---|---|---|
| | | Distribute brief *social validity surveys* to teachers, other school professionals and parents to query appropriate goals given area of concern and current functioning | | Pre-Intervention Planning |
| | | Convene Intervention Advisory Panel (IAP), comprised of school, student, parent & community representatives | | |
| | | IAP outline critical intervention targets and goals; based upon results of social validity surveys | | |
| | | Decide strategy to address each goal by (1) adopting a pre-packaged evidenced-based intervention OR (2) design intervention | | |
| | | Operationally define each skill/behavior to be taught to achieve each goal | | Intervention Design |
| | | List (1) essential components to attain each goal (2) intervention intensity and duration (3) benchmark goals, (4) methods to program contingencies for *generalization and maintenance* (5) responsible parties | | |
| | | Decide methods and intervals to (1) *monitor progress* and (2) *monitor treatment integrity* during intervention | | |
| | | Distribute *treatment acceptability* survey to teachers and parents; provide description of intervention goals and procedures. | | |
| | | Revise any goals or procedures deemed as not acceptable by a majority of surveys | | |
| | | Implementation of intervention components as designed. | | Intervention Phase |
| | | Collect *treatment integrity* measures at predetermined intervals. | | |
| | | Collect data to monitor progress at predetermined intervals. | | |
| | | Convene IAP to evaluate progress and treatment integrity data at regular intervals. IAP makes decision to adjust procedures if data provides evidence for need of change. | | |
| | | Implementation of changes as needed. | | |

**REPRODUCIBLE 7.2** *Continued*

| Check (√) when Done | Date(s) Complete | Task | Form # | Intervention Phase Component |
|---|---|---|---|---|
| | | Evaluate students resistant to intervention as indicated by no or low progress in comparison to peers. Consider for tertiary interventions, one-on-one intense treatment. | | Intervention Phase |
| | | Terminate intervention when goals are attained or at predetermined time. | | Post Intervention Assessment |
| | | Assess post intervention levels of newly trained skills/behaviors. Assess post intervention levels of any skills/behaviors targeted for decrease. | | |
| | | Assess *generalization* of skills/behaviors | | |
| | | Distribute *social validity* surveys to IAP, teacher(s), students and parents to assess (1) *treatment acceptability* and (2) *social significance* of intervention outcomes | | |
| | | IAP report intervention outcomes to students, teachers, parents | | |
| | | Assess *maintenance* of treatment outcomes after a reasonable time interval assuring effects are sustained or continuing to progress | | |
| | | Booster sessions of components assessed as not maintaining; consider tertiary intervention. | | |

IV.    Final Report by IAP of Intervention Process and Outcomes

A.    List components/procedures of intervention that were *not as successful* as planned; indicate those that were adjusted during intervention:

_____

_____

_____

_____

B.    List components/procedures of intervention that were *more successful* than planned

_____

_____

_____

_____

---

**REPRODUCIBLE 7.2**    *Continued*

C.   Summarize intervention outcomes by answering the following questions.

Question 1.  *To what extent did the secondary intervention help students improve academic performance?*

_____

_____

_____

_____

Question 2.  *To what extent did the secondary intervention help students improve behavioral performance and social competence?*

_____

_____

_____

_____

Question 3:  *Did the primary intervention differentially influence students?  If so, how?*

_____

_____

_____

_____

Question 4:  *If yes to #3, what decisions were made to implement more intense, tertiary interventions on a one-to-one basis for students who did not make progress?*

_____

_____

_____

_____

Question 5:  *To what extent were intervention components implemented with integrity? List percent of integrity by intervention component.*

(1) _____

(2) _____

(3) _____

(4) _____

**REPRODUCIBLE 7.2**   *Continued*

**Question 6:** *To what extent was treatment procedure judged overall as acceptable* **prior** *to intervention by the following people?*

Teacher(s): _____

Other school professionals: _____

Students: _____

Parents: _____

**Question 7:** *To what extent was treatment procedure judged overall as acceptable* **after** *intervention by the following groups of people?*

Teacher(s): _____

Other school professionals: _____

Students: _____

Parents: _____


**Question 8:** *To what extent did intervention agents/consumers/beneficiaries judge intervention outcomes as socially important?*

Teachers: _____

Other school professionals: _____

Students: _____

Parents: _____


**Question 9:** *To what extent did intervention outcomes generalize to other settings, times, people?*

_____

_____

_____


**Question 10:** *To what extent did outcome effects maintain after intervention was terminated?*

_____

_____

_____


D.    Rate the success of the intervention process overall.

| High | Moderate | Low |
|------|----------|-----|
| ←———|—————————|———→ |

**REPRODUCIBLE 7.2** *Continued*

272                    Copyright © 2004 by Allyn and Bacon.

## Tertiary Intervention
## A Planning Guide & Checklist

I.  Target Area of Tertiary Intervention
    List problematic skill/behavior(s):

(1) _____

(2) _____

(3) _____

(4) _____


II.  Pre-Intervention Evaluation/Assessment of Target Area:

A.  Conduct and evaluate assessment for following:

   • Present level of functioning for skills/behaviors listed above:

(1) _____

(2) _____

(3) _____

(4) _____

   • Nature of skill/behavior deficits (acquisition, performance or fluency):

(1) _____

(2) _____

(3) _____

(4) _____

   • Function of behavior:

(1) _____

(2) _____

(3) _____

(4) _____

C.  List appropriate replacement skills/behaviors:

(1) _____

(2) _____

(3) _____

(4) _____

REPRODUCIBLE 7.3   *Tertiary Intervention Planning Guide and Checklist*

B.  List levels deemed as proficient for each new skill/behavior component as well as normative levels for each skill/behavior that will decrease as a result.

(1) _____

(2) _____

(3) _____

(4) _____

III.  Use the checklist below to guide the intervention process AND as an overall intervention treatment integrity measure!  Use relevant forms to document procedures to validate intervention outcomes and accountability.

| Check (√) when Done | Date(s) Complete | Task | Form # | Intervention Phase Component |
|---|---|---|---|---|
| | | Conduct and evaluate **skills-based assessment** with student.  Review records. | | Pre-Intervention Assessment and Planning |
| | | Conduct observational assessments:  (1) ABC Event, (2) Reinforcement, (3) Environment | | |
| | | Conduct and evaluate **Functional Assessment Interviews** (FAI) with teacher(s), student, parents, other relevant people. | | |
| | | Assess *social validity* with teacher, student and parents to query understanding of problem and appropriate goals given area of concern, current functioning, and potential functions. | | |
| | | **Convene Intervention Team (IT)** comprised of teacher(s), administrator, psychologist, parents and student.  **Discuss & decide** (1) critical intervention targets and goals (2) strategy to address each goal | | Intervention Design |
| | | Interventionist:  **Operationally define** each skills/behaviors to be taught to achieve goals | | |
| | | List (1) essential components to attain each goal (2) intervention intensity and duration (3) benchmark goals, (4) methods to program contingencies for *generalization and maintenance* (5) responsible parties | | |
| | | **Decide methods** and intervals to (1) *monitor progress* and (2) *monitor treatment integrity* during intervention | | |

**REPRODUCIBLE 7.3**   *Continued*

| Check (√) when Done | Date(s) Complete | Task | Form # | |
|---|---|---|---|---|
| | | Assess *treatment acceptability* information by survey with teachers and parents; provide description of intervention goals and procedures. | | |
| | | Revise any goals or procedures deemed as not acceptable by a majority of surveys | | Intervention Design |
| | | Explain, train teacher(s) , student, and parents on components they will implement, monitor and graph | | |
| | | Implementation of intervention components as designed. | | |
| | | Collect *treatment integrity* measures at predetermined intervals. | | |
| | | Collect data to monitor progress at predetermined intervals. | | |
| | | Graph data about progress | | Intervention Phase |
| | | Convene IT to evaluate progress and treatment integrity data at regular intervals. IT makes decision to adjust procedures if data provides evidence for need of change. | | |
| | | Implementation of changes as needed. | | |
| | | Evaluate students resistant to intervention as indicated by no or low progress towards goals. Consider for formal evaluation for special education supports. | | |
| | | Terminate intervention when goals are attained or at predetermined time. | | |
| | | Assess post intervention levels of newly trained skills/behaviors. Assess and graph post intervention levels of any skills/behaviors targeted for decrease. | | |
| | | Assess *generalization* of skills/behaviors to other settings, people, situations | | Post Intervention Assessment |
| | | Assess *social validity* of intervention outcomes with teacher(s), student, parents; (1) *treatment acceptability* and (2) *social significance* of intervention outcomes | | |
| | | IT meets for report of intervention outcomes | | |
| | | Assess *maintenance* of treatment outcomes after a reasonable time interval assuring effects are sustained or continuing to progress | | |

**REPRODUCIBLE 7.3**   *Continued*

| | | Booster sessions of components assessed as not maintaining; consider formal evaluation for special education supports. | | |
|---|---|---|---|---|

IV.    Final Report by IAP of Intervention Process and Outcomes

A.    List components/procedures of intervention that were *not as successful* as planned; indicate those that were adjusted during intervention:

_____

_____

_____

_____

B.    List components/procedures of intervention that were *more successful* than planned

_____

_____

_____

_____

C.    Summarize intervention outcomes by answering the following questions.

Question 1.    *To what extent did the tertiary intervention help the student improve academic performance?* Compare pre-intervention to post-intervention levels.

_____

_____

_____

_____

Question 2.    *To what extent did the tertiary intervention help the student improve behavioral performance and social competence?* Compare pre-intervention to post-intervention levels.

_____

_____

_____

_____

**REPRODUCIBLE 7.3**    *Continued*

**Question 3:** *Did the intervention differentially influence the student?* (change vs. no change)

_____

_____

_____

_____

**Question 4:** *If yes to #3, what decisions were made to implement with more intensity, increase duration of the tertiary intervention, or consider for formal evaluation for special education?*

_____

_____

_____

_____

**Question 5:** *To what extent were intervention components implemented with integrity? List percent of integrity by intervention component.*

(1) _____

(2) _____

(3) _____

(4) _____

**Question 6:** *To what extent was treatment procedure judged overall as acceptable **prior** to intervention by the following people?*

Teacher(s): _____

Other school professionals: _____

Student: _____

Parents: _____

**Question 7:** *To what extent was treatment procedure judged overall as acceptable **after** intervention by the following groups of people?*

Teacher(s): _____

Other school professionals: _____

Student: _____

Parents: _____

---

**REPRODUCIBLE 7.3** *Continued*

**Question 8:** *To what extent did intervention agents/consumers/beneficiaries judge intervention outcomes as socially important?*

Teachers: _____

Other school professionals: _____

Student: _____

Parents: _____

**Question 9:** *To what extent did intervention outcomes generalize to other settings, times, people?*

_____

_____

_____

**Question 10:** *To what extent did outcome effects maintain after intervention was terminated?*

_____

_____

_____

**D.** Rate the success of the intervention process overall.

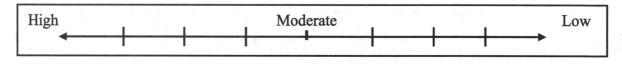

**REPRODUCIBLE 7.3** *Continued*

# Index

*Note:* Italicized page locators denote figures, forms, and tables.

**A**

Abbreviated Acceptability Rating Profile (AARP), 98
A-B-C data, 47, 217
ABC Event Record, *46, 234*
A-B-C relationship, in applied behavior analysis, 164
Absenteeism
  and linking interventions with assessments, 27, *28,* 29, 30–31
  and primary intervention, 26–27
Academically engaged (AE) behavior, 209, 218
Academically unengaged (AUE) behavior, 208, 218
Academic Engaged Time (AET), 213
Academic Excellence Indicator System (AEIS), 17
Academic interventions, progress monitoring of, 59
Academic underachievement, and antisocial behavior, 92
Accountability, 9, 10, 18
  demonstrating for student outcomes, 50
  need for demonstrating, 172
  and outcome-based education movement, 31
Accuracy, of skill and behavior, 64
Acquisition deficits, and social skills training, 5
Adaptive, replacement behavior, 153
ADHD. *See* Attention Deficit Hyperactivity Disorder
Administrative assessments, functional assessments *versus,* 19–22
AET. *See* Academic Engaged Time
Aggressive acts
  progress monitoring of, 55
  table of students participating in social skills group, *56*
Agran, M., 74
Airasian, P. W., 19, 22
Alberto, P. A., 66
Albin, R. W., 45, 97
Alexander, A. W., 5

Alexander, K. L., 78, 95
Algozzine, B., 133
Alper, S., 72
Anger management, 1, 8
Antecedents
  and functional contingencies, 151
  making less discriminable, 154, *155*
Antisocial behavior
  and academic underachievement, 92
  altering maladaptive consequences by reinforcement of, 153
Asarnow, J. R., 2
Assertive Discipline Plan, 204
Assessment, 19–25
  administrative *versus* functional assessments, 19–22
  intervention linked to, 5, 170
  linking to primary intervention, 25–27
  linking to secondary intervention, 27, 29
  linking to tertiary intervention, 29–31
  standardized *versus* skills-based tests, 23–24
  testing *versus,* 22–23
Assessment results
  importance of linking interventions to, 31–32
  linking interventions to, 221
  meaning of linking interventions to, 25–31
  ways of linking interventions to, 32–37
At-risk learners, and secondary prevention, 3
Attendance rates, multi-level intervention: summative findings, 220
Attention Deficit Hyperactivity Disorder (ADHD), 20, 21, 23
Ault, M. H., 47, 55
Ayllon, T., 30

**B**

Baer, D. M., 59, 93
Baker, E. L., 17
Baldwin, A., 77
Baldwin, C., 77
Bambara, L. M., 72
Barcikowski, R. S., 94
Bartko, W. T., 77

Batsche, G. M., 20, 23, 31, 32, 33, 36
Beatty, K. L., 130
Beck, R., 23, 30
Beebe-Frankenberger, M. E., 1, 5, 17, 24, 32, 87, 92, 131, 132, 169, 170, 210
Behavioral chain, *151*
Behavioral consultations, 32
Behavioral definition, example of, 64
Behavioral interventions, progress monitoring of, 59
Behavioral treatments, parental acceptability of, 96
Behavior intervention plans (BIP), 162
Behavior Intervention Rating Scales (BIRS), 98
Behavior Rating and Self-Evaluation Scale-Blank, *253*
Behavior rating scales, 45, 58, 89
    and treatment integrity assessment, 137, 144
Bergan, J. R., 32, 33, 90, 144
Best, A. M., 5
Betenbenner, D. W., 17
Bijou, S. W., 47, 55
Billingsley, F., 7, 172
Binns, W. R., 2, 25
BIP. *See* Behavior intervention plans
BIRS. *See* Behavior Intervention Rating Scales
Block-Pedego, A., 36, 55, 207
Bocian, K. M., 17, 132
Borthwick-Duffy, S. A., 95
Brody, G. H., 78, 95
Brown, B. B., 95
Bryant, B. R., 133, 137
Building in common physical stimuli, 156
Bursuck, W. D., 130
Bush, George W., 17
Busk, P. L., 57
Busse, R., 133
Butterworth, J., 24

**C**
Canter, L., 204
Canter, M., 204
Caplan, G., 2
Cartledge, G., 5, 72
Carver, R.P., 24
CBA. *See* Curriculum-based assessment
CBM. *See* Curriculum-based measurement
CEI. *See* Critical Events Index
Center, D. B., 1, 169
Chafouleas, S., 61, 62
Chang, C., 94
Changes
    importance of monitoring of, 57–58
    monitoring during intervention, 53–80
Charles, C. M., 204

Child characteristics, and assessments for secondary/tertiary interventions, 33, 34
Children's Intervention Rating Profile (CIRP), 98, *250*
Children's Social Validity Interview (CSVI), 98
Childs, K. E., 5, 19, 71, 217
Christenson, S., 133
CIRP. *See* Children's Intervention Rating Profile
Clarke, J. Y., 94
Clarke, S., 5, 19, 71, 217
Close, D. W., 5, 96
Cole, C. L., 72
Coleman, M., 74
Collateral effects, of intervention, 88
Colvin, G., 2, 25, 27, 61, 92, 207
Commitee for Children, 169
Common social stimuli, 158
Component checklists, 136
Component integrity, computing, 134, 136
Comprehensive Test of Phonological Processes (CTOPP), 47, 185, 216
Conflict resolution, 1, 8
Consequences
    and functional contingencies, 151
    making less discriminable, 154
Conway, T., 5
Cooper, L. J., 96
Core Components Model, *8*, 9, 10
    generalization and maintenance, 83, 147–165
    key tools for multi-level interventions, *222*
    social validity, 83, 85–124
    treatment integrity, 83, 128–146
Corrective Reading: Decoding Treatment Integrity Rating Scale, *138*, *139*
Correct words per minute (CWPM), 137
Coutinho, M. J., 5
Crimmins, D., 46, 217
Critical Events Index (CEI), 194, 212
Cronin, M. E., 72
CSVI. *See* Children's Social Validity Interview
CTOPP. *See* Comprehensive Test of Phonological Processes
Cultural values, and intervention, 93–94
"Curious double standard," 132
Curriculum-based assessment (CBA), 24, 31–32
Curriculum-based measurement (CBM), 24, 32, 55
Curriculum issues, assessing for secondary or tertiary interventions, 33, 34
Cushing, L. S., 7
CWPM. *See* Correct words per minute

**D**
Daly, E. J., 30, 32
Daly, E. M., 53
Darveaux, D., 98, 99, 210

Data collection, measurement of changes, *54*
Dauber, S., 96
Dawson, N. M., 72
DeBaryshe, B. D., 2, 77
Dejud, C., 220
Delayed reinforcement, 155
Deno, S. L., 32
Depression, self-monitoring example of pleasant events for students with, *73*
Derby, K. M., 96
*Diagnostic and Statistical Manual of Mental Disorders*, 20
DIBELS. *See* Dynamic Indicators of Basic Early Literacy Skills
DiGangi, S. M., 72
Dimensions, of skill and behavior, 64, *65–66*
Direct behavioral consultation, 32
Direct observation
    and social validity assessment, 97, 101
    and treatment integrity assessment, 133, 136–137, 144
Discrimination, 147–148
    continuum of generalization and, *149*
Discriminative stimulus, 156
Disruptive classroom behavior, 203
Distal effects, measuring, 88
District-level standards, student performance relative to, 172
District Literacy Plan (DLP), 203–182, 205
District multiple measures, 58, 59, 62
DLP. *See* District Literacy Plan
Dolstra, L., 132
Dool, E., 30
Doukas, G. L., 5, 47, 136, 172
Drug prevention, 1
Drummond, T., 181, 206
Duncan, B. B., 2
Dunlap, G., 5, 19, 45, 71, 217
Dunlap, L. K., 72
DuPaul, G. J., 19, 87
Durand, M., 46, 217
Duration, of skill and behavior, 64
Duration recording method, 66
Duration recording procedures, 213
Durnan, S. L., 76
Dwivedi, K. N., 5
Dynamic Indicators of Basic Early Literacy Skills (DIBELS), 47, 209

**E**
Eaton, M., 30
Eckert, T., 30, 87
Eddy, J. M., 203
Edelen-Smith, P., 72
Edgerton, M., 78, 95
Educational assessments, administrative or functional types of, 21
Effective interventions

designing, 1–10
    key features of, 5–8
Elbert, J., 1
Elliott, S. N., 3, 9, 24, 29, 32, 45, 55, 58, 89, 92, 95, 97, 98, 99, 132, 133, 182, 185, 194, 210, 204, 205, 216
Entwisle, D. R., 78, 95
Ervin, R. A., 19
Event recording method, 66
Evertson, C. M., 94
Evidence-based interventions, 1
External validity, treatment integrity and, 131

**F**
FAI. *See* Functional Assessment Interview
Falk, K. B., 5
Family/community factors, and assessing for secondary or tertiary interventions, 33, 35
Fawcett, S., 88, 101
Feil, E. G., 5
Feindler, E. L., 5
Ferro, J., 46
Finn, C. A., 97, 98
Fishbein, M., 24
Florida Comprehensive Assessment Test (FCAT), 17
Formative evaluation, 53
Forness, S. R., 1, 2, 5, 169
Foster-Johnson, L., 5, 19
Fournier, R., 17, 169
Frequency, of skill and behavior, 64
Frequency counts, 61, 70
Friman, P. C., 19, 137
Fryxell, D., 2
Fuchs, D., 1, 6, 9, 18, 24, 53, 55, 221
Fuchs, L. S., 1, 6, 9, 18, 24, 32, 53, 55, 221
Functional alternatives, generalized response suppression linked to, 164
Functional Analysis Interview Summary Form, 45
Functional approaches, to generalization and maintenance, 159–161
Functional Assessment Interview (FAI), 101
Functional assessments, 31
    administrative assessments *versus*, 19–22
Functional contingencies, incorporating, 151–153
Functional generalization, 160
Functionally equivalent behaviors, 160
Functional mediators, incorporating, 156, 158–159
Function of the behavior, 97

**G**
Galvin, G. A., 97
Gansle, K. A., 131
Generalization, 147, 204
    attending to issues of, 5, 7

Generalization (*cont.*)
continuum of discrimination and, *149*
defined, 148
errors, 159
importance of programming for, 150
programming for, 162–164
and secondary intervention: social skills target, 212
Generalization and maintenance, 9, 81, 83, 147–165, 170, 172
and data-based decision making, 161–162
description of, 147–148
importance of, 148, 150
and multi-level intervention, 221
and social validity measures, 93
Generalization and maintenance programming, 151–161
functional approaches to, 159–161
topographical approaches to, 151–159
Generalization failures, in terms of reliability/efficiency of competing behaviors, 160
Generalization Guidelines, *162, 259*
Generalization technology, incorporating, 163–164
Generalized response suppression, functional alternatives linked to, 164
Generic frequency count
sample form, *71*
by teacher, 70
Generic Frequency Count Form-Sample, *239*
Givner, C. C., 94, 128
Goal importance, 92–93
Golan, H., 72
Golly, A. M., 5
Good, R. H., 18, 47, 209
Gorman, J., 72
Graphs/Graphing
student self-monitoring with, 72
treatment integrity data using direct observation, 136
Greenwood, C. R., 18
Gregg, R. M., 5, 47, 136, 172
Gresham, F. M., 1, 2, 3, 5, 9, 17, 24, 25, 29, 32, 33, 45, 55, 58, 59, 69, 87, 88, 89, 90, 92, 93, 95, 96, 97, 101, 128, 131, 132, 133, 136, 137, 138, 141, 169, 171, 182, 210, 204, 205, 208, 221
Group contingency interventions, 97
Gumpel, T. P., 72
Gupta, A., 5

**H**
Habilitative validity, 90
Hall-Jamieson, K., 24
Hamburg, B. A., 92
Hamler, K., 30
Hamlett, C. L., 18

*Harry Potter and the Chamber of Secrets* (Rowling), 17
Haskins, R., 5
Hawkins, R., 90
Hayes, S., 25
Health awareness, 1
Heckman, K., 72
Heffer, R. W., 98, 99
Help, intervention and teaching student how to ask for, 94
Hinshaw, S. P., 92
Hintze, J., 30
Hollenbeck, J. R., 93
Homework Reminder Sheet, *157, 261*
Horner, R. H., 5, 7, 45, 97, 172
Horvath, B., 2, 25
Hughes, C. A., 5, 72
Hughes, M., 136

**I**
IAP. *See* Intervention advisory panel
IDEA, reauthorized (1997), 31
IEP. *See* Individual Educational Plan
Inclusive programming, for students with special needs, 1
Incremental student progress, monitoring, 61
Independent Group Contingency Plan with Response Cost, *140, 255*
Individual Educational Plan (IEP), 31
team, 128
Individualized educational plans, 162
Individualized transition plans (ITP), 162
*Individuals with Disabilities Education Act*, 9, 221
Intensity, of skill and behavior, 64
Intermediate/collateral effects, of intervention, 88
Intermittent reinforcement, 155
Internal validity, treatment integrity and, 131
Intervention advisory panel
Primary Intervention Worksheet, *175*
Secondary Intervention Worksheet, *183*
Social Secondary Intervention Worksheet, *189*
Intervention design, and planning for generalization, 162–163
Intervention monitoring roles, 69–72, 75, 76–77
parent, 77–80
student, 72–77
teacher, 70
Intervention outcomes
and meaningful changes, 165
presenting, 8, 172
Intervention planning activities, in hypothetical sample, 174, 203
Intervention process, *6, 129, 149, 171*

Intervention Progress-Monitoring Record
Sheet, *69, 238*
Intervention Rating Profile (IRP), 98, *106–107,*
205, 219
Intervention Rating Profile-15 (IRP-15), *249*
Intervention Rating Profile-20 (IRP-20), 98
Interventions
conducting in relevant environment, 163
degree of unresponsiveness to, *4*
effective, 5–8
importance of linking to assessment results,
31–32
linking to assessment information, 5, 170
linking to assessment results, 17–50, 221
meaning of linking assessment results to,
25–31
monitoring changes during, 53–80
process, *86*
resistance to, 68
ways of linking to assessment results, 32–37
Intervention Team (IT), Tertiary Intervention
Committee Worksheet, *197*
Intervention validity checklist (IVC), 136
Interviews, for social validity assessment, 97,
98, 101
IRP. *See* Intervention Rating Profile
Irvin, L. K., 92, 128
IT. *See* Intervention Team
ITP. *See* Individualized transition plans
IVC. *See* Intervention validity checklist

**J**
Jarrett, R., 25
Jenkins, A., 72
Johnson, S. B., 1
Johnston, J. M., 55, 185, 218
Jones, K. M., 137
Jones, R. N., 2, 25
"Just Say No" drug abuse campaign, 24

**K**
Kame'enui, E., 27
Kaminski, R. A., 18, 47, 209
Kamps, D., 2
Kartub, D. T., 2, 25, 35
Kauffman, J., 5
Kavale, K. A., 2
Kavanagh, K., 5
Kazdin, A. E., 7, 85, 87, 90, 97, 98, 99, 101,
169, 207
Kelley, M. J., 77, 98, 99,
Kellner, G., 5
Kendell, G. K., 87, 95
Keogh, B. K., 96
Kern, L., 5, 19, 47, 45, 71, 74
Kern-Dunlap, L., 217
Kerr, M. M., 94
Key tools, 170–172

King, N. J., 72
Kirby, P. C., 72
Kirkwood, M., 30
Klingner, J., 136
Knoff, H. M., 20, 23, 31, 32, 33, 36
Knoster, T., 2, 25
Knutson, N., 18, 24
Koegel, L. K., 72
Koegel, R. L., 72
Koeppl, G., 87
Korinek, L., 72
Kramer, J. J., 32
Kratochwill, T. R., 1, 32, 33, 90, 95, 144
Kravits, T., 2

**L**
LaFleur, L., 141
Lamborn, S. D., 95
Lambros, K. M., 5, 25, 32, 87, 92, 131, 136,
169, 210
Landon, T., 94
Lane, K. L., 1, 2, 5, 7, 24, 31, 32, 46, 47, 58,
87, 90, 92, 94, 95, 97, 98, 101, 128, 131,
132, 133, 136, 141, 169, 170, 172, 185,
205, 210, 219, 220
Lareau, A., 77
Latency, of skill and behavior, 64, 65
Latency recording method, 66
Learned helplessness, 97
Learning Environment Assessment, *49, 236*
Leave No Child Behind Act of 2001, 17,
169
Leonard, I. J., 74
Levinson, T. S., 76
Lewis, T. J., 1, 2, 5, 25
Liaupsin, C., 46
Likert-type scale, 101, 137, 203
Linn, R. L., 17, 31
Literacy programs, 2
Literacy skills, 203
Llewellyn, G., 2, 25
Lo, Y., 5
Loe, S. A., 5
Lohrmann-O'Rourke, S., 2, 25, 35
Lonigan, C., 1
Lopez, M. F., 87, 89, 90, 92, 93, 97, 101, 185,
219
Lovitt, T., 30

**M**
Maag, J. W., 72
Mace, F. C., 31, 62
MacGregor, R. R., 2
MacMillan, D. L., 1, 2, 17, 132, 133, 137, 141,
169
Mahdavi, J. N., 95
Maintenance
assessing, 213

Maintenance (*cont.*)
  attending to issues of, 5, 7
  defined, 148
Maladaptive behaviors, and teaching
    functionally equivalent behaviors, 164
Maladaptive consequences, altering those
    reinforcing antisocial behavior, 153
Manualized interventions, and treatment
    integrity assessment, 141
Marchand-Martella, N. E., 74
Marquis, J., 18
Marston, D., 32
Martella, R. C., 74
Martens, B. K., 30, 33, 61, 62, 98, 99, 132,
    205, 210
MAS. *See* Motivation Assessment Scale
Mash, E. J., 19
Massachusetts Comprehensive Assessment
    System (MCAS), 17
Mathematical problem solving, classwide
    progress on, *131*
Mather, N., 24, 216
Math progress, student permanent product
    progress-monitoring by graph for, *61*
Mayer, R., 25, 32, 58, 62, 64, 66
McCall, C., 74
McConnell, S., 58, 94
McGrew, K. S., 24, 216
McInerney, M., 5
McIntyre, L., 132
McLaughlin, V., 132
Mean bars
  examining "average" by drawing of, *60*
  on graphs, 59
Measurement systems, 61–62
Mediators, functional, 156
Menzies, H. M., 2, 5, 47, 136, 172
Mesinger, J. F., 94
Miltenberger, R. G., 98
Misra, A., 72
Moe, G. L., 97
Momentary time sampling method, 66
Monitoring changes, 58–62
  measurement system, 61–62
  outcome measures, 58–61
Monitoring method, defining, 66
Monitoring treatment integrity, 130–132
Moore, R. J., 72
MOOSES. *See* Multiple Option Observation
    System for Experimental Studies
Motivation Assessment Scale (MAS), 46, 217
Mounts, N., 95
Multi-level interventions, Core Components
    Model for, *222*
Multi-level intervention: summative findings,
    220–221
Multiple Option Observation System for
    Experimental Studies (MOOSES), 18

Munton, S. M., 5, 47, 136, 172
Murdock, J. Y., 72
Murphy, G. C., 72

**N**
Nabi, R., 25
Negative reinforcement, positive reinforce-
    ment *versus*, 47
Negative social interactions (NSI), 209, 210,
    213
Nelson, C. M., 1, 169
Nelson, J. R., 2
Nelson, R., 25
Newton, J. S., 97
Newton, K., 45
Noell, G. H., 29, 32, 53, 87, 88, 90, 92, 128,
    131, 138
Nonresponsive students
  to primary intervention, 207
  identifying for participation in secondary
    prevention efforts, 207
  identifying for participation in tertiary
    prevention efforts, 215
Nonsense word fluency (NWF), 209
Normative comparisons, 23
Norm-referenced standardized tests, 31
NSI. *See* Negative social interactions
NWF. *See* Nonsense word fluency

**O**
Observations, structuring, 47
Okagaki, L., 78, 95
Ollendick, T. H., 72
Olson-Tinker, H., 132
O'Neil, R. E., 45, 97
Operationalizing the skill, 63
Oral reading fluency (ORF), 209
  relationship between treatment integrity
    and, *136*
Oregon Statewide Assessments, 17
ORF. *See* Oral reading fluency
O'Shaughnessy, T. E., 1, 5, 24, 32, 47, 92, 136,
    169, 210
Oswald, D. P., 5
Outcome-based education movement, 31
Outcome measures, 58–61

**P**
Parent Post-Intervention Acceptability and
    Importance of Effects Survey, *119*
Parent Pre-Intervention Acceptability Rating
    Survey, *114*
Parents
  intervention monitoring by, 77–80
  and social validity assessment, 95–96
Parent's Child Social Validity Rating Survey,
    *109*
Parent-Teacher Association, 203

Partial interval recording method, 66
PATR. *See* Phonological Awareness Training for Reading
Patterson, G. R., 5, 78, 95, 96
Peer characteristics, and assessing for secondary/tertiary interventions, 33, 34
Pelander, J., 30
Pennypacker, H. S., 55, 185, 218
Performance changes, visual inspection of plotted data for changes in, *60*
Performance deficits, 216
Performance variability, during intervention, 59
Permanent products, and treatment integrity assessment, 141
Permanent products method, 66
Peterson, L., 132
Peterson, R. F., 47, 55
Phonics Chapter Books (Shefelbine), 209
Phonological awareness training, 4–5, 62
Phonological Awareness Training for Reading (PATR), 133, 137, *251*
  Treatment Integrity Checklist, *134*
  Weekly Treatment Integrity Checklist, *135*
Physical stimuli, building in, 156
Pianta, B., 133
Pierson, M., 5, 87, 94, 128, 131, 169
Plan evaluation, in consultation process, 32, 33
Plan implementation, in consultation process, 32, 33
Positive reinforcement, negative reinforcement *versus*, 47
Post, E. E., 76
Post-intervention social validity, and teachers, 95
Post-intervention: social validity components, 88–90
Prater, M. A., 72
Pre-intervention: social validity components, 85–88
Pre-intervention assessment: identifying intervention target areas, 174
Pre-intervention social validity measures, parents involved in, 96
Pre-intervention social validity surveys, teachers involved in, 95
Preliminary Functional Assessment Interview, *37–41*, 45, 217, *225–229*
Prereferral intervention plans, 162
Presenting intervention outcomes, 172
Presley, J. A., 5
Pretreatment social validity measures, and students, 97
Prevention levels, 2–5
  primary, 2–3

secondary, 3–5
tertiary, 5
Primary intervention, 221
  linking to assessment information, 18
  linking assessment results to, 33, 35–36
  linking assessments to, 25–27
  and social validity assessment, 92
  steps to link assessment data to, 36
Primary Intervention Plan: Design, Preparation, and Implementation, 203–205
  District Literacy Plan, 203–204
Primary Intervention Plan: Summative Example
  nonresponsive student participation in secondary prevention effor2s, 207
  results, 206–207
  Schoolwide Behavior Plan, 204
  Social Skills Plan, 204–205
  social validity, 205
  student progress monitoring, 205–206
  treatment integrity, 205
Primary Intervention Planning Guide, *173–174*
Primary Intervention Planning Guide and Checklist, *176–180, 262–266*
Primary Intervention Worksheet, *175*
Primary prevention, 2–3, 8, 62, 169
Primary prevention programs, 2
  and self-report rating scales, 98
Problem analysis, in consultation process, 32, 33
Problem identification, in consultation process, 32, 33
Problem-Solving Worksheet, *237*
  for design and progress monitoring, 66, *67*
Programming for generalization
  comprehensive guidelines for, 162–164
  topographical approaches, *152, 258*
Progress monitoring, 53–57
  graphical display of intervention, *63*
  graphing data and, 59
  by parents, 77
  problem-solving worksheet used for, 66, *67*
Progress Monitoring Grid, *243*
Proximal effects, 88

**Q**
Quinn, M., 5

**R**
Ramsey, E., 61, 78, 92, 207
Rankin, R., 94
Rasavage, C., 130
Rashotte, C. A., 5, 47, 207
Rate, of skill and behavior, 64
Rating scales
  self-report, 98

Rating scales  (*cont.*)
  for social validity assessment, 97
  for treatment integrity assessment, 137, 144
Reid, J. B., 5, 74, 78, 95, 96, 203
Reimers, T. M., 87, 96, 98, 99
Reinforcement
  positive *versus* negative, 47
  response maintenance linked to, 164
Reinforcement Assessment, *48, 235*
Reinforcement conditions, examining in environment, 163
Reinforcements, delivering when target behavior occurs beyond training setting, 153
Reinforcement slips, 154, 155
Reliability and efficiency, of competing behaviors, 160
Reliability of the independent variable, 128
Replacement skills/behaviors, 50, 208
  behavioral interventions and teaching of, 62
  and CBA data, 32
  defining and identifying, 24–25
  example of, 64
  and tertiary interventions, 29
Resistance to intervention, 68
Response examplars, and training broadly, 154
Response generalization, 159
Response generalization errors, 160
Response maintenance, reinforcement linked to, 164
Responses, and functional contingencies, 151
Response to intervention, description of, 68
Review, Interview, Observe, and Test (RIOT), steps in, 33
  Interview, 36
  Observe, 46–47
  Review, 36
  Test, 47
Reynolds, W. M., 72
Richardson, S. A., 5
RIOT. *See* Review, Interview, Observe, and Test
Risley, T. R., 93
Robbins, F. R., 217
Roberts, M., 30
Rosenberg, M. S., 130
Rosenfeld, S., 18, 24
Rowling, J. K., 17
Ruhl, K. L., 72
Rutherford, R. B., 1, 71, 169

**S**
Sabatine, K., 25
Sabatine, T., 2
Safran, J. S., 94
Safran, S. P., 94
Sameroff, A. J., 77
SARS. *See* School Archival Record Search

SBP. *See* School-wide behavior plan
Schaefer, E. S., 78, 95
Scheuermann, B., 74
Schloss, P. J., 72
School, as agent for change, 1
School Archival Record Search (SARS), 36, 55, 59, 194, 204, 216
School environment issues, and assessing for secondary or tertiary interventions, 33, 35
School-Home Note, 77, *257*
School-Home Note Card, *143*
School-Home Notes Guidelines, *142, 256*
School-Home Progress Note, *78–79, 244–245*
Schoolwide Behavior Plan, 182, 205
Schoolwide Intervention: Social Skills, *156, 260*
Schumm, J., 136
Scott, T. M., 2, 25, 35
Sechrest, L., 7, 128, 132, 171
Secondary intervention
  assessment linked to, 27, 29
  linking to assessment information, 18
  linking to assessment results, 36
  six conditions to assess for, *34–35*
  and social validity assessment, 92
Secondary Intervention: Academic Target
  intervention planning activities, 208
  pre-intervention assessment, 207–208
  results, 210–211
  student progress monitoring, 209–210
Secondary Intervention: Social Skills Target
  Intervention Planning Activities, 212
  nonresponsive students identified for tertiary prevention efforts, 215
  Pre-intervention assessment, 211
  results, 213–215
  Secondary Intervention Plan, 212–213
  student progress monitoring, 213
Secondary Intervention Plan: Summative Example
  academic intervention, 209
  intervention and assessment procedures, 208–209
  treatment integrity, 209
Secondary Intervention Planning and Checklist, *184–188*
Secondary Intervention Planning Guide, *181–182*
Secondary Intervention Planning Guide and Checklist, *190–194, 267–271*
Secondary Intervention to Improve Reading Comprehension, students mean score changes, *211*
Secondary Intervention Worksheet (IAP), *183*
Secondary prevention, 3–5, 8, 169, 221
Secondary prevention programs, 2
  progress monitoring example for, 55
  and self-report rating scales, 98

*Second Step Violence Prevention Curriculum*
(Committee for Children), 169, 170
Second Step Violence Prevention Plan, 170
Seifer, R., 77
Self-Control Social Skills Training, secondary
intervention in three groups, *214*
Self-mediated physical stimuli, 158
Self-mediated verbal and overt stimuli, 158
Self-Monitor for Neat and Complete Work
Assignments, *74, 241*
Self-monitoring
benefits of, 74
by students, 72
Self-monitoring behavior during class period
in middle school, 75
Self-monitoring grid, *76*
Self-reporting rating scales, for social validity
assessment, 98
Self-reporting strategies, and treatment
integrity assessment, 137–138, 140–141
Self-reports, and treatment integrity
assessment, 144
Semi-Structured Interview for Social
Validation, *100*
Semi-structured interviews, 98
Sensitivity to change, measurement systems
and, 61–62
Serlin, R. C., 57
Severson, H. H., 1, 2, 3, 5, 36, 55, 185, 210,
212
Shapiro, E. S., 71, 76
Shefelbine, John, 185, 209
Sheridan, S. M., 2, 25
Shimabukuro, S. M., 71, 74
Shinn, J., 32
Shinn, M. R., 18, 24, 32, 55, 94, 209
Sideridis, G. D., 92, 93
Simonian, S. J., 98, 99
Sindelar, P. T., 130
Singer, G. H., 92, 128
Skill deficits, determination of, 212
Skills-based tests, standardized tests *versus*,
23–24
Skills/behavior, dimensions of, *65*
Skills/behaviors measurement, 62–69
defining by dimension, 64–66
monitoring method definition, 66
and response to intervention, 68
topography, dimension, and method
combined, 66, 68
topography of skill/behavior, 63–64
Skinner, C. H., 130
Sladeczek, I. E., 97, 98
Smith, D., 2, 25
Social acceptability of intervention goals,
85, 87
Social acceptability of intervention
procedures, 89

Social comparisons techniques, for social
validity assessment, 97, 101
Social importance
and habilitative validity, 90
of effects resulting from intervention, 85,
87–88, 89, 90
Socially significant goals, 203
Social Secondary Intervention Worksheet
(IAP), *189*
Social significance of intervention goals, 85,
88, 90
Social skill interventions, poor generalization
of treatment outcomes with, 159
Social skills, 1, 8
Social skills groups, 158
progress monitoring data sheets for, *56, 57*
Table of Students in: Replacement Skill = #
Peer initiations, *56*
Table of Students Participating in: aggressive
acts, *56*
*Social Skills Intervention Guide: Practical Strategies
for Social Skills Training* (Elliott and
Gresham), 213
Social Skills Plan (SSP), 204–205
Social Skills Rating System (SSRS), 45, 55,
184, 204, 208, 221
Social skills training, 161
for children with acquisition deficits, 5
and self-monitoring, 72
Social validity, 9, 81, 83, 85–124
assessing, 5, 7
importance of assessing, 90, 92–94
meaning of, 85
measures, *99*
multi-informant method of assessment of,
94–92
post-intervention and components of,
88–90
practical applications of, 91
pre-intervention and components of, 85–88
primary intervention: summative example,
205
ways of assessing, 97–98, 101
Social validity assessment, 170
and multi-level intervention, 221
Secondary Intervention: Academic Target,
210–211
Secondary Intervention: Social Skills Target,
204, 205, 215
Tertiary Intervention: Summative Example,
208, 219
Social validity questionnaire, 174
Social validity surveys, interpreting, 101–102
Special needs students, inclusive programming
for, 1
Speece, D. L., 9
Spira, D. A., 94
Sprague, J. R., 45, 97

SRA Corrective Reading Program, 141
SRSS. *See* Student Risk Screening Scale
SSP. *See* Social Skills Plan
SSRS. *See* Social Skills Rating System
Standardized Testing and Reporting (STAR), 17
Standardized tests
  and academic problems analysis, 47
  skills-based tests *versus*, 23–24
Standards-based education, 169
Standards-based testing, 17
Stark, K. D., 72
State-level standards, student performance relative to, 172
Stecker, P. M., 6, 24
Steinberg, L., 95
Sternberg, R. J., 77
Stiller, B., 5
Stimuli examplars, and training broadly, 154
Stimulus conditions, examining in environment, 163
Stimulus control, stimulus generalization linked to, 164
Stimulus generalization, 159, 164
Stimulus generalization errors, 159–160
Stoiber, K. C., 1
Stolze, S., 2
Stoneman, Z., 78, 95
Storey, J. R., 45
Storey, K., 97
Student Assessment, *230–233*
Student Assessment Interview, *42–45*
Student Functional Assessment Interview, 45
Student Participant Interview, *123–124*
Student performance, evaluating, 5
Student Post-Intervention Acceptability and Importance of Effects Survey (Gr. 4-6), *121*
Student Post-Intervention Acceptability and Importance of Effects Survey (Gr. 7-12), *122*
Student Post-Intervention Acceptability and Importance of Effects Survey (Gr. K-3), *120*
Student Pre-Intervention Acceptability Rating Survey (Gr. 4-6), *116*
Student Pre-Intervention Acceptability Rating Survey (Gr. 7-12), *117*
Student Pre-Intervention Acceptability Rating Survey (Gr. K-3), *115*
Student progress monitoring, 7, 170, 203
  Primary Intervention: Summative Example, 205–206
  Secondary Intervention: Social Skills Target, 213
  Secondary Intervention: Summative Example, 209–210
  Tertiary Intervention: Summative Example, 219

Student relationships, negative consequences with lack of success in, 92
Student Risk Screening Scale (SRSS), 181, 184, 203–204, 220
Students
  intervention efforts and response of, 53
  intervention monitoring by, 72–77
  monitoring in target skills, *54*
  and social validity assessment, 96–97
Student Self-Assessment of Social Validity (Elementary Gr 4-6), *111*
Student Self-Assessment of Social Validity (Primary Gr K-3), *110*
Student Self-Assessment of Social Validity (Secondary Gr 7-12), *112*
Student Self-Monitoring My Own Behavior, *242*
Student Self-Monitoring of Events, *74, 240*
Sugai, G., 1, 2, 5, 25, 27
Sulzer-Azaroff, B., 25, 32, 58, 62, 64, 66
Support, three-tiered model of, *3*
Sutherland, K. S., 130
Swaggart, B., 2

**T**
TARF-R. *See* Treatment Acceptability Rating Form-Revised
TARP-R. *See* Treatment Acceptability Rating Profile-Revised
Target behaviors, antecedents and consequences with, 47
Tarnowski, K. J., 98, 99
Task Force on Evidence-Based Intervention in School Psychology, 1
Taylor-Greene, S. J., 2, 25, 35
TCAP. *See* Tennessee Comprehensive Assessment Program
TDB. *See* Total disruptive behavior
Teacher Post-Intervention Acceptability and Importance of Effects Survey, *118*
Teacher Pre-Intervention Acceptability Rating Survey, *113*
Teachers
  intervention monitoring by, 70
  secondary/tertiary interventions assessments and characteristics of, 33, 34
  rating scales, 62
  and social validity assessment, 94–95
Teacher's Child Social Validity Rating Survey, *108*
Teacher self-reports, and treatment integrity assessment, 144
Teaching strategy, skills affected by, 23
TEI. *See* Treatment Evaluation Inventory
TEI-SF. *See* Treatment Evaluation Inventory-Short Form
Tennessee Comprehensive Assessment Program (TCAP), 17